Praise for *Flag*

"Includes a number of tales well worth telling . . . scrupulously evenhanded."
— *The Washington Post Book World*

"Marc Leepson has written a highly readable and entertaining book about America's most recognizable symbol: the flag of the United States . . . HIGHLY RECOMMENDED."
—*American Vexillum*[TM] *Magazine*

"*Flag: An American Biography* is a valuable addition to American history, and Leepson, while never wrapping himself in Old Glory, certainly is due a portion of authorly glory for this absorbing account of America's national icon."
— *Richmond Times-Dispatch*

"[Leepson] provides an encyclopedic treatment of the flag in its various incarnations."
— *Chicago Tribune*

"Entertaining and informative."
— *The Star-Ledger* (Newark)

"The book brings depth to the origins and meaning of the flag and the patriotism and liberty that it represents."
— *GW Magazine*

"Leepson considers the abundant stories that purport to be the truth about Old Glory."
— *Booklist*

"Comprehensive, dispassionate chronicle of the potent banner that stirs up passions of every stripe. . . . Leepson (*Saving Monticello*, 2001) compiles the curious history of Old Glory and the special veneration it often evokes. . . . Unflaggingly straightforward vellixary law, lore, and legend, agreeably presented."
— *Kirkus Reviews*

ALSO BY MARC LEEPSON

*Saving Monticello: The Levy Family's Epic Quest to Rescue
the House that Jefferson Built*

*Webster's New World Dictionary of the
Vietnam War* (editor)

To Greg,
with thanks,

FLAG

An American Biography

MARC LEEPSON

FOREWORD BY NELSON B. DEMILLE

Marc Leepson

THOMAS DUNNE BOOKS

ST. MARTIN'S GRIFFIN NEW YORK

THOMAS DUNNE BOOKS.
An Imprint of St. Martin's Press.

www.stmartins.com

Design by Phil Mazzone

Library of Congress Cataloging-in-Publication Data

Leepson, Marc, 1945–
    Flag : an American biography / Marc Leepson.
        p. cm.
    ISBN-13: 978-0-312-32309-7
    ISBN-10: 0-312-32309-3
    1. Flags—United States—History.

CR113 .L44 2005
929.9'2'0973—dc22

                        2004065920

D 10 9 8 7 6 5

In memory of my grandparents:

Pauline Tarnovsky Leepson
Morris Leepson
Rose Friedenberg Levin
Herman Levin

Our flag carries American ideas, American history and American feelings. It is not a painted rag. It is a whole national history. It is the Constitution. It is the Government. It is the emblem of the sovereignty of the people. It is the NATION.

—Henry Ward Beecher, 1861

Your flag decal won't get you into heaven anymore.

—John Prine, 1969

Contents

Foreword   xi

Acknowledgments   xv

Introduction   1

ONE
Antecedents   7

TWO
The Birth of a Symbol   21

THREE
Mother of Invention   37

FOUR
First Additions   53

FIVE
Our Flag Was Still There   59

SIX
Additions and a Subtraction   77

SEVEN
A House Divided Against Itself   91

EIGHT
Flagmania   105

NINE
A Band of Brothers 125

TEN
The Hundredth Anniversary 135

ELEVEN
The Golden Age of Fraternity 143

TWELVE
One Nation Indivisible 163

THIRTEEN
The Great War 177

FOURTEEN
One Hundred Percent Americanism 193

FIFTEEN
United We Stand 205

SIXTEEN
The Cold War 219

SEVENTEEN
The Generation Gap 227

EIGHTEEN
United We Stand Again 245

Appendix: Stars and States 267

Notes 271

Bibliography 309

Index 319

Foreword

A BIOGRAPHY, according to most dictionaries, is an account of a person's life, written or told by another.

But here, Marc Leepson has expanded the meaning of the word and written a biography of an inanimate object: the American flag. And what a great job he has done.

Mr. Leepson begins at the beginning with the birth of the flag in 1777 during the American Revolution, and proceeds through the flag's infancy during the War of 1812, its childhood during the Civil War, its adolescence during the Spanish-American War, and its coming-of-age during the world wars.

And then there was the Vietnam War, when the flag, always venerated until then, became a symbol of the divisiveness that split the nation. The chapters that deal with the Vietnam period, at home and overseas, are worth the price of the book.

On a personal note, I served in Vietnam and during my year there, I rarely saw an American flag displayed at military installations or in combat operations. In fact, my photographs taken in Vietnam verify that memory. Mr. Leepson in his book writes:

> In Vietnam, some American troops flew the flag as their fathers did
> in Korea and in Europe and Japan during World War II and as their

grandfathers did in the trenches in World War I. The flag flew over American bases, remote outposts, and landing zones. Some troops carried small flags into battle, especially during the war's early years before it became controversial at home.

The key words there are "especially during the war's early years before it became controversial at home." By the time I got to Vietnam in November 1967, what was happening at home was starting to affect how newly arriving troops viewed the war, and thus conspicuous displays of patriotism, such as flying or carrying the American flag, were waning. This was in stark contrast to the Viet Cong and North Vietnamese troops as well as our South Vietnamese allies, who often carried flags into battle, and rallied around their flags, and also raised them in defiance of the enemy. I saw little of that on the American side during my tour of duty, and one might say that this period was the absolute low point of the American flag.

By the time of the first Gulf War, however, the flag had again become a unifying symbol, at least to most of the nation. And on September 11, 2001, the American flag flying over the ruins of the World Trade Center sprouted tens of thousands of new American flags across this country, Europe, and the world.

Many countries have more than one national symbol or emblem, some of which are religious, cultural, or pertain to royalty. In America, however, there are only two national symbols—the bald eagle, not known by everyone in other nations, and the American flag—known to the entire world. Marc Leepson explores the close identification of America and Americans with their flag and their country. A quote from Henry Ward Beecher in 1861 on the eve of the Civil War sums up this feeling:

Our flag carries American ideas, American history and American feelings. It is not a painted rag. It is a whole national history. It is the Constitution. It is the Government. It is the emblem of sovereignty of the people. It is the NATION.

Mr. Leepson also discusses "the cult of the flag," which swept the nation following the Civil War and led to the incorporation of the flag motif into many aspects of American life, art, home decoration, and public displays—a phenomenon that continues to this day and one that is rarely seen in other countries.

Flag: An American Biography is not a book with an agenda, or a subjective point of view; it is an objective history of the American flag, well researched, well presented, easy to read and understand, and very informative and entertaining.

One of the most entertaining aspects of *Flag* is its focus on personalities. For instance, Francis Hopkinson, a signer of the Declaration of Independence, is probably the designer of the American flag—not Betsy Ross. There are other such tidbits in the book, which keep us turning the pages, and probably causing us to read out loud to anyone nearby.

This is one of those books that seem as though someone should have written it years ago—but better late than never. *Flag: An American Biography* is a must read for scholars, history buffs, patriotic organizations, flag wavers, flag burners, anyone who owns an American flag or has seen a flag in the last forty-eight hours.

This iconic symbol of the nation, which is so ubiquitous in our lives, needs a history, and this is the definitive history of the Flag of the United States of America. Marc Leepson has done a wonderful job of making this inanimate object come alive and speak to us.

—Nelson DeMille

Acknowledgments

THE IDEA FOR THIS BOOK came from a series of conversations with my friend, literary agent, and fellow Vietnam veteran, Joseph Brendan Vallely. This book simply would not have come to pass without Joe's inspiration, encouragement, and advice. My undying gratitude goes to him.

Thanks, too, to my excellent editor at Thomas Dunne Books, Peter Wolverton, the associate publisher, who saw the merit in this book and steadfastly and expertly shepherded it through to publication. My appreciation for invaluable publishing assistance also goes to Thomas Dunne Books associate editor John Parsley, editorial assistant Katie Gilligan, to the copyeditor, Marcy VL Hargan, and David Stanford Burr, the production editor. Special thanks to Nelson DeMille for graciously agreeing to write the book's preface.

Several flag experts took time to answer my questions and provide insights into the history of, and the changing meaning of, the American flag. Thanks to Whitney Smith, the director of the Flag Research Center in Massachusetts, the world's No. 1 vexillologist; to Scot Guenter, the Coordinator of the American Studies Program at San Jose State University and the leading expert on the changing meaning of the American flag; to Henry Moeller, who has done pioneering research on the origins of the flag; and to

John W. Baer, the leading student of the history of the Pledge of Allegiance.

Thanks also to the following flag authorities who consented to interviews: Dr. Jeffery Kenneth Kohn, American flag collector and appraiser; Bob Heft, the designer of the fifty-star flag; Sally Johnston, the executive director, and Eric Voboril, the curator, at the The Star-Spangled Banner House in Baltimore; and Scott Sheads, park ranger/historian, and Anna von Lunz, cultural resources manager, at the National Park Service's Ft. McHenry National Monument and Historic Shrine in Baltimore. Thanks also to the artist Dread Scott, the creator of "What is the Proper Way to Display the American Flag?"

I owe a great deal to Marilyn Zoidis, the curator of the Star-Spangled Banner Project at the Smithsonian Institution's National Museum of American History who generously shared her knowledge about that flag and about the early history of the American flag, and to Suzanne Thomassen-Krauss, the project's chief conservator. Special thanks to Marilyn Zoidis for kindly agreeing to read and critique the chapter on The Star-Spangled Banner.

I have long been an ardent admirer of librarians and archivists. Many librarians and archivists helped me with invaluable research assistance. Thanks to: Sheila Whetzel, Tia Maggio, Tina Thomas, Mary Beth Morton, Heather Eickmeyer, Jeanine Raghunathan and Karen Warner at the Middleburg Library in Middleburg, Virginia; Mary Lou Demeo, Linda Holtslander, Robert Boley, and Michael Avera at the Loudoun County (Virginia) Public Library; Library Director Peggy Stillman at the Chesapeake Public Library in Chesapeake, Virginia; and to Steve Matthews and Alex Northrop at the Currier Library at Foxcroft School in Middleburg.

Also: Sam Anthony, director of lecture programs; Milton Gustafson, archivist, NWCTC; Rodney Ross, archivist, Center for Legislative Archives; and Darlene McClurkin at Museum Programs at the National Archives in Washington; Conley Edwards, the State Archivist; Tom Camden, director of Special Collections; Nolan Yelich, the Librarian of Virginia; Mary Dessypris, Government Reference Services & Outreach coordinator; Audrey C. Johnson, Picture Collection manager; and David Feinberg, reference librarian, at the Library of Virginia in Richmond; and my friends at the Library of Virginia Foundation: Mary Beth McIntire, Kathy Holmes, Heather Krajewski, and Richard Golembeski.

Also: My old friend and colleague Michael Koempel and his staff at the Library of Congress's Congressional Research Service Government

Division, and Patrick Kerwin, Manuscript Reference Librarian, at the Library of Congress's Manuscript Division; James W. Cheevers, associate director of the U.S. Naval Academy Museum in Annapolis; Carol Ganz, reference librarian at the Connecticut State Library; Rosemary Switzer, special collections assistant at Princeton University's Seeley G. Mudd Manuscript Library; my friend Bill Hammond, chief of the General Histories Branch at the U.S. Army Center of Military History; and Lynda L. Crist, editor of *The Papers of Jefferson Davis* at Rice University.

Also: Jane Ehrenhart, supervisor of Reference and Technical Services at the Illinois State Historical Library; Dr. Mark Benbow, resident historian at the Woodrow Wilson House in Washington, D.C.; Lisa Moulder, collections manager at the Betsy Ross House in Philadelphia; Howard M. Pollman, community relations officer at the State Museum of Pennsylvania in Harrisburg; and Andrea Ashby Leraris at the Independence National Historical Park Library in Philadelphia.

Also: Tom Sherlock, the historian at Arlington National Cemetery; Clare M. Sheridan, the librarian at the American Textile History Museum in Lowell, Massachusetts; Martha Mayo, director of the Center of Lowell History at the University of Massachusetts-Lowell; Rob Schoeberlein, director of Special Collections at the Maryland State Archives in Annapolis; Jon N. Austin, director of the Museum of Funeral Customs in Springfield, Illinois; Janie C. Morris, research services librarian at the Rare Book, Manuscript, and Special Collections Library at Duke University; Susan Pittman, press officer at the U.S. State Department; Bob Matthias, museum coordinator at the Grand Army of the Republic Museum in Lynn, Massachusetts; Tom Duclos, associate curator at the New York State Military Museum in Saratoga Springs; and Michael Moss, the director of the West Point Museum at the United States Military Academy.

I received much-appreciated support during the researching and writing of this book from a wonderful group of friends, family, and colleagues, especially Jay Adams, Xande Anderer, Tim Ashwell, Bernie and Linda Brien, Quentin Butcher, Bob Carolla, Chad Conway, Larry Cushman, John Czaplewski, Marianne and Tommy Dodson, Russell Duncan, Dale Dye, Bernie Edelman, Gloria Emerson, Carol Engle, Bill Fogarty, John Gardiner, Reno Harnish, John Hoffecker, Michael Kazin, Mike Keating, Liz Keenan, Michael ("M-60") Kelley, Evan Leepson, Peter and Ellen Leepson, Glenn Maravetz, Ashley Matthews, Kevin McCorry, Gregory McNamee, Dave Miller, Pete Nardi, Andre T. and Gayle Parraway, Angus Paul, Margaret Peters, Mokie Pratt Porter, Avrom Posner, Susan and Gray

Price, Dan and Margie Radovsky, Barbara and Pat Rhodes, Kathy Jo Shea, Margo Lee Sherman, Sally Sherman, Jaclyn Tamaroff, Angus Theurmer, Pam Turner, and Jim Wagner. Special thanks to all my valued colleagues at Vietnam Veterans of America's national office.

For help with understanding flag customs in other nations I would like to thank Caroline Toplis of New Zealand's Ministry for Culture and Heritage, Corinne Lyon Kunzle of the Swiss Embassy in Washington, D.C., and Joana Cavalcanti of the Brazilian Embassy's Cultural and Public Affairs Office. Thanks, too, to Johan Bonink and Peter Hans van den Muijzenberg, Holland; Roberto Toselli, Italy; Xavier Llobet, Spain; Conde Cargadito, Venezuela; Michael Adams and Bart Connolly, Ireland; Victor M. Martinez, Mexico; Tamer Olui, Egypt; Dan Palm and Jouni Maho, Sweden; Jukka Aho and Hiski Haapoja, Finland; Albert Reingewirtz, Israel; Steve Hayes and Moira de Swardt, South Africa; John Anderson, Germany; Greg Goss, J. R. Pelland and Rich Wales, Canada; Anthony Desportes and Eric Savary, France; Ammar A. Samandar, Syria; and Mark Terzano, Peru.

My wife, Janna, and our children, Devin and Cara, put up with me spending inordinately long periods of time researching and writing this book. I thank them for their patience, love, and support.

Introduction

AMERICANS HAVE a unique and special feeling for our flag. And that's putting it mildly. This is not to diminish the respect and pride people in other nations feel for their national emblems. However, no country in the world can match the intensity of the American citizenry's attachment to the fifty-star, thirteen-stripe Stars and Stripes, which is as familiar an American icon as any that has existed in the nation's history.

Nowhere on earth do citizens fly their national flags, as Americans do, everywhere they live and everywhere they go, from our front porches to our pickup trucks. The flag is a fixture in our nation's schools, in our mass media, and in our advertising. The flag flies in front of our government buildings and business establishments of all types, including countless automobile dealer showrooms throughout the land that specialize in flying extra large Stars and Stripes.

Nor does any nation turn to its flag as an emotional, political, and patriotic symbol in good times and bad the way Americans do. We display the red-white-and-blue American flag at festive cultural and social events to celebrate and, at times of national tragedy, to grieve and show our resolve.

No nation displays its national flag as ubiquitously or as proudly as Americans do at sporting events, from local Little League fields to the Super Bowl.

And no nation can match the widespread use of the American flag as a decorative part of countless items of apparel and accessories, from headbands to designer jewelry.

We Americans, alone among the nations of the world, have our school-children pledge their allegiance to the flag, and we have done so for more than a century. Our National Anthem is a hymn of praise to our flag. Our largest veterans' service organization, the American Legion, has had an Americanism division since it was founded in 1919. It promotes the display of, and dispenses advice about, the proper use of the American flag. The second largest veterans' group, the Veterans of Foreign Wars, similarly promotes the flag through its own Americanism program.

The proper use of the flag itself is detailed in a one-of-a-kind document, the official U.S. Flag Code, a long, detailed set of rules that was developed at the instigation of the newly formed American Legion in the early 1920s. The code has been a federal statute since 1942.

No other country can boast of well-organized, well-funded nonprofit nationwide organizations, such as the National Flag Foundation, the National Flag Day Foundation, and the Citizens Flag Alliance, which work full-time to promote respect for the nation's flag. The latter organization lobbies exclusively for congressional passage of a constitutional amendment to protect the flag from desecration. Legislation calling for the Flag Desecration Amendment, which would be the twenty-eighth amendment to the Constitution, has fallen short by just a handful of votes in recent years in Congress.

★   ★   ★

The flag's image has figured prominently in the national iconography since the War of 1812. Examples include the 1776 "Betsy Ross" thirteen-star flag, which has been memorialized in countless books and paintings and other widely disseminated images since 1870; the Star-Spangled Banner itself, which survived "the rockets' red glare" and "the bombs bursting in air" in 1814 at Fort McHenry; the hoisting of the red, white, and blue by six marines atop Mount Suribachi on Iwo Jima during World War II; and Neil Armstrong's proud planting of the flag on the Moon in 1969.

In recent years we have seen a damaged but intact American flag pulled from the debris of the World Trade Center following the September 11, 2001, terrorist attack; the huge American flag unfurled by firefighters from the roof of the Pentagon on September 12; and the widely disseminated media moment of the Iraq War in 2003 when a U.S. marine briefly placed a small American flag atop the face of a tumbling statue of Saddam Hussein in Baghdad.

Artists in every media have featured the American flag in their work, from folk artists to internationally renowned painters such as Jasper Johns and Childe Hassam. The flag also has been lionized in countless songs, including George M. Cohan's "You're a Grand Old Flag" and the nation's official national march, John Philip Sousa's "The Stars and Stripes Forever," as well as in poems, from the prosaic to the patriotic to the literary.

Tens of millions of Americans have served in the armed forces, and hundreds of thousands have given their lives in battle for the flag. In the wake of the events of September 11, 2001, the flag became an instant and widely used symbol of a nation united against terrorism as millions of Americans proudly and defiantly unfurled American flags in every corner of the country.

★   ★   ★

This unalloyed and unique feeling that Americans have for their flag is even more remarkable given the fact that the American flag's origins are murky and that Americans labor under several widespread misunderstandings about our national emblem. We do not know for certain, for example, who designed the first flag. Nor is it known who made the first flag—the Betsy Ross story notwithstanding. There is no document setting out the meaning of the flag's colors, even though pundits have promulgated their ideas about what the red, white, and blue stand for since the 1780s. We know why the first flag had thirteen stars and thirteen stripes—to represent the original colonies. But no document exists explaining why the flag's designers chose the stars and the stripes or why they picked red, white, and blue as symbols for those colonies.

The current feelings of near religious reverence many Americans have for the flag, which some have dubbed the "cult of the flag," date not from the Revolutionary War as is widely believed, but from 1861 and the start of the Civil War. Before the Civil War—for the first three quarters of this nation's history in fact—it was not customary for private individuals to fly the American flag. Until 1861, the flag was flown almost exclusively at federal facilities and by the American military, primarily on U.S. Navy ships. Contrary to images promulgated well after the fact, the Continental Army did not fight under the Stars and Stripes against the British; George Washington's troops displayed regimental flags.

It was not until the fall of Fort Sumter in 1861 that the American flag began to take on something approaching its current meaning to the American public. Soon after that fort fell to the Confederates, Northerners began displaying the flag ubiquitously as a symbol of the fight to keep the Union intact.

Another largely unknown factor in this equation is that the federal and state governments have not been the instigators in implementing the important milestones in the American flag's evolution. By and large it has been individual American businessmen, teachers, journalists, politicians, and private organizations—primarily but not exclusively veterans' groups and patriotic organizations—that have developed and pushed for many of the important changes in the evolution of the flag's cultural importance.

Those milestones include:

- The push to make "The Star-Spangled Banner," which was written in 1814, the official National Anthem, something that did not occur until 1931.

- The adoption of the Pledge of Allegiance, which was written by Francis Bellamy in 1892, but was not recognized by the federal government until 1942.

- The development of the Flag Code, which was put together primarily by the American Legion in 1923 and 1924 and not made into law by the government until 1942.

- The national June 14th Flag Day commemoration, which was the brainchild of a Wisconsin schoolteacher in 1885, was pushed by the American Flag Day Association in 1895 but did not receive presidential sanction until 1949.

What is not widely known today as well is that from the time the Continental Congress passed legislation establishing the flag's elements on June 14 (Flag Day) 1777, until June 24, 1912, there was no law setting out the exact order of the stars or the actual proportions of the flag. American flags during those 135 years often had different arrangements of the stars and differing proportions. Although most American flags had straight rows of stars and proportions similar to the official flag that was codified in 1912, the designs were left to the creative talents—and whims—of individual flag makers. And it wasn't uncommon for people to stitch all manner of symbols and slogans onto flags.

★   ★   ★

The question of why the American flag looms so large in the social, political, and emotional hearts and minds of millions of Americans has several answers. The flag, of course, stands for everything that is admirable in America's political history, especially our democratic form of government and the many freedoms Americans have enjoyed since 1776. It also has served as a unifying symbol for a relatively young nation made up predominantly of immigrants. And, it has been argued, the near religious fervor many accord to the flag derives from the fact that this nation has neither a state religion nor a royal family.

Alexis de Tocqueville, the acutely perceptive French aristocrat who visited these shores in 1831–32 and many of whose observations about this country ring true today, pointed to American democracy itself as the main force behind what he called Americans' tendency to "feel extreme pleasure in exhibiting" our "recently acquired advantages." People "living in democracies," de Tocqueville said of an era when the American flag was rarely exhibited by individuals, "love their country just as they love themselves, and they transfer the habits of their private vanity to their vanity as a nation."

Be it vanity, quiet pride, or boastful patriotism, there is little doubt that Americans have a special feeling for the red, white, and blue. This book looks at what's behind that special feeling by tracing the complete history of the American flag—it's biography, so to speak. It examines the many changes in the American flag and the evolution of its cultural importance beginning in the Revolutionary War and ending with the flag's prominent role as a symbol of American resolve in today's war against terrorism. It also traces the look of the actual flags themselves, which—like the meanings attached to the flag—changed over time.

The American flag is an unwavering part of life for untold tens of millions of Americans. My hope is that what follows will shine an informing light on what has become the object of veneration for so many Americans and the very visible symbol of this amazing nation.

CHAPTER ONE

Antecedents

★   ★   ★

The flag of today represents many centuries of development. Probably no other inanimate object has excited so great an influence over the actions of the human race. It has existed in some form among all peoples and from the earliest times.

—Frederic J. Haskin, 1941

HISTORY DOES NOT record the first time a human being attached pieces of cloth to a staff to use as a symbol. But wooden, metal, and cloth flaglike objects—statues, standards, banners, guidons, ensigns, pennons, and streamers—date from the ancient Egyptians who flew carved elephants and other symbols mounted on poles on boats and perhaps in front of their temples more than five thousand years ago.

Other early prehistoric cultures also placed carvings or animal skins atop poles, sometimes accompanied by streamers or feathers. Among the oldest is an ancient Persian metal flagpole that had a metal eagle perched at its top. There also are recorded uses of flag predecessors—nearly always as communications or identification devices on the field of battle or to signify religious affiliations—among the Assyrians, Phoenicians, Saracens, Indians, Aztecs, and Mongolians.

It is believed that the ancient Chinese first used cloth banners in the second century BC. The founder of the Chou dynasty (ca. 1027 BC), for example, is thought to have displayed a white flag to announce his presence. The main use of flags by the Chinese, though, was as a military communications device. "Because they could not hear each other, they made gongs and drums. Because they could not see each other they made pennants and flags," the ancient Chinese military general and philosopher Sun Tzu wrote in his classic *The Art of War.* "Gongs, drums, pennants and flags are the means to unify the men's ears and eyes."

That was the case in China in the fourth century BC, according to Sun Pin, the military strategist and Sun Tzu descendant. "Commands should be carried out by using various colored banners," he advised. "Affix pennants to the chariots to distinguish grade and status. Differentiate among troops that can easily be mistaken for each other by using banners and standards."

The ancient Roman legions carried banners called vexilla. These were small square ensigns, most often red in color, that were attached to cross-bars at the end of lances. They often were adorned with animal figures, such as horses, eagles, wolves, or boars. Flags in ancient India typically were carried on chariots and elephants. They were usually red or green triangularly shaped banners that had figures embroidered upon them and were surrounded by gold fringe.

The Vikings flew several types of flags, primarily on their famed sailing ships in the tenth and eleventh centuries AD. The most common was the Raven flag, in the shape of a triangle with two straight sides and a curved side. Historians believe that that emblem flew from the masts of Danish Viking ships and probably from the Norwegian Viking ships that landed in Newfoundland a thousand years ago. If so, the Viking Raven banner has the distinction of being the first flag to fly in North America.

The idea of flags as symbols of the rulers of nation states began to evolve in Europe in the Middle Ages and the Renaissance. One of the banners that Christopher Columbus displayed when he reached the West Indies in 1492, for example, bore the Spanish royal standard: two lions and two castles representing the arms of Castile and Leon. Columbus also carried a special white expeditionary flag with a green cross. It consisted of the letters F and Y for Ferdinand (Fernando) and Isabella (Ysabel), each of which was topped by a crown.

The English flag of the period, the red cross of St. George, the nation's patron saint, set on a white banner, dates from the Crusades and was considered a type of national emblem as early as 1277. It was not, however, considered a national flag as we know the concept today. The St. George's Cross rather was a royal banner—the symbol of the king's authority. It was flown on English ships and emblazoned on soldiers' shields. English ships also flew several types of rank-identifying pennants called ensigns, including the all-red, all-white and all-blue English naval ensigns. The word *ensign* itself derives from the British military rank of the same name; the "ensign" was the officer in charge of carrying the colors into battle.

Historical evidence about the use of flags in the fifteenth, sixteenth, and seventeenth centuries is scant and sketchy. Because flags did not have anything close to the meaning they took on as symbols of nations beginning in the late eighteenth century, primary documents rarely contain descriptions of flags. Much of our knowledge about flags during those centuries, therefore, is based on fragmentary evidence and historic supposition.

Historians believe that the first St. George's Cross to make its way to North America was brought by the Italian navigator and explorer Giovanni Caboto (known by his adopted English name, John Cabot), who sailed under the aegis of King Henry VII. The best historical evidence indicates that Cabot's small ship, the *Matthew*, reached Newfoundland in May 1497. When Cabot took possession of the land for England, he unfurled the St. George's Cross along with the Venetian flag of St. Mark.

The first explorers from the other nations who came to North America also sailed under various types of banners and ensigns, most often representing their countries' monarchs. That included the blue royal French flag adorned with three fleurs-de-lis likely carried by Giovanni da Verrazzano, the Italian-born navigator and explorer who sailed under the French king Francis I (François). Verrazzano made landfall off present-day Cape Fear, North Carolina, in March 1524 and sailed on to what is now New York harbor and New England. Jacques Cartier, who explored the Saint Lawrence River for Francis I in 1534, also is believed to have brought his monarch's banner to these shores.

Several types of French merchant flags—typically a white cross on a blue field with the royal arms at its center—were flown by the other pioneering French navigators who came to explore the New World: Samuel de Champlain in 1604; René-Robert Cavelier, Sieur de La Salle, and Jacques Marquette in 1666; and Louis Joliet in 1669.

The English navigator and explorer Henry Hudson, sailing for the Dutch, took his ship, the *Half Moon*, into what is now New York harbor on September 3, 1609. Hudson did so most likely flying the orange, white, and blue horizontally striped flag of the Dutch United East India Company. Hudson also probably carried the Amsterdam Chamber flag, a red, white, and black horizontal tricolor affair. Both flags also contained initials in the center white stripe.

The British Union Jack was created by King James I three years after he succeeded Queen Elizabeth I. James came to England to take the throne in 1603 after serving as James VI of Scotland, where the monarch's flag since the time of the Crusades had been the St. Andrew's Cross, a diagonal white cross on a blue background. On April 12, 1606, James decreed that all English and Scottish ships should fly the new red, white, and blue union flag on their main masts. That flag was known as the Union Jack and also as the "king's colors." It consisted of an amalgam of the crosses and colors of St. George and St. Andrew. The ships were directed also to fly either the banner of St. George or of St. Andrew on their foremasts.

It is believed that the *Mayflower* flew the red cross of St. George when it landed at Plymouth Rock on December 21, 1620, and it is possible that the ship also displayed the Union Jack. And it also is likely that one or both of those flags was flown by the members of the Virginia Company whose three ships—the *Susan Constant*, *Godspeed*, and *Discovery*—had landed on Jamestown Island in Virginia, on May 14, 1607, and began the first permanent British settlement in North America.

There is concrete evidence that the Union Jack flew in the Massachusetts Bay Colony as early as 1634. Court records show that John Endicott, a local government official who had previously served as governor, that year ordered the cross cut out of a Union Jack. This was not a protest against British rule however. Endicott, acting probably at the behest of the nonconformist pastor Roger Williams (who later founded the colony of Rhode Island), did so to spotlight his Puritan belief that the cross was an idolatrous and pagan symbol. Endicott was tried in a local court for the offense and censured.

The official Union Jack changed several times during the often-chaotic seventeenth century when England underwent two revolutions and a civil war. In 1707, when the turbulence ended under Queen Anne, the new Parliament of the United Kingdom of England, Scotland, and Wales officially adopted James I's Union Jack. "The ensigns armorial of our kingdom of Great Britain," Parliament decreed on January 16, 1707, shall be "the crosses of St. George and St. Andrew conjoined to be used on all flags, banners, standards, and ensigns both at sea and land." This flag, which was used exclusively on ships and on government buildings and military fortifications, came to be known as the "Union Flag."

★   ★   ★

English colonial governors and local military commanders in America, most often small militia companies, began designing and displaying their own flags not long after the establishment of the first settlements in Jamestown in 1607 and in Plymouth in 1620. Nearly all of the colors and symbols used in the earliest colonial flags were borrowed from the Union Jack and the various types of flags carried by British infantry units.

Not all were red, white, and blue, however, and not all used crosses. That is the case with one of the oldest flags of colonial America that still exists, the banner of the English troops based in the counties of Essex, Suffolk, and Middlesex, Massachusetts, known as the Bedford flag. Dating from about 1705, the Bedford flag was crimson in color and featured an arm reaching through a cloud, holding a sword. The arm, cloud, and sword were silver, gold, and black. The colors of Capt. Thomas Noyes's company of troops in 1684 in Newbury, Massachusetts, consisted of a solid green field. The upper left-hand corner (known most often as the canton or the union) contained a red cross on a white background.

Many other colonial flags of the seventeenth and eighteenth centuries contained a canton. That includes the Massachusetts Red Ensign, a red flag with a plain white canton, which flew from about 1636–1686. That flag, it is believed, was the first flown in America that contained the canton-and-field design combination.

The Saybrook, Connecticut, military company flag in 1675 was red with a white cross in the canton, augmented with a blue ball, most likely in a red field representing a bullet. The Newbury, Massachusetts, militia flag, as noted above, was green with a red cross in its white canton.

The flag with the canton that most resembled what would become the first American flag, though, was not directly associated with the British colonial government. It was the flag of the East India Company, which was formed on December 31, 1600, by Queen Elizabeth I following the 1588 defeat of the Spanish Armada. The East India Company was designed to be the official English entrant into the lucrative spice trade in East and Southeast Asia and India. But the company soon became much more than a commercial venture. It expanded into other commodities, including cotton and silk, and into other areas of the globe, including the Persian Gulf. In addition to its monopoly on trade in the East, the East India Company was given the authority to assume military and political power in the countries where it established itself.

The first reference to an East India Company flag was in 1616 when Japanese authorities complained about the cross on a flag flying from a company vessel. That cross likely was the St. George's Cross. Evidence indicates that in 1670 and in the 1680s the company's ships flew a flag with red and white horizontal stripes and the red St. George's Cross in a white canton. A book published in 1701 shows the East India Company flag with seven red and white horizontal stripes and the red cross of St. George in a white canton. Sometime after 1707, when the Union Jack was created, the company substituted it in the canton for the St. George's Cross. By 1732, the flag's number of stripes had grown from seven to thirteen.

★   ★   ★

By that time many in the thirteen American colonies were chafing under the heavy-handed British rule. As sentiment against King George grew and colonists banded together to protest against colonial rule, they adopted a variety of mostly anti-British flags as emblems of their rebelliousness. These flags featured three main images: the snake, variations on the theme of the word "liberty," and the pine tree. The idea for the "Don't Tread on Me" coiled snake flag came from the pen of Benjamin Franklin. In 1751 in his *Pennsylvania Gazette* Franklin wrote satirically that Americans should send rattlesnakes to England to thank the British for sending convicts to these shores.

On May 9, 1754, Franklin again used the snake in his newspaper, this time to induce the colonies to unite during the French and Indian War (1754–63), during which the English and French battled for control of colonial North America. Franklin, in what is believed to be the first political cartoon to appear in an American newspaper, drew a cartoon depicting a snake cut into eight sections, representing the colonies in a shape suggesting the Atlantic coast with New England as the head and South Carolina as the tail. The cartoon's caption read: "Join, or Die."

In the decades that followed, as discontent with British colonial rule intensified, Franklin's snake image became an expression of revolution. Christopher Gadsden, a patriotic South Carolinian who was a colonel in the Continental army, likely designed one of the first snake flags while serving in 1775 as a member of the Marine Committee of the Continental Congress. Gadsden appointed Esek Hopkins of Rhode Island to lead the first Continental Navy fleet in December of 1775. Hopkins, the first commodore of the U.S. Navy, took command of his five-ship fleet with a personal flag, which Gadsden likely had designed and given to him. That flag had a yellow field with a rattlesnake coiled in the middle and the words "Don't Tread on Me!" underneath.

Aside from what became known as "the Gadsden flag," the rattlesnake appeared on many other American colonial banners, including several flown by military units during the Revolutionary War. A flag used by the minutemen of Culpeper County, Virginia, for example, included the rattlesnake, the "Don't Tread on Me" motto, and the famous words of Virginia's Patrick Henry, "Liberty or Death."

Another similar banner was the 1775 flag of Col. John Proctor's Independent Battalion in Westmoreland County, Pennsylvania. That flag (more than six feet long and nearly six feet wide) consisted of a coiled rattlesnake and Gadsden's words painted directly on top of a solid red field with the British Union Jack in the canton. The snake's menacing tongue is pointed at the symbol of the British crown. Above the snake are the letters "J.P." and "I.B.W.C.P.," which stand for "John Proctor, Independent Battalion, Westmoreland County, Pennsylvania."

The flag of the Train of Artillery company in Provincetown, Massachusetts, also had Gadsden's words emblazoned under a coiled rattlesnake, as did the banner displayed by Major General John Sullivan's Life Guard in Rhode Island, also known as the Rhode Island Militia. That flag, which was used in 1778–79, had nine blue and white alternating stripes and a white canton with a coiled snake.

Although it did not have a snake, the Forster flag of 1775 is believed to have been the first flag with red and white stripes used to represent the colonial cause. Family lore has it that Maj. Israel Forster and the Minutemen captured a flag from the British at the Battle of Lexington on April 19, 1775. The patriots then replaced the Union Jack canton with six white stripes, spacing them over the red background to represent the thirteen colonies, and displayed the flag that day at that battle and the ensuing fighting at Concord.

★　★　★

Another popular theme that made its way onto anti-British flags during the years prior to the American Revolution was the word "liberty." Most often liberty flags were solid colored, usually white, with the word "liberty" spelled out in large capital letters. They date from the summer of 1765 and the secret revolutionary radical group the Sons of Liberty, which grew up that year throughout the colonies to protest the infamous British Stamp Act. The group took its name from a February 1765 Parliamentary speech in which rebellious Americans were mockingly referred to as "sons of liberty."

Sons of Liberty groups first met under "liberty trees," where they stirred up support for colonial resistance. When the colonial authorities cut down those trees, the rebels took to meeting under liberty poles, which often featured protest banners, such as one that contained the words "Liberty and Property." A flag displayed at Taunton, Massachusetts, featured the words "Liberty and Union" across a red field with the Union Jack in the canton. Another had the image of a tree, with the words "Liberty Tree" on top and "An Appeal to God" below. Another early liberty flag in New York contained the words "Liberty, Property and No Stamps."

Historians believe that one Sons of Liberty flag that flew from Boston's Liberty Tree contained nine red and white stripes in honor of the representatives of the nine colonies who attended the October 19, 1765, Stamp Act Congress. Those stripes likely were displayed horizontally. If so, that flag is the first recorded on the continent with alternating red and white stripes and could be the progenitor of the stripe design in the American flag. Thirteen horizontal stripes, in blue and silver, also appeared in the canton of the yellow silk regimental flag of Capt. Abraham Markoe's Philadelphia Light Horse Troop that accompanied George Washington to New York in the summer of 1775.

The third widely used symbol on anti-British colonial flags, primarily in New England, was the pine tree. The pine tree symbol in New England dates from the 1629 seal of the Massachusetts Bay Colony, which featured the images of an Indian and pine trees. The red 1686 New England flag contained a canton with the English St. George's Cross in it and a small green pine tree displayed in one corner of the cross. That banner was flown by Col. William Prescott, who commanded some one thousand American militiamen against a force of more than twice that number of British army regulars at the pivotal June 17, 1775, Battle of Bunker Hill, fought at Breed's Hill above Charlestown, Massachusetts.

The most popular image of that Revolutionary War battle—the 1786 painting *The Death of Warren* by John Trumbull—contains an image of the colonial troops flying a red flag with a green pine tree on a white background in the canton. But that image of the flag, minus the cross of St. George, is inaccurate. "Certainly Trumbull, like many artists of the Revolutionary War period, allowed his imagination free rein in the matter of depicting details in battle scenes," Whitney Smith, the nation's foremost vexillologist (flag expert), said of the Trumbull's artistic flag license in that painting.

Trumbull may have been influenced by the fact that not long after the Battle of Bunker Hill, pine tree flags began to be displayed on American Revolutionary War vessels. The first was in September 1775 when two heavily armed scows, called "floating batteries," flying the pine tree ensign adorned with the words AN APPEAL TO HEAVEN opened fire from the Charles River onto British houses in Boston.

The first six schooners commissioned by the Continental Congress to intercept British ships sailing into Boston in October 1775—the *Hancock, Lee, Franklin, Harrison, Lynch,* and *Warren*—flew the pine tree flag. An order dated October 20, 1775, from George Washington's secretary Col. Joseph Reed, proposed that the ships show a flag "by which our vessels may know one another," a flag with "a white ground and a tree in the middle, and the motto, 'An Appeal to Heaven.'" By January 1776 the *Franklin* was flying that pine tree flag. On April 29 the Massachusetts Council passed a resolution ordering its naval officers to wear green and white uniforms and that "the colors be a white flag with a green pine-tree and the inscription, 'An appeal to Heaven.'"

*   *   *

But it was not the rattlesnake, the pine tree, nor the word "liberty" that appeared on what is now considered the first American flag, although at the time it was not officially recognized as such. This is the flag that George Washington ordered hoisted on January 1, 1776, to recognize the birth of the Continental Army on Prospect Hill in Charlestown outside of his camp near Boston. The Second Continental Congress had named Washington commander in chief in June following the battles of Lexington and Concord.

On New Year's Day, Washington unfurled the improvised Continental Colors, also known as the Grand Union flag, the Continental flag, the Cambridge flag, the Somerville flag, the Union Flag, and the Great Union—the first flag that came into general use throughout the colonies. Washington, who referred to it as the "Union Flag in Compliment to the United Colonies," had the banner hoisted on a towering seventy-six-foot-high liberty pole so that it could be seen as far away as Boston. The flag had thirteen alternating red and white stripes. In the canton of the Continental Colors was the British Union Jack with its interwoven crosses of St. George and St. Andrew. Washington's flag was almost a carbon copy of the flag the East India Company had been flying since the 1670s.

*   *   *

The generally accepted explanation of the origins of the Continental Colors is that the thirteen stripes represented the colonies and the Union Jack the rebellious colonists' loyalty to the British crown, if not its Parliaments' policies. That sentiment held in general for most American rebels, at least

during this stage of the revolt, six months before the signing of the Declaration of Independence.

Still, the origins of the Continental Colors are not clear. Historians do
not believe that it was based on the strikingly similar East India Company
flag for two reasons. First, few colonists were familiar with the East India
Company flag because there is no evidence it ever flew in American waters.
Second, it seems highly unlikely that rebellious colonists would purposely
choose an emblem that stood for an organ of the British crown.

It also is not clear exactly who designed the Continental Colors. It may
have been the work of Benjamin Franklin, Benjamin Harrison, and
Thomas Lynch, who were appointed by the Continental Congress in the
summer of 1775 to advise Washington in forming his new army. The first
respected American flag historian, retired admiral George Henry Preble,
writing in the late-nineteenth century, ascribed to that theory. Franklin, et al.,
"were appointed to consider the subject" of "a common national flag," Preble wrote. They "assembled at [Washington's] camp in Cambridge." The
"result" of that meeting, he said, was the design for the Continental Colors.
However, no mention was made of the flag in the Franklin committee's detailed report to Congress on November 2, nor have historians been able to
find other concrete evidence to support Preble's proposition.

*   *   *

Esek Hopkins's small armada—the *Alfred*, *Columbus*, *Cabot*, and *Andrew
Doria*—the first regular American fleet, set sail from Philadelphia on January 4, 1776, flying several flags. One was his personal "Don't Tread on Me"
rattlesnake flag. Another was what Hopkins called "the strip'd jack" or
"striped flag," most likely a simple red and white striped flag used for identification. Also flying on the ships was the Continental Colors.

Before his fleet departed on December 3, 1775, the Continental Colors
was raised for the first time on an American fighting vessel, the fleet's flagship, the *Alfred*, under the command of Capt. Dudley Saltonstall. This was
about a month before Washington unfurled that flag in Charlestown. Just
who raised the *Alfred*'s flag is not completely certain. But the senior lieutenant on the *Alfred*, the renowned naval hero John Paul Jones, took credit
for it. "I hoisted with my own Hands the Flag of Freedom the First time
that it was displayed on board the Alfred on the Delaware," Jones wrote
in 1779.

Historians disagree about Jones's claim. Some believe that Jones raised the "Don't Tread on Me" rattlesnake flag, not the Continental Colors. Others believe Jones may have raised the Continental Colors on the *Alfred*, but that he was not the first American to do so. John Adams, among others, claimed that the "first American flag as hoisted," as he put it an 1813 letter, was the work of Capt. John Manly, who commanded the schooner *Lee* and the frigates *Hancock* and *Hague*. John Adams's after-the-fact claim notwithstanding, historians believe that in all likelihood the *Lee* flew the pine tree flag, not the Continental Colors.

Hopkins's fleet claimed other flag firsts. When Hopkins's small armada captured Forts Montagu and Nassau on the eastern end of New Providence in the British-owned Bahamas on March 17, 1776, it marked the first overseas victory for an American flag–flying navy ship. When Capt. John Barry's *Lexington* fought and defeated the British brig *Edward* on the seas off the Virginia coast on April 17, it marked the first time an American flag vessel captured a foreign flagged ship.

The American brig *Andrew* (sometimes called *Andrea*) *Doria* sailed into port on the small Dutch-owned West Indies island of Saint Eustatius (Sint Eustatius) on November 16, 1776, on a mission to obtain clothing, cannons, gunpowder, and other war supplies. The ship, under Capt. Isaiah Robinson, dropped anchor in the port city of Orangetown in front of Fort Orange. An English ship in the harbor reported that the Dutch flag at Fort Orange was lowered in welcome, and then the *Andrew Doria* lowered its sails and fired an eleven-gun salute. The fort's commander then sought advice about the efficacy of returning the salute from the Dutch governor. It was decided to return the salute with an eleven-gun reply. This marked the first foreign salute to an American flag.

The honor of presenting the Continental Colors to Europe for the first time went to the sixteen-gun brig, *Reprisal,* the first Continental navy vessel to reach European waters. Under the command of Capt. Lambert Wickes, the *Reprisal* set sail from Philadelphia on October 24, 1776, carrying Benjamin Franklin to assume his duties as the American Commissioner to France.

By the end of the year 1776, the Maritime Committee of the Continental Congress considered the Continental Colors as the de facto official flag of the American naval forces. The committee let all its commanders know early in 1777, for example, that "it is expected that you contend warmly All necessary occasions for the honor of the American flag."

Incorporating the Union Jack in the Continental Colors, Washington soon discovered, may have been a mistake. When British troops saw it, they took the Union Jack as a sign that the colonials were surrendering. "It was received in Boston as . . . a signal of submission," Washington wrote three days later.

Still the Continental Colors, although it was never formally adopted by Congress, remained the unofficial flag of the rebellious colonies until June 14, 1777. In the eighteen months following Washington's unveiling of that flag, it was used as a symbol of the rebellious colonies' unity—primarily, but not exclusively, on Continental navy ships.

The first Stars and Stripes—of whatever arrangement—to be raised in victory over a foreign force flew from the twenty-eight-gun frigate *Providence* on January 27, 1778, under command of Capt. John Peck Rathburne (sometimes spelled Rathbun). The *Providence*, sailing from North Carolina, captured the British Fort Nassau in the Bahamas, seized ammunition, and freed more than two dozen American prisoners. The ship also captured a British ship and reclaimed five other American vessels that had fallen into British hands.

Military units on land displayed the Continental Colors as well as a wide variety of other types of regimental flags. Many had single-color fields with emblems and cantons with various designs. The Second Rhode Island Regiment's flag, for example, had thirteen stars in its canton. The all-black Massachusetts unit, the Bucks of America, flew a flag with thirteen white or gold stars in a blue canton. The field featured a pine tree and an antlered buck. Troops of the Third Continental Infantry under Col. Ebenezer Learned, on the other hand, displayed the Continental Colors in Boston as they drove Gen. William Howe, the commander in chief of the British army, and his troops from that city in March 1776.

In his January 1776 report on the publication of Tom Paine's landmark pamphlet *Common Sense*, which passionately made the case for independence from England, the British spy Gilbert Barkley noted that armed colonial ships in Philadelphia flew "what they call the American flag," a banner that almost certainly was the Continental Colors. The ships commanded by Gen. Benedict Arnold flew a version of the Continental Colors at the ill-fated Battle of Valcour Island on Lake Champlain on October 11–13, 1776.

Joseph Hewes, a Continental Congress delegate from North Carolina, purchased a large Continental Colors from the Philadelphia flag maker Margaret Manny, who worked with the Wharton Ship Yard in Philadelphia, in February 1776. That flag subsequently flew in his hometown of Edenton. In April 1776 the Continental Colors was depicted on the North Carolina seven-and-a-half dollar bill. And it was flown in Williamsburg, the colonial capital of Virginia, on May 15, 1776. The occasion was the sendoff of Virginia's delegates to the Continental Congress in Philadelphia. The "union flag of the American states" flew from the colonial Capitol Building that day, according to one eyewitness. That "union flag" was the Continental Colors.

CHAPTER TWO

The Birth of a Symbol

★   ★   ★

Resolved, That the flag of the United States be thirteen stripes, alternate red and white: that the union be thirteen stars, white in a blue field representing a new constellation.

— Resolution adopted by the Second Continental Congress,
June 14, 1777

O N JULY 2, 1776, the Second Continental Congress approved a resolution declaring that the colonies "are, and of right ought to be, free and independent States." Late in the afternoon on July 4, the body approved the Declaration of Independence. Church bells chimed in celebration in Philadelphia, and copies of that seminal document made their way throughout the colonies to be read publicly. When the news hit Boston on July 18, the Union Jack and every other emblem of King George in the city were taken down and burned by the populace.

Despite the spirited celebrations, the Continental Congress took no immediate action to adopt a flag to represent the self-declared newly independent states. And no action would be taken on that front for nearly a year.

In the meantime the Continental Colors continued to serve as the de facto symbol of the newly created United States of America. Congress's Marine Committee certainly considered that to be the case. On September 27, 1776, the committee reported to Congress that it had given permission to a Francis Guillot to "equip and arm" a privateer (a private ship refitted to attack British ships) "under the colours of the United States."

During this time flag makers, including several in Philadelphia, continued to produce the Continental Colors, primarily for naval ship providers.

One of the earliest recorded flag makers was a Philadelphia seamstress, twenty-five-year-old Elizabeth Griscom Ross, who sold "ship's colours &c." to Capt. William Richards's store for fourteen pounds, twelve shillings in May 1777.

On July 4, 1777, celebrations took place throughout the United States to mark the young nation's first birthday. In Philadelphia all the naval ships in the harbor gathered together at one o'clock in the afternoon, and each one of them fired thirteen cannon to honor the thirteen states. The ships were festooned with streamers as well as the Continental Colors. Those colors also were proudly raised that day at all the forts, batteries, and ships in the harbor at Charleston, South Carolina.

Three weeks earlier, on Saturday, June 14, 1777, the Continental Congress had opened a short session in Philadelphia dealing with fiscal matters, including advancing several hundred dollars each to three Continental Army militia captains "for the use of their respective independent companies." After that came a Marine Committee matter: granting that panel permission to command Continental Navy ships in the Delaware River.

The next order of business was a brief resolution that read in its entirety: "Resolved, That the flag of the United States be thirteen stripes, alternate red and white: that the union be thirteen stars, white in a blue field, representing a new constellation."

Congress did not set the dimensions, the proportions, the size of the canton or field (the main body where the stripes are) or even the shape of the flag. Nor did the resolution say anything about the shape of the stars or the pattern for the stars in the constellation. The record does not show which member of Congress introduced the resolution or if a committee did so. The official record simply notes that the resolution was adopted without any debate, comments, or explanations.

Why did the Continental Congress seemingly pay such little attention to the Flag Resolution? Historians who have looked deeply into the matter have not discovered why Congress took so little time and expended such little energy with the piece of legislation that created our national flag. Nor has it been determined exactly what prompted Congress to act on June 14, 1777. There is speculation that navy officers were not happy with the Continental Colors because it contained the Union Jack, the sentiment that George Washington had expressed early in 1776. And flag suppliers, hearing those complaints, may have been pressing Congress to come up with a new all-American flag. William Richards, the Philadelphia ship outfitter, for example, had written to the Pennsylvania Committee of Safety, the state's governing body for military matters at the time, in August and in October of 1776, asking when a new design would be forthcoming.

Another theory holds that a petition to Congress by an American Indian may have precipitated the First Flag Resolution. On June 3, 1777, the Congress had received a petition from William Green, complete with "three strings of wampum." Green's request: "that a flag of the United States might be delivered to him to take to the chiefs of the nation, to be used by them for their security and protection." There is no record of the response Green received, although the wampum and the letter may have spurred Congress to act eleven days later.

The main reason the Flag Resolution was so little noted in the Congress or by the citizenry at large most likely has to do with the fact that in 1777 the flag was not looked upon as the archetypal symbol it would become a century later. It would be a stretch, in fact, to say that in 1777 Americans even recognized the Stars and Stripes as the national emblem or symbol.

"The American flag as a sovereign flag did not occur until 1782," says Henry Moeller, a marine biologist who has specialized in studying the usage of the flag during the Revolutionary War. "In the 1777 period, the flag was not a device that was used by the average citizen," according to Moeller. "It was used for communication," he said. Most historians concur with that assessment. But Moeller goes further, contending that the reason the Flag Resolution was enacted on June 14, 1777, was because the Continental Congress "needed a signal flag to communicate alarm" on the Delaware River.

"That flag that was being talked about on the floor of Congress was being discussed as some form of American identification to be used by the Navy or by the Army," he said. "They were getting ready for a threat in Philadelphia with British naval forces. They needed that device. They could distinguish the Continental Navy from the Pennsylvania State Navy and any other entity that was on the river or the bay. So there was a need for a flag that could be used to communicate. It wasn't until the end of the Revolutionary War when sovereignty was about to be obtained that they really got down to such things as the Great Seal and the formal flag of sovereignty."

★   ★   ★

Most of the summer elapsed before news of the passage of the Flag Resolution was reported in the nation's newspapers. The first newspaper to mention it, Benjamin Towne's *Pennsylvania Evening Post*, a triweekly, ran a brief item on August 30. The *Pennsylvania Packet,* or the *General Advertiser,* published by the printer John Dunlap (best known for printing the first copies of the Declaration of Independence), mentioned the resolution on September 2 in a column listing the proceedings of the Continental Congress. The news appeared in the *Boston Gazette,* that city's first newspaper, on September 1, and in the noted newspaper editor Isaiah Thomas's *Massachusetts Spy* three days later.

In one of history's intriguing coincidences, the Continental Congress's next order of business on June 14 after passing the Flag Resolution was to dismiss John Roach, the captain of the warship *Ranger,* because he was "a person of doubtful character." Congress immediately replaced Roach with an up-and-coming young navy officer, Capt. John Paul Jones. The Scottish-born Jones, who went on to become the top American naval hero of the Revolution, also claimed several flag firsts in his career, including two as captain of the *Ranger.*

He had been the first person to unfurl the Continental Colors on a naval vessel in December of 1775. On February 14, 1778, Jones arranged for the *Ranger* to exchange salutes with French Admiral of the Fleet La Motte Piquet in France's Quiberon Bay, marking the first time a foreign nation saluted the Stars and Stripes. On April 24, 1778, Jones captured the British sloop *Drake* off the Irish coast—the first victory at sea for a U.S. Navy ship flying the Stars and Stripes.

On September 23, 1779, in one of the most famous battles in U.S. naval history, Jones was in command of the frigate *Bonhomme Richard,* when the British frigate *Serapis* shot down his Stars and Stripes during a vicious four-hour battle in the North Sea. Jones's vaunted courage under fire eventually won the day, and he forced the *Serapis* to surrender. The *Bonhomme Richard* was so damaged in the battle that Jones abandoned it and sailed the captured English warship to port in Holland under the American flag, although that banner likely was not the one shot down during the battle. This was the battle during which John Paul Jones reportedly uttered the words: "I have not yet begun to fight."

★   ★   ★

A handful of militia units may have flown the Stars and Stripes during the Revolutionary War. But the flag never was officially supplied to George Washington's Continental Army. And apocryphal accounts and fanciful paintings notwithstanding, there is no evidence that Washington's troops flew the Stars and Stripes at the victorious Battles of Trenton and Princeton on December 26, 1776, and January 3, 1777, respectively, which took place before the Flag Resolution was passed.

The most famous artistic historic misrepresentation of the Stars and Stripes is German-born Emanuel Gottlieb Leutze's iconic 1851 painting *George Washington Crossing the Delaware.* In that much reproduced, twelve-foot-high, twenty-one-foot-long painting, Leutze depicts the flag being heroically clutched by Lt. James Monroe, the future president, standing behind a resolute George Washington on a small, wind-tossed boat.

Washington Crossing the Delaware, now in the Metropolitan Museum of Art in New York, does depict a real event, Washington's daring Delaware River crossing from Pennsylvania to New Jersey that took place on Christmas night, December 25, 1776, more than six months before Congress enacted the Flag Resolution. The truth is that Washington did not display the Stars and Stripes on that fateful journey. If he were carrying a flag on the Delaware crossing, historians believe, it would have been his personal headquarters flag, a blue field dotted with thirteen stars.

It is all but certain, moreover, that Washington and his commanders did not fly the Stars and Stripes at any of the big post–June 14, 1777, Revolutionary War engagements: the Battles of Saratoga on October 17, 1777, and Monmouth on June 28, 1778; the February–May 1780 siege at Charleston; and Corwallis's surrender at Yorktown on October 19, 1781. John Trumbull's famous oil paintings of Saratoga and Yorktown — *Surrender of General Burgoyne at Saratoga* and *Surrender of Lord Cornwallis at Yorktown* — which hang in the U.S. Capitol Rotunda, include prominently placed American flags. Trumbull, whose other heroic Revolutionary War paintings include *The Death of Warren* and *The Battle of Princeton* (which also contains the Stars and Stripes), painted the Saratoga and Yorktown oils long after the war was over, in 1817 and 1820 respectively. He admitted that he put his desire to commemorate those events heroically and patriotically over historical accuracy.

Trumbull received a commission from Congress in February 1817 to create the Saratoga and Yorktown paintings, as well as paintings of the signing of the Declaration of Independence and Washington resigning his military commission. Trumbull all but admitted that he used fanciful elements, such as including the Stars and Stripes, in these paintings in a June 11, 1789, letter to Thomas Jefferson. "The most powerful motive," Trumbull told Jefferson, "I had or have for engaging in or for continuing my pursuit of painting has been the wish of commemorating the great events of our country's Revolution."

There is evidence that some militia units fought in the Revolutionary War under flags that contained thirteen stars and thirteen stripes—although not the red, white, and blue stars and stripes. Two flags with thirteen stars have been associated with the August 16, 1777, Battle of Bennington in Vermont. In that engagement New Hampshire militia troops—including the famed Green Mountain Boys—under Brig. Gen. John Stark, a veteran of Bunker Hill and Trenton, and Vermont militiamen under Seth Warner defeated the British under Hessian mercenary Lt. Col. Friedrich Baum.

The Bennington flag, which is displayed today in the Bennington Museum, has seven white and six red horizontal stripes and a canton containing the number 76, above which are eleven stars in a semicircle and two additional stars above them. Each star has seven points. Some historians believe the Green Mountain Boys flew that flag—which is also known as the Fillmore flag after its original owner Nathaniel Fillmore, a veteran of that engagement—at the 1777 battle. Others say that the flag, which was handed down through three generations of the Fillmore family before it was donated to the Bennington Museum in 1926, was made in the nineteenth century. The consensus of opinion is that the latter argument in closer to the truth, and that the Bennington flag likely dates from the War of 1812 or to the celebration of the nation's jubilee in 1826.

There is another thirteen-starred flag, however, that historians do believe flew at the Battle of Bennington. It is the Stark flag, a green silk banner with a blue canton in which thirteen white or gold five-pointed stars are painted. That flag, too, came down through the family of a man who fought at the battle—in this case, Gen. John Stark. It was made public in 1877 by one of his granddaughters who testified that he owned the banner and that it had flown during the fighting at Bennington. It is not the Stars and Stripes, however, and is considered a militia flag.

A flag reputedly flown at the Battle of Brandywine on September 11, 1777, also has sometimes been referred to as the first Stars and Stripes used in battle. That flag—which is red with a small red-and-white-striped canton with thirteen red stars—supposedly was flying while some thirty thousand British and American troops under Washington and Howe faced off along the rolling hills near the Brandywine River in the hamlet of Chadds Ford, Pennsylvania. In one of the largest and bloodiest battles of the American Revolutionary War, the British outlasted the Continentals and forced Washington to retreat. Stories also have circulated that the flag flew at the September 3 Battle of Cooch's Bridge in Delaware, which took place just before Brandywine.

The Brandywine flag was, in fact, one of the first American flags with

A militia flag reputedly flown by the 7th Pennsylvania Regiment's Company at the Battle of Brandywine on September 11, 1777, is red with a small red-and-white-striped canton containing thirteen red stars. It is displayed today in Philadelphia's Independence National Historical Park. *Independence National Historical Park*

stars and stripes, but it was not an official flag of Washington's army. Historians believe that the Brandywine flag, which is displayed today in Philadelphia's Independence National Historical Park, was a militia color carried by Capt. Robert Wilson's seventh Pennsylvania Regiment's Company, which likely went on to carry the banner at the Pennsylvania Battles of Paoli on September 21 and Germantown on October 4.

Another early red, white, and blue flag made up of stars and stripes is the Easton flag—a silk banner with thirteen red and white stripes in the canton and thirteen white eight-pointed stars in its blue field arranged in a circle of twelve with one star in the center. That flag, which is displayed today at the Easton, Pennsylvania, Public Library, east of Allentown, at one time was thought to have been made for the July 8, 1776, reading of the Declaration of Independence in Easton. Historians believe, though, that it dates from the War of 1812 when Easton's citizens presented it to the city's First Company's First Regiment of Volunteers.

A red, white, and blue, thirteen-star, thirteen-striped flag with twelve stars arranged in a circle and one in the center of the canton was thought to have been carried at the January 17, 1781, Battle of Cowpens in the up-country of South Carolina. That flag, which today is housed in the Maryland State House in Annapolis, was said to have been carried by William Batchelor, the color bearer of the Third Maryland Regiment. In that crucial battle, Brig. Gen. Daniel Morgan led a force of some three hundred Continentals to victory against a British army force under Lt. Col. Banastre Tarleton in an area well known for pasturing cattle. Nine months later came the surrender of Cornwallis at Yorktown.

The flag was handed down in the Batchelor family, donated to the Society of the War of 1812 in 1894 and presented to the state of Maryland in 1907. However, an investigation of the flag by Maryland State archivists and by a Smithsonian Institution textile expert in the early 1970s concluded that the flag dated from the nineteenth century.

"The problem with Maryland's 'Cowpens flag' is that, first, there was no Third Maryland Regiment in the field at the Battle of Cowpens," Gregory A. Stiverson, Maryland's Assistant State Archivist, reported. "Second, despite repeated requests, there is no indication that General Washington ever received U.S. flags for the use of the army. Units of the army carried regimental, or state, colors." Stiverson went on to say that while Maryland regiments carried their own and state colors into battle during the Revolutionary War, the first Stars and Stripes made by the Maryland government "was not constructed until 1782, long after the Battle of Cowpens."

Because of those facts, as well as an examination of the thread and textiles used in the flag, he said, "we have concluded that Maryland's 'Cowpen's Flag' is in fact of nineteenth-century origin."

★　　★　　★

More evidence that the Stars and Stripes was not displayed at Bennington or Cowpens—or, in fact, used at all by Washington's army—is the fact that despite the June 14, 1777, resolution, the Continental Congress's Board of War never embraced the flag as the nation's emblem. "As for the Colours," Richard Peters, the Board's secretary, wrote to General Washington on May 10, 1799, "we have refused them."

Peters went on to explain that each Continental Army regiment "should have two Colours, one the standard of the United States which should be the same throughout the Army and [the] other a Regimental Colour which should vary according to the facings of the Regiment." There was one problem, though, with the "standard," he reported: "it is not yet settled what is the Standard of the U. States." Peters requested Washington's opinion so the board could ask Congress to "establish a Standard" and order enough made "sufficient for the Army."

Washington replied to the board four days later with a one-sentence answer at the end of a four-page letter. "The arrangement respecting Colours," Washington said, "is not [yet] made." The board and Washington never did come to an arrangement on the army's use of the colors before the final British troops left American soil in November 1783.

★ ★ ★

Two even bigger unanswered questions surround the June 14, 1777, Flag Resolution: Who came up with the thirteen-star, thirteen-stripe design? And why exactly did Congress choose the stars and stripes and the red, white, and blue color scheme? Historians have found no definitive answers to the latter question mainly because records either were not kept, were destroyed, or have not survived.

However a significant clue as to who designed the Stars and Stripes may be found by taking a look at the development of the Great Seal of the United States, the federal government's official emblem. Official seals were first used by monarchs in the seventh century. King John of England employed the first Great Seal during his reign in the early thirteenth century to differentiate his emblem from the privy seal used by his king's chamber. In this country the Great Seal (there are no lesser seals) is used by an officer in the U.S. State Department to seal documents. The Great Seal is impressed upon treaties and various presidentially signed documents, such as the appointments of ambassadors, cabinet officers, and Foreign Service officers. The Great Seal also is affixed on the outside of envelopes containing letters accrediting U.S. ambassadors and ceremonial presidential communications to the heads of other nations. The Great Seal has been depicted on the reverse of the dollar bill since 1935.

Almost immediately after adopting the Declaration of Independence, Congress took action on devising an official seal for the new nation. Late in the afternoon of July 4, 1776, Congress appointed a prestigious three-man committee—John Adams, Benjamin Franklin, and Thomas Jefferson—to come up with the nation's seal.

Franklin, Adams, and Jefferson had many gifts, but heraldry was not one of them. Congress did not accept the design their committee drew up with the help of the Swiss-born painter Pierre Eugène Du Simitière on August 20. It featured a shield with the emblems of England, Scotland, Ireland, France, Germany, and Belgium and the Goddess of Justice.

Congress set up a second Great Seal committee on March 25, 1780, consisting of James Lovell of Massachusetts, John Morin Scott of New York, and William Churchill Houston of New Jersey. That committee received significant help from its consultant Francis Hopkinson, a New Jersey lawyer and a signer of the Declaration of Independence, who also was an artist, and who was then serving as treasurer of the Continental Loan Office. Hopkinson's design, delivered to Congress on May 10, 1781, contained a blue shield with thirteen red and white diagonal stripes carried by a male figure holding a sword and a female figure holding an olive branch. The seal's crest, the device above the shield, contained thirteen six-pointed stars.

Historians believe that Francis Hopkinson (1737–1791), a signer of the Declaration of Independence, designed the American flag. Hopkinson also created the official seal of the State of New Jersey, and contributed to the design of the Great Seal of the United States. *Independence National Historical Park*

Francis Hopkinson's 1781 design for The Great Seal of the United States contained a blue shield with thirteen red and white diagonal stripes. The seal's crest has thirteen six-pointed stars. *National Archives and Records Administration*, Records of the Continental and Confederation Congresses and the Constitutional Convention

The Continental Congress turned down the second design, and on May 4, 1782, set up a third committee. It was made up of Arthur Middleton and John Rutledge of South Carolina and Elias Boudinot of New Jersey. Arthur Lee of Virginia replaced Rutledge and the committee received significant design input from Charles Thomson, the Congress's secretary, and from heraldry expert William Barton of Philadelphia. Congress accepted that committee's design—which has served since then as the nation's official seal—on June 20, 1782.

That familiar seal—a red, white, and blue eagle clutching thirteen arrows in one claw and an olive branch with thirteen leaves in the other, with thirteen stars arranged over its head—was primarily the work of Thomson. An ardent patriot and Philadelphia merchant, Thomson was born in county Derry in Ireland in 1729 and came to America as a young boy. He served for fifteen years, 1774–89, as the Continental Congress's secretary.

What is significant about the design process of the Great Seal vis-à-vis the design of the Stars and Stripes is the work of Francis Hopkinson, one of colonial America's most accomplished citizens. A friend of and correspondent with many of the Founding Fathers, including George Washington, Thomas Jefferson, and Benjamin Franklin, his mentor, Hopkinson was a lawyer, a member of the Continental Congress, and a signer of the Declaration of Independence. He also was a poet, artist, essayist, inventor, and musician. An accomplished harpsichord player, Hopkinson composed many religious and secular songs. Because he began writing sentimental love songs as early as 1759, some consider him to be the first American composer. He created what is believed to be the first American opera, *The Temple of Minerva*, in 1781. Hopkinson's "My Days Have Been So Wondrous," which he wrote in 1759, is thought to be the first secular song composed by a native-born American.

Francis Hopkinson was born in Philadelphia on October 2, 1737, the son of an English immigrant, a lawyer who was a friend of Benjamin Franklin and who died when Hopkinson was thirteen. Franklin took young Hopkinson under his wing after his father's death and shepherded him through the College of Philadelphia, which later became the University of Pennsylvania. Hopkinson became that institution's first graduate in 1757, and then studied law.

In 1766, when he was twenty-nine, Hopkinson visited his father's homeland and later in life used connections he made there to find good jobs in the colonies, first as collector of customs in Salem, New Jersey, and later in New Castle, Delaware. He married into colonial aristocracy, to Ann Borden of the New Jersey Bordens. The Hopkinsons lived in Bordentown, New Jersey, where Hopkinson plied his legal trade and then became active politically.

Hopkinson in 1774 was appointed to the New Jersey Governor's Council. Two years later he represented that state in the Continental Congress. Among his committee assignments in that body: the Marine Committee and the Secret Committee. After signing the Declaration of Independence, Hopkinson held several positions in the rebellious American government. In the fall of 1777, he became a commissioner on the three-member Continental Navy Board, which Congress had created on November 6, 1776, consisting of "three persons well skilled in maritime affairs" to "execute the business of the Navy under the direction of the Marine Committee." The other members were shipping merchant John Nixon and Philadelphia shipyard owner John Wharton. Hopkinson later served as the committee's chairman. He went on to become treasurer of the Continental Loan Office and Judge of the Pennsylvania Admiralty Court. From 1789 until his death two years later, Francis Hopkinson served as U.S. District Court judge for eastern Pennsylvania.

In addition to all his legal, governmental, and musical accomplishments, Hopkinson was a prolific and adept artist who had an affinity for designing seals and emblems. Among his designs: the seals of the American Philosophical Society, the state of New Jersey, and the College of Philadelphia. He also wrote many essays, anti-British satires during the Revolution, and works of fiction. His *A Pretty Story Written in the Year of Our Lord 2774*, which was published in 1774, is among the first works of fiction by an American writer.

Hopkinson habitually sent his writings and songs to Washington, Jefferson, and Franklin. Thomas Jefferson, for one, a man with well-known good taste, was impressed with the quality of Hopkinson's work — as were his daughters. The author of the Declaration of Independence thanked Hopkinson for sending him a packet of papers, pamphlets, and songs in 1789 while Jefferson was serving as U.S. Minister to France in Paris.

"Accept my thanks for the papers and pamphlets which accompanied them, and mine & my daughter's for the book of songs," Jefferson wrote from Paris on March 13. "I will not tell you how much they have pleased us, nor how well the last of them merits praise for its pathos, but relate a fact only, which is that while my elder daughter was playing it on the harpsichord, I happened to look towards the fire & saw the younger one all in tears. I asked her if she was sick? She said 'no; but the tune was so mournful.'"

★   ★   ★

"Francis Hopkinson," Whitney Smith said, "designed the flag." Smith's statement reflects the consensus of opinion of nearly all historians and flag experts who have studied and weighed the scant evidence that exists dealing directly with the Stars and Stripes' design.

On May 25, 1780, two weeks after the Second Great Seal Committee submitted his proposal to Congress, Hopkinson wrote a letter to the Continental Board of Admiralty containing his thanks that the seal he designed had been approved — something that later turned out not to be the case. He went on to mention his other patriotic designs, which he had completed during the previous three years. One was the Board of Admiralty seal, which contained a red and white–striped shield on a blue field. Others included the Treasury Board seal, "7 devices for the Continental Currency," and "the Flag of the United States of America."

In the letter Hopkinson noted that he hadn't asked for any compensation for the designs but was now looking for a reward: "a Quarter Cask of the public Wine." The wine would, he said, "be a proper & reasonable Reward for these Labours of Fancy and a suitable Encouragement to future Exertions of a like Nature."

The board sent that letter on to Congress. On June 6, Hopkinson forwarded a second, more detailed, bill to the Board of Treasury, dropping his bid for wine and asking, instead, for twenty-seven hundred pounds. Hopkinson submitted another bill on June 24 for his "drawings and devices." The first item on the list was "The Naval Flag of the United States." The price listed was nine pounds.

The Treasury Board turned down the request in an October 27, 1780, report to Congress. The board cited several reasons for its action, including the fact that Hopkinson "was not the only person consulted on those exhibitions of Fancy, and therefore cannot claim the sole merit of them and not entitled to the full sum charged."

However, the only design on his list that Hopkinson did not work on alone was the Great Seal, and it is likely that the final design was completely his work. The board cited no evidence—nor has any come to light since then—that Hopkinson's flag design was a collaborative effort. Hopkinson's itemized bill, moreover, is the only contemporary claim that exists for creating the American flag.

Why did Congress choose the colors and the stars and stripes to represent the states? One common theory, which has been discredited by historians and flag experts, is that the stars and stripes came from the Washington family coat of arms, which contains two horizontal stripes or bars on a white field topped by three red five-pointed stars.

The design came from George Washington's English descendants who lived in Northamptonshire. The coat of arms came to this country in the seventeenth century when Washington's great grandfather immigrated to Virginia. Washington displayed a wood carving of the family symbol above the mantel in the front parlor at Mount Vernon, his home in Alexandria, Virginia. He also used the coat of arms on the panels of his coach, on his personal bookplate, and on his silver.

Speculation that the Stars and Stripes is based on Washington's coat of arms appears to be an apocryphal attempt to add to Washington's patriotic legend. Historians can find no mention of the connection between the two symbols until 1876. The lack of contemporary evidence, the fact that the design of the Washington coat of arms is very different than the Stars and

Stripes, and Washington's well-known disdain for these kinds of trappings lead clearly to the conclusion that the two are not related.

As for stars, they have been used as a heraldic device since ancient times to symbolize humankind's strong desire to achieve greatness. Among the earliest use of the star symbol in the American colonies was the 1680 seal of Providence, Rhode Island, which contained a group of six-pointed stars. It is possible that the iconography of the secret fraternal order of Freemasonry influenced the choice of stars. The practice of Masonry, based on the guilds of stonemasons who built the Gothic cathedrals, abbeys, and castles of medieval Europe, was very common in eighteenth-century America. George Washington, eight signers of the Declaration of Independence, including Benjamin Franklin and John Hancock, as well as John Paul Jones, Robert Livingston, and Paul Revere, among many other influential early Americans, were Masons.

Stars are a prominent feature in Masonic iconography, as are arches, compasses, pyramids, and the "all-seeing eye." The Order of the Eastern Star, a charitable arm of Freemasonry for women, dates from the mid-nineteenth century. Historians believe that the stars in the Bennington flag of 1777 may have been inspired by Masonry, and there is no reason to doubt that the stars in the Stars and Stripes were as well.

As for the stripes, historians trace their American lineage to a 1765 Sons of Liberty flag that flew in Boston. That flag contained nine red and white stripes. Another early flag that used stripes was the 1775 flag containing thirteen horizontal blue and silver stripes flown by Capt. Abraham Markoe's Philadelphia Light Horse Troop. With the lack of any contemporary evidence to the contrary, it is most likely that whoever drew up the Flag Resolution's call for "thirteen stripes, alternate red and white" was influenced by those two flags.

As for the colors, no law, resolution, or executive order exists providing an official reason for the choice of red, white, and blue. The closest thing to an explanation consists of the personal views of Charles Thomson, the secretary of the Continental Congress who was instrumental in the design of the Great Seal. Thomson's report to Congress on June 20, 1782, the day the seal was approved, contained a detailed explanation of the seal's elements, including his ideas on the meaning of its colors.

"The colours," Thomson said, "are those used in the flag of the United States of America. White signifies purity and innocence. Red hardiness and valour and Blue . . . signifies vigilance, perseverance and justice."

Variations of Thomson's "meaning of the colors" have been expounded ever since 1782. Most often the explanation is stated as though it is official government policy. In a May 12, 1986, proclamation honoring the Year of the Flag, for example, Pres. Ronald Reagan said, "The colors of our flag signify the qualities of the human spirit we Americans cherish: red for courage and readiness to sacrifice; white for pure intentions and high ideals; and blue for vigilance and justice."

But the red, white, and blue do not have—nor have they ever had—any official imprimatur. What historians believe is the explanation of the derivation of red, white, and blue in the Stars and Stripes is the simple fact that those colors were used in the first American flag, the Continental Colors. And there is little doubt where the red, white, and blue of the Continental Colors came from: the Union Jack of England, the mother country.

CHAPTER THREE

Mother of Invention

Betsy Ross sewed the first American flag

—The Independence Hall Association, 2003

There is no substantiation for the legend that Betsy Ross was responsible for the Stars and Stripes.

—Milo M. Quaife, et al., *The History of the United States Flag,* 1961

WHY THE FOUNDING FATHERS chose stars, stripes, and the red, white, and blue colors for the American flag remains an open question. So, too, does the question of who made the first American flag. It is all but universally assumed today that Betsy Ross stitched together the first Stars and Stripes in her seamstress shop in Philadelphia. Betsy Ross was, indeed, a Philadelphia seamstress who made flags. But a careful reading of the facts reveals that the story that Betsy Ross—born Elizabeth Griscom on New Year's Day 1752 in the City of Brotherly Love—sewed the first flag is a myth.

Elizabeth Griscom was the eighth of seventeen children of Samuel, a builder, and Rebecca James Griscom. Elizabeth's great grandfather, Andrew Griscom, had immigrated to the United States from England in 1680. He was a member of the Society of Friends, a Quaker, who came to this country seeking freedom to practice his religion. Elizabeth Griscom likely attended the Friends elementary school on South Fourth Street in Philadelphia and then became an apprentice to an upholsterer, William Webster.

Two months before her twenty-second birthday, on November 4, 1773, Elizabeth Griscom ran off to Gloucester, New Jersey, where she married John Ross in Hugg's Tavern. The son of an Episcopalian minister from New Castle, Delaware, John Ross also worked as an upholsterer's apprentice at

Webster's. Six months later Elizabeth Ross was disowned by the Society of
Friends for marrying outside the faith. She became an Episcopalian and
worshipped with her husband at Christ Church in Philadelphia.

By March of 1775 John and Elizabeth Ross had opened a small shop on
Arch Street in the commercial district of Philadelphia, close to Independence Hall, several blocks from the bustling wharves along the Delaware
River. The young couple lived and worked in the house on Arch Street,
which they rented. Upholsterers of the day performed tasks other than
making and repairing chairs and other furniture, including seamstress
work, which Elizabeth Ross, known as Betsy, performed.

John and Betsy Ross's life together was cut short when John Ross was
killed on January 21, 1776, soon after he had joined a local militia company. He was on patrol near a wharf when a stockpile of gunpowder blew
up, injuring him fatally. Betsy Ross continued to work as a seamstress and
upholsterer after her husband's death. She married colonial war privateer
Joseph Ashburn on June 15, 1777, the day after the Continental Congress
enacted the Flag Resolution. Betsy and John Ashburn had two daughters
in 1779 and 1781, after which John Ashburn shipped out as first mate on
the armed merchant marine brigantine *Patty*. That ship was captured by
the British and the crew imprisoned in the Old Mill Prison in Plymouth,
where Ashburn died on March 3, 1782.

One of John Ashburn's fellow prisoners, John Claypoole, an old friend
of the Ross family, was released in a prisoner exchange and returned to
Philadelphia in June. Claypoole relayed the news of Joseph Ashburn's death
to his widow and her family. A Continental Army veteran of the Battles of
Brandywine and Germantown, John Claypoole had been wounded at the
latter battle and forced out of the army. He signed on to work on an American cargo ship, which the British captured on its way back from France.

Betsy Griscom Ross Ashburn married John Claypoole on May 8, 1783.
After the marriage, she continued to work as an upholsterer and seamstress
in the house on Arch Street. He worked for a time at the U.S. Customs
House in Philadelphia, then joined his wife in the family business. Contemporary business directories refer to the firm of "John Claypoole, upholsterer," although it is likely that Betsy Claypoole did the lion's share of the
work because of John Claypoole's war wounds, which grew worse as the
years passed.

Two years after they married, the Claypooles joined the newly formed
Society of Free Quakers, a breakaway Society of Friends group. Sometimes referred to as the "Fighting Quakers," that group was made up of

people who were "read out of meeting" by the pacifist main Quaker community for taking part in the American Revolution.

Elizabeth and John Claypoole had five daughters. John Claypoole died on August 3, 1817. After his death, until she retired at age seventy-five in 1827, Betsy Claypoole, working with her daughters, granddaughters, and nieces, continued to run her upholstery business and produce flags. After her retirement she lived with her daughter Susanna Satterthwaite in Abington, Pennsylvania, but moved back to Philadelphia in 1835 to stay with another daughter, Jane Canby. Betsy Ross died there on January 30, 1836, at the age of eighty-four.

★   ★   ★

Virtually every historian who has studied the issue believes that Betsy Ross did not sew the first American flag. Yet a significant number of others who have looked into the matter, such as the Independence Hall Association, the Philadelphia nonprofit group that supports that city's Independence National Historical Park, believes that Betsy Ross did, indeed, stitch the first American flag. That flag, widely known as "the Betsy Ross flag," contains thirteen stars arranged in a circle in the canton.

If you go to the Amazon.com Web site—or to any other online bookseller or bookstore for that matter—and type in the words "Betsy Ross" in the search field, you will discover many titles, nearly all for children, and nearly all carrying the same message: that Betsy Ross made the first American flag. While most qualify the claim by saying the story comes from oral tradition, nearly all of the children's books contain fanciful images of Betsy Ross sewing a flag with the thirteen stars in a circle in the canton, often with George Washington looking on approvingly. Some books also promote the message that Betsy Ross designed the Stars and Stripes. That is the case, for example, in Ann Weil's 1986 book aimed at children aged nine to twelve, *Betsy Ross: Designer of Our Flag*, which fancifully recreates Betsy Ross's childhood.

The message that Betsy Ross sewed or even designed the first American flag has generally been accepted among the American public for more than a century. And the name "Betsy Ross" has become an ingrained part of the national fabric. A popular playwright, Henry A. Du Souchet, produced a play on Betsy Ross's life in 1901 and went on to write the script for "Betsy Ross," a silent movie starring Alice Brady as the colonial seamstress, which appeared in September of 1917.

Another early Hollywood movie, starring the silent film stars Francis X. Bushman as George Washington and Enid Bennett as Betsy Ross, appeared in theaters in 1927. The twenty-minute Technicolor short—called *The Flag: A Story Inspired by the Tradition of Betsy Ross*—includes a scene in which George Washington asks Betsy Ross to design and make the first Stars and Stripes. Its last scene, a flash forward to a World War I battle, shows the American, British, and French flags flying side by side. That film regularly appears on television in the twenty-first century—most recently on July 4, 2004, on the cable channel, Turner Classic Movies (TCM).

In 1952 a three-cent U.S. postage stamp was issued marking the two hundredth anniversary of Betsy Ross's birth. The stamp shows Betsy Ross holding the American flag in her parlor. A heavily used bridge spanning the Delaware River between Philadelphia and New Jersey was renamed the Betsy Ross Bridge in 1973. There's a colonial-style hotel in the Art Deco National Historic District of Miami's South Beach named the Betsy Ross Hotel. And Timberland, the big footwear company, offers a women's no-nonsense black Betsy Ross shoe.

Bugs Bunny, the wise-cracking cartoon rabbit, added his special brand of humor to the Betsy Ross story. In the 1954 Warner Bros. cartoon "Yankee Doodle Bugs" and again in "Bugs Bunny: All American Hero" (1980) Bugs gives his nephew Clyde an American history lesson replete with tales of the important roles played by rabbits. In one scene Betsy Ross has just sewed a flag containing red, white, and blue stripes. Bugs steps into the picture and tells Betsy Ross that something else is needed to improve the banner. Whereupon he steps on a rake, which smacks him in the head. Bugs, of course, sees stars, and recommends that Betsy Ross add them to the flag.

When college students were asked in a study done in the 1970s and 1980s to name the first ten people they thought of in the category of "American history from its beginning through the end of the Civil War," excluding presidents, generals, and statesmen, Betsy Ross came out on top in seven of the eight surveys. She placed second in the eighth to Benjamin Franklin. In doing so Betsy Ross topped John Smith, Daniel Boone, George Washington Carver, Christopher Columbus, Lewis and Clark, Harriet Tubman, Eli Whitney, and Pocahontas, among others.

The name "Betsy Ross," however, was virtually unknown outside her circle of family and friends until 1870 when her last surviving grandson, William J. Canby, read his paper, "The History of the Flag of the United States," before the Historical Society of Pennsylvania in Philadelphia in

March of that year. Canby, who was a member of the society, announced that day that his maternal grandmother made the first Stars and Stripes at George Washington's behest and, moreover, that she helped come up with the flag's design. Canby based his paper on stories he had heard from family members since his childhood, along with his own memories of his grandmother's tales of her involvement in making flags. Betsy Ross had died when William Canby was eleven years old.

Canby reported that day that he had searched congressional and other records dealing with the June 14, 1777, Flag Resolution and could find nothing indicating the origins of the Stars and Stripes. "The next and last resort then of the historian (the printed and the written record being silent)," he wrote, "is tradition." That tradition turned out to be stories told by Betsy Ross to his mother and her sisters, to two of his aunts, and to one of Betsy Ross's nieces.

"According to a well sustained tradition in the family of Elizabeth Claypoole (the Elizabeth Ross), this lady is the one to whom belongs the honor of having made with her own hands the first flag," Canby said. His mother and her sisters learned this fact, he said, "from the recollection of their mother's often repeated narration and from hearing it told by others who were cognizant of the facts."

Canby reported that his grandmother made the flag after George Washington visited her "with her girls around her" in her shop on Arch Street in Philadelphia in June 1776. Washington was there with two other members of a congressional committee—Col. George Ross, Betsy's late husband's uncle, and Robert Morris, the merchant and Philadelphia banker and powerful member of Congress who played a pivotal role in financing the war effort. The three, Canby said, were charged by the Continental Congress to come up with the design of a flag for the new nation.

Canby said that George Washington had been a frequent visitor to Betsy Ross's shop. He "had visited her shop both professionally and socially many times," Canby said, "a friendship caused by her connection with the Ross family." Betsy "embroidered his shirt ruffles, and did many other things for him."

Canby's paper contended that Washington, Ross, and Morris told Betsy Ross that they were the members of a congressional committee appointed to "prepare a flag" and asked her if she could make one. She replied, Canby said, "with her usual modesty and self reliance, that she did not know but she could try; she had never made one but if the pattern were shown to her, she had no doubt of her ability to do it."

At that point the group adjourned to the shop's back room, a parlor, where Colonel Ross "produced a drawing, roughly made, of the proposed flag," Canby said. Betsy found that sketch "defective" and "unsymetrical" and "offered suggestions which Washington and the committee readily approved." Her exact suggestions, Canby said, "we cannot determine," but his grandmother's input caused Washington to redraw the design "in pencil, in her back parlor." As he was doing the new sketch, Betsy Ross interrupted and said that the stars in the flag should be five pointed rather than six pointed, as Washington had sketched them.

Could Betsy Ross make the more difficult five-star flag, the committee asked. " 'Nothing easier' was her prompt reply, and folding a piece of paper in the proper manner, with one clip of her ready scissors she quickly displayed to their astonished vision the five pointed star," Canby said, "which accordingly took its place in the national standard."

After he read the paper, Canby produced affidavits to back up his claims. They came from his first cousin Sophia B. Hildebrant, the daughter of Clarissa Claypoole Wilson; from Margaret Donaldson Boggs, a niece of Betsy Ross; and from Canby's aunt Rachel Fletcher, Betsy Ross and John Claypoole's then eighty-one-year-old daughter.

"I remember to have heard my grandmother, Elizabeth Claypoole, frequently narrate the circumstance of her having made the first Star Spangled Banner," Hildebrant said in her affidavit, which was taken on May 27, 1870. "It was a specimen flag made to the order of the committee of Congress, acting in conjunction with General Washington, who called upon her personally at her store in Arch Street, below Third Street, Philadelphia, shortly before the Declaration of Independence."

According to Hildebrant, Colonel Ross was so pleased with the flag that he gave Betsy Ross the congressional flag-making concession. "To my knowledge," Hildebrant said, "she continued to manufacture the government flags for about fifty years, when my mother succeeded her in the business, in which I assisted."

Margaret Donaldson Boggs, the daughter of Betsy Ross's sister Sarah, echoed that testimony in her affidavit, which she gave on June 3, 1870. "I have heard my aunt, Elizabeth Claypoole, say many times that she made the first Star Spangled Banner that ever was made with her own hands," Boggs said. "I was for many years a member of her family, and aided her in the business. I believe the facts stated in the foregoing article which has now been read to me are all strictly true."

Rachel Fletcher corroborated the entire story in her affidavit, which she gave on July 31, 1871. The first flag, her mother said, "was run up to the peak of one of the vessels belonging to one of the committee then lying at the wharf, and was received with shouts of applause by the few bystanders who happened to be looking on." Later that day, Betsy Ross reported, Washington's committee "carried the flag into the Congress sitting in the State House, and made a report presenting the flag and the drawing and . . . Congress unanimously approved and accepted the report."

★   ★   ★

The family version of the Betsy Ross story was made public when the nation was recovering economically, socially, and emotionally from the Civil War. It struck a chord among many individual Americans, and among the many patriotic and veterans groups that were formed in the last half of the nineteenth century. Another factor that influenced the Betsy Ross story's acceptance was the emergence of the American feminist movement.

It is possible to make a case that Betsy Ross's story—a strong-willed woman, twice widowed, running her own successful business out of her home while caring for her children—is a profeminist one. But in the latter half of the nineteenth century the story was regarded primarily as a rebuke to the emerging American feminist movement, which largely focused on women's suffrage beginning in the late 1860s.

The domesticity of the Betsy Ross story served as a sort of counterbalance to the message promulgated by organizations such as Elizabeth Cady Stanton and Susan B. Anthony's all-female National Woman Suffrage Association. That organization was founded in 1869 and considered by some to be too radical and dangerous and a threat to the future of the American family. The picture presented of Betsy Ross—doing a traditional woman's job of sewing at home, surrounded by her family, and doing the work for her country—contained the opposite message presented by the women who were outspokenly bold as they worked for the vote.

Betsy Ross "became America's founding mother to complement the Founding Fathers," said Morris Vogel, a Temple University history professor. "It was the immaculate conception: George Washington comes to visit and the flag literally issues forth from Betsy's lap."

The story was helped along also by several female descendants who, beginning in the 1870s, produced small "Betsy Ross" flags, known to collectors as flaglets. "The flaglets were made by her granddaughters or great granddaughters from the 1870s, and, as late as 1900–02," said Jeffrey

Kohn, a prominent Pennsylvania flag collector and dealer. "They sold as souvenirs for five dollars in 1890s. Now they go for between one and two thousand dollars, depending on condition."

The Betsy Ross story gained new momentum and took hold strongly across the nation in the 1890s, a period that marked the beginning of an era of widespread feelings of nativism and nationalism in reaction to large numbers of newly arrived emigrants from Europe. The backlash against the imigrant influx included a surge of nationalism and patriotism surrounding the American flag. Flag Day was born in 1885; the Pledge of Allegiance was written in 1892; a movement grew up during that time to require all public schools to fly the flag, and the Betsy Ross first flag story was memorialized and popularized in prominent magazine and newspaper articles and in books.

In "National Standards and Emblems," a long, detailed article on the history of flags that appeared in the July 1873 issue of *Harper's New Monthly Magazine*, for example, H. K. W. Wilcox relates the Betsy Ross story much as Canby told it. The "construction of the first national standard of the United States," Wilcox wrote, "took place under the personal direction of General Washington, aided by a committee of Congress." Wilcox repeated the story of Washington and the committee going to Betsy Ross's "little shop," putting the date "probably between the 23rd of May and the 7th of June, 1777," a year later than the time Canby reported.

Wilcox, echoing Canby, said that Betsy Ross suggested changing George Washington's choice of six-pointed stars to five-pointed ones because "the stars would be more symmetrical and pleasing to the eye if made with five points." She then demonstrated to the committee how easily it was to make five-pointed stars. After Washington approved the change, Wilcox wrote, Betsy Ross "at once proceeded to make the flag, which was finished the next day."

Betsy Ross, Wilcox reported, was then "given the position of manufacturer of flags for the government," something Canby never claimed, "and for some years she was engaged in that occupation."

The most influential book that dealt with the Betsy Ross story as fact is *The Evolution of the American Flag*, first published in 1909 by William Canby's brother George and his nephew Lloyd Balderson. The book was based on William Canby's first flag research, which ended when he died in 1907. It greatly expanded on Canby's 1870 paper and contained information about the American Flag House and Betsy Ross Memorial Association, which had been incorporated on, appropriately enough, June 14, 1898, to raise funds to purchase and start a Betsy Ross house museum on Arch Street in Philadelphia.

That group was founded by Charles H. Weisgerber of Philadelphia, who in 1893 had created the much-reproduced, life-size painting *Birth of Our Nation's Flag*, in which Betsy Ross is seated in her parlor, sunbeams pouring down on her, in the company of George Washington, George Ross, and Robert Morris. She is holding the thirteen-star Betsy Ross flag, which is draped across the floor and her lap and is meeting the admiring gaze of General Washington. The flag's stars are arranged in a circle in the canton, one of the first depictions of that arrangement. That painting "is the primary reason that the circle of stars has been identified with Betsy Ross," according to flag expert Edward W. Richardson.

Weisgerber's nine-by-twelve-foot work was reproduced on the three-cent stamp in 1952. Because no portrait of Betsy Ross existed, Weisgerber based his Betsy Ross on miniatures of her two daughters dating from around 1806. Those paintings have been attributed to Rembrandt Peale, the noted neoclassical artist and son of the American master Charles Wilson Peale (1741–1827), the preeminent painter of his generation.

Weisgerber's inspiration for the Betsy Ross painting, according to family lore, was a one-thousand-dollar prize offered by the city of Philadelphia in 1892 for the best artistic rendition of a local historical event. Weisgerber decided to enter the contest as he walked by the house on Arch Street. Outside was a sign that read: "Home of Betsy Ross: seamstress, upholsterer and maker of the first American flag." After consulting with William Canby, Weisgerber completed the painting, which won the prize.

Birth of Our Nation's Flag caused a minor sensation when Weisgerber exhibited the painting shortly after it was completed at the Columbian Exposition in Chicago in 1893. The attention the painting received generated a great deal of national interest in the Betsy Ross story. It was also at that large and well-publicized exhibition that the Pledge of Allegiance was introduced.

Weisgerber headed a group that in December 1898 purchased the house at 239 Arch Street where Betsy Ross lived from 1773–86, and where the scene in the painting supposedly took place. The price for the dilapidated brick row house was twenty-five thousand dollars. The plan was to turn the circa 1740 building—which most recently had been used as a combination general store and crude Betsy Ross museum by its previous owner, Charles P. Mund—into a shrine to Betsy Ross under the auspices of Weisgerber's American Flag House and Betsy Ross Memorial Association.

The building's future had been in doubt before Weisgerber's group acquired it. In December of 1895, The *Philadelphia Ledger* reported that the city's two councils had "declined to appropriate money for its purchase," and there were concerns that the building would "fall before the march of public improvements." Those concerns were temporarily allayed when the Schuylkill Council of the Junior Order of American Mechanics started a movement to purchase the house. When that effort did not materialize, Weisgerber's group stepped in.

Weisgerber's association's objectives, as his promotional literature put it, were "to purchase and preserve the historic building, situated at No. 239 Arch Street, Philadelphia, Pa., in which the *first flag* of the *United States of America* was made by Betsy Ross and subsequently adopted by Congress, June 14th, 1777, and to erect a national memorial in honor of this illustrious woman."

The main money raiser came from the sale of souvenir certificates of membership in the association—a way, the association said, "to have all Americans, *of every shade of religions and political opinion, affiliate alike,*" become "the preservers of the birthplace of the 'Stars and Stripes.'" The eight-by-fourteen-inch certificates contained a color reproduction of Weisgerber's painting, flanked by black-and-white drawings of the house on Arch Street "in which the first American flag was made," the certificate said, and of Betsy Ross's grave in Philadelphia's Mount Moriah Cemetery. The cost of a certificate was ten cents. Those who formed a "club" with thirty members received a larger, twenty-two- by twenty-eight-inch reproduction of the painting. More than two million of the certificates were sold, mainly to schoolchildren.

Weisgerber moved into the Betsy Ross House with his wife and brother around the turn of the century. When his son was born in 1902, Weisgerber named him "Vexil Domus" (Latin for "flag house") Weisgerber. The *New York Times* in 1908 called six-year-old Vexil Weisgerber "one of the most interesting of the house's attractions." On "state occasions," the paper said, "attired in a diminutive 'Uncle Sam' suit . . . he is lifted to the counter in the shoplike front room, and from that stage recites, with juvenile gestures, but a with flair quicker than that of the average child, what Nathan Hale said about the flag: 'My only regret is,' &c." and other famous patriotic and flag quotations.

Despite his big plans, within three years after gaining control of the house, Weisgerber tried to sell it to the federal government. A measure that would have made the house a government-run shrine to Betsy Ross was turned down by the House Committee on Public Buildings and Grounds in

The house on Arch Street in Philadelphia where Betsy Ross, then known as Elizabeth Claypoole, lived and earned her living as a seamstress. *American Flag House and Betsy Ross Memorial*

1905. In 1907, Weisgerber tried, again without success, to give the house to the City of Philadelphia.

Weisgerber died in 1932 and his association went out of business three years later. During the three decades of Weisgerber's ownership, the Betsy Ross house had fallen into serious decay. Weisgerber's association had raised and spent thousands of dollars purchasing the property and preserving it, but funds to maintain the building proved to be scarce. "Plaster is falling from the walls, exposing old hand-split laths," the *New York Times* reported on February 14, 1937. "The roof is leaking, the cellar kitchen where Betsy Ross cooked is damp and cluttered with waste material, and the treads of the stairs have been worn away with the use of two centuries." The savior of the house was A. Atwater Kent, who led a fund-raising effort to restore the building, which he donated to the city of Philadelphia in 1937.

"When I first learned of the condition of the Betsy Ross House through a newspaper story," Kent, who had made a fortune manufacturing automobile ignition systems and radios in the 1920s, said in 1937, "I thought it was a shame that so historic a shrine should be permitted to fall into decay. I felt that the house in its present dilapidated condition gave a very bad impression to the many thousands of visitors who come to visit it each year."

Today the house is known as the Betsy Ross House and American Flag Memorial. It is owned by the city of Philadelphia and managed by the non-profit group Historic Philadelphia, Inc. The house is one of the city's most visited historic sites, attracting more than 250,000 visitors a year. Only the Liberty Bell and Independence Hall draw more visitors.

Charles Weisgerber's "Birth of Our Nation's Flag" is not displayed in the Betsy Ross House. After the painting was vandalized while on exhibit in the old Pennsylvania State Museum in Harrisburg in the 1950s, it was placed in storage for more than four decades in a Delaware County, Pennsylvania, barn and later in a dye-making shop in southern New Jersey. The artist's descendants offered the painting to the city, but Philadelphia officials declined to exhibit it in the city's museums or other public buildings. After undergoing a forty-thousand-dollar restoration in 2000— during which the painting was cleaned, restretched, remounted, and retouched—the family donated the painting to the State Museum of Pennsylvania in Harrisburg, where it is on exhibit today. "We wanted it to be in a place that would guarantee accessibility to the public and give it the protection it needs for the long term," said the artist's grandson, Charles Weisgerber II.

"Birth of Our Nation's Flag," is "important not necessarily from an aesthetic point, but from an historic point," said Lee Stevens, the state museum's senior curator for art collections. "No other paintings quite inspired the rise of American patriotism at the time."

Visitors to the Betsy Ross House in Philadelphia may not actually be visiting the house where Betsy Ross lived. The evidence showing the exact house on Arch Street where Betsy Ross lived is unclear. That is due to the fact that Betsy Ross and her husbands rented; they never owned the property. One document indicates that Elizabeth and John Claypoole lived at 335 Arch Street. But because Philadelphia's street-numbering system changed several times in the nineteenth century, the best that can be said with certainty is that Betsy Ross lived either at the present day 239 Arch Street or next door at 241.

★   ★   ★

What is all but certain, however, is that Betsy Ross did not sew or help George Washington design the first American flag. George Canby's version of his grandmother's role as the nation's first flag maker was almost universally accepted for nearly forty years. Then, in 1908, William J. Campbell, the chairman of Philadelphia's Historic Sites Committee, published a report titled "The Betsy Ross House: Where Betsy Ross Did Not Design the American Flag," in which he called Canby's Betsy Ross story "a fake of the first water."

Campbell's committee had investigated the authenticity of many of Philadelphia's historic sites in preparation for a Founder's Day celebration in October 1908. "The story is nothing but a foolish tradition," the report said. "Betsy Ross never had any interview with George Washington, nor did she plan a five [pointed] star flag as the school books would have it." Betsy Ross, the report claimed, "was nothing more than an ordinary seamstress, and no doubt was glad to get a day's work sewing on any flag, five-starred or otherwise. She had absolutely nothing to do with the designing or planning of the flag."

That report was met with scorn by Weisgerber's association. "I have in my possession bills which show how much Betsy Ross received for making the flags, for she continued to make them and her daughters and granddaughters after her, down to 1856," said Col. John Quincy Adams, a member of the association's board who claimed to be a descendant of a cousin of Pres. John Adams. "And how do I know that Washington went to her house? Because she told George Canby, her grandson so, and he told me." Betsy Ross, Adams said, "did not die until 1836 and her story of the making of the flag was never doubted by her contemporaries."

Today some continue to claim that Canby's story is historical fact. That includes the message given to visitors at the Betsy Ross House in Philadelphia. Signs throughout that house museum are written as though the flag maker herself is telling her story. "So, of course, she's saying, 'I made the flag and I was visited by the flag committee,'" said Lisa Moulder, the Betsy Ross House collections manager. "But our brochure mentions that there is some controversy behind the story."

The brochure notes that "no official records exist to authenticate the story of Betsy Ross and the making of the flag." The "image of Betsy Ross sewing the first American flag has been imprinted in the minds of Americans since the late 1880s," the brochure says, "when the legend of Ross making the flag was first taught as a true historic event. The Stars and Stripes [is] one of our nation's most prominent symbols of national unity and common purpose, and the desire to know—with certainty—who made the first flag continues to this day."

The consensus among historians is that Betsy Ross undoubtedly made flags, but the earliest evidence shows that she did so in May 1777, when she was paid fourteen pounds, twelve shillings by a merchant for "ship's colours, &c," which, most likely, was the Continental Colors.

No evidence exists backing up the Ross descendants' claims that the Continental Congress set up any kind of committee to design a national flag in the spring of 1776. And if there were such a congressional committee it would have been extremely unlikely that George Washington would have been on it because he was commander in chief of the Continental Army, not a member of the Continental Congress, as Ross and Morris were.

Washington visited Philadelphia from May 22 to June 5, 1776. But he was there to consult with Congress on war matters. There is no evidence that he came to the Ross upholstery shop on Arch Street. There are no mentions of any discussions or debates or meetings about a national flag in the Journals of the Continental Congress in 1776, nor at any other time, except for the Flag Resolution of June 14, 1777. Nor is there any mention of national flag matters in any newspaper articles of the day or in any diaries or letters that have surfaced written by Washington, Robert Morris, Colonel Ross, or any other member of Congress.

Betsy Ross was known as an excellent businesswoman who kept detailed records of her transactions. Yet no invoice or other documents have surfaced linking her flag making to the Continental Congress or to George Washington. Betsy Ross is not mentioned in any shipping merchants' account books in 1776. And, notwithstanding the Betsy Ross descendants' oral history, historians have been unable to document the fact that Betsy Ross and George Washington knew each other.

The noted colonial era flag expert Edward W. Richardson, among others, studied the issue exhaustively and concluded that the story is not true. "There are elements of the Betsy Ross story which simply are not supported by recorded history," Richardson said. The "Betsy Ross family tradition probably became clouded with a number of embellishments and inaccuracies, which is a typical problem with most unrecorded and with some recorded history dependent on human memory and interpretation."

Whitney Smith, among others, believes that Betsy Ross "may have made some of the first Stars and Stripes just prior" to June 14, 1777. On the other hand, Smith said, "the popular image of the young girl in her shop showing Washington how to cut five-pointed stars in one snip undoubtedly began in the faulty recollections of an elderly lady and the impressionable mind of her young grandson."

Henry Moeller has a similar assessment. "Where there's smoke, there's fire," he said. "I think that Betsy Ross in her own way contributed to the actual manufacture of the flag, but how much she contributed to the actual design is a second question."

The question remains, then: Who did sew the first American flag? Historians and others who have researched the records cannot find any indication of the name of the first flag maker. More than a few other Philadelphia flag makers, both men and women, may have done so. Searches of the records of Philadelphia shipping supply merchants of the time, including an exhaustive study undertaken by Henry Moeller, show that at least seventeen upholsters and flag makers (including John Claypoole and Elizabeth Ross) worked in Philadelphia from 1775 to 1777. Most of them produced ensigns for ships.

The list includes:

- William Barrett, a flag painter;

- Cornelia Bridges, who appears to have made naval ensigns as early as December 22, 1775;

- Plunkett Fleeson, who set up his upholstery shop on January 18, 1775;

- Anne King, who was paid twelve pounds, thirteen shillings, eleven pence for 32 and 5/8th yards of "bunting for colors for the fleet" by the Navy Board of Pennsylvania on September 10, 1777;

- Rebecca Young, who made flags for the Quartermaster Department of the Continental army during the Revolution;

- Margaret Manny, who began making jacks and ensigns in December of 1774. A year after that, the records show, Manny made the Continental Colors for the *Alfred*—the first flag raised on an American fighting vessel by John Paul Jones on December 3, 1775.

Some historians, including the well-respected Barbara Tuchman, have bestowed the mantle of America's first flag maker on Margaret Manny. "Everyone knows about Betsy Ross, why do we know nothing about Margaret Manny?" Tuchman wrote in *The First Salute*. "Probably for no better reason than that she had fewer articulate friends and relatives to build a story around her."

A strong case can be made that Margaret Manny did make the first flag—although it was the Continental Colors, not the Stars and Stripes.

Pres. Woodrow Wilson, who presided over the first official national

Flag Day on June 14, 1916, may have best summed up the feelings of many Americans on the subject. Stories have circulated for years that when asked his thoughts on the Betsy Ross story, Wilson replied, "Would that it were true." Historians, though, have been unable to determine when, or even if, Wilson made that statement—which, ironically, mostly likely is another myth involving Betsy Ross and the making of the first American flag.

CHAPTER FOUR

First Additions

★   ★   ★

Be it enacted . . . that . . . the flag of the United States be fifteen
stripes alternate red and white. The Union be fifteen stars, white in a
blue field.

— The Second Flag Act, January 13, 1794

THE UNITED STATES OF AMERICA took a giant step in
its political evolution following the end of the Revolutionary War in 1783.
The weak federal authority created by the colonial Articles of Confederation gave way in 1787 to a new Constitution, which became the law of the
land the following year. The U.S. Constitution created a republican, federalist system of government with many powers shifted from the states to the
federal government. Two years later George Washington was elected the
new nation's first president and became the nation's leader for the next
eight years. During that time the American flag flew mainly on navy ships,
commercial sailing vessels, and American military installations on land.
And not all ships during the Revolution displayed the Continental Colors
or the Stars and Stripes.

"At this time we had no national colors, and every ship had the right to,
or took it, to wear what kind of fancy flag the captain pleased," Capt. John
Manly, then serving on the privateer *Cumberland*, wrote early in 1779.

Since the June 14, 1777, Flag Resolution did not specify the shapes of
the stars or their arrangements in the canton, and since all flags were made
by hand, there were many variations. Most stars on the flags had five or six
points, but others had four or eight points. Some stars were arranged in

a circle, some in horizontal rows of varying numbers, the most popular being four, five and four, and three, two, three, two, and three. But others had the stars arranged in the shape of a cross, a straight line, or a square with one star in the center.

Although most of the flags' stripes followed the wording of the Flag Resolution and were white and red, some had red, white, and blue stripes. A letter dated October 9, 1778, from Benjamin Franklin and John Adams, who were in Paris lobbying for French support for the Revolution, to the king of Two Sicilies, provides the best documentation of that fact. The "flag of the United States of America," Franklin and Adams wrote, "consists of thirteen stripes, alternately red, white, and blue." A "small square in the upper angle, next the flagstaff," they explained, "is a blue field, with thirteen white stars, denoting a new constellation."

Some flags had emblems sewn into them. Among the most popular was an eagle, often nestled in the canton below the stars. One of the busiest Stars and Stripes of the post–Revolutionary War years was a flag flown at the celebration of the end of the war on the public green in New Haven, Connecticut, on April 24, 1783. It was a "continental flag," a "grand silk flag," made by several local women, according to an eyewitness, Ezra Stiles, the president of Yale College. Stiles described the flag as having thirteen red and white stripes "with an azure blue field in the upper part charged with 13 stars."

The "upper part" also was crowded with words and symbols, Stiles said. Nestled below the stars were the words "Virtue, Liberty, Independence," Pennsylvania's motto (then and now), and among the stars were "a ship, a plough, and 3 sheaves of wheat," along with an eagle and two white horses.

That same motto was written on a flag flown at the Fourth of July celebration in 1783 in Princeton, New Jersey. "A flag was displayed, on a pole in the street before the college gate," Charles Thomson, the secretary of the Continental Congress, reported in a letter to his daughter Hannah the next day, "emblazoned with stars & stripes & with a motto, Virtue liberty & independence."

★   ★   ★

A twenty-four-year-old American, Elkanah Watson, on a business trip to London, claims to have hoisted the first American flag in England. The date was December 5, 1782, the day that King George III opened Parliament with a speech in which he formally recognized the victory of the American forces in the War of Independence. Watson, according to his journal, was having his portrait painted in the London studio of John Singleton Copley, the renowned Boston-born painter who had immigrated to England in 1775. Copley had painted his portrait, including the background that Watson requested, a ship flying "the stripes of the union." But the artist was not willing to paint the flag on the ship until the war was officially over because "the royal family and nobility" often came to his studio.

After King George's concession speech, Watson, who was in attendance at the House of Lords to hear it, hurried to Copley's studio. He made his case that the time was right for the flag to be added to his portrait. Through "my ardent solicitation," Watson said, Copley "mounted the American stripes on a large painting in his gallery—the first which ever waved in triumph in England."

Less than two months later the first American ship carrying the Stars and Stripes sailed into English waters. It was a commercial vessel, the *Bedford* of Nantucket, and it carried a huge cargo of whale oil. The *Bedford*, under Capt. William Mooers, sailed up the Thames on February 3, 1783, arriving at the customs house in London on February 6. It was "the first vessel which has displayed the thirteen rebellious stripes of America in any British port," a London periodical put it.

The first Stars and Stripes carried around the world was a banner that flew on two ships during the pioneering 1787–90 circumnavigation of the globe by the ships *Lady Washington* and *Columbia* under the command of Capt. Robert Gray and Capt. John Kendrick. A veteran of the Continental navy during the Revolutionary War, Gray was born in Rhode Island in 1755. He was working for a Massachusetts trading company in 1787 when he set sail from Boston with a cargo of buttons, beads, cloth, and other items. He reached the Oregon coast ten months later, then sailed across the Pacific to Asia before returning to his home port in August 1790. On a second trip in 1792, Gray explored what is now Gray's Harbor in the state of Washington and the Columbia River, which he named for his ship.

On March 4, 1791, Vermont joined the thirteen original colonies and became the fourteenth state. The fifteenth state, Kentucky, entered the Union on June 1, 1792. It was not until the end of 1793, however, that Congress set about changing the makeup of the American flag to reflect the newly added states. The fact that Congress took so long to get to the matter is another indication that the American people, as represented by their senators and congressmen, did not in general have strong feelings about their national flag.

On December 23, 1793, Vermont senator Stephen Row Bradley, who was elected to the Senate when his state was admitted to the Union, announced his intention to introduce a bill "making an alteration in the flag of the United States." The legislation called for a flag with "fifteen stripes, alternate red and white," with a union of "fifteen stars, white in a blue field." It would go into effect on May 1, 1795. The proposed measure was read for the first time in the Senate on December 26 and passed on December 30 without debate.

The House of Representatives took up the nation's second piece of flag legislation on January 7. A lively debate took place in the House that day. Congressman Benjamin Goodhue, a Massachusetts Federalist, opened the proceedings by ridiculing the idea of changing the flag. Goodhue called the proposed law "a trifling business which ought not to engross the attention of the House" because it had "matters of infinitely greater consequences" to attend to. He went on to say that he believed the thirteen-star, thirteen-stripe flag "ought to be permanent," and warned that if new stars and stripes were added every time new states entered the Union "we may go on adding and altering at this rate for one hundred years to come."

Israel Smith, a Vermont Republican, agreed with Goodhue, basing his opposition on fiscal grounds. "This alteration would cost [me] five hundred dollars," Smith said, "and every vessel in the Union sixty." Smith denounced the Senate for passing the bill, something he said was done "for want of something better to do." Nevertheless, Smith recommended the House endorse the measure, with one caveat. "Let us have no more alterations of this sort," he said. "Let the Flag be permanent."

William Lyman, a Republican from Massachusetts and a former major in the Continental army, spoke in favor of altering the flag. His main argument was that if Congress failed to do so, it would "offend the new states." That view was seconded by Congressman Christopher Greenup, a Republican from Kentucky who served in the war as an infantry colonel. Greenup said he considered adding two stars and two stripes in honor of his state and of Vermont "of very great consequence to inform the world that we had now two additional states."

Nathaniel Niles of Vermont also saw the matter as a trifling affair, "neither worth the trouble of adopting or rejecting." In order to get back to important congressional business though, Niles argued that the House should "pass it as soon as possible."

James Madison of Virginia, the nation's future fourth president, weighed in in favor of passage without elaborating on his reasons for doing so. Virginia Republican William Branch Giles argued for the bill as well, saying he "thought it very proper that the idea should be preserved of the number of our States and the number of stripes corresponding."

The debate continued the next day, January 8. After defeating a motion by Federalist Party congressman Benjamin Bourne of Rhode Island to refer the matter back to committee and a move by John Watts of New York to enact another bill calling for no future alterations of the flag, the matter was put to a vote. It passed 50–42. Pres. George Washington signed the bill into law on January 13, making it the first piece of legislation enacted by the Third Congress of the United States.

The fifteen-star, fifteen-stripe flag would be the nation's official emblem for the next twenty-three years. It flew on the ships of America's reconstituted navy beginning in the mid-1790s. That included the *Constitution,* one of six frigates authorized by Congress on March 27, 1794. The *Constitution* gained the nickname "Old Ironsides" during the War of 1812 for its extraordinary durability under battle conditions. One of the most celebrated warships in U.S. naval history, it was launched flying the fifteen-star, fifteen-stripe flag on October 21, 1797. Today the restored and preserved *Constitution,* the world's oldest commissioned floating warship, resides in the Boston's Charlestown Navy Yard.

The new flag made its way around the world in the 1790s. When future president James Monroe went to Paris as U.S. Ambassador to France during the French Revolution in August 1794, he presented the flag with great ceremony to the French National Convention, the assembly that governed the nascent French Republic during the most critical period of the French Revolution. The flag, according to Admiral Preble, was first displayed in Japan in 1797 by the American merchant ship *Eliza.* The frigate *George Washington* flew the Stars and Stripes for the first time in Turkey in 1800.

The fifteen-star, fifteen-stripe flag was the first American flag to be flown over a captured fortress outside the United States. The event occurred in the heavily fortified city of Derna (sometimes spelled Derne), the easternmost province of Tripoli (present-day Libya) on April 27, 1805, during the Tripolitan War. That undeclared war, sometimes called the Barbary War, was the first conflict waged by the new nation on foreign soil. It pitted American marines and naval forces against the Barbary pirates on Africa's Mediterranean Coast. The victory at Derna that day become legendary in the history of the U.S. Marine Corps.

The fight was waged by a heavily outnumbered force of American marines, working with European mercenaries and local forces, and supported by three U.S. Navy ships, the *Argus,* the *Hornet,* and the *Nautilus.* The

contingent of marines and mercenaries was led by Gen. William Eaton. He
commanded about sixty troops, plus cannon support from the ships at sea,
as he faced a heavily defended city with a force that outnumbered Eaton's
men by about ten to one.

Soon after the fighting began, Eaton was wounded. Marine Lt. Presley
N. O'Bannon took command of the American troops and led a frontal as-
sault that involved hand-to-hand combat. The marines won the day. When
they lowered the ensign of the city and replaced it with the Stars and
Stripes, the marines and sailors cheered lustily. The engagement turned
O'Bannon into the Marine Corps's first hero. The marines' actions that day
are honored with the words "to the shores of Tripoli" in "The Marine's
Hymn."

It was during the post–Revolutionary War period, too, that images of the
flag began to appear on consumer items for the first time. Among the first
was inexpensive china from England and China. Most often the flags that
appeared on the china made for the American market flew from the masts of
sailing ships. There is evidence, too, of the flag motif showing up in wallpaper. As far as textiles, such as kerchiefs and bandannas, the flag images that
were used were in nearly all cases part of depictions of sailing ships.

Still, in the post–Revolutionary War era, the flag, as a symbol of the nation, played a minor role. Other images of the nascent nation were used
much more widely. They included sculptures, paintings, and engravings of
George Washington, the universally revered "Father of Our Country," and
images such as the eagle and the female figures of Liberty and Columbia.

CHAPTER FIVE

Our Flag Was Still There

O say, does that star-spangled banner yet wave
O'er the land of the free and the home of the brave?

— Francis Scott Key, 1814

As Secretary of the Smithsonian Institution, I am often asked which of our more than 140 million objects is our greatest treasure, our most valued possession. Of all the questions asked of me, this is the easiest to answer: our greatest treasure is, of course, the Star-Spangled Banner.

— I. Michael Heyman, 1998

THE MOST FAMOUS fifteen-star, fifteen-stripe American flag — in fact, the most famous American flag and the banner that gave the American flag its most famous nickname — gained its place in American iconography during the War of 1812. Important milestones in the history of the American flag very often have been associated with armed conflict. That was the case with the Revolutionary War and the origins of the flag. And it was true with the War of 1812 and the American flag that gave this nation its National Anthem, "The Star-Spangled Banner."

The short but bloody War of 1812 pitted the young nation against its former colonial ruler in land battles in this country and in Canada and in sea battles along the Canadian-American border, in the Atlantic, and in the Gulf of Mexico. On June 12, 1812, Pres. James Madison signed a declaration of war against Great Britain in response to years of accumulating disputes over Britain's refusal to respect American sovereignty on the high seas, including the impressment of American sailors, as well as border disputes involving the Northwest Territories and Canada.

The war began in the summer of 1812 with the unsuccessful American invasion of Canada and ended in the early months of 1815 with the successful American defense of the city of New Orleans. Although the war generally was perceived in this country as a victory for the United States, it ended inconclusively, with losses and victories on both sides.

The events leading to the dramatic Star-Spangled Banner story began in the spring of 1814 when the War of 1812 took on a new complexion after Napoleon's defeat in Europe. That situation freed up large numbers of British troops to cross the Atlantic and do battle with the Americans. Their numbers included Maj. Gen. Robert Ross and his five thousand battle-hardened British army regulars and Royal Marines. Ross's men landed in this country on August 1, 1814, in Benedict, Maryland, near Washington, D.C. The British force also included a fleet of warships under Vice Adm. Sir Alexander Cochrane. That small armada entered the Chesapeake Bay on August 16.

Three days later Ross began a march toward the nation's capital. Just outside Washington, in the small town of Bladensburg, Maryland, on August 24, 4,000 of Ross's men faced off against some 6,000 American troops under the command of U.S. Army brigadier general William Winder. All but 350 of the American troops were inexperienced militiamen. The British routed the Americans in a four-hour battle. Ross's men then entered the city of Washington.

During most of the next two days, the British troops burned the Executive mansion (later known as the White House), the Capitol, the Library of Congress, and many other public buildings. The purpose of the destruction, the British said, was revenge against American troops' burning of government buildings in the city of York (now Toronto) in Canada in April 1813. President Madison and other American officials had fled before the British troops entered the city. They returned after Ross and his men left the capital during the night of August 25.

Meanwhile, some thirty-five miles north of Washington, in Baltimore, American forces under Maj. Gen. Samuel Smith made ready to defend that city. Smith had some 9,000 militiamen, which he massed on the city's eastern end. That included about 250 artillerymen and some 750 infantry regulars, sailors, and militiamen under U.S. Army major George Armistead in place at Fort McHenry.

That fort, named after former secretary of war James McHenry, stands on a narrow peninsula known as Whetstone Point on the Patapsco River, guarding the Baltimore harbor. Fort McHenry was built in 1798 on the site of the former Revolutionary War earthen mound fortress called Fort Whetstone.

After they left Washington, the British naval and ground troops repaired to Tangier Island in the Chesapeake Bay, where, on September 8, Admiral Cochrane and General Ross made their final plans to attack Baltimore, the nation's third largest city.

While the Americans prepared to defend Baltimore, a force of some six thousand British troops, including a naval brigade, under the overall command of Admiral Cochrane, landed at North Point, Maryland, some fourteen miles south of the city, in the early morning hours of September 12. At noon, Ross's troops encountered a small American force of Maryland militiamen. During the ensuing skirmish, Ross was shot and killed. Lt. Col. Arthur Brooke took over command of the British army after Ross's death and the Battle of North Point continued into the early afternoon. Dozens were killed and wounded on both sides in the fighting, which ended when the British broke off contact and made camp for the night in the nearby woods.

That evening, three British frigates, five British bomb vessels, and one rocket ship under the command of Admiral Cochrane sailed up the Patapsco and paused about two miles from Fort McHenry, just out of range of the fort's guns. At 6:30 the next morning, September 13, the ships began bombarding the fort with mortars and cannon. The relentless assault lasted throughout that entire day and into the night. When some of the British ships moved in closer, the guns at Fort McHenry opened fire and scored several hits. The Fort McHenry defenders also purposely sank some American vessels to block the British naval advance. The British ships retreated out of range of the fort's cannon. But they kept up the bombing, raining a nearly constant stream of shells onto the fort.

In the early afternoon of September 13, as the bombardment continued, the British ground troops circled into the city and came within sight of Fort McHenry. Brooke planned an assault on the American defensive lines. He held back, though, for three reasons: weather conditions—it was raining heavily; because Cochrane could not provide naval support; and because the army did not have the resources to carry off captured materiel if he had taken the city.

The bombing continued unabated into the night. The nearly constant stream of bomb, mortar, and rocket shells from the British Fleet was punctuated with loud thunderclaps as the rainstorm lashed the area. A two-hour diversionary attack by some twelve hundred British marines and sailors early in the morning of September 14 was repulsed by Fort McHenry's guns and by the artillery at two of the fort's nearby batteries. The British bombing recommenced after the attack at around 2:00 a.m. It continued relentlessly for several more hours until Cochrane called a halt to the onslaught at around 7:00. When the guns went quiet, the British war fleet turned away from the city and sailed back down the Patapsco, heading eventually for the island of Jamaica.

As the British ships retreated, the Americans at Fort McHenry "hoisted a splendid and superb ensign on their battery," a British sailor wrote, "and at the same time fired a gun of defiance." That ensign came to be known as the Star-Spangled Banner.

★   ★   ★

The man who named that flag, Francis Scott Key, witnessed the Battle of Baltimore aboard a sixty-foot sloop in the harbor. How Key found himself in the harbor while the battle raged is an intriguing and not widely known story.

Francis Scott Key was born on August 1, 1779, at his affluent family's estate called Terra Rubra in Frederick County in western Maryland. His great grandfather, Philip Key, had come to Maryland from England in the early 1720s. When he was ten years old, Key went to Annapolis to attend St. John's College. He graduated from that prestigious small liberal arts institution in 1796, then studied law under Judge J. T. Chase in Annapolis.

Francis Scott Key began practicing law in 1801 in Frederick, Maryland. His partner was Roger B. Taney, who married Key's sister Anne in 1806. Taney went on in 1836 to become the fifth chief justice of the U.S. Supreme Court. Shortly after Key married Mary Tayloe Lloyd in Annapolis 1802, he moved to the Georgetown section of Washington, D.C., to practice law with his uncle, Philip Barton Key. Francis Scott Key became one of the city's most prominent attorneys, eventually serving as U.S. Attorney for the District of Columbia, and arguing many cases before the U.S. Supreme Court. An amateur poet, Key also was a very religious man who was active in the Episcopal Church. He died in Baltimore on January 11, 1843.

The circumstance that led to Key's ringside seat at the Battle of Baltimore took place in the immediate aftermath of the British sacking of Washington. Before all of the British troops made their way aboard ships bound for Baltimore, a group of them raided several farms in Maryland outside

Washington. Dr. William Beanes, a prominent Upper Marlboro physician and a friend of Key, organized opposition to the renegade British troops. After Beanes's men captured some of the pillaging British troops, he and several other Americans were arrested and taken prisoner by the British.

A prisoner exchange followed, and everyone but Dr. Beanes was released. He was taken away in the *Tonnant*, Admiral Cochrane's flagship, as the British sailed toward Baltimore. Intermediaries contacted Key to ask him to arrange for Dr. Beanes's release. Key secured permission to negotiate the release from President Madison and Gen. John Mason, who was in charge of matters relating to military prisoners during the War of 1812. Key's orders were to go to Baltimore and rendezvous with U.S. Army colonel John S. Skinner, who had dealt with British rear admiral George Cockburn on prisoner exchanges and other issues in that city.

Key and Skinner met in Baltimore on September 4. The next day they sailed on a sixty-foot sloop carrying a truce flag in search of the British Fleet. They met up with the *Tonnant* and were welcomed aboard by General Ross and Admiral Cochrane. Key convinced the British commanders that Dr. Beanes was a civilian noncombatant. After what has been described as a cordial dinner on board the ship, the British agreed to Dr. Beanes's release. But there was a condition. Key, Skinner, and Beanes were not permitted to return to Washington until after the British attack on Baltimore.

The three men were first escorted to a British frigate, which towed their sloop toward Baltimore. On September 10, Key, Skinner, and Beanes were allowed to return to their vessel, accompanied by British marine guards. They set anchor in Baltimore harbor, about eight miles from Fort McHenry, and spent the next four days there, witnessing the fighting, including the relentless barrage during the stormy night of September 13–14. It was an emotion-laden experience. Key expressed his high feelings as the British Fleet sailed away from Fort McHenry by writing a poem, which he began to compose on the back of a letter he had in his pocket.

Key finished the four verses of the poem either while sailing back to shore or at a hotel—accounts differ—on September 16. The next day he presented the verses to his brother in law, Judge Joseph Hopper Nicholson, the chief justice of the Baltimore District of the Maryland Court of Appeals. Hopper had commanded the Maryland Volunteer Artillery's First Regiment, known as the "Baltimore Fencibles," at Fort McHenry during the Battle of Baltimore. Either Nicholson, his wife, Key, or Skinner took the poem to a printer, most likely Benjamin Edes, who also was a veteran of that battle, having commanded a Maryland militia company at the Battle of North Point. Edes owned and operated a print shop on the corner of Baltimore and Gay Street, from which copies of Key's poem, bearing the title "Defence of Fort M'Henry," were printed on handbills or broadsheets and distributed throughout the city. The text appeared in the daily afternoon newspaper, the *Baltimore Patriot*, and the *Evening Advertiser* on September 20.

The newspaper and broadsheets included a short introduction, probably written by Judge Nicholson. "The following beautiful and animating effusion, which is destined long to outlast the occasion, and outlive the impulse, which produced it, had already been extensively circulated," the introduction said. "In our first renewal of publication we rejoice in an opportunity to enliven the sketch of an exploit so illustrious, with strains which so fitly celebrate it."

The broadsheet and the newspaper went on to describe the "circumstances" under which the "song was composed." Key, who was described only as a "gentleman" and was not named, "was compelled to witness the bombardment of Fort M'Henry, which the Admiral [Cochrane] had boasted that he would carry in a few hours, and that the city must fall." Key "watched the flag at the Fort through the whole day with an anxiety that can better be felt than described, until the night prevented him from seeing it. In the night he watched the Bomb-Shells, and at the early dawn his eye was again greeted by the proudly-waving flag of his country."

The article indicated that the song was meant to be sung to the tune of "To Anacreon in Heaven," an English song, popular in pubs, that was composed by John Stafford Smith around 1775 and was well known in the United States. The tune was the theme song of the Anacreontic Society of London, a gentlemen's club that met periodically to listen to musical performances, dine, and sing songs. It was named after Anacreon, the ancient Greek poet known primarily for his verses in praise of love, wine, and revelry. Several similar organizations were formed in the United States, including the Columbian Anacreontic Society in New York, which had begun in 1795, and the Anacreontic Society of Baltimore, which would start in 1820.

On September 21, 1814, the *Baltimore American* published the song, and it soon became known, if not popular, throughout the nation. It was first performed publicly on October 19, 1814, in Baltimore at the Holliday Street Theatre, popularly known as "Old Drury," after the performance of a play. The song became known as "The Star-Spangled Banner" after it was published for the first time in sheet music form by Carr's Music Store in Baltimore in November. The title on the sheet music reads, "THE STAR SPANGLED BANNER," below which are the words "A PATRIOTIC SONG" and "Air, Anacreon in Heaven." The song was subsequently reproduced widely in newspapers and magazines and soon appeared in sheet music and in songbooks throughout the nation.

Fifty-seven years later "The Star-Spangled Banner" became the unofficial National Anthem of the North soon after the start of the Civil War. The widespread use of the song beginning in 1861 marked the first time that the nation widely and significantly embraced the flag as a symbol of American patriotism. In the decades following the war the song grew in popularity nationwide.

Although it remained popular from the time Key wrote the song in 1814—as evidenced by the cover of this 1861 sheet music—"The Star-Spangled Banner" did not become the official National Anthem until 1931. *The Library of Congress, Prints and Photographs Division*

The United States Naval Academy adopted "The Star-Spangled Banner" as its anthem in 1889, the same year in which navy bases and ships started playing it when the flag was raised each day at morning colors. The U.S. Marine Band began playing "The Star-Spangled Banner" at its public performances in 1890. The U.S. Army adopted the song for retiring the colors in 1895, and the U.S. Military Academy at West Point took the song as its official anthem in 1903. During the Spanish-American War in 1898, the American public for the first time began standing during the playing of "The Star-Spangled Banner." In 1916, just prior to America's entry into World War I, Pres. Woodrow Wilson issued an executive order calling for the song to be played at military and naval occasions. In 1917 the army and navy officially named "The Star-Spangled Banner" as "the National Anthem of the United States" for all military ceremonies.

There is anecdotal evidence that "The Star-Spangled Banner" was played at various sporting events, primarily baseball games, in the late nineteenth and early twentieth centuries. The first documented performance of the song being performed at a sporting event came during World War I at Comiskey Park in Chicago. The date was September 5, 1918; the occasion, the first game of the World Series between the Chicago Cubs and the Boston Red Sox. The Cubs were using Comiskey Park, the home of the White Sox, because their home, Wrigley Field (then called Weeghman Park), was deemed too small.

The historic event took place during the seventh-inning stretch. As the Cubs band played "The Star-Spangled Banner," the players and the nineteen-thousand-plus spectators stood, took off their hats, and sang along—much as they do today at professional and collegiate sporting contests. At Boston's Fenway Park on September 9 in the fourth game of the Series, the National Anthem was played before the first pitch. The Red Sox, led by pitching star Babe Ruth, prevailed in that post-season contest—and did not win another World Series until 2004.

"The Star-Spangled Banner" was played before the opening-day game and each World Series game the following season, 1919, but not at regular season games. That didn't take place until 1942, during World War II. Since then the National Anthem has been played before virtually every professional—and many collegiate and high school—baseball, football, basketball, hockey, and soccer contests in this country.

Members of Congress started introducing legislation to proclaim "The Star-Spangled Banner" the National Anthem of the United States around 1910. More than forty bills and resolutions were considered in Congress over the next two decades. On January 30, 1913, for example, Rep. Jefferson Levy, a New York Democrat, and the owner of Thomas Jefferson's Monticello, introduced such a joint resolution in the House. That measure, as was the case with dozens of other pieces of similar legislation, went nowhere.

The legislation did not succeed for several reasons. First, some believed that it was inappropriate for the nation to adopt as its National Anthem a song derived from an English drinking tune—especially after January 19, 1920, when Prohibition went into effect. Others objected to "The Star-Spangled Banner" because the music was not written by an American. Another objection had to do with the difficulty of singing the tune, which has a very wide range of notes. There also were arguments that Key's words were directed at a military enemy, Great Britain, that had become a close American ally. And some believed that the song was only appropriate as a martial air and not in times of peace.

" 'The Star-Spangled Banner' suggests that patriotism is associated with killing and being killed, with great noise and clamor, with intense hatreds and fury and violence," Clyde R. Miller, an administrator at Columbia University's Teachers College, said in 1930. "Patriotism may on very rare occasions involve all of these, but not everyday life."

There also was sentiment to designate other patriotic songs as the National Anthem. A popular favorite was "America the Beautiful," which Katharine Lee Bates, an instructor at Wellesley College in Massachusetts, wrote after climbing Pikes Peak, Colorado, in 1893. The words to that song were first published as a poem in 1895. The lyrics were revised twice, in 1904 and in 1913. Until 1910 the poem was sung to many different tunes, including "Auld Lang Syne." In 1910 Bates's words were put together with the tune we know today, "Materna," which was composed by Samuel A. Ward in 1882. The other song most frequently suggested for the National Anthem was the traditional folk tune "Yankee Doodle," which was written in the late 1760s.

A long lobbying effort by patriotic and veterans groups led by the American Legion and the Veterans of Foreign Wars won the day on behalf of Key's song. The VFW had been on record as early as 1917 favoring the "The Star-Spangled Banner" as the National Anthem. In December 1926 the group launched a lobbying campaign in support of a "Star-Spangled Banner" National Anthem bill pending in the House of Representatives. "There is a powerful and well-financed propaganda emanating from pacifist sources to replace Francis Scott Key's inspiring words with something more flowery and meaningless," said Herman R. La Tourette, patriotic instructor for the VFW's Department of New York, following a meeting in which the group asked the public to write to members of Congress urging them to support the bill.

That bill died in Congress, but the VFW continuing lobbying for subsequent similar legislation during the next four years. Representatives of more than sixty veterans and patriotic groups held a conference in Washington on January 30, 1930, to make a big push for another "Star-Spangled Banner" bill that had been introduced by Rep. J. Charles Linthicum, a Maryland Democrat who represented the congressional district in Baltimore that included Fort McHenry.

The following day the Veterans of Foreign Wars presented the House Judiciary Committee with a petition—which VFW commander in chief Walter I. Joyce called "fifty miles of names"—containing some five million signatures urging the adoption of "The Star-Spangled Banner" as the National Anthem. Sopranos Elsie Jorss-Reilley of Washington and Grace Evelyn Boudlin of Baltimore, backed by the U.S. Navy Band, performed the song for the committee that day "to refute," the *New York Times* said, "the argument that it is pitched too high for popular singing." The hearing room was packed with members of women's patriotic organizations decked out in what the *Times*, in a front-page article, described as "broad bands of red, white and blue."

The House approved the bill on April 21, 1930. The Senate voted for it unanimously on March 3, 1931, and on that same day Pres. Herbert Hoover signed into law a measure officially designating "The Star-Spangled Banner" as the National Anthem of the United States.

★   ★   ★

No flag sewn by Betsy Ross is known to exist today. But the flag that inspired the National Anthem, the flag known as the Star-Spangled Banner, today resides in the Smithsonian Institution's National Museum of American History in Washington. There is, moreover, indisputable evidence showing that Mary Young Pickersgill of Baltimore was the creator of that enormous and enormously influential, thirty-by forty-two-foot, fifteen-star, fifteen-stripe flag.

"She sewed the Star-Spangled Banner flag," said Sally Johnston, executive director of The Star-Spangled Banner Flag House in Baltimore. "We have the original receipt for the flag in our collection."

Mary Young Pickersgill (1776–1857), a Baltimore seamstress and flag maker, made the Star-Spangled Banner, the flag that flew over Ft. McHenry and inspired Francis Scott Key to write the National Anthem. *The Flag House and Star-Spangled Banner Museum*

That receipt, dated October 27, 1813, was given to Mary Pickersgill and her niece Eliza Young by the U.S. Army for making "1 American Ensign, 30 by 42 feet, first quality Bunting" and for another flag "17 by 25 feet." The army paid $405.90 for the larger flag, the Star-Spangled Banner, and $168.54 for the smaller one, which also flew at Fort McHenry.

Mary Pickersgill's home at 844 East Pratt Street in Baltimore, where she sewed the Star-Spangled Banner, opened in 1927 as the Star-Spangled Banner Flag House Museum. It became a National Historic Landmark in 1969. *The Flag House and Star-Spangled Banner Museum*

Mary Pickersgill was born on February 12, 1776, in Philadelphia. Following the death of her father two years later, Mary's mother, Rebecca Flower Young, supported the family by making flags in Philadelphia at her shop on Walnut Street and, later, in Baltimore. She made several dozen ensigns, garrison flags, and Continental Colors for the Continental Army and for the Pennsylvania navy. "All kinds of colours, for the Army and Navy, made and sold on the most reasonable Terms, By Rebecca Young," read her advertisement in the *Pennsylvania Packet* in 1781.

Shortly after Mary Young, who was nineteen years old, married John Pickersgill, a merchant, on October 2, 1795, the couple moved back to Philadelphia and had four children, only one of whom survived infancy. Two years after John Pickersgill died in 1805, his widow moved to what today is known is known as "The Star-Spangled Banner Flag House" at the corner of Albemarle and Pratt Streets in downtown Baltimore. It was in that house near the Baltimore waterfront that Mary Pickersgill lived with her daughter Caroline and her seventy-four-year-old widowed mother.

Mary Pickersgill supported her family by working as a seamstress and flag maker. She designed, sewed, and sold what a city directory of the time listed as "Ships Colours, Signals, etc." That included ensigns and other flags that she sold to the army, the navy, and to privately owned merchant ships.

Pickersgill was commissioned during the summer of 1813 by the army's Commissary Office in Baltimore to produce two large banners, a standard-sized garrison flag and a storm flag, for Fort McHenry. The fort's commanding officer, Maj. George Armistead, ordered the large flags primarily for identification purposes. He wanted anyone approaching the fort from the water to be able to see that the fort was flying the colors of the United States of America. Making the Star-Spangled Banner and the smaller flag was a cooperative effort. Pickersgill had help from her thirteen-year old daughter, Caroline, and from two nieces, Eliza and Margaret Young. She also probably received the assistance of her mother, Rebecca Flower Young.

It took several weeks to do the measuring, cutting, and sewing of the flags' components. The Star-Spangled Banner's fifteen stars were each about two feet long and the fifteen stripes measured just under two feet in width. The stars were made of cotton; the stripes and the blue canton of English woolen bunting. When the flags were ready to be put together, Pickersgill and company asked and received permission to use the malt house floor of nearby Claggett's Brewery to do the final assembling. They did the work in the evenings after the brewery ceased operations for the day.

"I remember seeing my mother down on the floor, placing the stars," Caroline Pickersgill Purdy wrote in an 1876 letter. "After the completion of the flag, she superintended the topping of it, having it fastened in the most secure manner to prevent its being torn away by [cannon] balls." The flag, she said, contained "four hundred yards of bunting, and my mother worked many nights until twelve o'clock to complete it in the given time."

The flags were delivered on August 19, 1813, to Fort McHenry. The larger flag, the Star-Spangled Banner, weighed about fifty pounds, and it took eleven men to raise it onto a ninety-foot flagpole at the fort. After the 1814 battle, George Armistead was promoted to lieutenant colonel and took possession of the Star-Spangled Banner. The fate of the smaller storm flag, which also flew over Fort McHenry during the Battle of Baltimore, is not known. After George Armistead died on April 25, 1818, his widow, Louisa Hughes Armistead, inherited the Star-Spangled Banner.

During the four decades Louisa Armistead possessed the flag she allowed it to be shown in public only on a few occasions. That included the emotional October 1824 visit to Baltimore by the Marquis de Lafayette, where the flag was displayed at Fort McHenry, and the 1844 Whig Party national convention in that city. Louisa Armistead also made an addition and a deletion to the flag. She cut out one of the stars and gave it to an acquaintance whom her daughter later described as "some official person," and whose identity is not known. And she sewed what appears to be a red chevron—an upside-down V—onto the third white stripe from the bottom of the flag. A small letter "B" is embroidered on one side of the chevron. The other side has an "M" inscribed on it in ink. Historians believe that the chevron was intended to be the capital letter "A" for Armistead. They are not certain what the "B" or "M" were meant to signify, although there has been speculation that they could stand for "Baltimore, Maryland."

After Louisa Armistead's death on October 3, 1861, the Star-Spangled Banner went to her youngest child, Georgiana Armistead Appleton, who was born at Fort McHenry on November 25, 1817. Over the years Louisa and Georgiana Appleton, who lived with her family in Baltimore, allowed veterans of the Battle of Baltimore and others to snip off small pieces of the flag as mementos. This was not an uncommon practice at the time. "Snipping," said Marilyn Zoidis, the Smithsonian Institution's curator of The Star-Spangled Banner Project, "appealed to the mentality of the nineteenth century." Several of the fragments have been acquired by the Smithsonian and are on display today at the National Museum of American History's Star-Spangled Banner exhibit.

By the mid-1870s, as the flag became nationally known and its value increased greatly, the family placed the Star-Spangled Banner in a vault in the New England Historical and Genealogical Society in Boston for safekeeping. Georgiana Appleton gave permission to have some pieces of the flag cut off for the society. It was moved in January 1876 to another vault in the Historical Society of Pennsylvania in Philadelphia with the idea that it would be exhibited at the Philadelphia Centennial Exhibition. But the Exhibition's organizers decided not to display it because of the flag's fragile condition. Later, on June 14, 1877, Georgiana Appleton allowed the Star-Spangled Banner to be exhibited publicly on the centennial celebration of Flag Day at Boston's Old South Meeting House.

Following Georgiana Appleton's death on July 15, 1878, the flag was bequeathed to her son, Eben Appleton, who also cut pieces from it as special favors. He soon thereafter placed the flag in a safe deposit box in New York City. Despite many requests to do so, it was leant out only once, on October 13, 1880, for the dedication of a monument to Eben Appleton's grandfather, George Armistead, in Baltimore as the city celebrated its sesquicentennial. With great pomp and ceremony the Old Defenders, the veterans of the Battle of Baltimore, paraded the flag through the streets of Baltimore.

The Smithsonian estimates that about eight feet of material was missing from the Star-Spangled Banner when Eben Appleton loaned the flag to the nation's museum in 1907. Appleton shipped the flag from New York to Washington, where it was hung outside on the wall of the old Smithsonian building known as the "Castle" for the benefit of newspaper photographers. The flag was then moved indoors and placed in a special exhibit case in the Arts and Industries Building. Five years later, in 1912, Appleton made the loan permanent, stipulating that the Star-Spangled Banner stay in the Smithsonian in perpetuity and giving the museum permission to do whatever was necessary for its preservation.

The flag was not in good condition when the Smithsonian took possession of it. Much of the flag was shredded and split and attached to a canvas backing. That backing had been sewn onto the flag in June of 1873 at the behest of Rear Adm. George Preble, the author of the first well-researched history of the American flag. Preble had convinced Georgiana Appleton to ship the flag to his office in the Boston Navy Yard. There he arranged for the new backing, hung the flag from four windows on the side of a building, and had it photographed for the first time for his book.

In an effort to stabilize the flag, the Smithsonian in 1914 hired a noted flag restorer and embroidery teacher, Amelia Bold Fowler of Boston. She oversaw the replacement of the canvas backing with a new one made of heavy, unbleached Irish linen, which was considerably lighter than the canvas. She was paid $1,243 for the work, including materials. It took ten seamstresses eight weeks, from May to July, to complete the job. In the end, some 1.7 million stitches were used to sew on the new backing.

After the seamstresses sewed the new backing in place, the museum created another specially designed and constructed case for the flag and displayed it near the main entrance of the Smithsonian's Arts and Industries Building. In 1931, it was moved to yet another case, which turned out to be too small for the entire flag, so about half of the banner had to be folded into the bottom of the case. All that was on view to visitors was the canton and the eight stripes next to it. Because of the way the backing was attached, the flag was displayed with the canton of blue stars to the right of the red and white stripes.

For two years during World War II museum officials moved the Star-Spangled Banner as a precautionary measure about 115 miles south to a warehouse in the Shenandoah National Park in the Blue Ridge Mountains near Luray, Virginia. The flag returned to the Arts and Industries Building in November 1944. It was taken out of the case in September 1961 in preparation for its move to a new museum, the National Museum of History and Technology on the other side of the National Mall. Three years later, in 1964, the flag was displayed prominently in the three-story main entrance hall, called Flag Hall, of that newly opened building, which is now known as the National Museum of American History. It hung there for thirty-four years, greeting tens of millions of visitors.

In 1982 Smithsonian conservators cleaned the flag thoroughly. When the banner was rehung, museum officials decided to expose the flag to limited amounts of light and dust. A protective shield made of gray linen painted with nineteenth-century American historical scenes was placed in front of the flag. It dropped down for a minute every half hour to allow for public viewing.

Despite preservation and conservation work done at the Smithsonian over the years, the Star-Spangled Banner in the early 1990s suffered from the effects of nine decades of public display and exposure to light and dust. In December 1998 the flag was taken down to undergo an extensive $18 million conservation treatment. It took eight conservators working with a team of riggers to remove the 1,020-square-foot flag from its display. The riggers were responsible for lowering the flag; the conservators for insuring the safety of the flag and for tilting it into a horizontal position and rolling it onto a 35-foot-long tube.

"We're not trying to restore the flag," Marilyn Zoidis said. "We're conserving it as a historical artifact."

The conservation work is being carried out in public in the museum's Star-Spangled Banner exhibit area in a customized two-thousand-square-foot laboratory behind a fifty-foot-long, floor-to-ceiling glass wall. After the laboratory opened in May 1999, a team of conservators began the enormous job of cleaning and stabilizing the flag. The first order of business was taking off the old linen backing one stitch at a time. Conservators did that painstaking job lying on their stomachs on a specially constructed gantry that hovered four inches above the flag. The job of removing the stitches took nearly a year to complete. When it was done, it marked the first time the covered side of the flag had been visible since 1914.

The conservators today are studying the best manner in which to display the flag permanently once the preservation effort is completed. It has not yet been determined exactly how one of the oldest surviving fifteen-star, fifteen-stripe flags will be displayed, but one thing is certain: the Star-Spangled Banner will not be displayed hanging vertically.

The journey of the Star-Spangled Banner from its beginnings in Mary Pickersgill's house in downtown Baltimore in 1813 to its hallowed place in the Smithsonian Institution today paralleled the changing ways that Americans viewed their flag. When it flew over Fort McHenry, the flag still was closely associated with the American military. Today the flag is viewed by many as the nation's ultimate symbol.

As Pres. Bill Clinton put it in 1998: The Star-Spangled Banner "and all its successors have come to embody our country, what we think of as America. It may not be quite the same for every one of us who looks at it, but in the end we all pretty much come out where the framers did. We know that we have a country founded on the then revolutionary idea that all of us are created equal, and equally entitled to life, liberty, and the pursuit of happiness."

CHAPTER SIX

Additions and a Subtraction

★   ★   ★

Be it enacted . . . that the flag of the United States be thirteen horizontal stripes, alternate red and white: that the union be twenty stars,
white in a blue field. And be it further enacted, that on the admission
of every new state into the Union, one star be added to the union of
the flag, and that such addition shall take effect on the fourth of July
then next succeeding such admission.

—The third Flag Act, April 4, 1818

WHEN THE FIFTEEN-star, fifteen-striped Star-Spangled Banner flew over Fort McHenry during the Battle of Baltimore, the number of
states had increased to eighteen. Tennessee had joined the Union in June 1,
1796; Ohio on March 1, 1803; and Louisiana on April 30, 1812. Still, no
one in Congress evinced interest in changing the look of the flag to reflect
the new number of states until December 9, 1816. On that day New York
representative Peter Wendover submitted a resolution in the House of
Representatives calling for a committee to be appointed "to inquire into the
expediency of altering the flag of the United States."

Peter Hercules Wendover was born in New York City August 1, 1768.
He spent most of his adult life in politics, holding several local and state offices, including serving as a member of the New York State Assembly in
1804. Wendover was elected as a Republican to the U.S. Congress from
New York City in 1814 and served three terms in the House. After leaving
Congress, Wendover served as sheriff of New York County from 1822 to
1825. He died in New York City on September 24, 1834.

On December 12, 1816, two days after Indiana became the nineteenth
state in the Union, the House took Wendover's advice and set up a panel
to determine the future makeup of the Stars and Stripes. The committee

consisted of Wendover, Burwell Bassett of Virginia, Henry Middleton of South Carolina, Artemas Ward Jr. of Massachusetts, and James Brown Mason of Rhode Island.

In his motion asking for the committee to be appointed, Wendover made it clear that he did not intend to make any "essential alteration" to the flag, something he hoped "no man in the House would consent to." He simply wanted, Wendover said, to make "an unessential variation" reflecting the fact that since the Second Flag Resolution of 1794 four new states had entered the Union.

Republican representative John W. Taylor of New York agreed that a change was needed, but for a different reason: for naval identification purposes. Taylor "had been informed," he said, "by naval gentlemen that our flag could be seen and recognized on the ocean at a greater distance than that of any other nation." If the number of stars and stripes were to be increased, Taylor said, "the flag would become less distinct to distant observation," something he "was desirous to prevent." Taylor therefore recommended permanently "restoring the flag to its original character" of thirteen stars and thirteen stripes.

Wendover's committee made its report to the House on January 2, 1817. The committee said that it had not considered changing the "general form" of the flag nor the "distribution of its parts." To do so, the report said, "would be unacceptable to" Congress "and to the people, as it would be incongenial with the views of the committee" because the stars and stripes "were truly emblematical of our origin and existence as an independent nation."

That said, the committee made its case for "a change in the arrangement of the flag" to reflect changes in the number of states in the Union. Looking ahead to the addition of future states, the committee said it would be "highly inexpedient to increase the number of stripes" every time a new state joined the Union. For one thing, a new, many-striped flag would be unwieldy and would "decrease [the stripes's] magnitude, and render them proportionally less distinct to distant observation." Since the flag, the committee said, was so widely used "by vessels of almost every description," it was also important not to make "great or expensive alterations."

A way to accomplish this would be to reduce the number of stripes to the original thirteen, the committee said, and to increase the number of stars "to correspond with the number of States now in the Union." For the future, the solution would be to "add one star to the flag whenever a new State shall be fully admitted."

The matter rested there for nearly a year, until December 16, 1817—six days after Mississippi had become the twentieth state. On that day Wendover asked the House to appoint a second flag alteration committee because the matter had been pushed aside due to "the pressure of business deemed more important." Again Wendover said that the flag "would be essentially injured" if new stars and stripes were added every time a new state joined the Union. He included a new argument, as well, complaining about "flags in general use" that greatly varied from each other. As examples Wendover pointed to the flags flying on Capitol Hill and in the Washington Navy Yard, "one of which contained nine stripes, the other eighteen, and neither of them in [conformance] to the law."

The House agreed to his motion and appointed a second flag committee that day. It was made up of Wendover, Mason, Thomas Newton Jr. of Virginia, John Ross of Pennsylvania, and George Poindexter of Mississippi. That committee reported a bill based on its predecessor's recommendations — calling for the flag to contain thirteen stripes and twenty stars and adding a star for each new state — to the House on January 6, 1818.

The American flag, the committee's report said, "was truly emblematical of our origin and existence as a nation" and therefore "having met the approbation and received the support of the citizens of the union . . . ought to undergo no change that would decrease its conspicuity, or tend to deprive it of its representative character." The report reiterated Wendover's complaint of December 16, decrying the "great want of uniformity" in flags, "particularly when used on small private vessels."

The matter came up for debate on the House floor on March 24. Wendover began with a long, flowery speech that again made his case for the slight alterations. "The importance attached to the national flag, both in its literal and figurative use, is so universal and of such ancient origin, that we seldom inquire into the meaning of their various figures as adopted by other nations and are in some danger of forgetting the symbolical application of those composing that of our own," Wendover said. "Suitable symbols were devised by those who laid the foundation of the Republic, and I hope their children will ever feel themselves in honor precluded from changing these, except so far as necessity may dictate, and with a direct view of expressing by them their original design."

The flag was adopted in 1777, he said, "as appropriate to and emblematical of" the first thirteen states, "contending for the rights of man and the rich boon of an independent government." The same principles, he said, were "retained and applied" in the second Flag Resolution. But continuing to add stars and stripes for each new state, he argued, would be "improper and inconvenient."

The proposed alteration with thirteen stripes and a star for each state,

Wendover said, "will direct the view to two striking facts in our national history," the number of original states and the current number of states. The arrangement also would honor those who fought in the Revolution, Wendover said. "In their memory, and to their honor, let us restore substantially the flag under which they conquered, and at the same time engraft into its figure the after-fruits of their toil."

Veterans of the Revolutionary War, he said, "have been preserved to see [the flag] acquire a renown which I trust will never fade; have lived to witness in their sons that heroic spirit, which assures them that their privations and their arduous struggle in defense of liberty have not been in vain." No disgrace, he said, "has attached to your 'Star Spangled Banner.' It has been the signal of victor on the land, of successful valor on the lakes, and waved triumphantly on the ocean."

He concluded: "The subject is plain and well understood. And though not of a character to be classed with those of the highest national importance, it still [is] proper to be acted on and worthy of the attention of the Representatives of a people whose flag will never be insulted for want of protectors, and which, I hope and believe, will never be struck to an inferior or equal force."

The bills, as reported, did not contain language addressing the arrangement of the stars. Wendover suggested adopting the committee recommendation that the stars be arranged in one of two ways: either "in the form of one great luminary," or, using the words of the 1777 Flag Resolution, in an unspecified arrangement that represented "a new constellation." He also noted that neither of the first two Flag Resolutions specified the direction of the stripes. The committee, therefore, he said, "deemed it advisable to direct that the stripes be horizontal." Words to that effect were contained in the resolution.

Gen. Samuel Smith, the commander of American forces at the Battle of Baltimore who was a congressman from Maryland, made a motion to table the bill before it could come to a vote. The House voted that motion down unanimously. At that point a flag—presumably one with twenty stars and thirteen stripes—was hoisted on the House floor. Poindexter then introduced an amendment calling for the number of stars to be reduced to seven to honor the seven states that had entered the Union after independence and to reduce the stripes to thirteen to honor the original states. Walter Folger Jr. of Massachusetts asked for an amendment to have the number of stars permanently set at thirteen. The House rejected those two proposed amendments with little debate.

The House went on to pass the nation's Third Flag Resolution that day with only a handful of negative votes. The Senate unanimously concurred a week later, on March 31. Pres. James Monroe signed the bill into law on April 4. A new twenty-star, thirteen-striped flag—with the stars shaped into one large star—arrived by mail on Capitol Hill on April 13. Even though the new law stipulated that it would not be official until July 4, that flag was promptly hoisted on the flagstaff of the House of Representatives.

"I am pleased with its form and proportions," Wendover wrote that day, "and have no doubt it will satisfy the public mind."

Peter Hercules Wendover is given credit for crafting the artful compromise that retained the stars and stripes of the 1777 Flag Resolution, and at the same time honored the thirteen original states with the stripes and each of the existing and new states with a star. He did not act alone, however. Shortly after his first flag committee submitted its report to the House in

U.S. Navy Captain Samuel Chester Reid, working with Congressman Peter Wendover of New York, drew up the guidelines for the third, and last, Flag Resolution that Congress passed in 1818. That measure set the number of stripes at thirteen and called for adding a new star for each new state. Reid is shown in an 1815 portrait by the artist John Wesley Jarvis. *U.S. Naval Academy Museum*

January 1817, Wendover sought out the advice of navy captain Samuel
Chester Reid, a hero of the War of 1812 who was living in Washington.
Samuel Reid deserves as much credit as Wendover does for coming up with
the guidelines that have shaped the American flag from 1818 to today.

Reid was born August 24, 1783, in Norwich, Connecticut. He joined
the U.S. Navy at age seventeen and was the commanding officer of the privateer *General Armstrong* during the War of 1812. On September 25, 1814,
while docked in the neutral Portuguese port of Fayal in the Azores, three
British warships attacked Reid's privateer. Although vastly outnumbered
and outgunned, Reid and his men put up a strong fight in a vicious battle
that included hand-to-hand fighting aboard the *General Armstrong.*

The British forced the Americans to abandon their ship, and Reid and
his crew took refuge in an old castle on shore where they awaited a British
attack. The British commander, though, who had suffered nearly two hundred casualties in the fight, chose not to engage the Americans. One of his
ships was completely out of commission and the other two transported
more than one hundred wounded sailors and marines to British bases.

Reid's actions are credited with delaying the British ships, which were
en route to the Gulf of Mexico, for more than a month. That gave Gen.
Andrew Jackson crucial time to organize the defense of New Orleans and
helped him defeat the British in the bloody Battle of New Orleans, which
began in December of 1814. Reid was honored for his wartime heroics
during a triumphal journey from Savannah, Georgia, to New York in the
spring of 1815. When he reached New York on April 7 the state legislature
presented him a ceremonial sword.

Two years later, in January of 1817, Reid worked hand in hand with
Wendover to shape the future of the American flag. According to his own
account of the matter, Reid was "a principal actor" in the decision to scale
back the number of stripes to thirteen and to add a new star for each new
state. Wendover, Reid said in a February 17, 1850, letter to his son, "call'd
on me" and "was in a dilema (*sic*) as to how the change should be made and
requested that I would help him out of it & give him my views."

Reid then went to work and sketched not one, but three, flags. The first,
which he called "the People's Flag," was the concept that Wendover and his
committee settled on, including Reid's recommendation (which did not appear in the final resolution) that the stars should be "formed into one great
star as forming one great Nation." That flag, Reid said, would be used by all
merchant ships and by "the Nation in general." He also proposed a "Government Flag" to be used by navy warships and "all other government vessels,

Forts, castles, & all gov't. Stations." That flag would have thirteen stripes with an eagle, rather than stars, in the canton.

Reid called his third flag the "Standard of the union" or "the great National Standard." It would be used, he said, on "gala days, to wave over the National Halls, to be hoisted at the installation of our Presidents, goveanors (*sic*), &c." That flag would be divided into four equal parts, containing the "great luminary" star made up of other stars in the upper left, the Great Seal below it, the stripes to its right, and the Goddess of Liberty in the upper right.

While Samuel Reid no doubt was a principal actor in the new design of the flag that was adopted in 1818, Wendover's committee never seriously considered his proposed eagle-bedecked Government Flag nor his busy National Standard.

★   ★   ★

In 1818 the flag was used primarily for government and military purposes. So it is not surprising that the first official order dealing with the arrangement of stars on the new flag following passage of the Flag Resolution came from the Navy Commissioners' Office. On May 18 the office issued a directive setting the size of American flags for U.S. Navy ships and naval installations—fourteen by twenty-four feet. It also stipulated that that the union (the canton) be one third the length of the flag, with six stripes next to the union and seven longer stripes below. That order also provided a sketch of the arrangement of the stars: four rows of five in a staggered pattern.

The commissioners slightly amended the pattern four months later, on September 18, at the behest of Pres. James Monroe. The new lineup of stars contained the same four rows of five, but the rows were aligned symmetrically. The circular also ordered naval commanders to fire a twenty-gun salute when the flag was first hoisted each day.

The U.S. Army didn't get around to adopting the Stars and Stripes as its official garrison flag until 1834. The directive came in the form of a general regulation that applied only to artillery troops. Infantry regiments received that order seven years later in 1841. Unlike the navy, the army did not describe the arrangement of the stars in the canton. The regulation said that the canton, or union, should contain one star for each state in the Union and that the canton should be in the upper left quarter, extending one-third the length of the flag. The regulation did not prescribe any dimensions for the flag nor did it set out the size or shape of the stars.

*   *   *

Despite the 1818 law—and because it was not specific about several key points, including the arrangement of the stars—American flags, which flag makers made by hand one at a time, varied widely in size, shape, and design in the decades following the measure's passage. Making the situation more complicated was the fact that the number of states grew from twenty in 1818 to thirty-four when the Civil War started in 1861. Each new state required one more star in the flag, and with no guidelines, flags contained many different arrangements of stars. The stars themselves often differed in size and style. Some flags had stars shaped into a larger star, or a diamond or a circle or into fanciful images such as an anchor. Emblems such as eagles often were sewed into the canton.

"Before the Civil War especially," Whitney Smith said, "flags were made to taste by each individuals since hand-stitching was then the common mode of manufacture."

Thirteen-star flags remained popular throughout the nineteenth century. Small boats in the U.S. Navy, for example, used the thirteen-star flag as their ensign from 1797 until at least 1916. Thirteen-star flags also were commonly displayed during holidays and other special commemorative events, and in fact continue to be used today on those occasions. That was true in 1826 when the nation celebrated its Jubilee, and in 1832 when the nation marked George Washington's hundredth birthday and at other patriotic occasions such as annual Fourth of July celebrations.

*   *   *

U.S. Navy lieutenant Charles Wilkes, flying under a twenty-six-star flag, led the first American expedition that explored Antarctica. That flag became official on July 4, 1837, following Michigan's entry into the Union. Wilkes commanded four naval vessels on an exploring and surveying expedition authorized by Congress that began in 1838. The pioneering Wilkes Expedition reached Antarctica in February 1839. During the next year, his ships sailed along fifteen hundred miles of Antarctica's ice pack, proving for the first time that Antarctica was a continental land mass.

The twenty-six-star flag that the Wilkes Expedition ultimately flew around the world was replaced by the twenty-seven-star flag on July 4, 1845. That followed Florida's entry into the Union on March 3 of that year.

One year later, on July 4, 1846, came the twenty-eight-star flag, recognizing Texas's entry into the Union on December 29, 1845.

Ten years earlier Texas had broken away from Mexico and formed an independent nation, the Republic of Texas. It had two official national flags: the first, a blue banner with a yellow star, was superseded on January 25, 1839, by the three-part, red, white, and blue "Lone Star" flag that remains the state flag today.

In January of 1846 the explorer and mapmaker John C. Frémont, on his third trip to the west for the U.S. Army's Topographical Engineers, carried with him a one-of-a-kind American flag. His wife, Jessie Benton Frémont, the daughter of Missouri senator Thomas Hart Benton, designed and made the flag, which featured the standard thirteen red and white stripes. She painted an eagle clutching a peace pipe and nine arrows in its claws in the white canton. Twenty-six five-pointed stars surrounded the eagle — thirteen above it and thirteen below. Frémont flew that flag from a fortified position atop Galivan Mountain in defiance of the Mexican military commander, who ordered him to leave the Salinas Valley in California.

Five months later Frémont received his commission as a U.S. Army major and joined forces with American settlers fighting for independence from Mexico. The conflict is sometimes known as the "Bear Flag Revolt" in honor of the banner flown by the rebels in their June–July 1846 war of independence in the Sacramento Valley. That white flag contained a grizzly bear standing on all fours facing a red star and featured the words "California Republic." After more American troops entered the fray, the California Republic dissolved and the Stars and Stripes replaced the bear flag.

Texas's entry into the Union in December 1845 precipitated the Mexican War, which began in April 1846 and ended less than two years later with the signing of the Treaty of Guadeloupe Hidalgo on February 2, 1848. In that war the United States defeated Mexico and took control of more than five hundred thousand square miles of territory that contained nearly all of what would become the states of New Mexico, Utah, Nevada, Arizona, and California, as well as most of western Colorado.

That conflict is significant in the history of the American flag because it was the first war in which American troops carried the Stars and Stripes into battle. It is not clear if the flag was flown in the skirmish that opened hostilities on April 25, 1846, in an area between the Rio Grande and Nueces Rivers that both nations claimed. That fight took place two days after Mexican president Mariano Paredes announced that a state of "defensive war" existed between the two countries. In the war's first major battle, a four-hour fight on May 8 in Palo Alto near Brownsville, U.S. Army general Zachary Taylor, the future president, flew the twenty-eight-star flag as his men defeated the Mexican army of the North.

The Mexican War also marked a milestone in the public perception of the American flag. In countless newspaper articles and personal accounts in books describing the war, the flag was depicted as the symbol of the American cause: a symbol of valor, patriotism, and victory. U.S. Army captain W. S. Henry, for example, in his account of the war published in 1848, referred to the Stars and Stripes as the "most beautiful of all flags, dyed in the blood of our fore-fathers, and redyed in that of their sons upon the fierce battle-field . . . an emblem of American possession to the Sierra Madre!"

The Mexican War, although costly in terms of lives lost (some ten thousand) and expenditures (some one hundred million dollars), was a popular one. As a result of the victory, the Stars and Stripes stretched from the Atlantic to the Pacific. It flew briefly in conquest in Mexico as well. On September 14, 1847, Gen. Winfield Scott and his men rode into Mexico City's main plaza flying the flag and stormed the Castillo de Chapultepec, the fabled residence of the nation's rulers, also known as the Halls of Montezuma.

Another indication of the jump in the flag's popularity occurred in 1847. Annin & Co., today the nation's oldest and largest flag manufacturer, began making American flags that year in a sail loft in New York City. The company had been producing signal flags for sailing ships since the 1820s. It incorporated in 1847. Two years later, when Zachary Taylor was sworn in as president, a flag made by Annin waved in Washington. An Annin & Co. flag has flown at every presidential inauguration since then.

The flag, while still primarily used by the government and the military, became in the pre–Civil War period more popular among the public in decorative arts and in early forms of advertising and promotion, as well as in political campaigns. The flag's image, primarily but not exclusively depicted as being flown on ships, also found its way onto consumer items such as hatboxes, wallpaper, and toys. In the 1830s the flag was used, for example, in the design of a game of Parcheesi, the backgammonlike board game, and on the covers of some needle books designed to teach young girls how to sew. In the 1840s hotels around the nation for the first time began flying American flags emblazoned with the hotel's name from their roofs and doorways.

The flag's image became part of a national political campaign for the first time in the presidential election of 1840, which pitted the Whig Party nominee William Henry Harrison, who was born in Virginia, and his running mate John Tyler against incumbent president Martin Van Buren, a New York Democrat. Van Buren, who was born in 1782, has the distinction of being the first American president born as an American citizen and under the Stars and Stripes.

Harrison had gained fame for his military exploits, especially his role in putting down a Shawnee Indian uprising at the Battle of Tippecanoe on November 7, 1811, in Indiana, and his leadership in the victorious War of 1812 Battle of the Thames in Ontario. Harrison's campaign dealt with few national issues and instead concentrated on building the candidate's image as a war hero and a man of the people. It featured political songs and slogans, including the famous "Tippecanoe and Tyler, too." And it featured the widespread distribution of miniature log cabins and jugs of hard cider.

The flag became part of a national political campaign for the first time in 1840 when William Henry Harrision and John Tyler used it on banners and broadsides, along with two other symbols of "Tippicanoe and Tyler Too," the log cabin and the jug of hard cider. *The Library of Congress, Prints and Photographs Division*

The log cabin logo was pasted on campaign banners, bandannas, ribbons, and broadsides. A Star-Spangled Banner flew prominently alongside some of the cabins—at a time when it was almost unheard of for private individuals to fly the flag. The campaign also employed Stars and Stripes banners with Harrison's name inscribed on them. Most had thirteen-star cantons. Some had his portrait in the center of the flag.

One campaign ribbon contained an image of Harrison, an eagle, and a display of battle flags. The ribbon's inscription read: "'Tis the Star-Spangled Banner! /O'Long May it Wave/O'er the Land of the Free and the Home of the Brave/Conquer We must—Our cause is just."

Harrison defeated Van Buren to become the nation's ninth president. His use of the flag in the campaign proved to be an important factor in that victory. More significantly, the campaign's use of the flag's image was a precursor of things to come in future presidential and other political campaigns.

The next presidential election, in 1844, saw the first widespread use of political parade banners. Both candidates—the winning Democrat, James K. Polk of Tennessee, and his Whig opponent, Henry Clay of Virginia—used the colorful banners. Polk and Clay also used flag banners in their political advertisements. Most commonly, the names of the candidates and their running mates—George M. Dallas, the Democrat, and the Whig Theodore Frelinghuysen—were emblazoned on the campaign flags. Sometimes the names were stitched in the canton with the stars removed; other times they were written across the stripes.

"Each new election [after 1844] brought some interesting variations," the historian Scot Guenter observed, "but the practice of advertising candidates on the American flag went unquestioned when it was introduced and it quickly became accepted as common procedure."

★　★　★

Another party that made an impact on the national political scene during the 1840s and 1850s, the Know-Nothings, used the American flag as one of its primary symbols. The Know-Nothings, the first anti-immigrant nativist movement in the United States, gained adherents following the large number of primarily Irish and German Catholics who came to this country beginning in the mid-1840s. The Know-Nothing movement began in New York City in 1849 with the founding of the Order of the Star-Spangled Banner and used that emblem liberally in its publications.

The group, which quickly gained adherents in the early 1850s, limited its membership to Protestant adults who pledged their belief in God and their willingness to abide by the order's rules. The order had its own members-only passwords, signs, and phrases of recognition. Its avowed purpose was "to place in all offices of honor, trust, or profit, in the gift of the people, or by appointment, none but native-born Protestant citizens."

When asked by established political leaders about their organizations, the members of the Order of the Star-Spangled Banner and the other groups had orders to say they "knew nothing." That led the noted newspaperman Horace Greeley to christen the movement the "Know-Nothings" in his *New York Tribune* in November 1853.

The flag-waving Know-Nothing parties went public under the banner of the American Party in the early 1850s. At its peak in 1853, the American

The anti-immigrant Know-Nothing Party, which made an impact on the national political scene during the 1840s and 1850s, used the American flag as one of its primary symbols. This illustrated sheet music cover, produced in May 1844, uses the flag to glorify the
party's nativist cause. *The Library of Congress, Prints and Photographs Division*

Party had some one million members in thirty-one states. The party reached
its height of influence in 1854 when it elected more than two dozen candidates to the House of Representatives. Despite the movement's election success, however, none of its stringent anti-immigrant policies became law. In
1856, when party members deeply split over the issue of slavery, the American Party and Know-Nothing movement collapsed.

CHAPTER SEVEN

A House Divided Against Itself

★   ★   ★

War! Young men your country calls, 'Tis duty to obey! All who are ready to volunteer, to serve their country, now in its hour of danger, to march in defence of the Government, and to protect our Glorious Flag, the Star Spangled Banner.

— Recruiting Poster, 104th Pennsylvania Infantry Regiment, August 1861

THE ISSUE OF SLAVERY and the broader issue of states' rights brought the United States into the Civil War in 1861, a cataclysmic event in the nation's young history—and an event that marked a sea change in the evolution of the cultural importance of the American flag. As soon as Americans began killing Americans on American soil, Americans from every strata of society in the North for the first time embraced the flag as a symbol of American patriotism. In short order the Stars and Stripes became a beloved, cherished icon in the North, a widely held symbol of the Union and the fight to keep it whole.

The bitterly contested, bloody Civil War dragged on for four long years and cost the lives of at least six hundred thousand Americans—almost as many as the number who died in all American wars combined. The magnitude of that national tragedy is reflected in the fact that never again would Americans, in the North or in the South, look upon the flag in the same manner.

The Civil War, Whitney Smith said, "became a fight for the flag, and it was expressed in those terms. The flag was everywhere. Every school flew a flag and prior to that there is only one known instance—in 1817—of a school flying an American flag. Union soldiers even carried miniature flags called Bible flags, small enough to fit in the Bible they would take with them to the battlefield. The start of the Civil War was the beginning of the sense we have today of the American flag as an everyday object and of something that belongs to everyone."

A hint of the flag's important role in the Civil War on both sides of the conflict may be found in the long, impassioned speech that Jefferson Davis made on the U.S. Senate floor on January 10, 1861. Davis, then a senator from Mississippi, would on February 18 be inaugurated as the first president of the Confederate States of America. A hero of the Mexican War, Davis had also served in the U.S. House of Representatives and was secretary of war under Pres. Franklin Pierce.

In his January 10 speech, which came the day after Mississippi seceded from the Union and the day that Florida seceded, Davis gave his assessment of the "state of the country." His main theme was a strong defense of states' rights, including his adamant belief that states had the right to withdraw from the Union. Davis spoke passionately about his wish to avoid armed conflict between the states. But he repeatedly warned that war would be inevitable if president-elect Abraham Lincoln and his Republican Party—whom he called "feeble hands" and "drivelers"—continued to act illegally and aggressively against the Southern states.

Davis peppered the speech with references to American history and the American flag. The last book Davis had checked out from the Library of Congress in December of 1860, in fact, was the then-standard work on the Stars and Stripes, Schuyler Hamilton's *History of the American Flag*. Early on in the speech Davis spoke of the "rich inheritance" given the nation by our Founding Fathers. He went on to invoke Fort McHenry, "memorable in our history as the place where, under bombardment, the Star-Spangled Banner floated though the darkness of night, the point which was consecrated by our national song."

In making his case for federal troops to withdraw from Fort Sumter in Charleston, South Carolina, Davis again invoked the flag. South Carolina had been the first state to secede from the Union on December 20, 1860. Five days later, U.S. Army major Robert Anderson moved federal troops into the fort. The next day, with great ceremony, he raised an enormous twenty- by thirty-six-foot, thirty-three-star American flag over the fort. As the flag was unfurled, Anderson wrote four days later, his troops presented arms and his band played "The Star-Spangled Banner," after which "three cheers were given for the flag and three for the Union," which Anderson called "a solemn, and to all, a most interesting ceremony."

Davis had heard, he said in his Senate speech, that the "greatest objection" to having the federal troops withdraw from Fort Sumter "was an unwillingness to lower the flag." He derided that argument, claiming that Southerners and Northerners had equally strong feelings about the Stars and Stripes. Southerners, he said, "are your brethren; and they have shed as much glory upon that flag as any equal number of men in the Union."

Davis spoke passionately about the Revolutionary War battle that took place near Fort Sumter in Charleston harbor on June 28, 1776, at what was then called Fort Sullivan. In that engagement colonial forces under William Moultrie fought off an attacking British Fleet in a nine-hour battle. The victory saved Charleston from British occupation and became a significant morale booster in the colonies, coming just six days before the Continental Congress adopted the Declaration of Independence on July 4.

Davis said that the defenders of Fort Sullivan (later renamed Fort Moultrie) "are the men, and that is the location where the first Union flag was unfurled," an event he said that had occurred in October 1775. (The consensus of historical opinion, however, is that the first Union flag, the Continental Colors, was unfurled by George Washington on New Year's Day of 1776 near Boston.) In the June 28 fight, Davis said, the "fort was assailed by the British fleet, and bombarded until the old logs, clinging with stern tenacity to the enemy that assailed them, were filled with balls, the flag still floated there . . ."

He then ridiculed the idea that there was any kind of shame in removing the American flag from Fort Sumter in 1861. "Can there be a point of pride," Davis asked rhetorically, "against laying upon that sacred soil today the flag for which our fathers died?" His pride, Davis said, "is that the flag shall not set between contending brothers." If the worst happened and war broke out, and the Stars and Stripes would no longer "be the common flag of the country," Davis recommended that the American flag be "folded up and laid away like a vesture [an article of clothing] no longer used; that it shall be kept as a sacred memento of the past, to which each of us can make a pilgrimage, and remember the glorious days in which we were born."

Later in the speech he returned to the Revolutionary War, referring to the flag as "the constellation," using the words of the 1777 Flag Resolution. Davis inserted his states' rights interpretation into his version of what the flag stood for. The flag, he said, "was set in the political firmament as a sign of the unity and confederation and community independence, coexistent with confederate strength." It "has served to bless our people," Davis said, and its "regenerative power will outlive, perhaps, the Government as a sign for which it was set."

He described his pride serving under the flag in the Mexican War and then lamented the fact that he would be turning away from "the flag of the Union." Davis spoke, too, of his "deep sorrow" as he contemplated "taking a last leave of that object of early affection and proud association, feeling that henceforth it is not to be the banner which, by day and by night, I am ready to follow, to hail with the rising and bless with the setting sun."

In his farewell speech to the Senate eleven days later, on January 21, Davis did not mention the American flag.

On January 11, 1861, the day after Davis's flag-heavy Senate speech, Alabama seceded from the Union. Georgia followed suit on January 19 and Louisiana on January 26. On January 29, Kansas joined the Union and on the Fourth of July 1861, the thirty-four-star flag became official. This was notwithstanding the fact that Texas, Virginia, Arkansas, Tennessee, and North Carolina had seceded in the interim, and that eleven of the thirty-four states did not consider themselves a part of the "constellation" any longer.

In the North, some people cut eleven stars out of their personal flags in protest. After the war began there was sentiment in Congress to remove the stars officially. Abraham Lincoln, however, stood steadfastly against removing stars from the flag because of his belief that the rebellious Southern states remained part of the national government.

The official national flag at the outset of the Civil War, therefore, contained thirty-four stars. On July 4, 1863, during the war, the flag gained another star in honor of West Virginia's entry into the Union on June 20. Nevada became the thirty-sixth state during the war, in October 1864. The thirty-six-star flag, which became official on July 4, 1865, typically contained five rows of stars. The first, third, and fifth rows held eight stars each; the second and four rows had six each.

★   ★   ★

Jefferson Davis was not the only prominent American who spoke out about the flag in the months before the Civil War began. Samuel F. B. Morse, the inventor of the telegraph, devoted considerable energy trying to stop the outbreak of war. In doing so, Morse came up with the idea of a secession or peace flag. Morse, who was sixty-nine years old and in his retirement in 1860, suggested that the states come together in a new national convention to try to iron out their differences. If that failed, he proposed two separate, allied nations, each with half of the United States flag.

Morse envisioned a Northern flag that would have the top six and a half stripes and half the canton divided diagonally with the corresponding number of stars. The Southern flag would have the six and a half stripes on the bottom and half the canton. If war with a foreign nation came, Morse said, "under our treaty of offence and defence the two separate flags, by national affinity, would clasp fittingly together, and the glorious old flag of the Union, in its entirety, would again be hoisted, once more embracing all the sister States."

Not surprisingly, the odd idea of secession or peace flags did not catch on. A few were raised in the North, but proved not to be very popular. In April, after the war had begun, a man who flew the secession flag in East Fairhaven, Massachusetts, was tarred and feathered by a mob, made to give three cheers for the Stars and Stripes, swear allegiance to the Constitution, and promise never to fly any flag other than the intact Stars and Stripes.

In the months prior to Fort Sumter, as it appeared that war was imminent, there were signs that the flag was becoming increasingly important as an everyday patriotic symbol in the North. Before a huge crowd outside Independence Hall in Philadelphia on February 22, 1861, for example, president-elect Abraham Lincoln, en route to Washington from Illinois, personally raised a Stars and Stripes flag that had been flown by American troops in the Mexican War. That act was greeted by a wave of intense emotion from the huge crowd that had gathered to hear him speak.

"I could not help hoping that there was, in the entire success of that beautiful ceremony, at least something of an omen of what is to come," Lincoln said later that night in Harrisburg. "I think the flag of our country may yet be kept flaunting gloriously."

On that same day in New Orleans, one of the last American flags flew in the South before the war began. The flag, inscribed "United We Stand, Divided We Fall," featured two clasped hands. A battle almost erupted between Southern patriots and the Northern sympathizers who unfurled the flag. It was averted when a group of armed men protected the flag throughout the day and then took it down voluntarily.

At Fort Sumter itself, Major Anderson received letters of support from friends and strangers, letters that typically mentioned the defense of the American flag. A Baltimore bricklayer wrote, for example, that he would be happy to come to Anderson's aid with other workingmen "who would not hesitate to lay the trowel if it became necessary and help to defend their country's flag."

*   *   *

On February 4, 1861, the Provisional Confederate Congress held its opening session in the Capitol Building in Montgomery, Alabama. The delegates' first orders of business were creating a Constitution for the breakaway Confederate States of America, electing a president and vice president, and choosing a flag and seal. Christopher Memminger of South Carolina presented the first proposed flag to the body on February 9—a banner, he reported, whose design came from "the ladies of South Carolina."

The Congress that day set up a select committee to choose a flag. That panel, the Committee on Flag and Seal, received scores of additional design suggestions from citizens from across the South during the next several weeks. A large percentage of the suggested flags were red, white, and blue. Many contained stars and stripes. Many envisioned the American flag's canton-and-stripes theme. Many had arrangements of seven stars, representing the seven Confederate states at the time. Several replaced the canton and inserted differing arrangements of stars on, above, below, or surrounded by red and white stripes.

A large percentage of the proposed flags were variations on the Stars and Stripes. But the Confederate Congress quickly dismissed a resolution by Walter Brooke of Mississippi on February 13, to instruct the flag committee "to adopt and report a flag as similar as possible to the flag of the United States." Brooke's proposal was met with derision in the Congress, and he withdrew the recommendation.

On March 4 Pres. Abraham Lincoln took the oath of office on the East Portico of the U.S. Capitol in Washington, D.C. On that same day in the Southern capital, Montgomery, William Porcher Miles, the chairman of the flag committee, presented the panel's recommendation to the Congress. Miles, who had argued heatedly against Brooke's proposal, reiterated his opposition to it in his report. First, there would be "practical difficulties" in a flag similar to the Stars and Stripes, Miles said. Second, there would be "no propriety in retaining the ensign of a government which, in the opinion of the States composing this Confederacy, had become so oppressive and injurious to their interests as to require their separation from it. It is idle to talk of 'keeping' the flag of the United States when we have voluntarily seceded from them."

Miles went on to lambaste those who spoke of the "glories of the old flag." He reminded those present that the battles of the Revolution, "about which our fondest and proudest memories cluster," were not fought under the Stars and Stripes. He spoke of Southerners' contributions to the War of 1812 and the Mexican War, but then derided any strong association with their service in that war and the American flag, which he called "a mere piece of striped bunting." He compared the Confederacy to the breakaway colonies who "did not desire to retain the British flag or anything similar to it." We "think it good to imitate [the colonies] in this comparatively little manner," he said.

Miles went on to mock two countries, Liberia and the Sandwich Islands, for choosing flags similar to the Stars and Stripes, saying they "had been pilfered and appropriated by a free Negro community and a race of savages." He said, though, that it would be appropriate for the Confederacy to "retain at least a suggestion of the old Stars and Stripes." Then Miles offered the committee's proposed flag, which the Congress adopted—the flag that has since become known as the Stars and Bars. It consists of three horizontal stripes, one white and two red, and a canton of blue containing a circle of seven white stars.

"If adopted," Miles said, "long may it wave over a brave, a free, and a virtuous people. May the career of the Confederacy, whose duty it will then be to support and defend it, be such as to endear it to our children's children, as the flag of a loved . . . a just and benign government, and the cherished symbol of its valor, purity, and truth."

The Confederate Congress approved the flag that day. The following day the Stars and Bars flew over the Capitol Building in Montgomery. The flag, however, so resembled the Stars and Stripes that Confederate commanders early on in the war stopped using it on the field of battle. By the end of the year, the Southern troops began displaying a different banner, the Confederate Battle Flag, known as the Southern Cross.

That came about as a direct result of the difficulty of distinguishing the Stars and Bars from the Stars and Stripes at the war's initial large engagment, the First Battle of Bull Run in Manassas, Virginia, on July 21, 1861. In that bloody and smoky fight the Confederates under Generals P. G. T. Beauregard and Joseph E. Johnston defeated the Union army under Gen. Irvin McDowell.

Because the Confederate troops had trouble seeing the colors through the heavy gun smoke at First Manassas, the Confederacy adopted an entirely new battlefield flag. Beauregard, Johnston, and Miles worked with the Confederate War Department to design the Battle Flag, which was presented formally in ceremonies to the troops in December. The red, white, and blue Battle Flag, consisting of a blue cross of St. Andrew containing thirteen white stars, with narrow white edges on the cross—sometimes known as the "Southern Cross"—became the Confederate war banner for the duration of the war.

A third flag, known as the Stainless Banner, was used mainly by the Confederate navy and maritime fleet. It consisted of the Battle Flag in the canton and a completely white field. The Confederate Congress adopted that banner as the official Confederate national flag on May 1, 1863. Near the end of the war, on March 4, 1865, it was modified with the addition of a wide red vertical stripe because it was reported that on windless days only the field showed, making the flag appear as if it were a white flag of surrender.

*   *   *

The event that launched the Civil War—the Confederate attack on Fort Sumter in South Carolina—also precipitated an unprecedented explosion of devotion to the Stars and Stripes that swept over the North when the flag was lowered in defeat in Charleston harbor. The bombardment of the fort on that man-made island of seashells and granite at the entrance to Charleston began at 4:30 in the morning of April 12. By that time the Confederacy had taken possession of all American military forts and arsenals in the seven-state South, with the exception of Fort Pickens on Santa Rosa Island on Pensacola Bay in Florida and Fort Sumter.

Fort Pickens, despite repeated attacks, never did fall to the Confederate army. But that was not the case at Sumter, a solidly built, five-sided ediface with fifty-foot-high walls as thick as twelve feet. Lincoln did not give in to the Confederate demand to evacuate the fort after he took office in March. Instead, he made plans to resupply Anderson's small garrison there in early April. That news was greeted by commanding Confederate general Beauregard's demand for the fort's immediate evacuation and surrender. When Lincoln refused, Beauregard received an order by telegraph from Secretary of War Leroy Pope Walker in Montgomery ordering the bombardment of the fort. Two days later, after thirty-four hours of being hit by some four thousand shells, Anderson surrendered.

Anderson, a Kentucky-born professional soldier, West Point class of 1825, and his men had put up a valiant fight. They raised the white flag of surrender at 2:00 in the afternoon on April 13, after Confederate guns had set the fort's barracks on fire, completely destroying the building, as well as the main gate, and seriously damaging some of the fort's walls and with the fort's food stores severely depleted. Anderson asked as part of the surrender terms that the Confederates allow him to give a one-hundred-gun salute as he lowered the fort's American flag.

Beauregard had agreed to that condition in his initial demand to Anderson to surrender. "The flag which you have upheld so long and with so much fortitude, under the most trying circumstances, may be saluted by you on taking it down," he said. "In recognition of the gallantry exhibited by the garrison," Beauregard said in his after-action report to President Davis, "I cheerfully agreed that on surrendering the fort the commanding officer might salute the flag."

Sumter's garrison flag had flown over the fort from December 26, 1860, until the first shots rang out at dawn on April 12. After high winds tore it in half, the flag was replaced by a smaller storm flag, which received the surrender salute. Ironically, it was during that salute—which began at two o'clock in the afternoon on April 14—that the first and only soldier on either side of the conflict was killed in action. During the loading of the forty-seventh salute cannon, an errant cartridge set off a pile of other shells that hit Pvt. Daniel Hough, who died instantly. Pvt. Edward Gallway, who was severely wounded, died three days later. Four other men were seriously wounded.

Anderson cut short the salute at fifty shots. At four o'clock, he and Capt. Abner Doubleday—who is sometimes credited with having invented the game of baseball—gathered the men on the parade ground. The Union troops then lowered the flag, and marched out of the fort as the small Union band played "Yankee Doodle Dandy." They boarded the steamer *Isobel*, which took them to the transport *Baltic*, upon which they sailed to New York, arriving on April 16. As he led his men out of Fort Sumter, Anderson had the garrison flag folded and tucked under his arm.

"At that hour," Beauregard reported, "the place having been evacuated by the United States garrison, our troops occupied it, and the Confederate flag was hoisted on the ramparts of Sumter with a salute from the various batteries."

Or, as the *New York Times* put it in the second paragraph of its front-page April 15, 1861, article headlined "FORT SUMPTER FALLEN": "The American flag has given place to the Palmetto of South Carolina."

Watching this unfold from the USS *Pawnee*, anchored outside the harbor, navy commander S. C. Rowan gave his version of events starting at

8:00 that morning: "Appearances of great rejoicing in Charleston Harbor. Smoke still rising from Fort Sumter. At 1 P.M. observed the American flag flying over Fort Sumter. At 2, a salute of fifty guns was fired and the flag was hauled down. At 4 P.M., the so-called Confederate flag . . . was hoisted on Fort Sumter amid a general fire from all the [surrounding] forts batteries."

★   ★   ★

Jefferson Davis had bitterly derisive—and only partially correct—words for those in the North who framed the fight at Fort Sumter in terms of an attack on the American flag, calling such sentiments the "disingenuous rant of demagogues." Davis, however, was completely correct in his assessment that the fall of Fort Sumter "was seized upon to inflame the mind of the Northern people."

A large part of that inflammation centered on feelings about the flag. "When the stars and stripes went down at Sumter, they went up in every town and county in the loyal states," Admiral Preble wrote in 1871. "Every city, town, and village suddenly blossomed with banners." What happened at Fort Sumter, he said, "created great enthusiasm throughout the loyal States, for the flag had come to have a new and strange significance. The heart of the nation swelled to avenge the insult cast by traitors on its glorious flag. It is said that even laborers wept in the streets for the degradation of their country. One cry was raised, drowning all other voices—'War! War to restore the Union! War to avenge the flag!'"

While Preble was not exactly an unbiased observer—a career officer, he served in various capacities with the U.S. Navy during the Civil War—his assessment of the "new and strange" role of the flag in the North following Fort Sumter is accurate. What happened at Sumter aroused bitterly strong feelings in the North and served as a unifying force for the war that was to come. A significant portion of the emotional component of the Union's war fever involved the flag.

"Romantic flag-waving rhetoric," in the words of the eminent Civil War historian James M. McPherson, swept through the North and South when the war began, as it does in virtually all societies during times of intense national strife. One example among many in the North: a letter written by James Welsh to his brother John shortly after the Stars and Stripes came down at Fort Sumter. The Welsh brothers grew up in Virginia, but John Welsh moved to Ohio in 1853 and was incensed by his brother's support of the Confederate cause. He never dreamed his brother would "raise a hand to tear down the glorious Stars and Stripes," James Welsh wrote, "a flag that we have been taught from our cradle to look on with pride. . . . I would strike down my own brother if he would dare raise a hand to destroy that flag."

Newspapers and magazines in the North ran red-hot flag-oriented editorials in the wake of the fall of Fort Sumter. An editorial in *Harper's Weekly*, the widely read news magazine published in New York, for example, vehemently condemned the Southern states for leaving the Union, partly framing the entire Civil War issue in terms of an assault on what the American flag stood for. The "rebels know," the magazine said, "that, as surely as the sun rises, the honor of the country's flag will presently be vindicated." The flag, the editorial announced, "is the symbol of the Government which secures and protects [the Southerner] in all his rights and interests; and when he excuses the crime [of warring against the Union], he invites anarchy and the universal destruction not only of all property, but of all the guarantees of civil society."

The editorial went on to express disgust that Southerners, who "have grown and prospered under [the flag] more than any nation in the world" would "strike their hands at the flag and their fangs at the peaceful and happy system which it symbolizes." It accused the Confederates of being "totally devoid of love of country," a feeling that "indicates the values" of "a moral monster," and "a lump of inhuman selfishness."

The *New York Times* offered an equally defiant, flag-waving editorial on May 6. "If anyone goes around among our soldiers now and asks the reason for their enlistment, they will very probably say, 'It was the insult to the old Flag at Sumter,' or 'It is for the Stars and Stripes,'" the newspaper said. Now "is the time of its peril, when the shot of traitors have pierced it, when it is discarded and outcast by those who have so long used it to protect their inequities, the feeling of the people springs towards it like a passion." The Stars and Stripes, the editorial predicted, "shall yet wave over Richmond and Charleston, and Mobile and New Orleans."

The editorial concluded with a plea to Northerners to fly the flag everywhere and for Union soldiers to pledge themselves to the flag. Let "the glorious banner flaunt from every housetop, from window and chimney, from monument and church—for no place is too sacred for it. In this time of its danger, we will wear it over our breasts, and bear it on our persons; and you who go forth to defend the Flag, remember that nothing can dishonor it but treachery and cowardice! Bear the old Stars and Stripes, as the emblem of your country, before you in battle, count it honor enough that you have been able to bleed and suffer for it, and a sweet and glorious thing if for that Flag you can die."

As Preble reported, all across the North citizens spontaneously began flying the flag from their homes and their businesses. The flag flew at public schools, colleges and universities, and in front of churches. Women wore small flags on their hats; men pinned small flags to their lapels and hat bands. Flags were tucked into horses' headstalls and wrapped around dogs.

"The patchwork of red, white, and blue, what had flaunted in their faces for generations without exciting much emotion, in a single day stirred the pulses of the people to battle," Preble wrote (breathlessly if not inaccurately), and "became the inspiration of national effort."

On April 12, the day the attack on Sumter had begun, a flag-bedecked rally took place in the city of Troy, New York, on the Hudson River north of Albany. "Will you permit that flag to be desecrated and trampled in the dust by traitors now?" one of the town's prominent citizens asked the crowd. "That flag must be lifted up from the dust into which it has been trampled, placed in the proper position and again set floating in triumph to the breeze."

In Boston flags "blossomed everywhere," according to Mary A. Livermore, who went on to serve as a Union nurse. The Stars and Stripes, she said, "floated from the roofs of the houses, were flung to the breeze from chambers of commerce and boards of trade, spanned the surging streets, decorated the private parlor, glorified the school-room, [and] festooned the church walls and pulpit."

On April 16, Livermore described the scene at Boston's Faneuil Hall where a large crowd of men had come to sign up for the Union cause. "I saw the dear banner of my country, rising high and high to the top of the flagstaff, fling out fold after fold . . . , and float proudly over the hallowed edifice," she wrote in her autobiography. "Oh, the roar that rang out from ten thousand throats! Old men, with white hair and tearful faces, lifted their hats to the national ensign, and reverently saluted it. Young men greeted it with fierce and wild hurrahs, talking the while in terse Saxon of the traitors of the Confederate States, who had dragged in the dirt this flag of their country, never before dishonored."

Maj. Robert Anderson and his men were greeted with an enormous display of American flags when they arrived in New York City by ship from Fort Sumter. The flag, one observer said, "flew out to the wind from every housetop" as "wildly excited crowds marched the streets demanding that the suspected or lukewarm should show the symbol of nationality as a committal to the country's cause." Tens of thousands of American flags flew throughout New York City that day. The city's artists joined in, immediately turning out engravings and lithographs prominently featuring the flag and other patriotic symbols. What the *New York World* on April 20 called "flag mania" soon gripped the city.

On April 19 Anderson had the Fort Sumter flag hung from a flagpole of a building on Broadway during a sendoff ceremony he took part in for New York's Seventh Regiment. The famed political cartoonist Thomas Nast memorialized that event in an oil painting, *Seventh Regiment Departing for the War,* which depicts the tattered Fort Sumter flag along with scores of Stars and Stripes being waved on the street.

The next day, April 20, a crowd of some one hundred thousand rallied in New York's Union Square where both Anderson and the Sumter flag made appearances. The center of attention was Henry K. Brown's large *Washington on Horseback* bronze sculpture. The tattered Fort Sumter flag was attached to a flagstaff allegedly taken from the fort and placed in George Washington's hands. "The national banners waving from ten thousand windows in your city today proclaim your affection and reverence for the Union," Republican U.S. senator Edward Dickinson Baker told the throng. Another speaker urged the crowd to "rally to the Star-Spangled Banner so long as a single stripe can be discovered, or a single star shall shimmer from the surrounding darkness."

Also in New York City a homemade thirty-foot flag flew on April 24 at a store on Maiden Lane. It was sewed by four generations of women of the Newcomb family. Also seen on the streets of New York: a flag over a sign painter's door with the words that eerily echo bumper stickers that appeared after the September 11, 2001, terrorist attacks: "*Colors* warranted not to run."

On April 25 U.S. senator Stephen Douglas of Illinois gave what has since come to be known as his "Preserve the Flag" speech to a joint session of the Legislature of Illinois in the Old Capitol Building in Springfield. Douglas and Lincoln were political enemies who had squared off in a historic series of debates during the 1858 Illinois Senate race over the issue of slavery. In his April 25 speech, however, Douglas urged Northerners to set aside their differences and unite under the flag against the Confederacy.

"For the first time since the adoption of the Federal Constitution, a widespread conspiracy exists to destroy the best government the sun of heaven ever shed its rays upon," Douglas told cheering state legislators.

"Hostile armies are now marching on the Federal Capitol, with a view of planting a revolutionary flag upon its dome," he said. "When all propositions of peace fail, and a war of aggression is proclaimed, there is but one course left to the patriot, and that is to rally under the flag which has waved over the Capitol from the days of Washington, and around the government established by Washington, Madison, Hamilton, and their compeers."

That was Douglas's last speech. He died on June 3, 1861, in Chicago. After his death, Americans in both the North and South took Douglas's admonition to "rally under the flag" to heart.

CHAPTER EIGHT

Flagmania

★ ★ ★

Yes, we'll rally round the flag, boys / Rally once again. . . .

— *"The Battle Cry of Freedom,"* George F. Root, 1862

TWO DAYS AFTER Douglas's farewell speech, Edward Everett—the former Massachusetts governor, ambassador to England, president of Harvard, and secretary of state in the Fillmore administration—gave a rousing speech at a flag-raising ceremony in Boston. "Why is it," Everett asked rhetorically, "that the flag of the country, always honored, always beloved, is now at once worshipped, I may say, with passionate homage of this whole people? Why does it float, as never before, not merely from arsenal and masthead, but from tower and steeple, from the public edifices, the temples of science, the private dwellings, in magnificent display of miniature presentiment?"

Everett answered his own question with two words: "Fort Sumter."

When word of the flag under siege at Sumter reached the Northern states, Everett said, "One deep, unanimous, spontaneous feeling shot with the tidings through the breasts of twenty millions of freemen, that its outraged honor must be vindicated."

Everett's oratory stood as a shining, if hyperbolic, example of what the *New Orleans Picayune* called the "flagmania" that swept both the Northern and Southern states in the weeks and months after the Confederate flag replaced the Stars and Stripes at Fort Sumter. In the South, the Confederate flag flew conspicuously in front of homes and businesses, much as the Stars and Stripes did in the North. Many women wore clothes embroidered with the Confederate flag or displayed small flags on their dresses.

"I wear one pinned to my bosom," twenty-year-old Sarah Morgan Dawson of Baton Rouge, Louisiana, wrote in her diary in 1862. "The man who says take it off will have to pull it off for himself; the man who dares attempt it—well! A pistol in my pocket fills the gap. I am capable too."

At send-off ceremonies in small and large towns and cities across the South, troops heading off to war were almost always presented with the Stars and Bars—and later the Southern Cross—most often by women who had sewn the flags themselves. Local politicians and clergymen often attended these events and made emotional speeches that were heavily covered in local newspapers. The Confederate soldiers went to war with florid, patriotic words ringing in their ears not to surrender the flag or, as a last resort, to destroy the banner rather than surrender it to the Yankees.

Send-offs were similar in the North. Milton Scott Lytle, a private in the 125th Pennsylvania Volunteers, described his unit's leave taking before a huge crowd of men, women, and children at the courthouse in Huntingdon County, Pennsylvania, as a flag-drenched, superpatriotic occasion. The second minister to speak, the Reverend. G. W. Zahnizer of the Presbyterian Church, Lytle said, "pointed to the American flag, and appealed to" the men "to return only when the dishonor heaped upon it shall be wiped out, and it again floats in triumph in every section of our country." Methodist minister S. L. M. Couser then "seized" the flag, Lytle said, and waved it over his head, declaring "his readiness to shoulder his musket in defense of the glorious emblem of liberty." The shouts that went up after he spoke those words "were deafening," Lytle said.

As the men marched to the train depot, the crowd followed along. "The scene there baffles description," Lytle wrote. "Mothers, wives and sisters weeping over their friends who thus willingly offer to lay down their lives in defense of their flag."

The Stars and Stripes began to appear on stationery and envelopes within weeks after the Confederate takeover of Fort Sumter. One of the first such images was a full-color American flag that covered the outside of an entire envelope. Printers in the South soon came up with a flag envelope of their own, using the Stars and Bars. The white stripe in the middle made a convenient place for the address. Envelopes and stationery in the North also featured patriotic slogans along with the flags. They included "Liberty and Union," "The Flag of the Free," and "Forever Float That Standard Sheet."

Other envelopes were adorned with flags and portraits of Abraham Lincoln and prominent military men such as John Frémont and Winfield Scott. Another popular envelope featured the flag and the words "I shall wave again over Sumter."

The actual Fort Sumter garrison flag itself became almost a holy relic in the North. Soon after it flew over Union Square, the flag was placed in a vault in New York City's Metropolitan Bank. It was loaned periodically during the war to the U.S. Sanitary Commission, a civilian group made up primarily of women set up by the Union government in June of 1861 to perform nursing and other medical and social work at field hospitals, soldiers' homes, and other venues. The commission, headed by the celebrated landscape architect Frederick Law Olmstead, used the flag as an effective fund-raising tool. The flag made a tour of cities around the country, where it was put up for "auction." The highest bidder then turned the money— and the flag—over to the commission.

As the war progressed, the flag became a visible and integral part of rallies and patriotic celebrations throughout the Union. The Fourth of July celebration in San Francisco in 1864, for example, turned out to be an especially flag-drenched affair. Mark Twain, then a reporter for the *San Francisco Daily Morning Call*, called the city's commemoration of the Fourth that year "the most remarkable day San Francisco has ever seen" in terms of "magnificence, enthusiasm, crowds, noise, wind and dust."

The "whole city," Twain reported, "was swathed in a waving drapery of flags—scarcely a house could be found which lacked this kind of decoration. The effect was exceedingly lively and beautiful." Montgomery Street, he said, "was no longer a street of compactly built houses, but simply a quivering cloud of gaudy red and white stripes, which shut out from view almost everything but itself. Some houses were broken out all over with flags, like small-pox patients; among these were Brannan's Building, the Occidental Hotel and the Lick House, which displayed flags at every window."

Poetry, stories, and songs about the flag became increasingly popular after the war began. Bands played "The Star-Spangled Banner" at patriotic rallies throughout the North, although Julia Ward Howe's "The Battle Hymn of the Republic," which first published in February 1862, became the Union army's de facto official anthem during the war. In July 1862, in a burst of patriotic spirit, the composer and lyricist George F. Root wrote "The Battle Cry of Freedom," which begins with the memorable words that later became a catch phrase: "Yes, we'll rally round the flag, boys / rally once again."

Root wrote the song following President Lincoln's July 2, 1862, call for three hundred thousand Union army volunteers. The song was performed for the first time on July 24. "The Battle Cry of Freedom" became an immediate hit and was performed at countless war rallies and other patriotic occasions. By war's end, more than a half million copies of the sheet music had been sold in the North.

Among the other songs published in 1861 extolling the American flag were "Defend the Stars and Stripes" by Gustave A. Scott; "The American Flag" by the Reverend J. D. Dickson; "The Red, White & Blue of '61", and

THE AMERICAN FLAG,
A NEW NATIONAL LYRIC.

BY
REVᴰ J. B. DICKSON
OF SCOTLAND

The start of the Civil War in 1861 precipitated an unprecedented explosion of devotion to the Stars and Stripes throughout the North. Its image was used extensively throughout the war, including in this patriotic 1862 Unionist sheet music illustration. *The Library of Congress, Prints and Photographs Division*

"Our Country's Flag" by G. Gumpert; "The Stars and Stripes" by James T. Field and O. B. Brown; "The Starry Flag" by John Savage; and "The Stripes and the Stars" by George A. Mietike.

These words from the Field-Brown "The Stars and Stripes" embody the tenor of those songs:

> *Let the Traitors brag;*
> *Gallant lads, fire away!*
> *And fight for the flag.*
>
> *Their flag is but a rag*
> *Ours is the true one*
> *Up with the Stars and Stripes!*
> *Down with the new one!*

With passions running so strong in the North and South, the flag inevitably became involved in violent, sometimes deadly, incidents. Southern sympathizers in the North risked mob violence if they displayed the Confederate flag publicly. The same was true with Northern patriots in the South. In some cases mobs in the North carried out attacks against individuals and businesses that failed to fly the Stars and Stripes.

A few days after the surrender of Fort Sumter, for example, an unruly throng in Philadelphia descended on the offices of the *Palmetto Flag*, a secessionist newspaper named for the state flag of South Carolina. The crowd dispersed only after the newspaper's employees displayed an American flag. Philadelphia's mayor Alexander Henry expressed the day's strong feelings for the flag but also cautioned the city's residents against violence. "By the grace of God, treason shall never rear its head or have foothold in Philadelphia. I call upon you, as American citizens, to stand by your flag and protect it all hazards," Henry told the crowd. "But in doing so, remember the rights due your fellow citizens and their private property."

In the South Union sympathizers who dared display the Stars and Stripes could be prosecuted under the Alien Enemies Act, which the Confederate Congress passed in August of 1861. That act ordered the departure of all Northerners and authorized the arrest of those considered to be hostile to the Confederate government. Private citizens in the South made their own anti-American flag sentiments known throughout the war. After Virginia seceded from the Union on April 17, for example, a crowd burned an American flag in the public square of Liberty, Mississippi. On April 21, a crowd cheered the public burial of an American flag in Memphis, Tennessee. On May 7, a riot broke out in Knoxville, Tennessee, after an American flag was hoisted; one man was killed in the ensuing melee.

What is believed to be the first fatal incident during a Civil War engagement involving a flag took place on May 24, 1861, the day that federal troops captured the city of Alexandria, Virginia, across the Potomac River from Washington, D.C. The commander of the New York Fire Zouave's First Regiment, twenty-four-year-old Col. Elmer Ellsworth, a close friend of Abraham Lincoln, was among the troops in the city that day. As they marched down one of Alexandria's main streets, Ellsworth and his men noticed that the Marshall House, an inn, displayed a large, sixteen-by thirty-foot Confederate Stars and Bars. Ellsworth entered the establishment to cut the flag down. After doing so, he was shot and killed by the innkeeper, James W. Jackson, with one close-in blast of his double-barreled shotgun. One of Ellsworth's men, Private Francis E. Brownell, then killed Jackson.

Lincoln was devastated by the news of his friend's death—the first union officer to die in the war. After recovering from the shock, Lincoln found some comfort in what occurred after the killings. "There is one fact that has reached me which is a great consolation to my heart and quite a relief after this melancholy affair," Lincoln told a group of White House visitors, including a reporter from the *New York Herald.* "I learn from several persons that when the Stars and Stripes were raised again in Alexandria, many of the people of the town actually wept for joy, and manifested the liveliest gratification at seeing this familiar and loved emblem once more floating about them."

Lincoln ordered that Ellsworth lay in state in the East Room of the White House where thousands attended his funeral. As the news of what became known as "The Marshall House Incident" spread—mainly through an illustrated, cover story in the June 15, 1861, issue of *Harper's Weekly*—Ellsworth was mourned throughout the North and became the Union's first Civil War martyr. Several regiments adopted the Zouave name in his honor, including the 44th New York Volunteer Infantry, which became known as "Ellsworth's Avengers," and Union troops took up the battle cry, "Avenge Ellsworth." Ellsworth's image appeared on stationery, sheet music, and in memorial lithographs. One envelope pictured Ellsworth attired in an idealized Zouave uniform holding a rifle and a large American flag. Above him were the words, "To Richmond," and below the words, "Remember Ellsworth."

The bloody Confederate flag that Ellsworth clutched in his hands was conveyed to the White House where Mary Todd Lincoln hid it away in a drawer. Tad Lincoln, the president's young son, enjoyed playing with the flag and sometimes displayed it during official occasions.

"When the President was reviewing some troops from the portico of the White House, Tad sneaked this flag out and waved it back of the President, who stood with a flag in his hands," Julia Taft Bayne, a playmate of Tad's, remembered. "The sight of a rebel flag on such an occasion caused some commotion, and when the President saw what was happening he pinioned his bad boy and the flag in his strong arms and handed them together to an orderly, who carried the offenders within."

When the captain of a U.S. Treasury Department revenue cutter ship, the *McClelland* in New Orleans, refused to obey orders from Washington in January of 1861, Buchanan administration treasury secretary John A. Dix telegraphed what would become a famous order to his agent in that city. In it Dix—a former U.S. senator and postmaster of the United States who later became a Civil War general—authorized the takeover of the *McClelland* and gave orders to treat those who disobeyed as mutineers.

"If any one attempts to haul down the American flag," Dix said on January 21, "shoot him on the spot." That order was not carried out, but Dix's words became something of a catch phrase among Union soldiers during the war. Not long after the war began, Dix's words appeared on stationery and envelopes, accompanied by images of the American flag.

New Orleans was the scene in 1862 of more threats of violence involving the flag, as well as the hanging of a Confederate supporter for the crime of taking the American flag down from the U.S. Mint. On April 25 Flag Officer David G. Farragut led his eighteen-vessel naval force to a decisive victory over the Confederate Mississippi River Squadron. After that battle some seven hundred of Farragut's troops landed to take over the city, the largest in the Confederacy. Farragut, who went on to compile a string of other naval Civil War victories, was born in Tennessee and raised in Virginia. He nevertheless was dedicated to the Union and ordered the city's mayor, John T. Monroe, to surrender the city.

Farragut also ordered, in Monroe's words, "the hoisting of the United States flag on the Customhouse, Post office, and Mint" and that "the Louisiana flag should be hauled down from City Hall." Monroe replied that Confederate general Mansfield Lovell controlled the city, and that as mayor he therefore didn't have the authority to raise the Stars and Stripes. Monroe also gave Farragut an "unqualified refusal" on his demand to lower the Louisiana flag from city hall.

Monroe was forced to concede defeat when Lovell pulled his disorganized troops out of the city. But the mayor vehemently and emotionally vowed that he would not replace the Confederate and Louisiana flags with the Stars and Stripes. "The man lives not in our midst whose hand and heart would not be palsied at the mere thought of such an act," Monroe replied to Farragut. "Nor could I find in my entire constituency so wretched and desperate a renegade as would dare to profane with his hand the sacred emblem of our aspirations."

From his flagship, the *Hartford*, Farragut again demanded the "unqualified" surrender of the city. And he again ordered that the American flag, "the emblem of the sovereignty of the United States," be hoisted over city hall, the Mint, and the Custom House. He also ordered that all flags, "or other emblems of sovereignty, other than those of the United States, shall be removed from all public buildings" by noon of the following day.

Farragut also expressed his concerns about New Orleans's citizens who taunted and threatened the Union troops in the city and about reports of attacks upon civilians who saluted the American flag. "I shall speedily and severely punish any person or persons who shall commit such outrages as were witnessed yesterday—armed men firing upon helpless men, women and children for giving expression to their pleasure at witnessing the old flag."

After the city's formal surrender on April twenty-eighth, Farragut sent a team of men to raise the flag at the Customs House and the Mint, ordering them not to fire unless fired upon. Citizens harassed the troops, but the military men refrained from firing their weapons. Upon hearing of the incident, Farragut fired off a dispatch to Mayor Monroe. His men, Farragut told the mayor, "have been insulted in the grossest manner and the flag which had been hoisted by my orders on the Mint was pulled down and dragged through the streets." If that continued, he warned, "the fire of this fleet may be drawn upon the city at any moment."

The mayor dared Farragut to fire at the defenseless city. Farragut replied on April 29 with the demand, again, that the city "haul down and suppress every symbol of government, whether State or Confederate, except that of the United States." The mayor finally capitulated. At noon that day a contingent of heavily armed marines went to city hall, removed the Louisiana flag, and replaced it with the Stars and Stripes. In the end Farragut did not order his fleet to fire on the city, but his threat to do so ranks among the strongest reactions to threats to desecrate the American flag.

On May 1 Gen. Benjamin Franklin Butler's fourteen-hundred-man army landed and occupied New Orleans. Butler, a brigadier general in the

Massachusetts militia who was appointed a major general in the Union army by President Lincoln on May 16, 1861, was vilified in New Orleans for what were considered his draconian measures as military governor. That—and a birth defect that caused one eye to be permanently twisted—earned him the nickname "the Beast." Reacting to constant harassment of his troops, Butler issued General Order No. 28 on May 15, 1862, ordering that any woman who insulted a Union soldier would "be treated as a woman of the town plying her avocation," that is, a prostitute.

That caused a furor. But what cemented Butler's nefarious legacy among the citizens of New Orleans—and throughout the South—was his insistence on court-martialing a man who pulled down the Stars and Stripes from the Mint and then desecrated the flag. Butler's troops arrested the man, twenty-one-year-old William Mumford. He was tried and sentenced to death. Butler had it in his power to stay the execution but chose not to do so.

Instead, Butler issued Special Order 10 on June 5. Mumford, the order said, having been "convicted before a military commission of treason, and an overt act thereof in tearing down the United States flag from a public building of the United States, for the purpose of inciting other evil-minded persons to further resistance to the laws and arms of the United States," would be executed. Mumford was summarily hanged. "His hanging of Mumford for hauling down the flag," according to a *New York Times* editorial, "effectually made the flag feared and respected from that time on."

Jefferson Davis reacted by issuing a death sentence for Butler. President Lincoln reacted on December 16, 1862, by relieving Butler of his command.

"The name of Mumford," Admiral Preble noted, "if we may believe the Confederate newspapers, was immediately added to their roll of martyrs to the cause of liberty."

★   ★   ★

Perhaps the most famous incident—which did not end in violence—involving a civilian and the American flag during the Civil War is the story of Barbara Frietschie of Frederick, Maryland. The famed American poet and ardent abolitionist, John Greenleaf Whittier, immortalized the story in his poem, "Barbara Frietchie," which the *Atlantic Monthly* published in its October 1863 issue. In it Whittier described how the townspeople of Frederick had taken down their American flags just before Robert E. Lee's

Army of Northern Virginia marched through that western Maryland city on September 10, 1862, two weeks prior to the bloody Battle of Antietam. The patriotic Frietschie, then ninety-five years old, according to Whittier, bravely defied the Confederates by brazenly flying the flag from her window.

"She took up the flag the men hauled down," Whittier wrote. "In her attic window the staff she set / To show that one heart was loyal yet."

When Confederate general Thomas J. Stonewall Jackson rode by her house, he saw the flag and ordered his men to shoot it down, which they did. The determined Barbara Frietschie took that fallen flag, "leaned far out on the window-sill," Whittier wrote, and "shook it forth with a royal will."

" 'Shoot, if you must, this old gray head, but spare your country's flag,' she said."

Her outspokenness shamed Jackson, who then told his men: " 'Who touches a hair of yon gray head / Dies like a dog! March on!' he said."

Barbara Frietschie proudly kept her lone flag flying.

"All day long through Frederick Street," Whittier wrote, "sounded the tread of marching feet. All day long that free flag tost / over the heads of the rebel host."

Mainly due to the popularity of that poem, the Barbara Frietschie story gained wide currency throughout the country during the decades after the Civil War and remains popular today. The story spawned a play, *Barbara Frietschie,* by the playwright Clyde Fitch (who was born in 1865), which had eighty-three performances on Broadway in 1899 and 1900. *My Maryland,* a musical based on the play, became a popular Broadway attraction in 1927 and 1928. Two silent Hollywood movies based on Fitch's play — both called *Barbara Frietschie* — came out in 1915 and 1924. The 1924 version featured twenty-nine-year-old Florence Vidor in the title role.

The 1922 book, *Poems of American Patriotism,* edited by Brander Mathews, contains the Whittier poem illustrated with a painting by the renowned illustrator N. C. Wyeth. It shows the gray-haired Frietschie leaning out a dormer with broken windows and a smashed flagpole, clutching a tattered Stars and Stripes in her right hand, her mouth open, shouting down to the street in defiance. Another Wyeth illustration in that book, *The Old Continentals,* depicts two Revolutionary War soldiers, with one unfurling the thirteen-star "Betsy Ross" flag — a banner that was never flown by the American fighters in that war.

Certainly no one doubted that Barbara Frietschie — born Barbara Hauer, the daughter of German immigrants eleven years before the First Flag Resolution of 1777 in Lancaster, Pennsylvania — was a very patriotic, strong-willed woman. But questions about the flag-waving episode arose soon after Whittier's poem was published. Critics claimed that Whittier's story was highly exaggerated at best. Historians now believe it is a myth.

They point to the fact, first, that there were no eyewitnesses to the scene, including the poet. Whittier learned the story from the popular sentimental novelist Emma Dorothy Eliza Nevitte Southworth, known as Mrs. E.d.e.n. Southworth, who lived in Washington, D.C., and had read newspaper accounts about it. So his information was third hand at best. It was soon determined, moreover, that Stonewall Jackson did not ride past the Frietschie house, which was razed during the Civil War but reconstructed in 1926 and today is known as the Barbara Frietschie House and Museum.

Historians now believe it is possible that Frietschie may have waved a small American flag from her porch or from a second-floor window and that that action morphed into the fanciful "shoot if you must this old gray head" story. There is stronger evidence, however, that the story evolved from an incident that day involving another Frederick woman who made a show of flying the American flag. The woman in question, Mary A. Quantrill, was the sister-in-law of the infamous Confederate captain William Clarke Quantrill, who led Quantrill's Raiders in guerrilla attacks against Union sympathizers in Missouri and Kansas during the Civil War.

Mary Quantrill, though, was a Union supporter who lived in Frederick. She and her daughter sat in front of her house on September 10, 1862, as Lee's men wended their way through town. They waved the Confederate flag and tied American flags to their horses' tails, Quantrill wrote in 1869, "as a warning to Unionists of what might occur thereafter." Quantrill heard a Confederate officer insult the American flag, shouting, "G_ d_ the stars and stripes to the dust, with all who advocate them." That, Quantrill said, was "too much." She took a "flaglet" from her daughter and "held it firmly" in her hand as the Confederate troops marched past.

Another officer rode up and ordered Quantrill to turn over the flag. She refused, he rode off, and she attached the small flag to the railing on her porch. Another Confederate soldier chopped it off with his bayonet and tore "the flag into pieces and [stomped] them in the dust." A neighbor, Mary Hopwood, produced a second small flag and they mounted it on the porch. It, too, was cut down by the same Confederate soldier.

Historians believe Quantrill's tale. Barbara Frietschie did not live to tell hers. She died in Frederick on December 18, 1862, two weeks after her ninety-sixth birthday.

Whittier's popular poem, however, immortalized Barbara Frietschie.

The tale of a frail old woman bravely defying the Confederates by flaunting her devotion to the American flag struck a nerve among Northerners. The story became an inspiration to millions during the Civil War, and for more than a century afterward. Whittier's work — perhaps the best-known American verse dealing with the American flag — provides a strong example of the powerful hold the Stars and Stripes has in the American psyche.

★   ★   ★

The other famed flag-defying tale that took place during the Civil War involves William Driver, a sea captain born in Salem, Massachusetts, in 1803. The story begins with a present that Driver received on his twenty-first birthday from his mother in 1824: a homemade twenty-four-star flag. When he first hoisted the flag and it unfurled in the wind, Driver was moved to name it "Old Glory." He proudly displayed that flag on board his small whaler, the *Charles Doggett,* as he sailed throughout the world. That ship's most notable voyage came in August and September 1831 when Driver and his crew transported sixty-five descendants of the survivors of the famed 1789 mutiny on the British ship the *Bounty* from Tahiti to their homes on Pitcairn Island in the South Pacific.

William Driver gave up the sea and moved to Nashville following the death of his first wife in 1837. He took his cherished flag with him to Tennessee, where he worked in a store owned by his brother, remarried, and had nine children, in addition to the three from his first marriage. Driver flew the flag on three occasions every year: Washington's Birthday, St. Patrick's Day (his own birthday), and the Fourth of July. He flew Old Glory on those days, "rain or shine," his daughter Mary Jane Driver Roland wrote in her privately published memoir, "on a rope suspended from the attic window [of his house] and stretching across the street, connecting with a pulley on a locust tree."

In 1860 Driver's wife and daughters repaired the tattered flag, removed the old stars, and sewed thirty-four new ones onto it. According to his daughter, Driver "supplemented our labor with the anchor, which he sewed on." That small white anchor still adorns Old Glory in the lower right corner of the canton.

After Tennessee seceded on May 7, 1861, the Driver family hid the flag away, sewing it inside a quilt used as a bed comforter. Twice during the war Confederate partisans came to the Driver house and demanded that he surrender the flag. He adamantly refused. "If you want my flag," Driver told the second group (according to his daughter), "you'll have to take it over my dead body."

Old Glory made its first public appearance after the war began on February 25, 1862, when federal troops occupied Nashville. Driver celebrated that event by liberating Old Glory from inside the quilt, taking it with an escort of troops from the Sixth Ohio Regiment to the Tennessee State Capitol Building and hoisting it from the Capitol's dome. The event was greeted with "frantic cheering and uproarious demonstrations by soldiers and a sprinkling of civilians," Mary Driver Roland, an eyewitness to the scene, said. That event also popularized the name "Old Glory" as a nickname for the American flag.

It received more publicity when James Whitcomb Riley's poem, "The Name of Old Glory," came out in the *North American Review* in December 1898. The poem by Riley—the prolific and popular Indiana poet known as "the poet of the common people"—is an ode to the flag and a rumination on the answer to the question: "Who gave you the name of Old Glory?" Riley did not mention William Driver in his ode. He concluded in the poem's fourth and final stanza that the fluttering of the flag itself provided "an audible answer" to his question.

> And it spake, with a shake of the voice, and it said:
> By the driven snow-white and the living blood-red
> Of my bars, and their heaven of stars overhead
> By the symbol conjoined of them all, skyward cast,
> As I float from the steeple, or flap at the mast,
> Or droop o'er the sod where the long grasses nod,
> My name is as old as the glory of God.
> . . . So I came by the name of Old Glory.

The Driver family took Old Glory home the day after flying it over the Tennessee Capitol. They kept it out of sight again until the two-day Battle of Nashville in December 1864, when Confederate general John Bell Hood tried to retake the city and the Union troops under Gen. George H. Thomas fought back the attack. "The morning of the battle, December 15," Mary Roland wrote, "my father hung Old Glory out of the third-story window, in plain sight." Before he left the house to help defend the city at nearby Fort Negly, the sixty-one-year-old Driver "called together the entire household and said, 'If Old Glory is not in sight, I'll blow the house out of sight, too.'"

Captain Driver died on March 3, 1886, and was buried in Nashville's

City Cemetery. Although his grave is not one of the places authorized by Congress where the flag may be flown twenty-four hours a day, the caretakers of Driver's grave fly the flag there night and day in honor of the man who came up with the storied nickname of Old Glory.

Thirteen years before his death, on July 10, 1873, William Driver had given Old Glory to his daughter Mary. "This is my ship-flag Old Glory," he said as he turned the flag over, according to Mary Roland's recollection of the event. "I love it as a mother loves her child; take it and cherish it as I have always cherished it; for it has been my steadfast friend and protector in all parts of the world—savage, heathen and civilized."

Old Glory remained in Mary Roland's possession until December of 1922, when she donated it to Pres. Warren Harding, who turned it over to the Smithsonian. The museum did not put the flag on exhibit, however, because of its fragile condition, its large size—about ten feet by seventeen feet—and because of the Smithsonian's limited conservation budget. After a series of articles on the state of Old Glory appeared in the Nashville *Tennessean* newspaper in 1980, four Tennessee American Legion posts and the Tennessee Society of the Daughters of the American Revolution undertook a fund-raising effort for the flag's preservation.

After the money was raised, a team of Smithsonian textile conservators went to work on Old Glory in June 1981. The flag was spread out on a large table and photographed, and a technical analysis was undertaken of the fabric. Then the conservators vacuumed the flag, steamed it to smooth out wrinkles, and removed the backing material. They covered the flag with crepeline, a loosely woven, almost invisible type of silk imported from France that is often used as a backing support for fragile textiles. Old Glory went on public display in a custom-made exhibit case on December 10, 1982, in the Smithsonian's National Museum of American History in Washington where it remains today.

★   ★   ★

Barbara Frietschie and William Driver made names for themselves during the war for their devotion to the flag. But countless numbers of Union and Confederate soldiers whose names were barely known outside their units risked their lives—and in some cases were killed or wounded—symbolically or physically defending the flag. Many were flag bearers, assigned to carry the American flag and the regimental colors into battle.

All Union infantry regiments had color companies or color guards. The colors were an integral part of the regiments since they were used in battle to mark positions and to serve as morale boosters and rallying points for the troops. Bearing the national colors into battle was considered an honor, and members of the color guards were chosen based on their courage under fire.

Courage was necessary because those who carried the Stars and Stripes—known as color sergeants—went into battle unarmed. Color corporals, who did carry weapons, nominally protected the flag bearers. The corporals had orders, however, not to fire unless the flag itself came under attack. Losing the flag in battle was considered catastrophic. Capturing the enemy's flag was a high honor. On many occasions, more than one color sergeant was killed or wounded in the war's larger engagements. Two Fifth New Hampshire Regiment color sergeants, for example, were

This *Harper's Weekly* cover in 1862 featuring a Thomas Nast drawing of a gallant Union Army color-bearer illustrates how the flag was used in the North to bolster the Civil War effort. *The Library of Congress, Prints and Photographs Division*

severely wounded at the Battle of Fredericksburg, on December 11–13, 1862, and a third sergeant gave up his weapon to fly the flag for the rest of that bloody engagement in which the Union suffered thirteen thousand casualties.

The same was true with Confederate color bearers. On July 1, 1863, for example, on the first day of the Battle of Gettysburg, F. W. Faucette, the color bearer of the Thirteenth North Carolina Regiment, was shot in the right arm during a charge. That arm, "with which he bore the colors, was shivered and almost torn from its socket," said Maj. Gen. John B. Gordon in his war memoir. "Without halting or hesitating, he seized the falling flag in his left hand, and, with his blood spouting from the severed arteries and his right arm dangling in shreds at his side, he still rushed to the front, shouting to his comrades: 'Forward, forward!' "

Union prisoners of war also regularly rallied around the flag. On July 4, 1864, for example, at the Confederate prison camp in Macon, Georgia, a captain from the Eighth New Jersey Volunteers unfurled a small American flag he had hidden in his hat. The other prisoners cheered its appearance and broke into "The Star-Spangled Banner" and "The Battle Cry of Freedom." The American flag, historian Scot Guenter observed, "was a vital symbol for the prisoners, and the telling of such incidents in the North only further contributed to its importance at home."

★　　★　　★

The American flag also had a significant impact among African Americans, both in the North and South, during the Civil War. After 1863, when Lincoln allowed blacks to fight in the Union army, flags became "every bit as central to the wartime experience of African Americans as they were to other Civil War participants," noted the historian Robert E. Bonner. "Despite unequal treatment, black troops entered Union service as citizen-soldiers and as full participants in the flag culture of the Union cause." There were flag presentation ceremonies for the free blacks in the North as they went off to war, just as there were for whites in the North and South. Black women typically presented homemade flags to the departing soldiers just as their white counterparts did.

In South Carolina thousands of former slaves flocked for protection to the Union troops that landed on the island town of Beaufort in late 1861 to anchor the blockade of the ports of Charleston and Savannah, Georgia. A year later black volunteers were accepted in the Union army and formed the First Regiment of South Carolina Volunteers, the first black unit to serve in the war. Their commander, Col. Thomas Higginson, a Harvard-educated Unitarian minister and ardent abolitionist, was white.

Higginson's troops took part in flag-waving rallies late that year and early in 1863. During one such occasion, on December 6, 1862, Cpl. Price Lambkin "brought out one of the few really impressive appeals for the American flag that I have heard," Higginson wrote in his journal. He quoted Lambkin in black dialect speaking of how Southern slave owners who lived under the flag, "got dere wealth under it," and used their slaves to enrich themselves. But as soon as Southerners thought that the flag "mean freedom for we colored people, dey pull it right down and run up de rag ob dere own." Lambkin concluded with a plea to his men never to "desert de ole flag, boys, neber; we had lib under it for eighteen hundred sixty-two years, and we'll die for it now."

During a rally on New Year's Day 1863—the day that President Lincoln's September 22, 1862, Emancipation Proclamation took effect—Higginson picked up an American flag, "which now for the first time meant anything to these poor people," he said, and began waving it. "There followed," he wrote, "an incident so simple, so touching, so utterly unexpected & startling that I can scarcely believe it when I recall it, though it gave the keynote to the whole day." As Higginson waved the flag, he said, "there suddenly arose, close beside the platform, a strong male voice (but rather cracked and elderly), into which two women's voices instantly blended, singing." The song they sang began with the words: "My country 'tis of thee / Sweet land of Liberty."

The crowd sang along, and Higginson said, "I never saw anything so electric; it made all other words cheap; it seemed the choked voice of a race, at last unloosed." The event marked, he said, "the first flag they had ever seen which promised anything to their people."

The actions of Sgt. William Carney of the Fifty-fourth Massachusetts Colored Regiment at the assault on Fort Wagner, South Carolina, on July 18, 1863, are perhaps the best-known example of an African-American Union soldier's devotion to the flag. During that bloody assault—which is depicted in the 1989 Hollywood film, *Glory*—the unit's flag bearer was wounded, and the twenty-three-year-old Carney dropped his rifle and grabbed the Stars and Stripes before it hit the ground. Carney then was shot in the leg. Despite his wounds, he carried the flag and led the advance on the fort. He hoisted the flag over Fort Wagner and suffered another wound before the battle ended.

On May 25, 1900, William Carney was awarded the Medal of Honor, the military's highest award for valor for "most distinguished gallantry in action." He was the first African American to receive the award. The official citation reads: "When the color sergeant was shot down, this soldier grasped the flag, led the way to the parapet and planted the colors thereon. When the troops fell back, he brought off the flag, under a fierce fire in which he was twice severely wounded."

★   ★   ★

When Robert E. Lee surrendered to Ulysses S. Grant on April 9, 1865, at Appomattox Courthouse in Virginia, the Confederate troops, in addition to their weapons, had orders to surrender their battle flags. The "torn and tattered battle-flags were either leaned against the stacks [of weapons] or laid upon the ground," said Maj. Gen. John B. Gordon, who had risen through the ranks to command the Confederate Second Corps. "Some of the men who had carried and followed those ragged standards through the four long years of strife rushed, regardless of all discipline, from the ranks, bent about their old flags, and pressed them to their lips." Others tore their flags from their staffs, Gordon—who later became Georgia's governor and a U.S. senator—said, "and hid them in their bosoms, as they wet them with burning tears." They "loved those flags," he said, "and will love them forever, as mementos of the unparalleled struggle."

Union Brevet Maj. Gen. Joshua Lawrence Chamberlain of Maine, a veteran of twenty-four battles and a recipient of the Medal of Honor, received the formal surrender. Chamberlain described the scene in similar words. The Confederate soldiers, Chamberlain said, came forward at the end of the surrender ceremonies "reluctantly, with agony of expression." They "tenderly fold their flags, battle-worn and torn, blood-stained, heart-holding colors, and lay them down; some frenziedly rushing from the ranks, kneeling over them, clinging to them, pressing them to their lips with burning tears. And only the Flag of the Union greets the sky!"

★   ★   ★

Five days after the Confederate surrender, on April 14, 1865, Robert Anderson, the commanding officer at Fort Sumter in 1861 who had been promoted to major general, came out of retirement for one reason: to reraise his flag at the South Carolina fort where the war began. Sumter had been under intermittent attack by Union forces from July 1863 to February 1865, when it was retaken. On February 18, 1865, Union troops raised an American flag at the fort, which had suffered extensive damage and had been nearly reduced to rubble.

Edwin M. Stanton, the U.S. Secretary of War, issued an order in Washington on March 27 directing that at twelve noon on April 14, 1865, Anderson "will raise and plant upon the ruins of Fort Sumter, in Charleston Harbor, the same United States flag that floated over the battlements of that fort during the rebel assault" exactly four years before. The order also called for a one-hundred-gun salute and "a national salute from every fort and rebel battery that fired upon Fort Sumter."

On April 14, which happened to be Good Friday, Stanton's orders were carried out. A fleet of U.S. Navy vessels, each decked out in full dress colors, sat in Charleston harbor. A large crowd assembled around the flagstaff at the fort. They sang "Victory at Last" and "The Battle Cry of Freedom." Prayers were read. Then the old flag, Admiral Preble wrote, "was attached to the halyards, when General Anderson, after a brief and touching address, hoisted it to the head of the flag-staff amid loud huzzas, which were followed by singing 'The Star-Spangled Banner.' "

The guns then blazed in salute on land and on the sea. The ceremony ended with an address by Henry Ward Beecher, the prominent Congregational minister who had been an outspoken abolitionist and was one of the nation's most popular orators of the day.

John G. Nicolay, President Lincoln's private secretary who had just been appointed U.S. Consul General to France, was among a large group that had sailed from New York to be among the crowd at Sumter that day. When Nicolay returned to New York, he learned that at about 10:15 p.m. on the day that Anderson's flag was reraised at Sumter Abraham Lincoln had been shot and killed during a performance of the play *Our American Cousin* in his flag-bedecked box at Ford's Theatre.

The box was decorated with two American flags on staffs on each end and two American flags draped as bunting over the box's railings. The regimental flag of the U.S. Treasury Guards hung from a staff attached to the box's center pillar. The Treasury flag played a role in the escape and eventual capture of Lincoln's assassin, John Wilkes Booth.

After Booth shot Lincoln, Union army major Henry Rathbone—a guest of the Lincolns that evening with his fiancée Clara Harris—grappled with Booth. As the actor attempted to jump over the railing toward the stage, he caught the spur of his boot heel on the fringe of the Treasury flag, which came tumbling down. Booth lost his balance and fell nearly twelve feet onto the stage, breaking his left leg in the process.

The end of the Civil War marked another significant step in the evolution of the meaning of the American flag. Although animosities remained in the North and South, the nation once more united under one banner, the Stars and Stripes. In the years that followed, as American unity was slowly re-established, the American flag played an important role in that achievement.

CHAPTER NINE

A Band of Brothers

★   ★   ★

... patriotic groups like the Union veterans who formed the Grand Army of the Republic dedicated themselves to gaining mass and official support for everything from anthems to holidays, but most important, they promoted enshrinement of the flag as the nation's most sacred symbol.

—Cecelia Elizabeth O'Leary

ON MARCH 2, 1865, during the waning days of the Civil War, Congress passed and President Lincoln signed into law a measure requiring that the federal government purchase bunting—the lightweight, loosely woven woolen fabric used to make flags—only from American manufacturers. Until then virtually all the bunting that went into flags in this country was imported from England. That law led to the creation of what some called "the first American flag," meaning that it was the first (or among the first) flags made in this country entirely with American-made wool bunting.

That flag was produced by the newly founded United States Bunting Company in Lowell, Massachusetts. Its founder, U.S. army general Benjamin Franklin Butler, is the same General Butler who ordered the execution in 1862 of a man in New Orleans for desecrating the American flag. Butler had been a very prosperous businessman in Lowell before the war. Among other interests, he had purchased the Middlesex Company, a large woolen manufacturer, in 1859. Butler founded U.S. Bunting in 1865 after he played a leading role in lobbying Congress to enact the law requiring American flags used by the government to be made exclusively of domestically produced bunting.

Butler, who was still in the Union army, presented that twelve-by-six-foot first flag, which had thirty-seven stars (in anticipation of the Nebraska Territory's entry into the Union), to President Lincoln on April 11, 1865, two days after Lee's surrender at Appomattox, and four days before Lincoln's death. The stars were arranged in a centered diamond of twenty-seven flanked on both sides by vertical rows of five stars. On February 2, 1866, a large thirty-six-star flag manufactured by U.S. Bunting made of all American materials flew over the Capitol Building in Washington, D.C.

U.S. Bunting was the first factory in this country to develop a process to dye blue bunting successfully. Before 1865, flags were made by sewing strips of red, white, and blue bunting together and then stitching the white stars onto the blue field. DeWitt C. Farrington, the manager and one of Butler's partners at U.S. Bunting, helped develop a new process, known as clamp dyeing. In it, the bunting "is first woven like the old, but in dyeing the stripes, stars, or other designs are colored in the piece so that no sewing is necessary," a *Scientific American* magazine article reported in 1869. In that year, the magazine said, nearly all American flag makers used American-made bunting and the new method of flag making, and "no less than three thousand yards per day are now made at the works of the company."

That was a very good thing, the magazine said. When all of America's flags were made of English bunting, "our national banner was a humiliating witness to our dependence upon the industry of other nations." American genius, the magazine said, had "triumphed over the disabilities which involved such a necessity. Now the American flag may be made of American wool by American labor, and 'long may it wave' over a land independent in deed as well as in name."

In December 1865, nine months after the law requiring all government flags to be made of all-American materials, U.S. Bunting signed a contract with the government to be its sole manufacturer of flags. The company retained that contract until the 1920s, long after Butler died in 1893. "Wherever the flag of the United States flies over government property, either in this country or in the farthest reaches of the world, there the name of the [U.S.] Bunting Company is represented," a 1930 history of Massachusetts industries proclaimed, "inasmuch as the concern makes all the bunting for the United States government which is fashioned into the flags used by the nation."

The Reconstruction period after the Civil War was an era of often bitter antagonism between many white Southerners and the Northerners (known as carpetbaggers), Southern blacks and cooperating Southern whites who administered the state governments of the former Confederacy. But that bitterness did not, in general, spill over to feelings about the American flag. While it was by no means universal, a large majority of Southerners, including veterans of the Confederate army, figuratively pledged their allegiance to the Stars and Stripes after the Civil War ended. Some, echoing the feelings expressed by Jefferson Davis in 1861, played down the fact that the flag had been the emblem of the Confederacy's enemy during the Civil War and concentrated on the flag as a symbol of the Revolutionary War. Some white political leaders took a pragmatic route, embracing the American flag in an effort to try to secure a place for themselves at the table in national affairs.

Many acts of reconciliation involving the flag took place in the months and years after the war. Sometimes the respect came grudgingly. On May 16,1865, for example, when the Stars and Stripes was officially raised in Atlanta to honor President Lincoln, it was immediately lowered. At other times the respect was fulsomely displayed. At the annual Charleston, South Carolina, fire department parade on April 27, 1867, for example, the city's fire chief noticed that the American flag was conspicuously absent among the many banners on display. He stopped the parade, found a flag, and displayed it prominently. "Every person in the column readily and cheerfully saluted it by lifting his hat or cap in passing," Admiral Preble reported.

★   ★   ★

One of the clearest examples of the widespread respect for the Stars and Stripes in the South took place beginning in January 1868 when Union veteran Gilbert H. Bates, acting on a bet, undertook a now almost-forgotten, amazing, four-month, fourteen-hundred-mile trek on foot through the old Confederacy carrying an American flag. Bates, a former sergeant in the First Wisconsin Heavy Artillery, was a shopkeeper in Edgerton, Wisconsin. He believed that such a journey would be met with a warm reception. Fellow Civil War veterans thought otherwise, claiming that Southerners felt nothing but antipathy for the American flag and would attack anyone— especially a former Union soldier—who dared to display it.

Bates undertook what some called his "star-spangled march" to try to prove them wrong. "Bates is to carry the flag unfurled," the marching orders he and his fellow veterans drew up, said, "except at night, during storms, or when eating but is not to pass through cities or collections of people with it furled. He is to travel only during the day time; to be always unarmed, to go on foot; not to employ anybody to protect him; may employ one person as a guide when necessary; if any parties choose voluntarily to escort him, they are at liberty to do so."

Bates went South without a dime in his pocket, wearing old farmer's clothes. He said he would sell photographs of himself for twenty-five cents along his route and would turn the proceeds over to a fund for Civil War widows and orphans of soldiers from both sides of the conflict. Telegraph operators reported his progress to newspapers across the country.

Mark Twain, the great American humorist and writer, made light of Bates's endeavor. Bates, Twain predicted late in January, "will get more black eyes down there among those unconstructed rebels than he can ever carry along with him without breaking his back." Twain said he expected to see Bates "coming into Washington some day on one leg and with one eye out and an arm gone. He won't amount to more than an interesting relic by the time he gets here and then he will have to hire out for a sign for the Anatomical Museum." Southerners, Twain, said, "have no sentiment in them. They won't buy his picture. They will be more likely to take his scalp."

Whether Twain was being satirical or not, his prediction was completely wrong. At the thirty-year-old Bates's first stop, in war-ravaged Vicksburg, Mississippi, he received a warm welcome from the mayor and the town's leading citizens. A group of women made him an American flag, which replaced the tattered regimental Stars and Stripes Bates had brought with him from Wisconsin. As Bates began his march out of Vicksburg, the mayor and the town councilmen escorted him on horseback, along with a brass band, and townspeople along the route cheered him heartily.

Bates met similarly warm receptions throughout his trek, in small towns and large cities. "Joyful multitudes everywhere hail his advance as though it were the advance of an Emperor," a New York Times editorial said. People invited Bates into their homes and offered food and shelter. Strangers gave him warm clothing to fight off the cold weather. Bates received a hero's reception in Jackson, Mississippi, where he gave a speech and waved his flag from the balcony of the state capitol. In Meridian, Mississippi, he was paraded through the streets. Bates received a welcoming reception as he marched through Alabama and even when he waved the Stars and Stripes in Montgomery, Alabama, the first capital of the Confederacy.

The story was the same as the Union veteran made his way through Georgia, South and North Carolina, and Virginia, receiving nothing but an outpouring of Southern hospitality from women, children, and former Confederate soldiers all along his route. Welcoming cannon fire and five hundred people greeted him at the end of his Southern sojourn when Bates arrived in Virginia's capital, Richmond, on April 8. After checking into a hotel, Bates jogged to the State Capitol Building, where the Confederate Congress once met—and which Thomas Jefferson designed—and waved his American flag to the cheers of a large crowd that had gathered in an adjoining park.

Bates again received a hero's welcome when he arrived in Washington, D.C., on April 14, three years after the Stars and Stripes had been reraised at Fort Sumter. A large crowd and a brass band ushered him to the White House where Pres. Andrew Johnson greeted Bates on the front steps and took him into the East Room. When Johnson and Bates came out of the White House, the band broke into a rendition of "The Star-Spangled Banner."

Bates intended next to plant his flag on the Capitol dome. When he arrived on Capitol Hill with a crowd of followers, however, police officers would not permit him to enter the building because he didn't have the proper authorization from the House of Representatives' Sergeant-at-Arms. Bates and his followers then decided to plant the flag at the Washington Monument, but were thwarted again when, after arriving on the Monument grounds, they couldn't find a halyard. So they took his flag to his hotel, the Metropolitan, where it was placed on public exhibit.

Bates's American flag journey was more than a footnote to history. It proved that the Stars and Stripes could be a healing, all-American symbol during the difficult days of Reconstruction. As the *New York Times* put it, if those who were skeptical of Bates's reception "would start out a-marching with their waving flags, as the Sergeant has done, they would render their country a better service than by staying at home and growling at the rebels."

After his Southern tour, Gilbert Bates tried to make a living out of displaying the national colors. But he was less than successful in turning his goodwill triumph into a paying profession. During the summer of 1868, Bates charged admission for flag-waving personal appearances at venues such as the Holiday Street Theatre in Baltimore, a Civil War veterans' convention, and at the New York Democratic Party Convention. At the latter event Bates met "no recognition whatever on the part of the delegates," one observer said, "and after hiding a few moments behind the rostrum celebrities, he groped his way unattended and unnoticed out of the hall."

Bates did have personal—if not financial—success in a second flag-bearing pilgrimage in 1872. That year, probably as the result of another bet, Bates went overseas, where he set out on another star-spangled walking tour, this time from Gretna Green in Scotland to London. He had the same goal: to show that the British people harbored no ill will against the reunited United States since the English ruling class had strongly sympathized with the South during the Civil War. His reception in Scotland and England mirrored what he had found four years earlier in the old Confederacy; adoring crowds and spontaneous celebrations greeted him wherever he went.

When Bates arrived in London, "the populace of England were wild in their demonstrations," a *Philadelphia Times* reporter said. As he "stood up in a magnificent carriage drawn by six beautiful dapple gray horses, the turnout elegantly festooned with American and British flags, he was the lion of the day, and all London turned to gaze upon the eccentric American soldier . . . So enthusiastic and excited were the populace of London, that when Bates appeared upon the scene they seemed to lose all control over themselves."

In 1878 Bates conceived of a second Southern trip for the summer of 1880—one it appears he did not undertake—to carry an American flag containing the names of all the Republican candidates throughout the South. In the summer of 1881, a reporter tracked Bates down in the central Illinois town of Saybrook. Bates, who appeared to be drinking heavily, lived in a "miserable, tumble-down looking sort of a house," the reporter said. "He was a lantern-jawed and sallow-faced, hungry looking sort of a fellow" who wore "an old pair of dilapidated boots, which were, like the wearer, run down at the heel." He "continually dwells on the flag business, and he never seems to tire of talking of his trips through the South and England."

Sergeant Bates seemingly pulled himself out of that stupor a few years later. In 1883 Buffalo Bill Cody hired Bates to appear in his Stars-and-Stripes-bedecked Wild West Show. Not surprisingly, Buffalo Bill hired Bates to be the flamboyant show's flag bearer.

★   ★   ★

Another act in the postwar period that might be considered in the reconciliation category was the issuance in 1869 of the first American postage stamp containing an image of the American flag. It was a thirty-cent stamp with a ferocious-looking eagle perched atop a shield, flanked on both sides by the Stars and Stripes. Other U.S. postage stamps issued that year contained images of Benjamin Franklin, George Washington, Abraham Lincoln, Christopher Columbus, the signing of the Declaration of Independence, and the Pony Express.

★   ★   ★

Union veterans of the Civil War, who began to organize on an unprecedented scale almost immediately after the shooting stopped in the spring of
1865, turned into a social force that propelled the movement known as the
"cult of the flag" into full flower by the end of the nineteenth century. These
groups had several functions. They started as social and fraternal organizations. They then began helping needy veterans and their families and lobbying the federal and state governments for veterans' programs. By the
1890s, the veterans' groups had become potent political entities, focusing
on veterans issues and flag-waving patriotism.

The nation's first veterans' organization, the Order of Cincinnati, also
known as the Society of the Cincinnati, was formed in 1783 and was made
up of officers who fought in the Revolution. Two veterans' groups formed
after the War of 1812 mainly to lobby for pensions. The Aztec Club of 1847,
a group of Mexican War officers, was primarily a social organization.

The American veterans' movement came into its own following the Civil
War. The two-day, flag-bedecked Grand Review of Union troops victory
parade in Washington, D.C., on May 23 and 24, 1865, was a precursor of
sorts of the soon-to-be powerful movement. Some 150,000 soldiers from
Gen. George Meade's Army of the Potomac and Gen. William Tecumseh
Sherman's Army of Georgia and the Army of the Tennessee marched
through the nation's capital on those two days.

The marches ended at a presidential reviewing stand in front of the
White House bedecked with Stars-and-Stripes bunting and over which
flew a huge American flag. The city, still mourning President Lincoln's as-
sassination, did not go all out during those two days in the flag-display department however. Some citizens did display flags, floral arches, banners,
and bunting; but many buildings were still draped with black crepe. In a
matter of days following the march the two huge armies disbanded.

Soon after, the first Civil War veterans' groups were born. They included the Union Veteran Legion, the Veteran Brotherhood, the Veterans'
Rights Union, the Society of the Army of the Cumberland, and the Society
of the Army of Ohio. Gen. John A. Logan of Illinois organized the Society
of the Army of the Tennessee in August 1865. A veteran of the Mexican
War, a lawyer, and a member of Congress, Logan had become one of the
top Union generals in the Civil War, serving under Gen. U. S. Grant at
Vicksburg. In 1866 Logan, a Democrat before the war, was elected as a

Republican to Congress. That year he also helped found by far the largest and most influential Civil War veterans' group, the Grand Army of the Republic, an organization that spearheaded the movement to spread the cult of the flag across the country.

The GAR was open to all honorably discharged veterans—officers and enlisted men—who served in the Union army between April 12, 1861, and April 9, 1865. Logan served as the GAR's commander in chief for four terms beginning 1868. The first of what would become thousands of local GAR posts formed on April 6, 1866, in Decatur, Illinois.

The GAR soon far eclipsed all the other veterans' groups. Within three months, thirty-nine posts formed in Illinois alone. Then the GAR went nationwide rapidly. Ten states and the District of Columbia sent delegations to its first national convention—called an encampment because many members bedded down in tents—in Indianapolis on November 20. The flag-bedecked encampments took place annually beginning in 1867 on the state and national levels.

The Grand Army of the Republic's motto was "Fraternity, Charity and Loyalty." Its posts offered fraternity among fellow Union veterans; charity for needy veterans, widows, and orphans of veterans; and steadfast loyalty to the United States in the form of ardent, flag-waving patriotism. Working on the local level, GAR posts helped found veterans' homes and lobbied for veterans' issues. The group soon became a powerful social and political force in the country. GAR posts helped build memorials to Union veterans across the country and helped preserve Civil War sites and artifacts, including regimental and national flags. GAR state departments and the national organization led the late-nineteenth-century movement to have flags flown at all the nation's schools and to teach schoolchildren to venerate and respect the flag. GAR members also worked to have the Stars and Stripes displayed in the nation's churches.

The GAR was primarily responsible for creating an American institution of which the American flag is an integral part, Memorial Day. Springtime cemetery ceremonies honoring those who died in the Civil War had taken place in the South during the war. In 1866, the year after the war ended, such ceremonies also took place in cities in the North and the South. On April 25, 1866, in Columbus, Mississippi, for example, a group of local women placed flowers on the Friendship Cemetery graves of Confederate and Union soldiers who had perished at the nearby 1862 Battle of Shiloh. The Ladies Memorial Association of Petersburg, Virginia, which was formed on May 6 of that year, set aside June 9—the anniversary of the 1864 Siege of

Petersburg—as an annual Memorial Day to honor the men of the Petersburg militia. On May 5 the citizens of Waterloo, New York, honored their Civil War dead with a city-wide commemoration in which businesses closed for one hour, flags flew at half staff, and townspeople decorated the graves of Union soldiers with flowers, wreaths, and crosses.

Similar ceremonies took place throughout the spring of 1866 in Macon and Columbus, Georgia; Richmond, Virginia; Boalsburg, Pennsylvania; and Carbondale, Illinois. After Mary Simmerson Cunningham Logan, the wife of John Logan, had visited Petersburg in March 1868 and learned of the annual observance there, General Logan issued a general order on May 5 to all GAR chapters. The order instructed the chapters to set aside May 30, 1868, as Decoration Day, a day to remember the Union dead by placing flowers on their graves. Historians believe that Logan chose May 30 because flowers generally are in bloom throughout the country at that time.

"The 30th of May, 1868," General Order No. 11 said, "is designated for the purpose of strewing with flowers, or otherwise decorating the graves of comrades who died in defense of their country during the late rebellion, and whose bodies now lie in almost every city, village and hamlet churchyard in the land." The order prescribed no specific ceremony, advising local GAR posts "in their own way, [to] arrange such fitting services and testimonial of respect as circumstances may permit."

Along with garlanding graves with "choicest flowers of springtime," the order also said: "let us raise above them the dear old flag they saved."

"The most notable act of [Logan's] administration, indeed of any [GAR] administration was the order ... designating May 30 as Memorial Day," Maj. George S. Merrill, GAR commander in chief from 1881 to 1882, said in 1890. "To the bright offerings of springtime the Grand Army has very generally added the flag in miniature. ... Through the months of summer the tiny flag is kissed by the breezes as it marks the resting place of one of the nation's dead."

The first formal, official observance of Decoration Day took place on May 30, 1868, at the National Cemetery in Arlington, Virginia. General and Mrs. U. S. Grant and other officials, including congressman James A. Garfield, opened the ceremonies with speeches from the verandah of Robert E. Lee's former house overlooking the cemetery. GAR members then decorated graves, both Union and Confederate, with flowers.

In subsequent years Decoration Day was commemorated in many different ways. In some communities ceremonies were held at schools featuring visits by war veterans who wore their uniforms and told war stories.

Many cities held parades in which flag-waving veterans led marches to local cemeteries where they decorated graves and photographs were taken of the soldiers posing with American flags. In some communities flags and military insignia were placed at soldiers' graves along with flowers.

"Patriotic color," the historian Robert E. Bonner noted, "was a centerpiece of commemorative [Memorial Day] activities" after the Civil War. Bonner and others have argued that the use of flags at Memorial Day commemorations paved the way for the outpouring of American flags following national tragedies such as the September 11, 2001, terrorist acts. Memorial Day flag rituals "perpetuated what would become an instinctive reliance on flags to give solace during times of national tragedy," Bonner said.

In 1873, New York became the first state to make Decoration Day a holiday; many other states soon followed suit. The GAR lobbied successfully in 1882 to have the holiday renamed Memorial Day, although many continued to call it Decoration Day because of the occasion's grave-decoration origins. After World War I the commemoration was broadened to honor those who perished in all American wars. Since 1971 it has been celebrated on the last Monday in May.

The nation's official Memorial Day ceremony takes place at Arlington National Cemetery across the Potomac River from Washington, D.C. It features speeches, veterans' organization color guards, and the laying of a wreath at the Tomb of the Unknowns. Beginning in the late 1950s, the American flag has played a prominent role in the Arlington National Cemetery Memorial Day commemoration. In the early morning hours of the Friday before Memorial Day, the twelve hundred soldiers of "the Old Guard," the Third U.S. Infantry Regiment that guards the Tomb of the Unknowns, place small American flags on every one of the more than 280,000 gravestones at the nation's largest cemetery, a task that takes about three hours to complete. The Old Guard then mounts a twenty-four-hour guard for the balance of the Memorial Day weekend to make sure the flags remain in place.

CHAPTER TEN

The Hundredth
Anniversary

★   ★   ★

you, mottled Flag I love

— Walt Whitman, *Leaves of Grass*, 1891–92

THE AMERICAN FLAG played a prominent role in the Centennial year of 1876 as Americans celebrated the nation's evolution into a world power and looked back with pride on one hundred years of independence. Individual flag makers around the nation used the occasion to create a wide variety of unique celebratory flags, many of which included the dates "1776" or "1786." One popular flag had both dates spelled out with stars in the canton. Others contained the word "Centennial," typically nestled among the strips. Some Centennial flags had thirteen stars to commemorate the original states. Most had thirty-seven stars, the official number, arrayed in various patterns.

Some businesses used the occasion of the Centennial to create advertisements incorporating the flag. The Baltimore & Ohio (B&O) Railroad, for example, produced an ad that consisted of a waving thirty-eight star flag. The words "Go to the Centennial via the Baltimore and Ohio R.R. and Washington City" were printed in blue capital letters on the white stripes. In addition to a fanciful arrangement of the stars, the canton contained the date "1876" in gold, along with a golden wreath and red ribbon.

Many flags celebrated Colorado's entry into the Union on August 1, 1876, by adding a thirty-eighth star. Others contained thirty-nine stars in the mistaken belief that two states would be added that year. As it turned out, there never was an official thirty-nine-star flag. That's because four states—North and South Dakota, Montana, and Washington—came into the Union in 1889 and Idaho became a state on July 3, 1890. So the official flag changed from thirty-eight stars on July 4, 1877, to forty-three stars on July 4, 1890.

Officials made plans all across the country to usher in 1876 with lavish ceremonies that prominently featured the Stars and Stripes. In San Francisco, for example, Mayor A. J. Bryant issued a proclamation calling for the flag to be "displayed on all public buildings, places of amusement and business, and on the shipping in the harbor, from sunrise to sunset" on New Year's morning. The city of Philadelphia put on an elaborate celebration on New Year's Eve. At the stroke of midnight Mayor William S. Stokley ushered in the New Year by raising the Continental Colors over the old State Capitol Building. The city then erupted with the ringing of church bells, the firing of cannons, and a massive fireworks display.

The City of Brotherly Love played host later that year to the mammoth Centennial Exhibition, a world's fair officially known as the International Exhibition of Arts, Manufactures and Products of the Soil and Mine. It opened on May 10 at Fairmount Park. Before it closed six months later some nine million people had entered the turnstiles to take in the fair. The American flag was one of the most prominent features of the Centennial Exhibition. Hundreds were displayed on the exhibition's buildings, including four eleven-by-eighteen-foot flags at the main entrance of the enormous Main Exhibition Hall, which covered twenty acres and was the largest building in the world in 1876. Popular souvenir items included paper hand fans decorated with American flags. "No one," the noted writer and critic William Dean Howells said, "can see the fair without a thrill of patriotic pride."

Thirty-seven nations took part in the exhibition, which showcased American culture and the emergence of the United States as a thriving industrial world power. The *Philadelphia Public Ledger* called the May 10 opening-day ceremonies "the grandest ever witnessed in America." Whether or not it was the grandest, the ceremonies certainly were impressive. Pres. U. S. Grant presided, addressing a huge, boisterous crowd. At the end of his welcoming speech, Grant declared the exhibition officially open, and as he did, hundreds of flags were unfurled throughout the grounds and an orchestra and a thousand-voice choir performed the "Hallelujah Chorus."

The city of Philadelphia decked itself out in American flags and red, white, and blue bunting for the fair's opening. "All the public buildings, many stores, and private residences had the American colors floating from the house-tops or windows, and some were profusely decorated with small flags," the *New York Times* reported on May 11. "Broadway looked as though it had been prepared for the entry of a triumphal procession. The City Hall, the shipping in the harbor, and all the ferry-boats were gayly decorated with bunting."

The Trans-Continental Hotel, near the fairgrounds, a *Philadelphia Public Ledger* reporter wrote, "is brightened up by numbers of flags, which hang from its many windows and flutter in the breeze." The nearby Globe Hotel also was "decorated with the National colors," the newspaper reported. Restaurants and small hotels also flew "banners and flags in profusion," as did the Pennsylvania Railroad depot.

Inside the fair grounds one of the most popular attractions was an enormous "Origin of Our Flag" exhibit in the U.S. Government Building. That exhibit traced the history of the American flag using an elaborate display of some two dozen historic banners, including the Union Jack, early colonial flags, and the Continental Colors. The building itself was decorated with American flags and bunting inside and out.

★ ★ ★

In the celebratory and patriotic climate of the year 1876, several specious stories dealing with the American flag were promulgated and widely accepted. Some persist to this day. That year saw the publication, for example, of *Washington: A Drama in Five Acts*, a drama in verse by the popular English poet Martin Farquhar Tupper. In it Benjamin Franklin proclaims that the design of the Stars and Stripes was based on the coat of arms of George Washington. "We, and not he—it was unknown to him," Franklin says, "took up his coat of arms, and multiplied and magnified it every way to this, our glorious national banner."

The play was widely performed, and its false message resonated with the American public. The story was repeated many times, including regularly in the popular children's magazine *St. Nicholas*. In 1882, for example, the magazine published "The Origin of the Stars and Stripes," an article by Edward W. Tuffley, which was later reproduced in booklet form. In the article and booklet, Tuffley described his visit in the 1860s to the church in Brington, in Northhamptonshire, England, where George Washington's forefathers worshipped.

"On passing down the middle aisle of the church the parish clerk called our attention to the memorial brass plate of the Washingtons,'" Tuffley wrote, pointing out that the plate "bears the arms of the family—the Stars and Stripes."

"Do you mean to say," Tuffley quoted himself as responding, "that the family arms of the Washingtons were the Stars and Stripes?"

"Certainly they were," the clerk replied. He went on to tell Tuffley that a monument to a Washington family member "has the Stars and Stripes on, too."

While the Washington family coat of arms has two horizontal stripes and three red stars, there is no evidence whatsoever that it was the basis for the flag's design. Nevertheless, Tupper's apocryphal tale set in motion a myth that still is reported as the truth today.

Another flag falsehood that gained widespread currency in the Centennial period centered around a twelve-star flag that was billed as the banner that flew on John Paul Jones's *Bonhomme Richard*. That flag, which was shot down during the famed "I have not yet begun to fight" battle in September 1779 was said to have been saved from the sea by the daring act of James Bayard Stafford, a seaman on the ship. Stafford's family claimed that Congress's Maritime Committee had bestowed the flag on him in 1784 as a reward for his meritorious service.

The flag surfaced during the Civil War when Stafford's daughter, Sarah Smith Stafford, allowed it to be used at U.S. Sanitary Commission fundraising events. She later cut off a piece of the flag and presented it to President Lincoln. The flag was displayed at the Philadelphia Centennial Exhibition in 1876 and described as John Paul Jones's flag from the *Bonhomme Richard*. After Sarah Stafford's death in 1880, her brother Samuel Bayard Stafford and his wife inherited it. They took the flag to the 1887 national encampment of the Grand Army of the Republic where it was billed as "the first Stars and Stripes ever made."

The family donated the flag to Pres. William McKinley, who turned it over to the Smithsonian Institution in Washington. Although some flag experts and historians expressed doubts about the flag's authenticity, the Smithsonian exhibited it as John Paul Jones's flag until the 1930s. That's when Georgetown University history professor George Tansill examined the flag, determined it was a fraud and the museum withdrew it from public display.

Another widely viewed object exhibited at the Centennial Exhibition in Philadelphia also presented a false picture of the American flag: Ohio artist

Archibald M. Willard's *The Spirit of '76*, originally titled *Yankee Doodle*. Willard, whose grandfather had served with the Green Mountain Boys in the Revolutionary War, was a color bearer in the Civil War with the Eighty-sixth Ohio Regiment. Before the war he had worked in a wagon and carriage shop in Wellington, Ohio, painting peddlers' wagons with landscapes and images of animal heads.

After the war Willard turned to canvas and created several paintings of Civil War scenes. The artist began what his business partner James F. Ryder called his "greatest achievement and his crowning success" in 1875 at his studio in Cleveland specifically for the Centennial Exhibition. Willard "was deeply stirred by the impulse to do something to mark the great event," Ryder said. "He wished to express in a painting for publication the highest sense of patriotic fervor."

Willard gave a somewhat different account of the painting's genesis. "The centennial year was approaching and Mr. Ryder and I agreed that that year ought to be made memorable and financially profitable by a humorous picture," Willard said in a 1912 interview. "The title 'Yankee Doodle' suggested itself and I set to work to make a picture to fit the title." After he began the painting, however, Willard changed his mind about the humorous nature of the work. Something "of self-condemnation came over me that I had ever treated this theme as a humorous one," he explained.

The inspiration for the oil painting came from patriotic parades Willard had witnessed growing up in small Ohio towns. "I had boyhood memories of a country Fourth of July celebration, in which the local musicians bore their conspicuous share," he said. "There was a 'three-fingered Dick'; who tossed the drumsticks. . . . I made him the central figure."

The Spirit of '76 depicts three heroic figures: a drummer boy in a tri-corner hat; a hatless older man—the central figure—with a drum who slightly resembles George Washington but was based on Willard's father; and a fife player with a white headband. They are resolutely marching in step, clouds of smoke from a battle hovering over them, as they pass a wounded soldier raising himself on his elbow in salute.

Behind them is a Continental Army flag bearer. He is flying the "Betsy Ross" flag, with thirteen stars arrayed in a circle in the canton. "The man who had carried the Stars and Stripes," Ryder said, "marching under the same thrilling tune, put his heart into the picture."

Ryder first exhibited the painting in the window of his Cleveland art gallery. It caused an immediate sensation. "The crowds which gathered about it blockaded the entrance to the gallery and obstructed the sidewalk" so much, Ryder said, that he was forced to move the painting to the back of the store, where it was on view for several days. During that time, he said, "all business in the store was discontinued on account of the crowds, which filled the place."

Ryder and Willard then took the painting to Philadelphia, where it was displayed prominently at Memorial Hall, the Centennial Exhibition's art gallery, and the only significant building from the 1876 fair that still stands today. "It was a life-size canvas, and hung on the line and crowds thronged it day after day," Willard said. Ryder created chromolithographs of the painting to promote the exhibit. He sold hundreds of thousands of them. After the fair ended, the painting was exhibited for several weeks at the Old South Meeting House in Boston. It then went on to Washington, Chicago, San Francisco, and other cities, "so great was the desire of the public to see the painting, which had such welcome in the hearts of patriotic people," as Ryder put it. *The Spirit of '76*, he said, "stirred the heart of a nation."

The fact that the Continental Army, as we have noted, did not fly the Stars and Stripes had seemingly no effect on the extremely positive public reaction to the painting. The continuing widespread popularity of *The Spirit of '76* to the present day has had the unintended side effect of contributing to the commonly held misconception that Washington's army defeated the British under the Stars and Stripes.

The Centennial era, too, saw the widespread acceptance of the Betsy Ross myth, which began in 1870 with the speech by her grandson William Canby at the Historical Society of Pennsylvania. The story was in widespread circulation as Betsy Ross's popularity zoomed in the 1880s and 1890s, as we noted in chapter 3.

*   *   *

Americans celebrated the centennial Fourth of July with particularly profuse displays of the Stars and Stripes. New York City, for example, was ablaze in American flags and bunting. The Bowery's "exhibition of patriotism is of the most effusive sort," the *New York Times* reported. "There is not an undecorated building its entire length." On Canal Street, "nearly every one of [the] large furniture warehouses is crowded to its utmost capacity with emblems of various kinds." In Los Angeles, bunting and flags "were liberally used" throughout the city that day, "a triple arch adorned Main Street; statues of national heroes and pictures of Washington bedecked the town, and . . . a truly typical American Fourth of July procession of the Victorian epoch paraded through the streets. . . ."

Fifteen thousand men, including five thousand Union veterans marching with the Grand Army of the Republic, paraded through Philadelphia's streets in a nighttime Independence Day celebration. "The streets over which the procession passed were crowded with spectators, and at many points hearty applause was bestowed," the *Philadelphia Public Ledger* reported. The American flag was very much in evidence, as were old battle flags, proudly carried by GAR members from posts in Pennsylvania, New Jersey, and other states. One of the oldest was the Eutaw flag, a rough-hewn banner of crimson cloth that William Washington flew at the Revolutionary War battles of Cowpens and Eutaw Springs.

A group of those veterans that day founded a new organization, the Centennial Legion of Historical Military Commands. Its founders, Maj. George W. McLean of New York and Capt. Robert C. Gilchrist of South Carolina, fought on opposite sides in the Civil War. Their new organization, which still exists today, was formed to keep alive the memory of the military organizations that served in the Revolutionary War. Part of its mission was fostering patriotism; one of its primary objectives was teaching respect for the American flag.

A patriotic group called the Sons of Revolutionary Sires also was organized on the Centennial Fourth of July in San Francisco. That group became the first state society of the organization that came to be known as the National Society of the Sons of the American Revolution, which incorporated fourteen years later, in 1890, in Connecticut. The SAR, which remains active today, formed to honor the memory of those who fought in the Revolutionary War. Membership is open only to descendants of those who served in the American military in that war or otherwise fought the British during the conflict.

The seeds for the name of Flagstaff, Arizona, were sowed on July 4, 1876, when Thomas F. McMillan and a group of settlers from Boston raised the Stars and Stripes in that northern Arizona town at the base of the San Francisco Peaks. The town had been named Agassiz by a group of settlers from Boston, known as the First Boston Party, when they had laid out the town's plan three months earlier. Local lore holds that those men had raised an American flag on a flagpole they had fashioned by stripping the branches off a pine tree growing near their camp.

The Tennessee-born McMillan, known as the father of Flagstaff, had started a sheep ranch at about the same time in Antelope Valley just north of the city. His cabin there was the first structure built in the town. On the Fourth of July, 1876, McMillan and the Bostonians who camped out in his corral, known as the Second Boston Party, decided to do something special to celebrate the nation's one-hundredth birthday. So they reputedly cut down a pine tree, stripped off its limbs and bark, mounted it on the cabin, and attached an American flag to it. McMillan's spread thereafter became known as Flag Staff Ranch. In 1881, the town officially changed its name to Flagstaff.

As many as twenty thousand people turned out for the Fourth of July parade on Gay Street in Knoxville, Tennessee, on July 4, 1876. One of the highlights of that big celebration was the ride by some two hundred horsemen across the Tennessee River where they displayed a silk American flag with the words "South America"—the nickname for the South Knoxville section of the city—embroidered on it. In Portland, Oregon, a Mexican War veteran named Thomas S. Mountain unfurled a huge, forty-foot by eighty-foot American flag that day on a two-hundred-foot flagpole. Mountain, a former gold miner, paid $365 for the enormous flag.

★   ★   ★

The nation did not go all-out to celebrate the one-hundredth anniversary of the First Flag Resolution of June 14, 1777. Congress took note of the occasion and asked that the flag be flown on all public buildings that day, and remembrances took place in several cities. The biggest celebration took place in Boston. The "flag," Admiral Preble wrote, "was displayed from all the public buildings, from the shipping in the harbor, and numerous private buildings were ornamented with bunting and miniature flags." A celebratory cannon was fired at noon at Boston Common.

A well-attended rally took place that evening at the historic Old South Meeting House, where the Boston Tea Party began, presided over by Boston mayor Frederick O. Prince. The original Star-Spangled Banner made a rare public appearance and "The Star-Spangled Banner" was performed with "the audience joining in the chorus," Preble said.

That event was not named but it is now viewed as the first Flag Day celebration held in this country. Flag Day would not be officially recognized by Congress and the president until 1949.

CHAPTER ELEVEN

The Golden Age of Fraternity

*   *   *

The American people "regard the flag as a symbol of their country's power and prestige, and will be impatient if any open disrespect is shown towards it."

—U.S. Supreme Court justice John Harlan, 1907

SOMETIMES REFERRED TO as the "Golden Age of Fraternity," the 1880s and early 1890s saw the emergence of scores of patriotic, veterans, hereditary, and fraternal organizations, many of which took a keen interest in promoting the American flag. Most of the groups established national organizations, augmented with affiliated groups in the states.

The Grand Army of the Republic underwent a remarkable rebirth during those two decades, both in numbers of members and in its influence on patriotic matters, including encouraging veneration of the American flag. GAR membership had dropped during the 1870s to some twenty-seven thousand adherents nationwide. By 1890, however, membership soared to a peak of more than four hundred thousand in some seven thousand local posts in small and large towns and cities.

GAR posts were set up in all the states that remained loyal to the Union, in the states that came into the Union after the war, and even in most of the former states of the Confederacy. Virtually every prominent Union veteran of the Civil War joined the Grand Army of the Republic. That included five U.S. presidents: U. S. Grant, Rutherford B. Hayes, James Garfield, Benjamin Harrison, and William McKinley.

Former GAR commander in chief George S. Merrill characterized the

rapid growth of the organization in the 1880s and 1890s as "the most conspicuous and convincing monument of patriotism which American pos-
sesses." Merrill called GAR members "the survivors of the grandest army
the word has ever seen," who were "animated alone by a sprit of loyalty to
liberty and a devotion to the flag." In addition to its work memorializing the
war effort and its charitable acts, the GAR, Merrill said, "inculcates lessons
of gratitude and awakens the sweet sympathies and patriotic impulses of
the whole people."

The GAR's devotion to the Stars and Stripes was most visible at parades
and at the state and national encampments. Old and new flags were prominently and profusely displayed at the encampments, where veterans reverently saluted them. During the Twenty-sixth National GAR Encampment in
Washington, D.C., in September 1892, for example, the nation's capital was
"dressed in flags from the dome of the Capitol, where four great banners
float under the feet of the Goddess of Liberty, to the humblest negro cabin,
with its tiny cotton streamers," according to one newspaper account.

GAR parades also were flag-saturated occasions. "American flags fluttered everywhere" during the Thirty-seventh National GAR Encampment
parade in August 1903 in San Francisco, a newspaper in that city noted,
"from hundreds of street poles, from tops of buildings, from innumerable
windows, and from tens of thousands of right hands raised in tribute" to the
marching Union veterans.

In 1897 one observer estimated that some 5.4 million Americans belonged
to secret, fraternal orders—about one in eight adult males. That did not include the 400,000-plus members of the GAR and other veterans and military
groups. The newly formed organizations included patriotic groups that
worked to foster an appreciation of the nation's history by supporting historic
preservation, love of country, and respect for and adoration of the American
flag. The most active were hereditary societies that looked to the American
Revolution for inspiration: the Sons of the Revolution, the Colonial Dames of
America, the Society of Colonial Wars, the Sons of the American Revolution
(SAR), and the Daughters of the American Revolution (DAR).

The General Society of the Sons of the Revolution (SR), which first came
together in Washington, D.C., in 1876, incorporated in New York in 1884,
and began organizing state societies in the early 1890s. A women's group, the
National Society of the Colonial Dames of America, was established in 1891
in Philadelphia. The American Society of Colonial Wars, which organized in
1892, became the General Society of Colonial Wars in 1893. The National Society of the Sons of the American Revolution (SAR, which was not affiliated

with the SR) was formally established on April 30, 1889, the one hundredth anniversary of George Washington's first inauguration. The National Society received a charter from Congress on June 6, 1906 signed by Pres. Theodore Roosevelt, himself an SAR member.

The SAR, which had allowed women to join, changed its policy in 1890 and admitted only men. That led to the founding on October 11, 1890, of the women-only Daughters of the American Revolution. The DAR offered membership to women who were directly descended from someone who fought in the Revolutionary War. The organization grew steadily in power and influence in the 1890s and received a congressional charter on December 2, 1896. By the turn of the twentieth century, the DAR had more than thirty thousand members and some five hundred local chapters. The DAR's mission included working for the establishment of patriotic holidays and for "the enshrinement of the flag as the nation's most sacred symbol," as the historian Cecilia Elizabeth O'Leary put it.

The Grand Army of the Republic had several affiliated groups. The largest and most influential was the Woman's Relief Corps, which formed in July 1883. The Woman's Relief Corps still exists and has as its mission to perpetuate the GAR's memory and to promote patriotism, which includes, as the organization puts it, "the love and honor of our flag."

*   *   *

The patriotic and veterans groups threw their support, beginning in the late 1880s, behind the movement to make June 14 a national holiday in honor of the first Flag Resolution of 1777, which became law that day. The first call for what would become known as Flag Day had come in 1861. On June 8, less than two months after the Civil War began, Charles Dudley Warner, the editor of the *Hartford Evening Press*, wrote an editorial calling for two new American holidays, Constitution Day on September 17, and Flag Day on June 14. Flags flew in Connecticut on June 14, 1861, and there was a flurry of media interest in the North. Warner's idea did not take hold in the North or nationwide after the Civil War, but the custom of displaying flags on June 14 continued for several years throughout the city of Hartford.

"The day was a beautiful one," the *Hartford Courant* noted on June 14, 1870, in an editorial lamenting the fact the city no longer celebrated Flag Day. "Our streets were decked with the colors, flags waved from every conspicuous point; in city and country the windows were gay with the bright show, and life, for a day, took on a festive air."

On the hundredth anniversary of the first Flag Resolution, June 14, 1877, the *New York Times* called for "a general display of the American flag throughout the country," but stopped short of recommending a national holiday. "There will not be any very general celebration of this peculiar anniversary," a *Times* editorial said, "but every citizen may signify anew his love for 'the old flag' by hoisting its folds to the breeze today."

Several notable Flag Day ceremonies did take place around the nation. In Boston, the original Star-Spangled Banner was displayed at the city's official celebration hosted by Mayor Frederick O. Prince at the Old South Meeting House. "I wish that every citizen of our great republic could gaze upon this very flag we are so fortunate as to have here tonight," Nathan Appleton, a cousin by marriage of the flag's inheritor, Georgiana Appleton, said in his speech. "Let us all take it with us in thought at least, as we travel through these United States." The New York City Teachers' Association held a large Flag Day commemoration that day at the Academy of Music.

The idea for a national Flag Day was revived in 1885 by Bernard John (B.J.) Cigrand, a nineteen-year-old, forty-dollar-a-month teacher at the one-room Stony Hill Schoolhouse in Waubeka, Wisconsin. Cigrand, the son of immigrants from Luxembourg, was a very patriotic man who kept a small American flag in his classroom. On June 14, 1885, he asked his students to write an essay about what the flag meant to them. The exercises he held that day in the classroom in Waubeka—which is about midway between Chicago and Green Bay—are generally recognized as the nation's first Flag Day observance.

Organizing the Flag Day exercises set Cigrand on a long quest to lobby for the creation of a national Flag Day holiday, which he initially called Flag Birthday. "He was a historian and he loved the flag," Barbara Trayer Michael, Cigrand's great granddaughter, said in 2002. "His parents came over from Luxembourg and they loved the country. They instilled that love of the country in him and really took it to the pinnacle." The patriotic Cigrand, who joined the navy in his forties to fight in World War I, was—like Francis Hopkinson and other flag aficionados—an expert on seals and heraldry. He designed several official seals, including those of the city of Chicago and Cook County, Illinois.

Beginning with "The Fourteenth of June," an article he wrote in June 1886 in the Chicago newspaper *Argus*, Cigrand penned countless pro–Flag Day newspaper and magazine articles and pamphlets, along with several books. He also made hundreds of speeches espousing his Flag Day cause. Soon after his first Flag Day commemoration, B. J. Cigrand left teaching to attend dental school. Although he practiced dentistry in Aurora, Illinois, and taught at the Dental College of the University of Illinois, lobbying on behalf of Flag Day remained Cigrand's passion throughout his life.

Soon after he had graduated from dental school, Cigrand made a flag speech before the Chicago branch—called a "camp"—of the Patriotic Order Sons of America, which had been formed in 1847 in Pennsylvania and was part of the anti-immigrant Know-Nothing movement. Soon thereafter Cigrand began editing a new patriotic magazine, The *American Standard*, published by the Order. He wrote many articles in the magazine on his favorite cause, calling attention to the American flag and the date of the first Flag Resolution. The Order made securing a law making Flag Day a national holiday one of its highest priorities.

Beginning in the early 1890s, Cigrand's flag celebration idea took hold in many cities and towns. Flags flew from public and private buildings, ceremonies took place at city halls and other municipal venues, streetcars in big cities were decked out with flags and bunting, and flag commemorations took place in public schools. A Flag Day ceremony was held at the Betsy Ross House in Philadelphia on June 14, 1891. In 1894 Cigrand's missionary work on behalf of Flag Day—which included helping found the Illinois Flag Day Association and the American Flag Day Association with William T. Kerr of Pittsburgh—resulted in its first big success in Chicago. On June 14 some three hundred thousand schoolchildren took part in citywide Flag Day activities held in five parks, the first public school celebration of its kind.

That same year New York Gov. Roswell P. Flower signed an order directing that all public buildings in the Empire State display the flag on June 14. The following year, 1895, Charles R. Skinner, a former member of Congress who was then superintendent of the New York State Department of Public Instruction, recommended that all schools in New York hold "appropriate" Flag Day "exercises" on June 14. "I would specially recommend that the flag be raised on each school building at precisely 9 o'clock, and that, if locality and weather permit, a part of the morning programme take place in the open air, in connection with the raising of the flag," New York City public school superintendent John Jasper wrote to the principals of that city's schools in 1896.

Veterans and patriotic groups played a large part in lobbying for Cigrand's cause and helped spread the Flag Day concept around the nation. In 1890, the Connecticut SAR Society proposed that that state set aside June 14 as Flag Day and promoted the idea of flying the flag every day at all public buildings, in courtrooms and in post offices. The idea caught on the following year when thousands of flags were displayed widely on Flag Day throughout New England and in New York City, Philadelphia, Baltimore, Chicago, and Washington, D.C.

The Pennsylvania Society of Colonial Dames, along with the Pennsylvania SR branch, lobbied successfully to have the city of Philadelphia display the flag on June 14 on all public buildings in 1893. That same year Flag Day exercises took place in Philadelphia's Independence Square for the city's schoolchildren. In March 1895 the Massachusetts SAR Society petitioned the Boston city government to enact an ordinance mandating that American flags be flown on all public buildings and grounds on June 14. It was passed and signed into law by Mayor Edwin Curtis at the end of the year. On June 14, 1895, Boston held its first official Flag Day commemoration, which included special exercises in the city schools.

The GAR initially rebuffed attempts to support a June 14 Flag Day holiday. The leadership believed that the date was too close to Memorial Day and the Fourth of July. But sentiment for Flag Day grew within the organization and in its sister group, the Woman's Relief Corps, which signed on in support of the work of Cigrand's American Flag Day Association. In 1892, the Iowa GAR called for a Flag Day holiday—but chose February 22 in honor of George Washington's birthday.

The flag and Flag Day played a prominent role in the 1896 presidential election campaign between Ohio's Republican governor William McKinley and the Democrat and Populist Party nominee, William Jennings Bryan of Nebraska. Flags had been used by virtually every presidential candidate in all the post–Civil War presidential elections. McKinley's campaign manager, the industrialist Mark Hanna, however, linked his candidate to the flag in a new and unprecedented manner in a campaign that cost a record $3.5 million. Hanna figuratively wrapped McKinley, a Civil War veteran, in the American flag.

During the campaign the Republicans handed out hundreds of thousands of flags at rallies across the country. Hanna devised a campaign button that contained the image of the American flag. He also created what he called the Patriotic Heroes' Battalion, which was made up primarily of revered Civil War generals. The Battalion undertook an extensive train tour throughout the Midwest and West under banners that read "1896 is as Vitally Important as 1861." The train was bedecked with oceans of flag bunting. Two thirty-foot collapsible flagpoles sat atop one of the train's flat cars, and a campaign worker unfurled the Stars and Stripes at countless stops.

At a rally on September 4 in New York City, American flags and banners emblazoned with the names of McKinley and running mate Garret A. Hobart flew in profusion along a six-block-long stretch of Broadway. "There was a dazzling display" of flags from Seventeenth Street to Twenty-third Street, the *New York Times* reported the next day. "A half dozen large banners and hundreds of small ones were flung to the breeze at 5 o'clock." Enormous flags, "some of them thirty-six feet long, were unfurled, and at the same time the smaller flags were waved furiously. It presented a beautiful and impressive sight. Most of the banners were the National colors, having at the end a strip bearing the names of McKinley and Hobart."

A military band playing "The Star-Spangled Banner" led a procession of "several thousand business men" marching up Broadway, according to the *Times*. "The procession halted at every block, and as it paused, more banners were unfurled. There was a large crowd along the line of march, which cheered lustily whenever another group of banners was displayed."

On October 26, Hanna declared October 31, 1896, national Flag Day. He called on Republican state central committees throughout the nation to "make a special effort" that day to "assemble in the cities, villages, and hamlets nearest their homes and show their patriotism, devotion to country and the flag, and their intention to support the [Republican Party] by having patriotic speeches and such other exercises as will be appropriate for the occasion and tend to make the day a general holiday as far as possible."

Republicans heeded Hannah's call by holding Flag Day events across the country that day, just three days before the election. Large events took place in cities such as Washington, D.C., Chicago, San Francisco, and New York. They featured mass displays of flags and appearances by former Union generals. The message was that the Republican Party of McKinley saved the nation under the flag by prevailing in the Civil War and that voting Republican was the proper patriotic thing to do.

"The flag was everywhere" at the enormous New York City Flag Day demonstration, the *New York Tribune* reported. "It flaunted from every window; it waved from every portico; it flew from every roof; it floated over almost every street, and many times in every block. The marching thousands trampled between walls of human faces that were almost entirely folded in the stripes and dotted with the stars, while every man in the whole vast line carried a flag of his own."

A *New York Times* editorial that day expressed the view that the display of flags was more than a political strategy. Showing the flag "is not merely a proclamation of the politics of him who displays it," the editorial said, "but it is the celebration in advance of a victory. Confidence in that victory is simply trust in the American people and belief in their capacity for self-government." Those who flew the flag proclaimed "their fealty to the Republic and their defiance of its enemies, and to celebrate in advance the victory it will win" on Election Day, the editorial said.

But that is not the way Democrats and Populists saw it. Some reacted indignantly to the ploy and tore down flags at McKinley rallies that day. In Sedalia, Missouri, according to a report the next day in the *New York Times*, Bryan supporters seized a flag from a young boy and burned it, along with a pile of McKinley campaign literature. Most Democrats, however, responded with flag-waving ceremonies of their own that day.

The red, white, and blue display by the Democrats in Washington, D.C., that day had an impact on Mabel Hubbard Bell, Alexander Graham Bell's wife. A staunch Republican, she nevertheless had had qualms about flying the flag on October 31 from their house on Connecticut Avenue in Washington. But Mabel Bell wound up displaying "a lot of flags," she said in a letter to her husband. "A whole lot of houses on Connecticut Ave. were decorated and Penna. Ave. and F Street were very gay with flags," she reported. "At first, I did not approve for I did not believe in the bringing of our national emblem in party strife." Mabel Bell changed her mind, she said, after she saw the flags displayed at the Democratic headquarters and remembered that Bryan had endorsed Hanna's suggestion.

"I didn't see why I shouldn't show my interest in the election, why in fact it wasn't meritorious," she said, "so I stopped at a flag store and got some."

Mabel Hubbard Bell's cautionary note about bringing the flag into "party strife" was prescient. She realized that she was taking part in something unprecedented. Even though the Democrats and Populists also celebrated Flag Day and tried to make the point that the flag was not the property of one party, their effort came too late, and the Republicans succeeded in tying their candidate to the flag and the patriotic feelings that went along with it.

"Although members of both parties demonstrated their patriotism by flying the flag that day," Scot Guenter noted, "the attempt to appropriate it for one partisan ideology by creating a special Flag Day illustrated the power political strategists recognized in the symbol."

★   ★   ★

Flag Day celebrations picked up steam following McKinley's election. A large, city-wide celebration took place, for example, on June 14, 1897, in

New York, sponsored by the Empire State Society of the Sons of the American Revolution. "On all of the Federal and municipal buildings the flags were hoisted at sunrise, as they were also on the Liberty Pole at the Battery and at the old fort in Central Park." The *New York Times* reported the following day. "As the city awakened, the rainbow effect was extended till it reached the entire length of Broadway and of the avenues, through the cross streets, and along the water front, on piers and on shipping." The Stars and Stripes also was "displayed from every schoolhouse" and "draped in the assembly rooms, and in many of the up-town schools the children were provided with small flags, which they waved in time with the singing of the National airs."

Beginning at the turn of the twentieth century, many states and localities officially celebrated Flag Day. In Michigan, for example, the legislature approved a Flag Day resolution in 1901. The state's governor, Aaron T. Bliss, then issued a proclamation designating June 14, 1902, as Flag Day in the Wolverine state.

"The breezes stealing in from the Great Lakes and the rising sun should find Old Glory waving from every home, from every schoolhouse, from every church and every public building," the governor proclaimed. "Every flag staff should bear aloft the banner which has never known a stain. There should be appropriate exercises in every school" and "each child should have for his own a flag to be treasured and revered through the passing years."

On May 30, 1916, as it became increasingly likely that American troops would soon be fighting a world war, Pres. Woodrow Wilson established a national Flag Day through a presidential proclamation. Wilson made a Flag Day speech on June 14 that year near the Washington Monument after having led a flag-saturated Preparedness Parade in which some sixty-six thousand marchers took part from the Capitol along Pennsylvania Avenue to the White House. Wilson himself carried the Stars and Stripes at the head of the parade.

"I regard this day as a day of rededication to all the ideals of the United States," Wilson said. "As I see the winds lovingly unfold the beautiful lines of our great flag, I shall seem to see a hand point the way of duty, no matter how hard, no matter how long, which we shall tread while we vindicate the glory and honor of the United States."

In 1918, responding to a plea by the National Security League, a private organization made up primarily of bankers and industrialists, nationwide Flag Day celebrations took place in an effort to boost patriotism after

Before the United States entered World War I, flag-bedecked Preparedness Parades took place throughout the country, including this one in Washington on June 14, 1916, in which marchers passed before a reviewing stand in front of the White House. *The Library of Congress, Prints and Photographs Division*

President Woodrow Wilson led the parade, leading some 66,000 marchers from Capitol Hill to the White House, carrying the Stars and Stripes. *The Library of Congress, Prints and Photographs Division*

America entered World War I. In many states audiences in movie theaters sang "The Star Spangled Banner" and one other patriotic song that day and special celebrations, proposed by the federal government's Bureau of Education, took place in factories. They included the raising of the flag accompanied by a bugle call, a recitation of the Pledge of Allegiance, and singing patriotic songs.

Despite the popularity of Flag Day celebrations, President Wilson did not make Flag Day a legal public holiday. Nor has any president done so since then. Only Pennsylvania, which took action in 1937, has chosen to make June 14 a legal state holiday. Even though it is not an official national holiday, Flag Day observances have taken place every year since Wilson's proclamation. On August 3, 1949, Pres. Harry Truman signed into law a resolution passed by Congress designating June 14th of each year National Flag Day. That measure calls upon the president to issue an annual proclamation calling for a Flag Day observance and for the display of the flag on all federal government buildings. In 1966 Congress passed a Joint Resolution asking the president to issue an annual National Flag Week proclamation as well, and to call on American citizens to display the flag during the entire week in which June 14 falls.

Every year since then our presidents have issued Flag Day and Flag Week Proclamations, directing U.S. government officials to fly the flag on all government buildings and asking all Americans, as Pres. Ronald Reagan put it in his 1981 Flag Day Proclamation, to fly the flag "from their porches, windows and storefronts."

★   ★   ★

The veterans and patriotic organizations—led by the Grand Army of the Republic and by the Sons and Daughters of the American Revolution—played the leading role in what became known as the flag protection movement, which grew up in the late 1880s. The movement came about as a result of what many saw as the out-of-control commercialization of the use of the flag.

In the absence of laws governing the use of the flag's image or any accepted rules of flag etiquette, marketers and advertisers routinely printed the Stars and Stripes directly on their products and on advertisements for them and had no qualms whatsoever about printing their messages directly on American flags. A 1878 advertisement for McFerran's Magnolia Hams, for example, had Uncle Sam pointing to a ham sitting in front of a flag with

the words "The Magnolia Ham is an American Institution" printed across
the stripes.

Politicians also took liberties with the American flag, including inserting
candidates' names and messages across the stripes and nestled among the
stars. The practice dated to before the Civil War. A flag made for the 1860
Abraham Lincoln–Hannibal Hamlin Republican Party presidential ticket,
for example, had a likeness of Lincoln in the canton surrounded by twenty-
nine small stars in a circle and four larger stars in the canton's corners. Four
white stripes contained the words: "For President, Abram Lincoln. For Vice
President, Hannibal Hamlin." The stripes of a flag produced for the Republican ticket in the 1884 presidential campaign included the slogan, "For
President James G. Blaine. For Vice President John A. Logan 1884." The
canton contained the requisite thirty-eight stars, as well as likenesses of

By 1860, it had become common practice for politicians to use American flags as campaign posters. This flag promotes the candidacy of Abraham Lincoln and his vice presidential running mate that year, Hannibal Hamlin. *The Library of Congress, Prints and
Photographs Division*

Blaine and Logan, who had been the GAR commander in chief from 1868 to 1871.

As the nation rapidly industrialized in the last third of the century, color printing developed on a large scale. Low-cost color postcards proliferated in the 1880s and 1890s; many of them featured red, white, and blue American flags. Flag business cards also were popular, and the flag was a common letterhead theme embossed on private and commercial stationery. Advertising in newspapers and magazines and on billboards and signs also flourished in this period.

Images of the flag found their way into an astonishing number of advertisements for scores of different types of products. The long, long list includes baking powder, bicycles, beer, cigarettes, corned beef, toilet paper, tobacco products, window shades, and whiskey barrels. As one late-nineteenth-century reference book for advertisers put it, flags "are admirably adapted to all purposes of heraldic display and their rich, glowing colors appeal to feel-

The first laws enacted by the states and the U.S. Congress against flag desecration came in the early 1890s in reaction to the rampant use of the Stars and Stripes in advertising, including this late 19th century ad for Young America hams and breakfast bacon. *The Library of Congress, Prints and Photographs Division*

ings of patriotism and win purchasers of the merchandise to which they are affixed."

The rampant use of the flag for commercial purposes did not sit well with the veterans' and patriotic organizations nor with some members of Congress. The first attempt to legislate against misuse of the flag in advertising and political campaigns was a bill introduced in the House of Representatives in 1878 by Congressman Samuel Sullivan Cox of Ohio. Cox's measure called for criminal penalties for anyone who "shall disfigure the national flag, either by printing on said flag, or attaching to the same, or otherwise, any advertisement for public display." That bill died in committee.

So did a similar measure introduced in 1880 by Congressman Hiram Barber Jr. of Illinois. Barber's bill was designed to "protect the national flag from desecration" by banning the flag's image for "advertisement of merchandise or other property or of any person's trade, occupation or business." Cox and Barber's measures failed mainly because they were ahead of their time. Significant sentiment in favor of enacting a federal law outlawing flag desecration did not manifest itself in Washington until the early 1890s.

That sentiment was much stronger in the House of Representatives than in the Senate. In 1890 the House for the first time passed a flag-desecration bill, which was introduced by Congressman John Alexander Caldwell of Ohio. That measure made it a misdemeanor punishable by a fifty-dollar fine or thirty days in jail to use the flag in any way in "advertisements for public display or private gain." The Senate did not take action on the measure, however, and it did not become law.

Beginning in the mid-1890s the patriotic and veterans' groups launched a strong nationwide campaign to lobby the state and federal governments to enact flag protection laws. The first shot in the campaign was fired in 1895 by U.S. Army captain Philip H. Reade, an amateur historian who served as a historian for the Society of Colonial Wars (whose Illinois branch he headed) and the Sons of the American Revolution. Reade (1844–1919), who claimed that he was descended from two dozen colonial ancestors, had graduated from West Point, served in the Union army in the Civil War, and went on to fight in the Indian wars and in the Spanish-American War.

In 1895 Reade—whom the political scientist Robert Justin Goldstein called the "Johnny Appleflag" of the flag protection movement—helped shape a Society of Colonial Wars resolution that called on Congress to enact legislation reining in the commercial use of the flag. In that same year he set up a society committee headed by Charles Kingsbury Miller that compiled a list of the names and addresses of companies and organizations that used the flag for commercial purposes. The committee published a pamphlet called "Misuse of the National Flag," which described advertising excesses using the flag and distributed it widely to politicians, colleges, clergy, and newspaper editors, as well as to patriotic and veterans groups.

Reade heavily lobbied other patriotic and veterans organizations to join the movement to protect the flag with legal sanctions. He traveled extensively speaking to many organizations, urging them to support desecration legislation. And he achieved great success, winning support from many state branches and from the national organizations of the leading groups, including the SAR, SR, DAR, GAR, and the Loyal Legion. From 1897 to 1899, those groups established committees to work for flag protection legislation and later formed the American Flag Association to coordinate the effort.

Another of the movement's most effective leaders was Frances Saunders Kempster of the Milwaukee DAR chapter. Her lobbying on behalf of flag protection legislation bore fruit in 1897 when the DAR National Convention endorsed the idea and she was named the head of a new DAR National Flag Committee. A third important player in the movement, Col. Ralph E. Prime, a Civil War veteran and the former deputy attorney general of New York, headed the national SAR Flag Committee.

In February 1898, Prime brought representatives of the flag committees of the other patriotic and veterans' organizations together in New York's City Hall. That meeting resulted in the founding on February 12 of the American Flag Association, which was made up of representatives of thirty state and national flag committees. The group included national and state SAR and DAR flag committees, along with representatives of several other veterans and patriotic groups. The association soon attracted many more groups, including eight states and the national GAR Flag Committee. Prime became the Flag Association's founding president, serving in that position until 1908 and leading the effort to foster "public sentiment in favor of honoring the flag of our country and preserving it from desecration, and of initiating and forwarding legal efforts to prevent such desecration."

The association and the many national flag committees worked hard to convince Congress to enact legislation. Despite decades of lobbying, however, no legislation would be passed on Capitol Hill until 1968. Crucial roadblocks came from the powerful Republican chairmen of the Senate and House Judiciary Committees throughout most of the 1890s, Sen. George F. Hoar of Massachusetts and Rep. David B. Henderson of Iowa. Hoar objected to flag desecration legislation for several reasons, including the possibility of lawsuits from firms that had registered their commercial flag images with the United States Patent and Trademark Office. Hoar, who said he initially favored flag desecration legislation, also believed that politicians would strongly object if they were no longer permitted to put their images on campaign posters featuring the flag.

Henderson, who also served as Speaker of the House from 1899 to 1903, said that prohibiting the use of the flag on commercial products would not be good for business. Henderson, a colleague said, "hoped the American people would continue to wrap hams in the flag, not to teach patriotism, but to teach ham eaters to eat American hams."

With legislation for a national law solidly bottled up in Congress, the advocates for flag desecration legislation turned their attention to the states. In 1897, Pennsylvania, Illinois, and South Dakota enacted flag protection laws; by Flag Day of 1905 thirty-two states and the Arizona and New Mexico Territories had followed suit.

There were other successes, as well. U.S. Army inspector general Joseph C. Breckinridge, a member of the American Flag Association's executive committee, in 1899 ended the long-standing military practice of inscribing flags with unit names and the battles they took part in. Four years later, the U.S. Commissioner of Patents and Trademarks ruled that his office no longer would register any trademarks on commercial products that made use of the flag. Congress in 1905 codified that ruling into law.

On March 4, 1907, the U.S. Supreme Court, in the case of *Halter v. Nebraska,* upheld state flag protection laws when it ruled that a 1903 Nebraska flag protection measure did not violate the Constitution. That law, among other things, made it a misdemeanor, punishable by a fine or imprisonment, to "sell, expose for sale, or have in possession for sale" any merchandise "upon which shall have been printed or placed, for purposes of advertisement" the image of the American flag. This marked the first time the nation's highest court offered its views on flag protection laws.

Justice John M. Harlan, delivering the opinion, ruled against the appeal of a Nebraska company that had been convicted and fined fifty dollars for painting the American flag on beer bottles for advertising purposes. "It would seem difficult," Harlan said, "to hold that the statute of Nebraska, in forbidding the use of the flag of the United States for purposes of mere advertisement, infringes any right protected by the Constitution of the United States."

In his opinion Harlan gave a short history of the American flag and noted that every "true American has not simply an appreciation, but a deep affection" for the flag. "No American, nor any foreign-born person who enjoys the privileges of American citizenship, ever looks upon it without taking pride in the fact that he lives under this free government."

States, he said, have the power "to strengthen the bonds of the Union, and therefore, to that end, may encourage patriotism and love of country among its people." A state, he said, would be ignoring "the well-being of its people if it ignores the fact that they regard the flag as a symbol of their country's power and prestige, and will be impatient if any open disrespect is shown towards it." He characterized using the flag in advertising as "a purpose wholly foreign to that for which it was provided by the nation."

Such use, he said, "tends to degrade and cheapen the flag in the estimation of the people, as well as to defeat the object of maintaining it as an emblem of national power and national honor." The court, he said, could not hold that "any privilege of American citizenship or that any right of personal liberty is violated by a state enactment forbidding the flag to be used as an advertisement on a bottle of beer."

★   ★   ★

In the middle of the first decade of the twentieth century, amid the veterans' and patriotic groups' clamor for flag protection, the American flag played a leading role in two of Broadway's most popular stage musicals, *Little Johnny Jones* and *George Washington, Jr.* Both of those smashingly successful shows were written and produced by Broadway's first superstar, George M. Cohan, who also starred in the productions. *Little Johnny Jones*, which opened on November 7, 1904, at the Liberty Theater, went on the road and ran for two more years. It is the story of an American horse jockey, played by Cohan, trying to win the English Derby. It was Cohan's third Broadway show and the one that made his reputation. Its songs were wildly popular, especially "Give My Regards to Broadway" and "Yankee Doodle Dandy," which Cohan performed surrounded by an American flag-waving retinue.

George Washington, Jr. opened in 1906. Cohan wrote the script, coproduced the show, starred in it, and wrote the words and music to all the songs, including the show stopper, "You're a Grand Old Flag." Cohan, playing the title character, a senator's son who out of patriotism refuses to marry a British nobleman's daughter, belted out that tune with a large American flag in hand marching back and forth across the stage. The song was a huge success; it became the first tune from a musical to sell more than a million copies of sheet music.

Cohan had written the song after a chance meeting with a Civil War veteran of the Battle of Gettysburg. They were sitting next to each other at a funeral when Cohan noticed that the veteran had an old American flag folded in his lap. In the ensuing conversation, the man referred to the tattered flag as "a grand old rag." That inspired Cohan to write the song he called "You're a Grand Old Rag," which is how the song was performed when *George Washington, Jr.* opened. Cohan soon changed the words after complaints from critics, veterans, and patriotic and veterans' groups.

The word change satisfied those who took offense, and *George Washington, Jr.* and Cohan's succeeding shows became huge hits. Still, he was not immune from criticism for his use of the flag. The drama critic James Metcalfe, for example, lambasted *George Washington, Jr.* for its "mawkish appeals to the cheapest kind of patriotism." If Cohan "can bring himself to coin the American flag and national heroes into box-office receipts," Metcalfe said, "it is not his blame but our shame." That criticism did not stop Cohan from repeating his flag-waving routine in subsequent shows.

One composer who received not a whit of criticism for his use of the flag in his music was John Philip Sousa. The man known as "the March King" composed 136 military marches, including "The Stars and Stripes Forever," which became the nation's official march by an act of Congress in 1987. Sousa led the U.S. Marine Band from 1880 to 1892 and was resoundingly popular in this country and Europe for the next four decades as he presented countless concerts with his own band. Sousa wrote "The Stars and Stripes Forever" in December 1896; it became a national sensation within a year. Sousa's band typically played the song at the end of its concerts, at which point audiences rose in tribute to the song and the flag. It remains a popular, stirring patriotic tune that is widely performed today.

*   *   *

The United States went to war with Spain in April of 1898, and handily defeated the Spanish in Cuba and the Philippines by the end of the year. The Spanish-American War is significant in the evolution of the American flag for several reasons. First, and most important, it was the first war fought by the entire nation under the Stars and Stripes since the Mexican War ended fifty years earlier. Americans from the states that fought each other under the Confederate flag and the Stars and Stripes during the Civil War came together under the forty-five-star American flag to fight in Cuba and the Philippines against the Spanish in 1898. Former Confederate general John Brown Gordon, expressing a common sentiment as the war began, pledged that southerners would fight in the Spanish-American War "wrapped in the folds of the American flag."

The "greatest good" the Spanish-American War did, then New York governor Theodore Roosevelt said in August 1899, "was that beneath the same banner marched the sons of the blue and the gray. The nation is now united in deed as well as well as in name. After being the son of a man who wore the blue, the next best thing is to be a son of a man who wore the gray. We are now all Americans, proud of our forefathers and their bravery on both sides."

That conflict, the nation's first declared war fought entirely overseas, also stirred up tremendous patriotic fervor in the United States following the sinking of the USS *Maine* in Havana harbor on February 15. That fervor often was expressed using the American flag. After the United States declared war on Spain on April 25, Americans put on a "great display of flag flying, flag waving, and flag saluting," Scot Guenter noted.

"The demand for bunting within the last ten days is in excess of the supply," the *Wall Street Journal* reported on May 2. "The demand is such that orders have been taken for delivery from three to four months ahead." The demand for bunting and flags led to price increases of fifty cents for bunting and twenty-five cents for flags, the *Journal* reported.

When the American Fifth Army Corps under Gen. William Shafter took Santiago de Cuba on July 17 after three weeks of bloody fighting, forcing Spain to sue for peace, the American flag flew in triumph over the Governor's Palace. "The ceremony of hoisting the Stars and Stripes was worth all the blood and treasure it cost," the *New York Times* opined the next day. "A vast concourse of ten thousand people witnessed the stirring and thrilling scene that will live forever in the minds of all the Americans present."

The Spanish-American War also saw the display of a spate of extraordinarily large flags. That included the 120-foot by 43-foot Stars and Stripes raised in Havana on January 1, 1899, and the massive 500-foot flag that Comm. George Dewey's flagship, the USS *Olympia*, flew when it steamed home in triumph after the Battle of Manila Bay.

By the turn of the twentieth century, the American flag had secured a strong place in the hearts and minds of the American public. That was due mainly to the influence of veterans' and patriotic groups, the easing of lingering tensions left over from the Civil War, and a national climate that was ready to embrace patriotism and its symbols. The next important step in the flag's history took root during this period as well: the birth, growth, and nationwide acceptance of the idea of schoolchildren making a daily vow to pledge their allegiance to the flag and what it stands for.

CHAPTER TWELVE

One Nation Indivisible

* * *

I pledge allegiance to my flag and the Republic for which it stands;
one nation indivisible, with liberty and Justice for all.

—The Youth's Companion, September 8, 1892

THE YOUTH'S COMPANION began publishing in Boston in 1827.
By 1890, it had become one of the most popular magazines in the nation,
with a circulation of nearly five hundred thousand. Its content initially was
geared toward children, but in 1857 the weekly magazine also began to appeal to adults. It attracted some of the best writers of the day, including
Ralph Waldo Emerson, Harriet Beecher Stowe, John Greenleaf Whittier,
William Dean Howells, Jack London, and Emily Dickinson. The magazine's owner from 1867 to 1899, Daniel Sharp Ford, filled the Boston-based
The Youth's Companion with essays and articles on diverse subjects, along
with poetry, humorous stories, and fiction.

The Youth's Companion also was a highly commercial operation. Advertisements filled its pages and the Premium Department gave flags and other
items as incentives to new and renewing subscribers. In 1886, Ford appointed his nephew James B. Upham to head that department, as well as a
subsidiary called the Perry Mason Company. Soon thereafter, Upham, who
was born in New Hampshire in 1845, spearheaded a mission known as the
school flag movement or schoolhouse flag movement. It was designed to
put American flags in all of the schools in the country—flags that, it was
hoped, would be purchased from *The Youth's Companion*.

"At that time," said John W. Baer, the author of a history of the Pledge of Allegiance, "a flag was considered an unnecessary expense, especially for one-room schoolhouses. A flag pole and a flag amounted to expenses school committees didn't want."

The Grand Army of the Republic and its auxiliary organization, the Woman's Relief Corps, joined the movement to bring American flags to the public schools beginning in 1889. The Rochester, New York, GAR Post that year presented flags to all of that city's public schools to mark George Washington's birthday. At the national encampment in Milwaukee that year the GAR voted to ask each post to provide a flag to every public school that did not have one. "Let the eight million boys and girls in our elementary schools be thus imbued with a reverence for the flag and all it represents," GAR commander in chief William Warner, a former Missouri U.S. congressman, said in 1892. "Then the future of the Republic is assured and that flag shall forever wave."

Patriotic ceremonies revolving around the flag took place in New York City public schools beginning in early 1888. They were introduced by Col. DeWitt C. Ward, a New York City school trustee. George T. Balch, the Board of Education's auditor, embraced the idea and publicized it and other patriotic school endeavors in his 1889 book, *Methods of Teaching Patriotism in the Public Schools.* Balch worked closely with Margaret Pascal, who taught primarily immigrant children. Pascal fostered patriotism among her students by, among other things, encouraging girls to sew flags and boys to make flagstaffs. Balch, who also was a teacher and a Civil War veteran, called for schools to display the flag and to institute flag ceremonies that included what he called "The American Patriotic Salute." The historian Scot Guenter calls Balch's idea "the first known organized [flag] salute designed for use in American public schools."

Balch's salute began with students touching their foreheads and then their hearts and saying: "We give our Heads! —and our Hearts! —to God! and our Country!" The students then extended their right arms, palms down, and said, "One Country! One Language! One Flag!" By 1893 some six thousand students—many of them the children of immigrants—who attended New York City's twenty-one Children's Aid Society schools recited Balch's salute every morning. Teachers in the U.S. government's Indian schools in the West also adopted the salute. The GAR and the Women's Relief Committee enthusiastically endorsed Balch's school flag salute concept.

The Youth's Companion magazine offered for sale many sizes of flags, including small pocket-sized versions with carrying cases. It sold six-foot-long flags, "just right for a 'little country school,'" an advertisement in the magazine said, for $3.50 and nine-foot-long flags for $5.35. "At these prices," the ad said, "we pay postage. The boys can cut the flag-staff." Staffs were favored over flagpoles because poles were deemed too expensive and because, outside of military bases, they were rarely used to display the Stars and Stripes at the time.

The magazine also offered free "flag certificates" to schools to sell as a way to raise money to purchase flags. "By the sale of these Flag Certificates for ten cents each to the friends of the pupils," the ad said, "your school can raise money for its Flag in one day." The certificates read: "This Certificate entitles the holder thereof to one share in the patriotic influence of a Flag over the schoolhouse."

The magazine promoted the endeavor heavily, pitching it as a way to foster love of country, especially among foreign-born children and the children of immigrants who came to this country primarily from southern and eastern Europe by the millions in the 1880s and 1890s. The "school house flag," Upham wrote in *The Youth's Companion*, "seen so often so constantly present in the pupil's thoughts, has a marked influence, as several teachers report, upon foreign born children and the children of foreign born parents."

In 1890, the magazine ran an essay contest on the theme, "The Patriotic Influence of the American Flag When Raised over the Public Schools." The prize for the winner in each state was a nine-by-fifteen-foot American flag. The magazine sold some 25,000 flags to schools by mid-1892. Upham in 1891 had formed the Lyceum League of America, a patriotic and debating society made up primarily of high school students, to help the cause. And the magazine prominently featured the flag in graphics and illustrations in many flag-inspired articles and stories. That included "George Washington II," the story of a brave, patriotic boy, which appeared in 1891; "The Story of a War Song," a history of the song "The Battle Cry of Freedom" by George Root, which appeared in the August 25, 1892, issue; and "His Day for the Flag," the story of children who raise money to purchase a flag for their school, which also ran in 1892.

The magazine also heavily promoted state laws mandating that school boards provide flagstaffs and flags for the schools in their jurisdictions. That campaign was successful. In 1895, Massachusetts—the home of the magazine—became the first state to mandate compulsory flags and flagstaffs in its public schools. Wisconsin followed suit in 1889. By 1905, nearly two dozen states, all of them in the North and West, had laws making school flags compulsory.

In 1891, Ford had hired a new assistant editor, thirty-six-year-old Francis Bellamy, who was a close friend, a Baptist minister, and—along with Edward Bellamy, his famous cousin—an adherent of Christian socialism.

The year before, James Upham had come up with the idea of what he called a Public School Celebration, a patriotic commemoration of Columbus Day 1892. In 1891 Upham presented the organizers of the Columbian Exposition (also known as the Chicago World's Fair of 1893) with a plan for the event, which he renamed the National School Celebration. It was designed to take place at the same time as the fair's proposed groundbreaking on October 21, 1892, marking the four-hundredth anniversary of Christopher Columbus's voyage of discovery to America. Upham's plan, which the Exposition accepted in January 1892, was to have all the nation's schoolchildren take part in a flag-raising and flag-saluting ceremony that day. The National Education Association (NEA) and William Harris, the U.S. Commissioner of Education, endorsed the idea. The NEA formed a committee to promote the celebration; Francis Bellamy was chosen to be its chairman.

Former president Grover Cleveland, the Democratic nominee for president in 1892, also endorsed the National School Celebration. After intense lobbying from Bellamy, Congress passed a resolution on June 29 calling for the nation to observe Discovery Day on October 21 with "public demonstrations" and "suitable exercises in the schools and other places of assembly." October 21 was chosen because changes that were made in the calendar in the sixteenth century moved the date of Columbus's landing from October 12 to 21. Bellamy had been lobbying Pres. Benjamin Harrison to sign on to the idea, as well. As part of that campaign Bellamy wrote a letter to the president, urging Harrison to support a nationwide observance of Columbus Day in the schools.

"I am very much pleased with the idea," Harrison replied in a letter he wrote to Bellamy from the White House on May 23. "Properly conducted, such exercises will be very instructive to the pupils and will excite in every village in the land an interest in this great anniversary."

On July 21, Harrison issued a presidential proclamation making October 21 a "general holiday," and calling on schools to take part in the National Columbian Public School Celebration. *The Youth's Companion* published Harrison's proclamation in its September 8 issue. "Let the National Flag," the president proclaimed, "float over every schoolhouse in the country, and the exercises be such as shall impress upon our youth the patriotic duties of American citizenship."

The magazine promoted the upcoming celebration heavily. And it used it as an opportunity to sell flags. An advertisement for flags offered to send the celebration's official program—written by Francis Bellamy—to teachers for free. "Your school," the ad said, "will not let itself be left out of the Celebration. It must have a Flag."

One aspect of *The Youth's Companion* campaign to promote the celebration called for students across the land to ask their teachers and school boards to set up committees to organize local celebrations. Bellamy wrote many press releases and other materials, distributing them to thousands of newspapers and magazines pushing the idea. The Grand Army of the Republic signed on to help promote the event. "It is an immense thing," the GAR commander in chief John Palmer wrote to Bellamy. "It is the best thing the public school has ever thought of doing. It will impress all these pupils that they've got a country and it will make our people understand what a thing our free public school system is for America."

Bellamy also won the support of many members of Congress and other prominent national figures, including Theodore Roosevelt, who was then a U.S. Civil Service commissioner and a big supporter of the Lyceum League. "The part the Flag is to play appeals to me tremendously," Roosevelt wrote to Bellamy. "We are all descendants of immigrants, but we want to hasten that day, by every possible means when we shall be fused together. . . . Consequently, by all means in our power we ought to inculcate, among the children of this country, the most fervent loyalty to the Flag."

Public schools and the flag, Roosevelt continued, "stand together as the arch-typical of American civilization." The flag, he said, "represents not only those principles of equality, fraternity and liberty, but also the great pulsing nation with all its hopes, and all its past, and all its moral power. So it is eminently fitting that the Common School and the Flag should stand together on Columbus Day."

★   ★   ★

The "Official Programme for the National Columbia Public School Celebration of October 21, 1892," which Francis Bellamy wrote under Upham's direction, appeared in a page-and-a-half spread in the September 8 issue of *The Youth's Companion.* The program called for a flag raising by a group of veterans, a prayer, a Columbus Day song, and several speeches. It also included a "Salute to the Flag." Bellamy, John Baer said, built the program "around a flag ceremony and they built the flag ceremony around this new Pledge of Allegiance."

The salute contained twenty-two words: "I pledge allegiance to my Flag and the Republic for which it stands, one nation, indivisible, with liberty and justice for all." Bellamy looked for inspiration in choosing those words, he later wrote, in the Declaration of Independence and "the salient points of our national history," including "the meaning of the Civil War."

The "true reason" for allegiance to the flag, Bellamy said, "is the 're-public for which it stands.'" Bellamy said he considered "the republic" to be "the concise political word for the Nation—the One Nation which the Civil War was fought to prove. To make that One Nation idea clear, we must specify that it is indivisible, as Webster and Lincoln used to repeat in their great speeches." As for "liberty and justice for all," Bellamy said he was inspired by "Liberty, Equality, and Fraternity," the "historic slogan of the French Revolution which meant so much to Jefferson and his friends."

Bellamy drew up specific instructions for the entire ceremony, including what later was dubbed "the Bellamy salute." "At a signal from the Principal, the pupils, in ordered ranks, hands to the side, face the Flag. Another signal is given; every pupil gives the military salute: right hand lifted, palm downward, to a line with the forehead and close to it. Standing thus, all repeat together slowly [the Pledge]. At the words 'to my Flag,' the right hand is extended gracefully, palm upwards, toward the Flag, and remains in this gesture till the end of the affirmation; whereupon all hands immediately drop to the side. Then, still standing, as the instruments strike a chord, all will sing AMERICA—'My Country, 'tis of Thee.'"

The pledge was first recited at New York City's ceremony on October 12, when some thirty-five-thousand schoolchildren took part in the first of three days of Columbus Day celebrations. The rest of the nation celebrated on October 21, which was believed to be Christopher Columbus's true birthday. Millions of children all across the country took part. After Bellamy heard thousands of students in Boston recite the Pledge that day he added a twenty-third word, changing the Pledge slightly to read "I pledge allegiance to my Flag and *to* the Republic . . ."

All forty thousand public school students took part in Bellamy's special Columbus Day activities at their schools in Washington, D.C. The Pledge also was recited that day at a pomp-filled ceremony at the end of a three-day celebration in Chicago dedicating the Manufactures and Liberal Arts Building of the World's Columbian Exposition. Some 140,000 people, including many foreign visitors, attended. Two days earlier Chicago's schoolchildren had taken part in large-scale gatherings to pledge allegiance to the flag.

A National Liberty Pole and Flag Raising Ceremony held at the Navesink Atlantic Highlands Light Station in New Jersey, on April 25, 1893, featured the first massive adult Pledge recitation. The ceremony was the brainchild of William McDowell, one of the founders of the Sons and the Daughters of the American Revolution. Upham and Bellamy attended the ceremony, which took place several days before the Chicago World's Fair's opening. The site was chosen because it was one of the highest points on the eastern seaboard. A large flagpole was erected for the occasion. The Lyceum League donated the flags for the event.

At the ceremony a DAR member raised a flag, and it received a salute from U.S. Navy ships at anchor offshore. The attendees then saluted the flag with their right arms outstretched. Bellamy, with Upham beside him, led the recitation of the Pledge. In Upham's address he spoke about the importance of training patriotic young Americans to help America "fulfill her divine mission."

The World's Columbian Exposition, popularly known as the Chicago World's Fair of 1893, opened in the Windy City on May 1 that year. As was the case with the 1876 Centennial celebration in Philadelphia, the Chicago World's Fair celebrated the Industrial Age's progress in science, industry, and culture. The Ferris wheel was unveiled for the first time in America at the fair, as were the ice cream cone, Aunt Jemima pancakes, and the popcorn concoction known as Cracker Jack.

Pres. Grover Cleveland opened the fair by pushing an ivory-and-gold "electric button" that turned on the electric power for the exposition. Cleveland's action instantly illuminated a hundred thousand incandescent light bulbs and removed the shroud covering a statue of the *Republic* in the fair's main fountain. It also unfurled a large American flag. "The first tangible sign of the accomplishment of a conception which took 15,000 men and $33,000,000 three years to accomplish was then breaking loose at the top of the tapering mast in front of the grand stand of the Stars and Stripes as the sailor at the front pulled the halyards," the *New York Times* reported. "The glorious emblem threw its folds wide to the breeze, and cheer rose on cheer from 600,000 throats." From "every flagstaff along the upper edges of the buildings and on the towers and pinnacles, 2,000 flags and banners and pennants were unfurled. In the lagoons the steam launches blew their whistles, and a cloud of white vapor rose to the sky."

The act that marked the official closing of the fair on October 30: the lowering of the American flag.

★   ★   ★

Five years later, in 1898, New York became the first state to mandate that students recite the Pledge of Allegiance in public schools at the beginning of each school day. In 1916, the New York State Department of Education produced a textbook, *The Citizen Syllabus,* which was used in night school for adult immigrants nationwide. The forty-eight-page book contains a section on the American flag that includes the Pledge of Allegiance. By 1918, Rhode Island, Arizona, Kansas, and Maryland had enacted mandatory Pledge laws.

Delegates to the National Flag Conference in Washington, D.C., in 1923

The Pledge of Allegiance, which Francis Bellamy wrote in 1892, did not become officially recognized until 1942 when Congress included it in the U.S. Flag Code. New York City public school students are shown saluting the flag in January 1943. *The Library of Congress, Prints and Photographs Division*

and 1924 made two changes to the wording of the Pledge. At the behest of representatives from the American Legion and the Daughters of the American Revolution, the words "my Flag" were replaced with, first, "to the Flag of the United States," and, then later "to the flag of the United States of America."

On June 22, 1942, Congress officially recognized the Pledge of Allegiance by including it in the U.S. Flag Code, which also abolished the "Bellamy salute" because it resembled the salute used by the Nazis in Hitler's Germany. In October of that year the DAR's National Committee on the Correct Use of the Flag sponsored nationwide ceremonies marking the Pledge's fiftieth anniversary.

Section 4 of the Code states that the Pledge "should be rendered by standing at attention facing the flag with the right hand over the heart." Those not wearing a military uniform "should remove their headdress with their right hand and hold it at the left shoulder, the hand being over the heart." Those in uniform "should remain silent, face the flag, and render the military salute." The code also mandates that all future changes in the Pledge's wording—as well as any other flag "rule or custom"—may be made by the president, acting as commander in chief of the armed forces, "whenever he deems it to be appropriate or desirable; and any such alteration or additional rule shall be set forth in a proclamation."

Two years earlier, on June 3, 1940, the U.S. Supreme Court had ruled that a Pennsylvania law making it mandatory for teachers and students to salute the flag as part of daily school exercises was constitutional. That case, *Minersville School District v. Gobitis,* involved two children, Lillian and William Gobitis, who were expelled from school after refusing to salute the flag because their religion, Jehovah's Witnesses, considers the American flag an icon and follows the biblical injunction not to "bow down to graven images."

On January 9, 1942, the West Virginia Board of Education instituted a new policy in that state, ordering that the Pledge Allegiance become "a regular part of the program of activities in the public schools" and requiring that teachers and pupils "participate in the salute honoring the nation represented by the flag." Those who refused to salute the flag would be expelled and not permitted to return to school unless they agreed to take part in the daily Pledge of Allegiance.

That action prompted another legal challenge from Jehovah's Witnesses after several children were expelled from West Virginia public schools for refusing to recite the Pledge. This time the Supreme Court reversed its earlier ruling. By a 6–3 vote, the court voted to overturn the *Gobitis* decision. On Flag Day, June 14, 1943, the court, in *West Virginia State Board of Education v. Barnette,* ruled that schoolchildren could not be compelled to recite the Pledge.

Civil libertarians see that ruling as a precedent-making freedom of speech decision—and one that used the American flag to make its point. The historian Arthur M. Schlesinger Jr., for example, said the decision "clarified the meaning of the flag as the symbol of patriotism." The decision showed, Schlesinger said, that saluting the flag and pledging allegiance to the flag are "forms of speech," and that requiring "people to do these things violated their constitutional rights to freedom of speech."

Supreme Court justice Robert H. Jackson, in fact, prominently cited the First Amendment in writing the majority's decision. "If there is any fixed star in our constitutional constellation, it is that no official, high or petty, can prescribe what shall be orthodox in politics, nationalism, religion, or other matters of opinion, or force citizens to confess by word or act their faith therein," Jackson said. "If there are any circumstances which permit an exception, they do not now occur to us. The action of the local authorities in compelling the flag salute and pledge transcends constitutional limitations on their power, and invades the sphere of intellect and spirit which it is the purpose of the First Amendment to our Constitution to reserve from all official control."

Although the court had ruled on the unconstitutionality of mandatory pledge laws, state legislators nevertheless have enacted many such laws since the 1943 ruling. In 1970, for example, the Maryland General Assembly and the Massachusetts Legislature passed mandatory Pledge bills. Gov. Francis W. Sargent of Massachusetts vetoed the legislation in his state, and a Maryland Circuit Court overturned the Maryland law.

In the wake of the September 11, 2001, terrorist attacks, state legislatures across the country took a new interest in mandatory pledge laws. In the 2002 and 2003 legislative sessions, seventeen states enacted new pledge laws or amended existing Pledge of Allegiance policies. That brought the total number of states with some form of mandatory Pledge laws to thirty-five. The laws either required school districts to have teachers lead the Pledge or to have students to recite it. Nearly all of the state laws, because of the 1942 Supreme Court decision, contained language making the Pledge optional for students who objected to saying it on religious or other grounds.

Pennsylvania's 2003 law, which required the parents of students who refused to say the Pledge give written notification to that effect, was struck down by U.S. District Court judge Robert F. Kelly on July 15, 2003. Kelly ruled that the parental notification abridged students' First Amendment rights because it could put coercive pressure on their decision whether or not to recite the Pledge. The Pennsylvania statute, one of the most stringent Pledge laws in the nation, required public and private school students in the state, from preschool through high school, to face the flag and recite the Pledge or sing the National Anthem at the beginning of each school day. Kelly had blocked implementation of the law on February 6, 2003, after public and private school students challenged its constitutionality. The state of Pennsylvania appealed the case to the United States Court of Appeals for the Third Circuit, which heard arguments on March 9, 2004, and upheld the ruling on August 19, 2004.

★   ★   ★

The third change in the Pledge's wording came in 1954 when, prodded by a national campaign led by Luke E. Hart, the Supreme Knight of the Knights of Columbus, the Catholic men's fraternal benefit society, Pres. Dwight D. Eisenhower added the words "under God" after "one nation indivisible."

Congressman Louis C. Rabaut, a Michigan Democrat, had introduced a resolution in the House of Representatives the previous year calling for the addition of the words "under God" in the Pledge. But no action was taken on Capitol Hill on the matter until February of 1954. The catalyst for congressional action was a sermon given by Rev. Dr. George M. Docherty on February 7, 1954, at the New York Avenue Presbyterian Church in Washington, D.C. There was "something missing" in the Pledge of Allegiance, Reverend Docherty said. "Apart from the mention of the phrase, 'the United States of America,' this could be a pledge of any republic. In fact, I could hear little Muscovites repeat a similar pledge to their hammer-and-sickle flag in Moscow with equal solemnity."

Among the parishioners in church that day was President Eisenhower. Within days after the sermon, seventeen resolutions were introduced in the House and Senate to add "under God" to the Pledge. Both houses approved the resolutions in June. "At this moment in our history the principles underlying our American government and the American way of life are under attack by a system that does not believe in God," Congressman Charles Wolverton, a New Jersey Republican, said during the House floor debate on June 7. "The inclusion of God in our Pledge of Allegiance rightly and most appropriately acknowledges the dependence of our people and our government upon that divinity that rules over the destinies of nations as well as individuals."

President Eisenhower signed the measure into law on Flag Day, June 14, 1954. "From this day forward," he said, "millions of our schoolchildren will daily proclaim in every city and town, every village and rural school house, the dedication of our nation and our people to the Almighty. To anyone who truly loves America, nothing could be more inspiring than to contemplate this rededication of our youth, on each school morning, to our country's true meaning."

Including the words "under God," Eisenhower said, reaffirmed "the transcendence of religious faith in America's heritage and future. In this way we shall constantly strengthen those spiritual weapons which forever will be our country's most powerful resource, in peace or in war."

The inclusion of "under God" came during the Cold War with the Soviet Union. Two years later, in 1956, the words "In God We Trust," which first appeared on the two-cent coin in 1864, became the nation's national motto. "Since the Soviet Union was avowedly atheistic, many believed that the United States needed vigorously to support religion—specifically Christianity—in order to be successful in the titanic struggle," Whitney Smith of the Flag Research Center said.

The decision to include "under God" in the Pledge was not controversial in 1954. It, however, soon was challenged by parents, teachers, students, and others who argued that those two words violated the concept of separation of church and state. In 1964, the U.S. Supreme Court refused to review a New York state court's 1960 decision that upheld the use of the words "under God" as constitutional. In June 2002, the United States Court of Appeals Ninth Circuit, however, ruled in favor of Michael A. Newdow, an atheist, who sued the public school district in California where his daughter attended classes, arguing that the mandatory recitation of the Pledge with the words "under God" in schools violated the Establishment Clause of the First Amendment to the Constitution.

The U.S. Supreme Court agreed to hear the case on October 14, 2003, and heard arguments on March 24, 2004. On Flag Day, June 14, 2004, the court issued its decision in the case, unanimously reversing the Court of Appeals for the Ninth Circuit's ruling. The court, however, did not base its ruling on the constitutional question. Instead, it ruled that Michael Newdow—who was not married to his daughter's mother but shared custody of the ten-year-old—lacked the legal standing to sue on behalf of his daughter.

The Flag Day 2004 Supreme Court ruling, U.S. attorney general John Ashcroft said in a prepared statement, "insures that schoolchildren in every corner of America can start their day by voluntarily reciting the Pledge of Allegiance."

The ruling, though, left open the question of whether the words "under God" made the Pledge unconstitutional. Observers expected that more litigation would follow to force the courts to rule on that issue. "The justices ducked this constitutional issue today," the Reverend Barry W. Lynn, executive director of Americans United for Separation of Church and State, said on June 14, 2004, "but it is certain to come back in the future."

★   ★   ★

When *The Youth's Companion* published the original Pledge no credit was given for its authorship. An article in the magazine in December 1917 claimed that James Upham wrote the Pledge. For many years, until his death in 1931, Francis Bellamy spoke out strongly, claiming that he was the Pledge's author. The matter was settled in 1939 when the United States Flag Association, an organization formed in 1924 to promote the proper use and display of the flag, appointed a committee of distinguished historians to look into the matter. The committee weighed all the evidence and unanimously agreed on May 16, 1939, that Bellamy wrote the Pledge. A seventeen-month study undertaken by the Library of Congress in 1957 came to the same conclusion.

In 1985, President Reagan signed a law recognizing the pause for the Pledge of Allegiance, encouraging all Americans to recite the Pledge on Flag Day. In 1988, the Pledge became an issue in the presidential campaign between Republican George H. W. Bush and Democrat Michael Dukakis. Bush criticized Dukakis for vetoing a bill that would have required the Pledge to be recited in Massachusetts's public schools when Dukakis was the governor of that state in 1977. Dukakis, Bush said, "isn't willing to let the teachers lead the kids in the Pledge of Allegiance." Dukakis responded that he vetoed the legislation after being advised by the Supreme Judicial Court of Massachusetts and his state attorney general Francis X. Bellotti that a mandatory pledge law was unconstitutional and unenforceable.

During the height of the campaign, on September 13, 1988, the Pledge was recited on the floor of the House of Representatives for the first time. Republican members of the House, who were in the minority, offered a resolution to that effect; and Speaker of the House Jim Wright, a Texas Democrat, accepted it. Congressman G. V. Sonny Montgomery, the chairman of the House Committee on Veterans' Affairs, a Mississippi Democrat, recited the Pledge that day. Speaker Wright ruled that from that day forward the Pledge would be recited at the start of business each day the House of Representatives was in session.

The U.S. Senate did not adopt the daily recital of the Pledge until June 24, 1999. Republican senator Strom Thurmond of South Carolina recited the Pledge that day for the first time in that legislative body after the Senate unanimously adopted a resolution offered by Sen. Bob Smith, an Independent from New Hampshire. It went into effect the same day that the House of Representatives had voted to adopt an amendment to the Constitution to ban flag desecration.

"The U.S. Senate started reciting the Pledge in 1999; the House in 1988. Essentially, it's moved from a children's procedure to one that adults use," noted John Baer. "Local governments and state legislatures now recite the Pledge. You have a fascinating phenomenon there."

That phenomenon also includes the fact the United States is the only nation in the world that has codified the use of a pledge of allegiance to its national flag. As Baer put it: "The verbal flag salute is unique and has something to do with the fact that we are a republic. It's right up there with the Declaration of Independence and the Gettysburg Address."

CHAPTER THIRTEEN

The Great War

★   ★   ★

As I see the winds lovingly unfold the beautiful lines of our great flag,
I shall seem to see a hand pointing the way of duty, no matter how
hard, no matter how long, which we shall tread while we vindicate the
glory and honor of the United States.

—**Pres. Woodrow Wilson, Flag Day, June 14, 1916**

HAVE NAILED THE STARS and Stripes to the Pole." Those
were the words of a telegram sent from the Smoky Tickle telegraph station
at Indian harbor in Labrador on September 6, 1909, by U.S. Navy rear admiral Robert Edwin Peary to his wife, Josephine, at their summer home on
Eagle Island in Casco Bay off the Maine coast. The pole the veteran polar
adventurer referred to was the North Pole, which he and his associate and
fellow explorer Matthew Henson and their four Inuit guides had reached
five months earlier, on April 6—the first humans to do so.

The American flag "had a certain sacred symbolism to" Peary, his daughter Marie Peary Stafford explained. "In a sense, the flag *was* the country,
and flags had always played an important and thrilling part in his exploration work."

In 1898 Josephine Peary made a large, gold-fringed, taffeta, forty-five-star American flag for her husband as he was about to embark on a four-year expedition into the Arctic. That silklike homemade flag, his daughter
said, "meant more to him than all the replicas in the world. He carried it with
him always when in the field, wrapped around his body underneath his fur
clothing because he did not wish to trust it to a sledge," which might break
through the ice. Peary cut out five pieces of the flag to leave as markers at

noteworthy places "whenever he had attained one of his objectives," as his daughter put it, in northern Greenland and northern Ellesemere Island in Canada in 1900 and 1906. The "Stars and Stripes" that the Peary party planted at the North Pole actually was the sixth piece of Josephine Peary's flag, a four-inch-wide diagonal strip of that flag cut diagonally to include both stars and stripes.

That act captured the popular imagination in this country. Even though the flag placed at or near the North Pole (probably by Henson) was but a fragment of an entire flag, the image of an intact Old Glory flying on a pole at the top of the world became instantly accepted when the news of Peary's feat reached the American populace. That image has resonated with the American public since then. Newspaper and magazine accounts helped spread the idea. That included the newspaper columnist and poet Leigh Mitchell Hodges's ode to Perry and Henson's achievement, "The Flag That Tops the World." It contained the stanza:

> *You may sing a song of banners that are brave against the breeze,*
> *Of flags that ne'er in time of need are furl'd;*
> *You may boast the battle ensigns that have swept the seven seas,*
> *But I toast the starry flag that tops the world!*

Had Peary's flag been official and up to date, it would have had forty-six stars, in recognition of Oklahoma's entry into the Union in 1907. A government study undertaken when Oklahoma became a state found that federal agencies were flying sixty-six different-sized and proportioned American flags. That situation prompted the federal government to set up a special panel to consider the look of the forty-six-star flag. The panel was put together by the War Department—the predecessor of the Department of Defense—and consisted of army and navy officers. Eighty-year-old admiral of the navy George Dewey, who was then serving as the president of the General Board of the Navy, headed up the effort. Dewey's panel recommended a flag with six rows of stars in the canton: four rows of eight and two rows of seven.

The Territories of New Mexico (on January 6) and Arizona (on February 14) became the nation's forty-seventh and forty-eighth states in 1912. That prompted another session of Dewey's panel to consider the arrangement of the forty-eight-star flag, which would become official on July 4, 1912. The committee recommended a flag with the stars arranged in six horizontal even rows of eight stars each, with one point of each star facing upward.

On June 24, 1912, Pres. William Howard Taft accepted the Dewey committee's recommendation and signed a groundbreaking executive order setting out the star arrangement for the forty-eight-star flag. That executive order marked the first time since the Stars and Stripes was born in 1777 that a president officially clarified exactly what the American flag should look like and what dimensions the government would accept for its flags. Taft's order cut the number of official government flag sizes to twelve and used the Dewey panel's recommended forty-eight-star arrangement.

Taft's executive order applied only to government flags, but it also served to curtail the number of creatively designed flags by private individuals. One exception was the Whipple flag of 1912, the creation of Wayne Whipple, a Germantown, Pennsylvania, author who had written a hagiographic history, *The Story of the American Flag,* for children in 1910. Whipple designed a flag in a heraldry contest and had high hopes that it would become the official forty-eight-star flag. He took his flag to President Taft. The president, Whipple said, "went into ecstasies over it," and recommended it to the War and Navy Departments. Whipple also lobbied veterans' and patriotic groups across the nation on behalf of his creation.

In his flag thirteen stars were arrayed midcanton in the shape of a six-sided star; twenty-five stars circled that star, with ten additional stars sitting in an outer circle. The thirteen stars symbolized the original states; the twenty-five stars stood for the states that entered the Union in the nation's first one hundred years; the ten stars represented the states that joined after 1876. Whipple referred to his creation, which was not chosen as the nation's official banner, as the "Peace Flag."

World peace, however, was shattered in Europe in 1914 with the outbreak of World War I, the mammoth "war to end all wars" that forever altered the world's political landscape and caused unprecedented loss of life and carnage in western Europe and Russia. The Great War, as it was called—along with the 1918 influenza pandemic—resulted in the deaths of some 8.5 million combatants and some 13 million civilians, in addition to some 21 million wounded and 7.7 million missing or imprisoned. The United States entered the war in April 1917.

Shortly after war broke out in Europe in August 1914, former president Theodore Roosevelt and U.S. Army chief of staff Gen. Leonard Wood, among others, formed the preparedness movement. The idea was to lobby the Wilson administration and to convince the American public of the need to get the nation ready for war. The movement called for compulsory military training for all able-bodied young men. In conjunction with organizations such as the National Security League, the American Defense Society, and the League to Enforce Peace, it organized a series of preparedness parades around the nation to publicize the cause. These parades prominently featured the Stars and Stripes.

The first preparedness parades took place in 1914. For the next three years, until the United States entered the war in April 1917, similar parades were put on all over the country, mostly in cities, from Buffalo to San Francisco. Preparedness parades reached a peak in 1916 as it became clear that this country would be sending troops to Europe to fight in the war.

Some seven thousand people marched in Baltimore's preparedness parade on May 17, 1916, and more than one hundred thousand flag-waving spectators cheered them on. On Saturday, June 3, 1916, more than fifty-two thousand men and women took part in a massive, flag-waving, seven-hour preparedness parade in Providence, Rhode Island. That same day some thirty-five thousand men marched in New Orleans's preparedness parade. Only two banners were permitted in that parade: the Stars and Stripes and the Stars and Bars held aloft by Confederate veterans.

An even larger preparedness parade had taken place in New York City on May 13, 1916. The eleven-hour parade began at City Hall Park and moved up Broadway and Fifth Avenue. It featured some 125,000 marching civilians and dozens of brass bands and drum corps. An estimated crowd of a million people lined the march. The parade was led by an enormous, ninety-five-foot by fifty-foot American flag that had been made by the Amoskeag Manufacturing Company in Manchester, New Hampshire, in 1914.

That huge flag was far from the only one flying that day. "Almost every marcher carried an American flag," the *New York Times* reported. "Almost every building along the line of march was covered with the red, white and blue bunting of the national colors. Every spectator wore 'Old Glory' or carried a tiny flag. The effect was a sea of red, white and blue that billowed and moved. Probably never before in history has there been such a showing of the flag and its colors."

The profusion of flags in the city and at the parade proved to be an inspiration to Childe Hassam, the nation's leading Impressionist painter. Soon after the May 1916 New York parade, the prolific and influential Hassam began a series of paintings that featured the streets of New York decorated with American flags. "I painted the flag series after we went into the war," Hassam told an interviewer in 1927. "There was that Preparedness Day, and I looked up the avenue and saw these wonderful flags waving, and I painted the series of flag pictures after that."

Hassam, whose studio was on West Fifty-seventh Street near Sixth Avenue, turned out thirty flag paintings during the next three years, inspired by that first preparedness parade and the many patriotic parades held in the city thereafter during the war. The paintings featured flags mounted on buildings along Fifth Avenue between Thirty-third and Fifty-seventh Streets and other nearby New York streets. The subjects included the Waldorf-Astoria Hotel, the Union League Club, the Friar's Club, and St. Patrick's Cathedral.

Hassam executed "Allies Day, May 1917" following the visit of the French and British war commissioners to this country the month after the United States entered the war. It showed a grouping of the British Union Jack, the French Tricolor, and the Stars and Stripes, which likely was the first time those three flags had been displayed together in public. Hassam's goal was to keep the flag paintings together as a tribute to the American war effort, but they were sold individually. Today the paintings are in private collections and art museums, including the National Gallery of Art in Washington and the White House.

Childe Hassam was not the only American artist who used the flag in his work during World War I. A group of artists, led by the famed illustrator Charles Dana Gibson, in April 1917 organized the Division of Pictorial Publicity for the federal government's Committee on Public Information. In the next eighteen months Dana and many other artists turned out 700 posters, 287 cartoons, and 432 newspaper advertisements. All were designed to build public support for the war effort. The Stars and Stripes was used widely in those works. "The American flag," the art critic Ilene Susan Fort noted, "was an extremely potent symbol of unity and liberty and often appeared [in the Pictorial Publicity works] in conjunction with other stock subjects," such as the Statue of Liberty.

One of the committee's contributors, the serendipitously named James Montgomery Flagg, had created one of the nation's most famous and enduring posters for the cover of the July 6, 1916, *Leslie's Weekly*. Titled "What Are You Doing for Preparedness?" the poster shows a scowling "Uncle Sam," replete with a red- white- and blue-starred hatband, pointing an accusatory finger at the viewer. More than four million copies of that poster with the inscription "I Want You for U.S. Army" underneath were printed by 1918. The poster went on to become an icon of American culture.

The figure of Uncle Sam, usually clad in striped pants and a white jacket festooned with stars, dates from the War of 1812. Historians believe

The aptly named James Montgomery Flagg created one of the nation's most famous and enduring posters for the cover of the July 6, 1916, *Leslie's Weekly*. More than four million copies of that poster with the inscription "I Want You For U.S. Army" underneath were printed by 1918. The image soon became an icon of American culture. *The Library of Congress, Prints and Photographs Division*

he was based on Samuel Wilson, a patriotic meat packer in Troy, New York. Wilson supplied food to the U.S. military, stamping his shipments with the letters "U.S." for the United States government. Wilson soon became known as "Uncle Sam" Wilson. Thomas Nast and other political cartoonists made frequent use of a stylized, stars-and-stripes-clad figure of Uncle Sam throughout the nineteenth century as a symbol representing the United States and patriotism.

The flag also was a prominent feature on many other World War I home-front posters, including military recruiting posters and those produced by civic groups such as the YMCA and the Red Cross, the United War Work Campaign, the U.S. Department of Labor, and the U.S. Food

Administration. "Rally 'Round the Flag with United States Marines," said a Marine Corps recruiting poster that featured an image of marines storming a beach with a large American flag waving overhead. A 1918 Red Cross poster by Harrison Fisher depicts a beautiful young woman volunteer clasping a large American flag to her bosom with the U.S. Capitol in the background. Her mouth is open and the words "I summon you to Comradeship in the Red Cross" are emblazoned on the poster.

The flag was a prominent feature on many World War I home-front posters, including military recruiting posters and those produced by civic groups such as the YMCA and the Red Cross. *The Library of Congress, Prints and Photographs Division*

In many ways the outpouring of affection for the flag prior to and during World War I resembled the outburst of flag waving in the North that began at the start of the Civil War in 1861 and lasted until the fighting ended four years later. Within hours after World War I was declared on April 6, 1917, flags were displayed from public and private buildings all across America. "Though the city has been besprinkled with flags in the

last weeks, a veritable flood of bunting broke forth yesterday" in New York
City, the *New York Times* reported April 7. "Now is the time above all others
that citizens should show their country's colors," the *Los Angeles Times* edi-
torialized on April 6. "The Stars and Stripes should wave from every business, house and residence in the city."

In Washington, D.C., in response to a nationwide public outcry, American flags began flying twenty-four hours a day over the east and west
fronts of the U.S. Capitol. Flag-waving patriotic pageants, with names
such as "Building of the Flag, or Liberty Triumphant" and "A Pageant of
the Stars and Stripes," took place in communities and schools throughout
the nation.

A joint resolution Congress passed on May 8, 1914, authorizing the
president to designate the second Sunday in May as Mother's Day contained language calling for the American flag to be displayed that day
"upon all Government buildings," as well as for "the people of the United
States to display the flag at their homes or other suitable places" as "a public expression of our love and reverence for the mothers of our country."
President Wilson issued the first Mother's Day holiday proclamation the
next day. Two years later he established June 14 as national Flag Day
through a presidential proclamation.

Not long after the United States entered the war in April 1917, the New
York commissioner of education, Henry Sterling Chapin, organized a
nation-wide contest to choose a national creed, what Chapin envisioned as
"the best summary of the political faith of America." Some three thousand
entries were submitted. Baltimore's mayor, James H. Preston, offered a
one thousand dollar prize. The winning entry was the work of William
Tyler Page of Chevy Chase, Maryland, a descendant of U.S. president
John Tyler. Page worked in the U.S. House of Representatives and in 1919
became the Clerk of the House.

Page's winning entry, now known as the American's Creed, was published in the *Congressional Record* on April 3, 1918, the day Page was awarded
his one-thousand-dollar prize on Capitol Hill by Mayor Preston. The federal
government has never accepted the creed officially; but many patriotic
groups, including the Daughters of the American Revolution, have adopted
it. The creed contains words and phrases borrowed from Lincoln's Gettysburg Address, the Declaration of Independence, and the Preamble to the
Constitution. It ends with a pledge of allegiance to the nation and its flag: "I
believe it is my duty to my country to love it, to support its Constitution, to
obey its laws, to respect its flag, and to defend it against all enemies."

World War I created an "unprecedented demand and runaway market" for American flags, the Federal Trade Commission reported in July 1917. Sales of flags reached an all-time high during the war. Businesses, including Wanamaker's Department Store in Philadelphia and Marshall Field & Company in Chicago, produced and distributed written materials promoting the flag. Marshall Field's sixteen-page pamphlet, *Laws and Customs Regulating the Use of the Flag of the United States*, was written by B. J. Cigrand, the Chicago dentist and national Flag Day proponent.

"In presenting to the public this booklet for distribution, it is with the hope that it may prove to service in making readily available such information as will tend to increase the evidences of public respect for our national emblem," Cigrand wrote in his introduction.

National Geographic magazine devoted an entire special issue in October 1917 to flags, concentrating on the history of the American flag. The navy's top flag expert, Lt. Cmdr. Byron McCandless, an aide to the chief of naval operations William S. Benson and to the secretary of the navy Josephus Daniels, edited the issue. It contained a sixteen-page history of the American flag with illustrations and photographs, including one of the Star Spangled Banner being restored by "expert needlewomen" at the Smithsonian. Another photo, with the caption, "The French Army's First Salute to the Stars and Stripes on French Soil," showed a flag ceremony on the French front in June 1917 with members of the American Ambulance Corps and the French army. Five thousand copies of the issue were distributed free of charge to American troops on their way over to France.

Men went off to war with flag-inspired patriotic words ringing in their ears. "The American flag and the many things that it stands for should be their constant thought," former senator J. C. Pritchard of North Carolina, then a judge of the U.S. Court of Appeals, Fourth Circuit, told a patriotic gathering of citizens in Raleigh on September 23, 1917. "Let them cherish this glorious emblem of our liberty."

African Americans, the overwhelming majority of whom supported the war effort, also exhibited affection for the American flag. Some 350,000 black Americans served in World War I in segregated units. Although most of the black units were support troops, several fought in the trenches in France. "True Sons of Freedom," a 1918 poster by Charles Gustrine, depicts black American fighting men in hand-to-hand combat with German soldiers. The American flag waves prominently in the background, with Abraham Lincoln looking down benignly on the scene. The words "Liberty and Freedom Shall Not Perish" are inscribed under Lincoln's visage. The poster also contains the words: "COLORED MEN: The First Americans Who Planted Our Flag on the Firing Line."

At home, many black women were active in efforts to support the war. The thinking among most black Americans was that patriotically taking part in the war effort would lead to more freedom at home after the fighting ended. On June 14, 1918, large numbers of African Americans marched in several flag-saturated parades in honor of Flag Day, including a large parade in Wilmington, Delaware. "Material manifestation of the patriotism of the Negroes of Wilmington was given," the *Cleveland Advocate* reported, "when in honor of the Flag Day—the anniversary of the Stars and Stripes—5,000 local members of the race, men women and children, gave a decidedly credible parade, which was applauded by thousands of white persons who lined the streets over which it passed."

The startling success of a fund-raising event for Liberty Bonds (U.S. government war bonds) in New York City in 1918 featuring an American flag flown in battle in Europe offers a good illustration of the unfettered veneration Americans held for the flag during the war. The flag in question actually consisted of two streamers cut from an American flag and flown on the struts of a British Royal Flying Corps (RFC) plane by the first American air ace of the war, Frederick Libby, an all-but-forgotten American military hero.

Libby grew up on a ranch in Sterling, Colorado. As a young man he became one of the last of a dying breed, a true American cowboy who made his living roping, punching cattle, and taming horses in Arizona, New Mexico, and in his home state. Libby found himself in Calgary, Alberta, Canada, when the war broke out in 1914. He promptly joined the Canadian army and went to France where he signed up as an aerial observer/machine gunner with the RFC, immediately taking to the air in a wooden two-seater FE 2b biplane.

In May 1916, Libby moved to the pilot's seat, where he took part in some of the world's first aerial battles, going head to head with, among others, the legendary German ace Manfred von Richthofen. Libby survived his showdown with the Red Baron and went on to shoot down fourteen enemy aircraft before transferring to the U.S. Air Service in September 1917.

At Buckingham Palace in November 1916 King George V awarded Libby the British Military Cross for conspicuous gallantry in action. In 1917, Libby took the streamers from an American flag and hooked them onto the struts of the plane he flew in battle. An English RFC major "suggested that I use [the flag] as a streamer or streamers just to show the Hun that America had a flyer in action," Libby said in his memoir. "This I did—from May 28 until my return to America" in October. "During this period, there were always one or two streamers of an American flag over the German lines." It was not done "with any idea of a stunt to be first with anything," Libby said. "It was done in the line of duty and at the suggestion of my squadron commander."

Libby came back to this country in October 1917 and brought the streamers to New York City, where he donated them to the Aero Club of America to auction off at a Carnegie Hall fund-raiser for Liberty Bonds. "The action wasn't intended by me as a stunt for publicity," Libby said. "In fact, I had a feeling of embarrassment, as these streamers had been a part of my plane for many, many hours of combat service."

When Libby took the Carnegie Hall stage at the October 17, 1918, fund-raiser, the crowd "rolled forward in tumult of noise, men and women with welcome in their voices and tears in their eyes," the *New York Tribune* reported. "Then a girl reached out and over the crowd, caught hold of the tattered thing, held it hard and with swimming eyes raised it to her lips. The voices stopped and the air was silent as a prayer." Then the crowd "sought to grasp the precious stripes" of the flag and to shake Libby's hand. "And so the procession passed along," the article said. "Some touched it lightly, some shook it as if it were a paw. The women kissed it, the soldiers saluted it."

The enthusiastic reception given Libby's American flag streamers was reminiscent of the situation in the North during the Civil War when Major Anderson's Fort Sumter Stars and Stripes was used as a highly effective fund-raising tool at auctions supporting the war effort. Libby's streamers outdid the Fort Sumter flag, however. The streamers were auctioned at Carnegie Hall following the bidding on a French Legion of Honor cordon. As the bidding on Libby's streamers began, someone in the audience shouted, "If the cordon of the French Legion of Honor is worth a million dollars, how much is Old Glory worth?" The answer was provided by the National Bank of Commerce, which bought Libby's tattered streamers for $3,250,000—the equivalent of more than $40 million today. The winning bid contained the proviso that Captain Libby would be allowed to keep the streamers.

The American flag also was popular in Canada, England, France, and Belgium and elsewhere outside of Germany in western Europe after the United States entered the war. On April 6, 1917, the day the United States declared war on Germany, the American flag flew for the first time ever alongside the Union Jack on the Canadian Parliament Building in Ottawa.

The Stars and Stripes also was raised over Ottawa's city hall and many other public buildings that day. The citizens of England expressed their gratitude to this country in the days after the United States declared war with an unprecedented display of the American flag. That included, for the first time in history, the flying of a foreign flag next to the Union Jack outside of Parliament.

"The Stars and Stripes almost instantaneously broke out on private dwellings, shops, hotels, and theatres" in London when the United States declared war on Germany, one observer wrote. "Street hucksters did a thriving business selling rosettes of the American colours, which even the most stodgy Englishmen did not disdain to wear in their buttonholes; wherever there was a band or an orchestra, the Star Spangled Banner acquired a sudden popularity."

U.S. ambassador Walter H. Page organized what he called "an American Dedicatory Service" at St. Paul's Cathedral in London in April. The royal family attended, as did British government officials, members of Parliament, the ambassador corps, and a hundred wounded Americans serving in the Canadian army. My "Navy and Army staff went in full uniform," Page said in a May 3, 1917, letter, "the Stars and Stripes hung before the altar, a double brass band played the Star Spangled Banner and the Battle Hymn of the Republic, and an American bishop preached a red-hot American sermon, the Archbishop of Canterbury delivered the benediction; and a foreign flag flew over the Houses of Parliament."

The situation was similar in France. When the United States entered the war, the American flag flew at the French National Assembly at the Palais Bourbon in Paris next to the French Tricolor and along the streets of Paris and other French cities. On April 11, Raymond Poincaré, the president of the French Republic, joined with many other government officials, French military officers, and others in ceremonies commemorating the American entry into the war. "Great crowds surrounded the building" where the ceremonies were held, the *Washington Post* reported. "There were many tiny American flags, and vendors had a lively traffic in postcards of Uncle Sam and President Wilson and rosettes of French and American flags entwined." That same day the Lafayette Flying Squadron (or Escadrille), a group of Americans fighter pilots serving with the French, received orders to don American uniforms and thereby became the first American unit to take the Stars and Stripes into battle in World War I.

By the summer of 1918, the American flag was a common sight in the streets of the French capital. "In Paris, the red, white and blue of France is so blended with the red, white and blue of America that it is difficult to tell at a glance where one flag begins and the other ends," *New York Times* correspondent Charles A. Seldon reported on July 3. Sheldon described the American flag flying at several of Paris's famed landmarks, including the Louvre, the Place de la Concorde, and the Hotel de Cluny. He found the flag as well "in regions where English will never be spoken" and "in obscure little streets that were streets long before America was discovered, in streets of old Paris, of the Franks and the Romans."

★   ★   ★

Not long after the United States entered the war, the U.S. Department of Justice let it be known that Germans and other aliens who were discovered "abusing or desecrating" the American flag "in any way" would be subject to "summary arrest and confinement" as a "danger to the public peace or safety" during the duration of the war. In 1918 Congress passed and President Wilson signed into law an addition to the June 1917 Espionage Act, called the Sedition Act. That measure, among other things, made it illegal to "willfully utter, print, write or publish any disloyal, profane, scurrilous, or abusive language" about the Constitution, the government, or the American flag. The Sedition Act also banned the willful display of the flag "of any foreign enemy." Those acts were punishable by a fine of not more than ten thousand dollars or twenty years in jail. The law also mandated that any U.S. government employee or official who, "in an abusive and violent manner criticizes the Army or Navy or the flag of the United States shall be at once dismissed from the service."

During World War I several states strengthened the language and increased the penalties of their flag protection laws—which originally had been designed mainly to cut down on the commercial use of the flag. And Congress, on February 8, 1917, approved a bill making it a misdemeanor punishable by a one-hundred-dollar fine or thirty days in jail for manufacturing, selling, or advertising items decorated with the American flag in the District of Columbia. That included canned goods, post cards, and sheet music, as well as stores' show-window decorations.

Kansas enacted a law in 1915 making it a misdemeanor to "publicly mutilate, deface, defile, or defy, trample upon, or cast contempt, either by words or act upon any" American flag. Three years later Frederick Shumaker Jr. of Wetmore, Kansas, was convicted under the statute for making "a very vulgar and indecent use of the flag." He was accused of using language in a blacksmith's shop so foul that the court would not spell it out because the words would become part of the official record. Shumaker apparently had referred to the flag as "a rag." He appealed his case to the Kansas Supreme Court and lost.

Texas's Disloyalty Act, which became law on March 11, 1918, made flag desecration punishable by up to twenty-five years in jail. The law imposed that strict penalty on those convicted of using "any language" in public or private that "cast contempt" on the American flag.

Montana enacted a similarly worded law in February 1918. Six months later a man named E. V. Starr was arrested, tried, and convicted in Montana for the words he said after a mob tried to force him to kiss an American flag. "What is this thing anyway, nothing but a piece of cotton with a little paint on it and some other marks in the corner there," Starr said. "I will not kiss that thing. It might be covered with microbes."

It is unclear from court records and newspaper accounts if the mob turned on Starr for political reasons. What is clear is that federal and state officials enforced flag protection laws during the war primarily against those who spoke out against the war effort—most often labor activists, pacifists, socialists, anarchists, and communists—as well as German immigrants, German-Americans, and those who expressed sympathy for the German cause. A New York City woman was arrested and sent to jail for six months in March 1918, for example, for displaying a German flag and for taking down an American flag put in her window and then saying the words: "To hell with the American flag. I want my own flag."

Outside of the law, citizens took measures against German-Americans and others who spoke out against the war effort. Vigilante actions of this sort typically involved forcing a suspected unpatriotic person to salute the flag, to recite the Pledge of Allegiance, or to kiss the flag. The self-appointed flag defenders may have taken their cue from the stern words of President Wilson in his April 2, 1917, war message to a special session of Congress. Speaking about Americans "of German birth and native sympathy who live among us," Wilson warned what would happen if they were not loyal during the upcoming war. "If there should be disloyalty," he said, "it will be dealt with with a firm hand of stern repression."

Shortly after the war began in April 1917, a man thought to have insulted a flag in Santa Cruz, California, was forced to kneel on the sidewalk and kiss it. At around the same time, a mob of angry citizens attacked a socialist and two suffragists who would not rise for the playing of "The Star-Spangled Banner" at a New York City supper club. On April 12, 1918, in Collinsville, Oklahoma, a mob forced a German-American, Henry Rheimer, to kiss an American flag and then tried, unsuccessfully, to hang him with an electrical cord.

The day the war ended, November 11, 1918, five carloads of men drove eleven miles outside of Burrton, Kansas, and ransacked the house and farm of John Schrag, a German-speaking Mennonite who had immigrated to this country when he was thirteen years old in 1874. The men took Schrag into town where he faced a larger mob, unhappy over the fact that he had refused to buy Liberty bonds. Schrag offered, instead, to donate money to the Red Cross or Salvation Army. The mob then demanded that Schrag salute the American flag and parade it through town. He refused.

When a flag that was forced on him dropped to the ground, the crowd set upon Schrag, covered him with yellow paint, and attempted to hang him. He was saved by the head of the local Anti-Horse-Thief Association. Schrag escaped with his life but was arrested for violating the Espionage Act because he allegedly desecrated the American flag. He was tried in federal court in Wichita and found not guilty.

The most egregious incident involving the flag and a German-American's supposed criticism of the war occurred near St. Louis in April 1918. Robert Paul Prager, a thirty-year-old German-American, was taken from his home in nearby Collinsville, Illinois, by a mob of some three hundred people — members, the *Chicago Daily Tribune* said, "of the local loyalist committee." Prager was forced to march down the street barefoot carrying two small American flags. He was wrapped in a large American flag and made to kiss the flag as he walked. An unemployed miner, Prager had given a speech earlier in the evening at a socialist meeting in which he allegedly made disloyal remarks.

Collinsville police placed him in custody for his own safety. Outside the jail, the mayor of Collinsville talked the mob into dispersing. But the group reformed, broke into the jail, and hanged Prager to death from a tree just after midnight on April 5. At his funeral on April 10, a large American flag was draped over Prager's coffin. Police arrested eleven men and charged them with Prager's murder. A jury found them not guilty in Edwardsville, Illinois, on June 8.

As the Prager case showed only too well, the American flag evoked exceptionally strong emotions during World War I. When the war ended in 1918, most Americans continued to feel very strongly about the flag and what it stood for. Those strong feelings continued unabated in the 1920s, pushed along in large part by veterans of the Great War who banded together to form the powerful veterans' service organization, the American Legion.

CHAPTER FOURTEEN

One Hundred Percent Americanism

★   ★   ★

The Flag of the United States—a beautiful, artistic, inspiring emblem, standing for our National sovereignty, ideals, traditions, and institutions; a sacred symbol of our political faith, appealing so strongly to every American—affords, indeed, an ideal rallying point for the citizens of the Republic—rich and poor, high and low—to assemble and join hands in working together for lofty Americanism, sturdy patriotism, and good citizenship which shall make stronger and more secure the foundations on which this Government is built.

—United States Flag Association, 1924

WORLD WAR I ended with the armistice on November 11, 1918, thanks in no small measure to the battlefield contributions of the two-million-strong American Expeditionary Force under U.S. Army general John Joseph "Black Jack" Pershing. Not long after hostilities ended, state legislatures began enacting laws declaring November 11 Armistice Day to remember the sacrifices of those who served in Europe. Twenty-seven states had made November 11 a legal holiday by 1926.

On June 4 of that year Congress passed a resolution asking the president to issue an annual proclamation for a federal Armistice Day holiday. The resolution called for the American flag to be displayed on all government buildings that day and urged all Americans to observe the day "in schools and churches, or other suitable places, with appropriate ceremonies of friendly relations with all other peoples." On May 13, 1938, Congress approved legislation that made November 11 an annual legal holiday.

When World War I ended, American troops helped occupy Germany and remained in Europe throughout the first half of 1919. On March 15, 1919, at the behest of U.S. Army lieutenant colonel Theodore Roosevelt Jr., the son of the nation's twenty-sixth president, a group of army officers and enlisted men met at the Cirque de Paris, a large building bedecked with American flags and red, white, and blue bunting for the occasion. This was the Paris caucus at which Roosevelt and company founded the American Legion, a veterans' service organization that became the spiritual successor of the Grand Army of the Republic, which by the 1920s was rapidly declining in membership and influence.

The American Legion was born at the end of that three-day caucus in Paris and immediately began attracting large numbers of World War I veterans. A thousand delegates showed up at the Legion's first American caucus on May 8 in St. Louis, where the organization pledged itself to work for "God and Country." When Congress granted the Legion its national charter of incorporation on September 16, there already were 5,670 local posts in every state in the Union and in Europe. By 1920, some 840,000 World War I veterans had joined, about a fifth of those eligible for membership. Within a year after the Paris caucus met "the Legion established itself . . . as the most powerful veterans organization in American history," as the historians John Lax and William Pencak put it.

Today the American Legion has nearly three million members in some fifteen thousand local posts, making it the largest veterans' organization in the world. The Legion's posts are organized into fifty-five departments in the fifty states, the District of Columbia, Puerto Rico, France, Mexico, and the Philippines. The Legion's national headquarters is in Indianapolis, and it maintains a large additional office in Washington, D.C.

From the beginning the American Legion, as was the case with its spiritual predecessor the GAR, had several agendas. At its heart the organization was an advocacy group working on behalf of disabled veterans and their families. It was also a fraternal organization that offered fellowship and companionship at local posts across the country. But the American Legion also was a political organization. Its constitution pledged that the Legion would be "absolutely nonpolitical" and not be used "for the dissemination of partisan principles" or to endorse political candidates. However, the constitution also said that the Legion would work to "maintain law and order; to foster and perpetuate a one hundred percent Americanism," and to "combat the autocracy of both the classes and the masses."

The Legion's 100 percent Americanism agenda came about in reaction to the 1914 communist revolution in Russia and to the leftist social and political movements related to Bolshevism and Marxism in the United States that had gained many adherents by 1919. The Legion's political agenda included a heavy attachment to the flag, a deep involvement in promoting respect for the flag, and teaching proper flag etiquette. In one of its first actions, in January of 1921, the Legion successfully lobbied the Massachusetts Boxing Commission to issue a ruling prohibiting boxers from wearing the American flag in the ring during state-sanctioned boxing matches.

A political cartoon that appeared in the Memphis *Commercial Appeal* in 1919 clearly illustrates the importance of the American flag to the American Legion. Titled "The New National Figure," the cartoon by James P. Alley depicts a giant of a man attired in a World War I army hat and britches, his face resolute, his well-muscled arms crossed at his chest, and the words "American Legion" on his shirt. Behind him a large American flag is unfurled. At his feet are small, shiftless human figures labeled "Anarchy," "Lawlessness," "Class Autocracy," and "Petty Politics."

This was a time of severe social conflict in the United States that included anarchist bombings, extreme labor unrest, race riots, and lynchings of African Americans in the South and elsewhere. Many believed Communists were behind the unrest. What was called the Red Scare—a fear of communists, socialists, anarchists, labor radicals, and a xenophobic reaction against immigrants—spread throughout the nation. That fear often was expressed as an assault on the American flag by political cartoonists in the nation's top newspapers. A Fred Morgan cartoon in 1919 in The *Philadelphia Inquirer*, for example, consisted of a large American flag (with only thirty-six stars) being attacked by a bearded, evil-looking man clutching a large knife with the word "Bolshevism" on it and a flaming torch labeled "Anarchy."

A 1919 Raymond O. Evans cartoon in the Baltimore *American* showed an anarchist tossing a bomb that was blocked by a large American flag and sent on its way back to blow him up. A John H. Cassel cartoon in the New York *Evening World* in 1920 depicted an evil Karl Marx–like figure holding an emasculated American flag that consisted only of the red stripes—red being the color of communism.

The flag itself often was used as a symbol in the fight against the Red Scare. That was the case, for example, during a three-day strike by local unions that nearly shut down the city of Seattle in February 1919. Mayor Ole Hanson, calling the strikers anarchists and comparing them to Bolsheviks, threatened to impose martial law to end the strike. To boost his cause, the mayor draped a large American flag over his car as he led a detachment of U.S. Army troops from nearby Fort Lewis to confront the strikers.

The world's largest American flag of its day, measuring 71 feet by 37 feet and weighing 90 pounds, hung from the interior courtyard of the old U.S. Post Office Building in Washington, D.C., in the summer of 1922. *The Library of Congress, Prints and Photographs Division*

One of the first orders of business for the American Legion in 1919 was setting up its Americanism Committee, which later became the National Americanism Commission. The committee's goal was to promote what it termed "100 percent Americanism" by fighting what it believed were anti-American activities, by teaching immigrants and American citizens the principles of Americanism, and by spreading the word on Americanism in the nation's schools. The American flag was the primary symbol of the Legion's Americanism effort. Other groups, including the American Protective League and the Ku Klux Klan, used similar Americanism tactics as a way to counteract the influence of political radicals.

In 1917, the National Conference of Commissioners on Uniform State Laws—an organization that since the early 1890s had been drawing up suggested model laws for state legislatures—approved a Uniform Flag Law. It was almost identical to New York's flag protection law, which that state had adopted in 1905. That measure provided that "No person shall publicly mutilate, deface, defile, defy, trample upon, or by word or act cast contempt upon any such flag, standard, color, ensign or shield." Even though the conference approved the proposed law, it was adopted by only a handful of states.

Garland W. Powell, a World War I veteran and former Maryland state senator who had a strong interest in the American flag, became the American Legion's National Director of Americanism in 1919. In his book, *Service for God and Country,* Powell offered a treatise on Americanism, including advice about flag etiquette. Powell contacted other groups interested in the flag, proposing that they meet in a national conference to put together a uniform national code of flag etiquette.

Even though President Taft's 1912 executive order had cut down drastically on free-lance American flag designing, "there were a lot of flags being used during and directly after World War I," Whitney Smith said. "A lot of people thought [the flag] was being used improperly. The Army and Navy had regulations regarding the flag because they have regulations regarding everything. Various veterans' organization had their own ideas. So . . . they all decided to get their act together."

Powell's organizing efforts came to fruition on June 14, 1923, when the Legion's Americanism Committee convened the first National Flag Conference. It took place at Memorial Continental Hall, located in the DAR's national headquarters complex near the Washington Monument and the White House in Washington, D.C. In addition to the Legion and the DAR, sixty-six other groups took part in the gathering. The U.S. Army and Navy sent representatives. Samuel Gompers, the president of the American Federation of Labor, attended, as did representatives from groups such as the DAR, the Sons of the American Revolution, the Boy Scouts of America, the National Congress of Mothers and Parent-Teachers Associations, the United Daughters of the Confederacy, and the Ku Klux Klan.

"I hope you will succeed in forming a code that will be welcomed by all Americans," Pres. Warren G. Harding said during his forty-minute speech at the opening ceremonies, "and that every patriotic and educational society in the republic will commit itself for the endorsement and observance and purposes of that code." American Legion national commander Alvin Owsley, in a statement issued from the organization's Indianapolis headquarters, said the conference "will develop a definite code of rules so that every man, woman and child in this country may know how to honor and revere the American flag. Let us not be ashamed to demonstrate our loyalty and affection for the flag. May we take pride in revealing this sentiment before our fellow countrymen, for it is a worthy and manly emotion."

The conferees did, indeed, agree on the nation's first Flag Code. They based it heavily on a War Department *Flag Circular* that had been published earlier in the year. Much of what the code contained was apolitical and had to do with practical matters, such as the proper ways, times, positions, and occasions to display the flag. The code also included the Pledge of Allegiance and the proper ways to render it, as well as a section on the proper ways to respect the flag. The conference agreed to replace the words "my Flag" in the Pledge of Allegiance with "to the Flag of the United States." The Second National Flag Conference on May 15, 1924, amended that language slightly to read: "to the flag of the United States of America."

There was, however, an antisocialist, anticommunist political dimension to the conference. Harding administration secretary of labor James J. Davis expressed the gist of that feeling when he warned the conference that "disrespect for the flag" was one of the "first steps" toward communist revolution.

The Flag Code that the conference came up with became big news. In the weeks after the 1923 conference, virtually all of the nation's large newspapers published the new code. Other newspapers followed suit on the Fourth of July. The American Legion and the other organizations that took part in the conference published their own booklets explaining the new code and distributed them by the millions. Fifty-one additional patriotic, hereditary, and veterans organizations took part in the Second National Flag Conference in Washington in 1924. That gathering, however, made only minor revisions to the work done the year earlier.

The Flag Code did not become the law of the land until 1942 during World War II. On June 22 of that year, Congress passed a resolution, which Pres. Franklin D. Roosevelt signed into law, adopting the code with several small changes as part of Title 36 of the United States Code. The code was slightly amended in December 1942 and several other times in subsequent years. It remains in effect today. Although the Flag Code is a national public law, it does not call for penalties for violations of its provisions.

"It is a set of guidelines for proper flag usage, but it is not illegal to display the flag in contravention of the Code," Whitney Smith noted. "Military and civil branches of the government have their own regulations, but in the private sector it is appropriate that the freedom symbolized by the flag itself should be reflected in the way citizens display it."

★   ★   ★

When the white supremacist Ku Klux Klan—which formed late in 1865 and had been virtually dormant since the early 1870s—was revitalized in the 1920s the group soon took a strong interest in promoting the American flag. Klansmen dressed in white robes, hoods, and sheets decorated with Klan symbols and, later, the American flag. The group had disbanded in 1869 as Klan violence veered out of control but was reborn with a vengeance in the fall of 1915 under Col. William Joseph Simmons. The former preacher led a group of men flying the American flag to the top of Stone Mountain, Georgia, where they set a pine cross on fire and proclaimed the Klan's rebirth. The KKK gained hundreds of thousands and then millions of adherents, primarily in the South, Midwest, and West, by the early 1920s.

The Klan crusaded against Catholics, Jews, immigrants, African Americans, political corruption, labor unions, and immorality, and pushed for prohibition and traditional family values. Violence and physical intimidation sometimes were used. But the Klan of the 1920s also often worked openly. It staged parades, marches, conventions, and social events that included the prominent display of the American flag and the organization used the flag as one of its primary symbols. Members, for instance, were required to swear allegiance to the flag and to the U.S. Constitution.

Local Klan groups, known as klaverns, typically gave flags—and Bibles—to Protestant churches and schools. The KKK "stands for the two greatest gifts that Heaven has bestowed, namely the Holy Bible" and "the American flag handed down by our forefathers who fought and died to keep it clean and spotless." Those words were contained in a letter presented to the minister of the Methodist Church in Prescott, a small town in southwest Arkansas, by a group of ten white-robed Klansmen who made an appearance during Sunday services there in the fall of 1922. Another example of many: At the April 1923 dedication of the Riverside Church of Christ in Wichita, Kansas, the local KKK chapter presented the congregation with a large American flag and a flagstaff.

The Klan lobbied for legislation requiring schools to fly the flag. It endorsed the Flag Code and required its Junior League members to learn proper flag etiquette. Local Klan groups took part in Flag Day parades, often on horseback, always with the American flag flying prominently. At Klan rallies members flew American flags from their cars and Klanswomen wore dresses made from American flags. A KKK meeting in Sidney, Ohio, in August 1923 ended with a display of cross burnings and "the American flag in fireworks," according to an account in the *Sidney Daily News*. In Oregon and other states robed Klansmen nailed American flags to the doors of Catholic schools.

The Klan featured the American flag prominently on its paraphernalia. A KKK poster of the era, entitled "We are all Loyal Klansmen," depicts a stars-and-stripes-clad Uncle Sam holding a large American flag with five white-hooded-and-robed Klansmen standing behind him. A 1920s KKK pewter commemorative coin featured a night rider on one side and an American flag and a fiery cross on the other, along with the words "America First" and "Preserve Racial Purity." A 1920s Klan bronze belt buckle shows a Klansman holding a Bible and carrying an American flag in front of a burning cross on a hillside.

The KKK used distortions and outright lies about the flag to deliver its message. A report in the May 31, 1924, Klan publication, *The Fiery Cross*, for example, made up stories about clashes with University of Notre Dame students that supposedly took place at a May 17 KKK parade in South Bend, Indiana. Under the headline, "Roman Students of Notre Dame Trample Flag," an article reported that the Catholic students had stoned a flag that flew over the Klan headquarters building, insulted and ridiculed Klan women, and assaulted an elderly Klan couple.

The Klan's power and influence began to wane significantly in the late 1920s. The organization won few supporters during the Depression and disbanded in 1944. There was a second rebirth during the mid-1960s in reaction to the Civil Rights Act of 1964. The KKK still exists today with comparatively few members in several separate and competing groups. At its public gatherings, KKK members continue to fly the American flag, often alongside the Confederate battle flag and the flag of Nazi Germany.

★   ★   ★

On April 24, 1924, retired U.S. Army colonel James A. Moss, a West Point graduate and a veteran of the Spanish-American War and World War I, founded the United States Flag Association in Washington, D.C. Moss headed the foundation until his death in 1941. His association soon became an influential national voice that focused on promoting flag etiquette and patriotism based on veneration for the flag and what it symbolized. The association also worked to counteract the spread of communism, crime, and anarchy.

When asked why there was a need for the association, Col. Thomas Denny, the governor of the Society of Mayflower Descendants and an officer of the association's New York State board, said: "Growing influences and forces which are detrimental to the ideals, traditions, institutions and principles on which the Republic is founded and which are symbolized by the flag of the United States."

The association had a national council of forty-eight members, one from each state. Moss recruited thirteen prominent men and women — "typifying the 13 stripes of the flag," he noted — to be the organization's titular sponsors. The group included former Supreme Court justice (and future chief justice) Charles Evans Hughes, then serving as U.S. Secretary of State; Wilson administration vice president Thomas R. Marshall; Card. William Henry O'Connell of Boston; Rabbi Abram Simon of Washington Hebrew Congregation; Bishop James E. Freeman of the Washington Cathedral; union leader Samuel Gompers; and New York governor Alfred E. Smith. Pres. Calvin Coolidge agreed to be the association's honorary president; Pres. Herbert Hoover followed suit in 1929; and Franklin D. Roosevelt did so in 1933.

Moss also named Elihu Root, the 1912 Nobel Peace Prize recipient who had been William McKinley's Secretary of War and Theodore Roosevelt's Secretary of State, the organization's "active president." The presidents and the sponsors, though, did little more than lend their names to the United States Flag Association. "The Association was mostly a one-man effort that Moss ran as director-general," Scot Guenter said. "Financial support came mostly from Washington politicians whose aid Moss procured. The Association's main activity was the production and distribution of pamphlets and books that Moss wrote on proper flag etiquette."

The association also lobbied for Congress to enact flag protection legislation. In December 1924, the association linked that message to a call for the American public not to buy Japanese-made American flags. "Flags made in Japan," the association said, "are of such cheap material that, when they become wet, the colors run and the result is something that looks more like the red flag of Bolshevik Russia than the flag of the United States." The statement noted that the association issued the public appeal because Congress had "refused to enact a national law prohibiting the improper use of the flag."

One of the association's first publications, *Today's Flag Day, June 14th,* was a combination brochure and membership application published in 1924. The brochure painted an unabashedly positive picture of the American flag's history and meaning, showering accolades on the flag in flowery, ultrapatriotic prose.

On its front page the brochure repeated the Betsy Ross myth as if it were fact. Under a drawing of Betsy Ross with the flag on her lap was the caption: "George Washington, Colonel Ross, and Robert Morris, committee appointed by Congress 'designate a suitable flag for the Nation,' commissioning Betsy Ross to make the first Flag." The caption under an accompanying drawing of a thirteen-star "Betsy Ross" flag contained the completely fanciful statement that the arrangement of the stars "in a circle typifies that the Union shall be without end."

The brochure also set out Moss's vision of what his organization would do to promote the flag. The flag, he said, "should be brought into greater consideration and more appreciative regard by the citizenry of the Republic." Schoolchildren, he said, "should be taught what the Flag stands for" and "they should be taught to pay it proper respect and reverence." The association's "aims and purposes," Moss said, were "in the interest of lofty Americanism, sturdy patriotism, and good citizenship: To bring into greater consideration and higher appreciative regard by the citizenry of the Republic the Flag of the United States as the visible, symbolic representation of our National sovereignty, ideals, traditions, and institutions."

Life membership in the association, which Moss referred to as a "great American patriotic society," was open only to American citizens. The membership fee was one dollar for adults and twenty-five cents for children. All members signed on to the association's pledge: "I pledge myself to assist in carrying out the aims and purposes of The United States Flag Association, encouraging the paying of reverence to the Flag and helping to prevent it from being subjected to disrespect or improper use."

In the 1930s the association became more involved in crime fighting and fighting communism in the United States. Moss set up what he called the Steering Committee of the National Council of '76 to work on the effort. The committee sponsored a National Anti-crime Conference in 1933. It focused on "helping to create and galvanize into action public sentiment for the enforcement of law and the defeat of communism in the United States," as Patrick J. Hurley, the former secretary of war, put it at an association program held on July 4, 1935.

In 1938 Moss began a campaign to have the second week of June celebrated as Flag Week. He called for a week-long commemoration of the flag and what it stands for with rallies at schools and patriotic, civic, and social clubs, along with parades and community celebrations. By 1941, thirty of the forty-eight governors had proclaimed National Flag Week, along with some 650 mayors.

James Moss died in an automobile accident in New York City on April 23, 1941. A little more than a year later the U.S. Flag Association ceased to exist. Its mantle was taken up, however, by several other organizations, including the American Flag Movement and the United States Flag Foundation, which was established in December 1942. The latter organization was the predecessor of the National Flag Foundation, the Pittsburgh-based nonprofit group that was founded in 1968 and today is, in many ways, the twenty-first-century equivalent of Moss's United States Flag Association.

The National Flag Foundation bills itself as "America's flag authority" and "the voice of patriotic education." George F. Cahill, a patriotic World War II veteran who headed the Boy Scouts of America's regional council in Pittsburgh, founded the foundation. The nonprofit group promotes the display of the flag, as well as "love of country, respect for the flag and civic responsibility to all Americans." It maintains a Flags of America art collection at its headquarters in Pittsburgh's Flag Plaza, and sells prints of flag artwork.

The foundation aims its main programs at schoolchildren. That includes its Young Patriots educational program, which provides teachers with videos, Web sites, and teachers' guides that contain the flag's history, teach respect for the flag, and encourage students to recite the Pledge of Allegiance.

The foundation's Flags Across America program promotes establishing flag plazas in cities and towns across the land. The main feature of each plaza is an enormous thirty-foot-by-sixty-foot American flag and its 120-foot flagpole. The first such site, in Johnstown, Pennsylvania, was dedicated in 1989 to commemorate the one-hundredth anniversary of the devastating Johnstown flood. The purpose of the program, the foundation says, "is to boost patriotism, unite citizens, and build greater respect for our national symbol." Several dozen plazas have been dedicated and many more are in the planning stages.

The Veterans of Foreign Wars of the United States (VFW), which was formed when several Spanish-American War veterans' organizations merged in 1913, also heavily promotes reverence for the American flag and proper flag etiquette through its flag-oriented Americanism Program. The VFW, which today has some 1.8 million members in some nine thousand local posts around the world, is open to veterans who have served overseas in war zones or other hazardous duty areas around the world. The VFW's

Americanism Program grew out of the VFW's Americanization Committee's drive to "Americanize America" in the 1920s by promoting the use of the English language among immigrants, encouraging immigrants to become American citizens, instituting a nationwide "Buy American" campaign, and working to take "un-American" textbooks out of the nation's schools.

"The fact that our population is becoming more varied as immigration continues presents [a] problem," Herman R. La Tourette, Patriotic Director for the VFW's Department of New York, told a crowd of some five thousand on June 14, 1926, at the fifth annual Americanization rally in Prospect Park in Brooklyn. "We repudiate all who profess even the smallest degree of loyalty to any other nation. We assert that no man is an American who bears in his heart the slightest allegiance to any flag except the Stars and Stripes, and we mean not only the flags of foreign powers, but the red flag of anarchy and the black flag of international socialism."

The VFW's Americanization Committee produced a booklet, "Etiquette of the Stars and Stripes," which it distributed widely to schools, local VFW posts, and to other organizations. The VFW also was a leader in the movement to have "The Star-Spangled Banner" declared the National Anthem.

Today flags and flag education remain important elements of the VFW's Americanism Department's Citizenship Education Program, which promotes the teaching of citizenship in the nation's schools. The VFW's School Flag Education Program brings members of the organization into the nation's schools to teach respect for the flag and flag etiquette. Color guards from local posts take part in flag presentation ceremonies at many events, including get-out-the-vote drives and Veterans Day, Pearl Harbor Day, Memorial Day, Fourth of July, and other commemorations. The VFW's Emblem and Supply Department sells flag patches, flag information booklets, as well as some 250,000 flags each year.

CHAPTER FIFTEEN

United We Stand

★　★　★

Take every other normal precaution for the protection of Army headquarters, but let's keep the flag flying.

— Dispatch from Gen. Douglas MacArthur, December 15, 1941,
U.S. Army Far Eastern Forces Headquarters, Manila

THE AMERICAN FLAG, Pres. Herbert Hoover said in his Flag
Day 1932 message, "stands for all that has been accomplished by our people in the century and a half of this nation's existence. That accomplishment
was based on and made possible by faith, fortitude, resolution, courage,
and character." Hoover went on to make a plea to the American people to
"renew" that faith and to resolve "that we will hand on to the next generation, unimpaired by the passing emotions of temporary distress, these national traits and the American system which they have built."

The "temporary distress" Hoover referred to was the Great Depression,
which had begun in 1929 and would turn out not to be temporary. By the
end of 1932, the year Hoover uttered those words, manufacturing output in
the United States had dropped to more than half of what it was in 1929,
and the nation's unemployment rate reached nearly 30 percent. Economic
and social conditions did not improve until the late 1930s. America's entry
into World War II in December 1941 ended the Great Depression, the
longest and most severe economic downturn in American history.

The American flag was an important symbol of the war effort for American troops on the fields of battle in Europe, Africa, Asia, and the Pacific, as
well as on the home front. On December 8, 1941, the day the United States

declared war on Japan following the December 7 attack on Pearl Harbor, Americans used the flag as they did at the outbreak of World War I and of the Civil War: to show solidarity in time of national crisis.

"As if by magic, Fifth Avenue and other thoroughfares [in New York City] showed a spontaneous display of American flags" on December 8, the *New York Times* reported that day. Loudspeakers broadcast President Roosevelt's "a date which will live in infamy" radio address that afternoon to outdoor crowds. "Men removed their hats when 'The Star-Spangled Banner' was played," following the speech, the newspaper said, "in restaurants and offices, every one stood up."

John Cashmore, the borough president of Brooklyn, issued a proclamation on December 11 urging all Brooklynites to fly the flag every day during the war. Flying the flag, the proclamation said, would be "visible evidence of the determination of the people of America to remain steadfast in their resolve that this nation under God will stamp out the treacherous forces of tyranny and aggression which are now attempting to enslave the world."

Soon after Pearl Harbor, dry cleaners across the country announced that they would clean American flags without charge. The first cleaning establishment that offered that patriotic service was the C. G. Howes Company of Boston, which had begun free flag cleaning in August 1940. Upon doing so, the company was deluged with more than a thousand flags a week from churches, schools, American Legion posts, and businesses. "If there was ever a time in the history of the Nation when the Stars and Stripes should be universally displayed, it is in these crucial days," the United States Flag Association wrote to Howes's general manager. "We wish to commend you for your patriotic efforts to encourage and stimulate the display of our Country's Flag."

Citizens everywhere flew flags as a sign of support for the war effort. The residents of one block in New York City's South Bronx—158th Street between Melrose and Courtlandt Avenues—displayed 146 large American flags on gleaming white poles every day during the war in honor of the men from the street who were serving in the armed forces. On Memorial Days the residents—nearly all of them of Irish, Italian, Polish, and German ancestry—added four more flags suspended from ropes across their street.

As it did during World War I, the flag also resonated with America's allies in the war against Germany and Japan. On New Year's Day 1942 the American flag flew alongside the British Union Jack at Westminster Abbey in London in observance of a special day of prayer. Eight days later

Royal Air Force planes dropped nearly two million propaganda leaflets over German-occupied Paris and its environs and the city of Lille in France. The leaflets, printed in French, contained a photograph of the Statue of Liberty—a gift to the United States from France—and of the American flag. In December 1941 the official Tass news agency in the Soviet Union produced large anti-German posters prominently featuring images of the American, British, and Soviet flags and distributed them throughout that nation.

"Until recently," Walter B. Kerr, the *New York Tribune* foreign correspondent reported from Moscow, "the American flag seldom has been seen in this country, except over the American Embassy at Moscow and the consulate at Vladivostok."

Pres. Franklin D. Roosevelt, on June 22, 1942, approved the U.S. Flag Code that had been passed by Congress. On February 19, 1944, Roosevelt issued a presidential proclamation allowing the use of the flag's image on items exported to American allies, exempting those items from the portion of the code that prohibited placing images of the flag on commercial products. Roosevelt's decree authorized use of the flag on labels, packages, cartons, and containers intended for export as Lend-Lease Aid, as relief and rehabilitation aid and as emergency supplies for American territories and possessions. Such use, his proclamation said, "shall be considered a proper use of the flag of the United States and consistent with the honor and respect due the flag."

Roosevelt took that step, he said, after five U.S. senators had made a battle-front tour in 1943 and reported that British firms put the image of the Union Jack on food items sent to the Allies. American companies had been hesitant to take the step because they were afraid some flag-embossed food containers would inadvertently be distributed in the United States, thereby violating the Flag Code. The flag, Roosevelt said in his proclamation, is "universally representative of the principles of the justice, liberty, and democracy enjoyed by the people of the United States." People "all over the world recognize," the Stars and Stripes, he noted, "as symbolic of the United States."

Allowing the image of the American flag to be used on products shipped to our Allies, Roosevelt said, would foster "a proper understanding by the people of other countries of the material assistance being given by the government of the United States." Not to mention help with the "effective prosecution of the war."

Back at home, in San Francisco, the city Park Commission ordered that the Japanese Tea Garden in Golden Gate Park fly the American flag for the first time. The commission also changed the Tea Garden's restaurant's bill of fare from tea served by young women in kimonos to coffee and donuts served by women in "American garb." In Los Angeles, the city council enacted an ordinance on March 11, 1942, making it illegal to sell American flags and other "patriotic emblems" that were not endorsed by the city's Social Service Commission. The action was taken after City Councilman Carl Rasmussen had purchased a small American flag from a street vendor and then noticed that it was made in Japan.

Americans at home did not tolerate the few recorded instances of disrespect to the flag during the war. Five days after Pearl Harbor, for example, two factory workers at the Hatfield Wire & Cable Co. in Hillside, New Jersey, were fired for refusing to salute the flag at a lunch-hour flag raising. The dismissals of the unidentified workers, the *New York Times* reported on December 12, "were demanded by other employees who said they would not return to work if the two were retained by the company." The plant's United Electrical Radio and Machine Workers Union affiliate approved the action. A New York magistrate fined Dietrich Meyer, a naturalized German citizen, fifty dollars in May 1945 for displaying an upside-down American flag in his delicatessen in the Bronx. The charge was disorderly conduct.

In the nation's capital, the outbreak of war changed the custom of lowering the American flag at the White House when the president was not in residence. Instead, the White House staff, in an effort not to make President Roosevelt's itinerary public, raised the flag in the morning and lowered it at sundown every day. The practice of flying two flags twenty-four hours a day at the Capitol Building, which began during World War I, continued with one change. The flags no longer were illuminated at night because of blackout regulations.

Some patriotic observers felt that Americans did not display the flag in sufficient numbers in the first months after the United States entered World War II. "Everybody flew the flag during the last war, but this time people have hardly realized yet that we are at war," W. A. Mandelberg, the manager of the soon-to-be disbanded United States Flag Association's New York City office, said in January 1942. "Look out my office window. You can see . . . four flags on a dozen flagstaffs." That, he said, was "not enough. In wartime, every building ought to fly the flag."

Two weeks after war was declared, the demand for flags was heavy, but not at World War I levels. Flag sales "are now showing increases of between 15% and 25%," the *Wall Street Journal* reported on December 17, 1941, "as compared with a 100% increase when this country entered World War I." In Chicago, on the other hand, flag dealers sold out their entire inventories a day after war was declared. That came despite the fact that the dealers had stocked up on flags during the spring and summer of 1941. A survey of flag manufacturers and dealers in New York City the next summer found "an industry besieged with orders, from both civilians and the government," the *New York Times* reported August 2, 1942, "most companies reporting a demand that was either 'terrific' or 'very high.'"

President Roosevelt issued a proclamation on May 10, 1942, directing the federal government and asking state and local governments and individual Americans to fly the Stars and Stripes on Flag Day, June 14, in honor of "the nation's mothers and their valiant sons in the service." He also took the unprecedented step of encouraging Americans "where feasible" to fly the twenty-six flags of the nation's World War II allies that day.

As was the case in World War I, scores of colorful, patriotic posters urging Americans at home to back the war effort featured a flag motif. Artists working for the government, patriotic groups, and private industries produced the posters. One of the first issued by the Office of War Information after it was created to serve as the federal government's main wartime propaganda agency was a painting by the artist Allen Saalburg of a tattered American flag flying at half-mast. The poster featured the famous phrase from Lincoln's Gettysburg Address: ". . . we here highly resolve that these dead shall not have died in vain . . ." at the top and "REMEMBER DEC. 7th!" in red capital letters on the bottom.

Large corporations pitched in by commissioning posters designed to build morale, increase industrial production, and conserve materials needed for the war effort. Those posters were distributed to the military, to government offices, and to defense plants. One such poster, produced by the General Cable Corporation, consisted of Uncle Sam's accusatory finger bursting through the stripes of an American flag with the words: "Are YOU doing all you can?"

Military recruiting and government war bond posters, not surprisingly, also featured the flag. That included the women's branches of the armed services. "Are you a girl with a Star-Spangled heart?" asked a Women's Army Corps (WAC) poster. Below those words a large American flag flew behind the image of a beautiful, resolute-looking Army WAC. A Navy WAVE poster had a similar design: a young, attractive woman in uniform staring purposefully, with a large Stars and Stripes making up the poster's background.

"Follow the Flag" were the words on a navy recruiting poster that contained the image of an athletically built, determined male sailor planting a
large American flag on a faraway island. "Let's Go Get 'Em!" topped a U.S.
Marine Corps recruiting poster, which depicted two marines in battle with
the Stars and Stripes and the Marine Corps flag waving behind them. A war
bond poster contained the image of an American soldier grasping a large
Stars and Stripes with the caption, "To Have and to Hold!" Another depicted
the Statue of Liberty, an American flag, and a city skyline along with the
words, "Keep Old Glory Forever Free. Buy More Bonds for Victory."

Magazine advertisements often bore patriotic messages and the image
of the American flag. An ad for Camel cigarettes that appeared in *Life* magazine in 1943, for example, focused on a Pan American Airways employee,
Patricia Garner, who worked as a ground traffic controller. She was pictured waving her guiding flags in front of a Pan Am aircraft with the American flag painted on its fuselage. "Behind those flags in her hands there's a
flag in her heart," the ad says, "the Stars and Stripes she's serving while
working at a war job. A man's job! —but she's the *real* All-American girl,
1942 model."

★   ★   ★

The most extensive home front display of the American flag during the war
came in July 1942, seven months after Pearl Harbor. That month more
than four hundred magazines put versions of the Stars and Stripes on their
covers in a coordinated effort called "United We Stand." The name came
from a line in "The Liberty Song," a 1768 tune written by the Pennsylvania
patriot and statesman John Dickinson. The song, which was popular during the American Revolution, contained the words:

> *Then join in hand, brave Americans all!*
> *By uniting we stand, by dividing we fall.*

Paul MacNamara, a Hearst Corporation publicist, conceived the 1942
"United We Stand" campaign. He envisioned it as a way of selling more
magazines and boosting home-front morale during a time when the U.S.
war effort had yet to produce much positive news. Roosevelt administration treasury secretary Henry Morgenthau Jr. supported the endeavor,
seeing it as an opportunity to sell war bonds. The Treasury Department un-
derwrote special displays for the magazines in some twelve hundred stores

nationwide. Walter Winchell, whose blunt-talking gossip column appeared in some eight hundred newspapers across the nation, backed the campaign by warning magazine publishers of the consequences if they didn't get on board.

Hundreds of publishers, large and small, did get on board. That included all the popular magazines, such as the *Saturday Evening Post*, *National Geographic*, *Life*, *Look*, *Time*, *Vogue*, *Esquire*, *Harper's Bazaar*, *The New Yorker*, *Popular Mechanics*, *Business Week*, *Family Circle*, *Gourmet*, and *Ladies Home Journal*. The covers of children's comic books depicted superheroes clutching American flags. Specialty magazines such as *Steel* and *The Lutheran* also joined in. *The Ring* magazine's cover had a photograph of heavyweight boxing champion Joe Louis and his challenger Billy Conn in army uniforms, saluting, with an American flag in the background. *Screenland*, the movie magazine, offered a photograph of the sultry movie star Veronica Lake in a red-and-white bathing suit, alongside an American flag. The cover of *Poultry Tribune* showed a young boy saluting a phalanx of eggs aligned in platoon formation with the lead egg flying a small American flag. Many magazines also used the words "United We Stand" on their covers and urged readers to buy war bonds.

The United States Flag Association, then in its last year of existence, supported the "United We Stand" magazine campaign by sponsoring a contest to reward the best covers. A panel of judges, including the photographers Margaret Bourke-White and Edward Steichen and the artist Norman Rockwell, chose *House & Garden*'s cover as the overall winner. It consisted of an image by Allen Saalburg of a large American flag folded back at one corner with Mount Vernon, George Washington's home, in the background.

The 1942 "United We Stand" campaign used the American flag to enforce the message that the home front was a crucial part of the war effort. "The flag was a rallying point," said Paul Kreitler, a retired Episcopal priest who owns a collection of about 325 of the magazines. "People saw in the red, white, and blue certain meanings: White represented purity, blue loyalty, red the blood that generations before us shed to preserve our freedoms. The flag became identified with the fact that we might lose these freedoms if we all don't participate."

During the war singing "The Star-Spangled Banner" became a standard feature at movie theaters across the country. Theater owners and the Hollywood studios cooperated in that patriotic endeavor. In addition to producing a steady stream of war films idealizing the American effort, the studios also produced National Anthem trailers designed to be shown before the feature films started. The trailers depicted patriotic images including the American flag, or simply the image of a waving flag. The Fox Movietone News version, sung by Merrill Miller, included a crawl with the words to the song. When the trailer came on the screen, audiences stood, placed their right hands over their hearts and sang along. Some theaters repeated the ritual after the feature film ended.

One of the most popular movies released during World War II was 1942's *Yankee Doodle Dandy*. That ultra-flag-waving musical told the story of the life of George M. Cohan, who had made his reputation with a series of flag-waving hits on Broadway four decades earlier. James Cagney starred as Cohan in a film that featured lavish, flag-drenched production numbers of the title song and of "You're a Grand Old Flag."

Audiences also sang the National Anthem before performances by symphony orchestras around the country, as well as before Broadway shows. "They did it in every Broadway theater. If it was a musical, the orchestra would play and everyone in the audience would stand and sing along," a New York City woman said. "If there wasn't an orchestra, someone would come on stage and lead the audience in singing."

★   ★   ★

More than sixteen million American men and women served virtually everywhere around the globe during the Second World War. Nearly everywhere they went, American troops displayed the Stars and Stripes. Paratroopers of the U.S. Army's 82nd Airborne Brigade and 101st Airborne Division, for example, wore red, white, and blue American flags on their jump suit sleeves when they parachuted behind enemy lines on D day, June 6, 1944. "They wore American flags on their right shoulder to identify themselves to French citizens in occupied areas who had never seen an American soldier, but would recognize the Stars and Stripes," said Dale Dye, the former marine who is Hollywood's leading military technical adviser. "They generally kept the flag on their uniforms until later in the hedgerow fighting when some removed the patch to assist in camouflage efforts."

Within a day after the D day invasion, U.S. troops had anchored American flags on the Normandy cliffs. As they took French towns from the Germans in the ensuing days, the troops often displayed American flags; some were the same flags the troops had raised in triumph as they fought their way up the Italian peninsula in 1943 and 1944.

American troops taken prisoner by the Japanese when they captured the Philippine island of Mindanao in 1942 managed to bring the canton of an American flag with them to their prison camp in Japan. They kept it hidden for three years. Then, in 1945, using materials that had been dropped by parachute from American planes, the prisoners fashioned a complete Stars and Stripes. That flag now is on exhibit in the Admiral Nimitz Museum and Historical Center in Fredericksburg, Texas. The flag "exemplifies all that they struggled for," said Helen McDonald, the center's curator. "Had they been found with those stars, as prisoners of war, they would have been punished, or even executed."

American pilots and crews carried small American flags with the words "I am an American" printed on them in Russian on bombing raids over eastern Germany near the end of the war. "They gave us small American flags to put in one of the zippered pockets of our flight suits," said Harry A. Dooley, who served as a B-17 navigator in the Eighth Air Force's Ninety-first Bombardment Group. "If you [were shot down and] thought you might be in friendly territory, but weren't sure because of the language barrier, you'd show them the flag, and they'd understand you weren't Russian or English. That flag was your universal I.D. There aren't too many people who don't recognize the American flag."

The Stars and Stripes flew in triumph in cities across Europe as the American forces defeated the German army in Italy and moved into Germany in the spring of 1945. U.S. troops also unfurled American flags in the war against Japan in the Pacific. In his World War II memoir, the historian William Manchester described the American flag that a fellow marine hung and flew during the fierce August 1942 battle of Tanambogo Island during the first part of the Guadalcanal Campaign against the Japanese. American flags were planted as U.S. forces landed and took over other Japanese-occupied islands in the South Pacific.

That included the seven-mile-long island of Iwo Jima, located in the Bonin volcano group in the Western Pacific. That small island of volcanic rock dominated by an extinct volcano, the 556-foot Mount Suribachi, held strategic significance. It contained an airfield that the Japanese used as a base for fighter aircraft—and which the Americans planned to use to launch bombing raids over Japan. Some twenty-one thousand Japanese troops defended the island from an elaborate system of tunnels and caves.

On the morning of February 19, 1945, the first wave of Fourth and Fifth Marine Division troops landed on Iwo Jima. The fighting went on for thirty-six days and Iwo Jima became one of the bloodiest battles of World War II. When it was over, of the more than 71,000 marines who had landed on the island, 5,910 were killed in action and 17,372 wounded. Only 216 Japanese troops were taken prisoner; the rest perished. The Medal of Honor, the nation's highest award for courage under fire, went to twenty-two marines, four navy corpsmen, and a navy landing craft commander for their actions on Iwo Jima. Nearly half were awarded posthumously.

As brutal and as strategically significant as the fighting was on Iwo Jima, the island's name will forever be associated in American history with the American flag and the actions of five marines and one sailor on February 23, 1945, four days after the initial landing. That's when marines Ira Hayes, Franklin Sousley, Harlon Block, Michael Strank, Rene Gagnon, and navy corpsman (medic) John Bradley raised a large American flag on a long drainage pipe left behind by the Japanese atop Mount Suribachi.

The most reproduced image of the American flag is Associated Press photographer Joe Rosenthal's Pulitzer Prize–winning photograph of U.S. Marines raising the Stars and Stripes atop Mount Suribachi on February 23, 1945, at the bloody Battle of Iwo Jima. *AP World Wide Photos*

Associated Press photographer Joe Rosenthal, on assignment with the military's Still Picture Pool, caught them in the act. "People ask, 'Was the picture posed?'" Rosenthal said in a 1950 interview. "No, it wasn't. I went into the beach on a [landing craft]. I heard the boys were going to plant the flag, so when we landed I dashed right up the hill. I had a couple of minutes to get set while they were getting the flag ready, but they didn't pose. I just caught them in a candid shot. The light and the wind were with me. It was a million-to-one lucky break."

Rosenthal did not know that at the time however. After shooting the marines atop Mount Suribachi, Rosenthal put his exposed film on a military transport and it was flown to Guam that night. The film was developed, and prints sent by radio signal to the Associated Press headquarters in New York. The photo appeared in hundreds of newspapers on February 25. It caused an immediate sensation. Responding to demands from readers, newspapers across the nation published special editions that contained only the image of the stirring photo. It became the most recognized image of the war, won the Pulitzer Prize and other top photojournalism awards, and became one of the most reproduced images of the twentieth century.

"People would always remember where they were the moment they saw the photo," said James Bradley, John Bradley's son, in his book *Flags of Our Fathers*. "The flag-raising photograph signaled victory and hope, a counterpoint to the photos of sinking ships at Pearl Harbor that had signaled defeat and fear four years earlier."

The Iwo Jima flag raising also served to bolster the morale of the marines on the island. "It meant we secured the island and that we were going home soon and in thirty-plus days we did," former marine Bernard Dobbins of Lebanon, Connecticut, said in 2004. "We had just happened to look at the mountain and it was in all its glory."

Only three of the men—Bradley, Hayes, and Gagnon—survived the fighting on Iwo Jima. President Roosevelt issued an order for them to come to Washington, where they were greeted as national heroes. Roosevelt recruited the men to be the centerpiece of the Seventh Bond Tour. The Treasury Department commissioned a color poster of the photo by the artist C. C. Beall. Some 3.5 million copies of the poster were distributed to about a million retail stores around the nation. The poster also was displayed in tens of thousands of theaters, banks, factories, railroad stations, billboards, and other public venues.

The Seventh Bond Tour was a rousing success, raising millions of dollars for the war effort. Bradley, Hayes, and Gagnon met newly installed

Pres. Harry Truman at the White House on April 20, 1945, eight days after Roosevelt's death, to kick off the tour. On May 9, their Iwo Jima flag, which had been badly damaged during the fighting, was hoisted over the U.S. Capitol dome in ceremonies attended by a thousand people. Two days later, at the Bond Tour event in New York City, the three Iwo Jima survivors raised the flag over a fifty-five-foot statue based on the Rosenthal photo at ceremonies in Times Square and on Wall Street before a huge, roaring crowd estimated at 1.4 million. The tour went on to similarly enthusiastic receptions in Chicago, Boston, Indianapolis, Detroit, Cleveland, Phoenix, Los Angeles, and several other cities.

The statue was the work of Austrian-born sculptor Felix de Weldon, who served as a U.S. Navy aviation artist in Virginia. De Weldon, one of the first to see the photo, was immediately captivated by it. De Weldon was so taken by the image that, on his own, he worked virtually nonstop for three days to create a three-foot-high model, using a mixture of floor and ceiling wax because modeling clay was not available. De Weldon's work made an impression on Defense Department officials.

"When it was sent to Washington, the navy had it," de Weldon said in 1998. "The two-star admiral at the time had four Navy captains escort it to the other end of the Navy Annex to show it to the Commandant of the Marine Corps with the instructions to 'make sure it comes back.' When it got there [Marine Corps Commandant] General Alexander Vandegrift pointed to it and said, 'This statue better stay right here.'"

De Weldon was then commissioned to create a nine-foot version of the model in plaster, which the government sent across the nation on the war-bond fund-raising tour. The three survivors posed for that statue and de Weldon used Rosenthal's Iwo Jima photo and other photographs for the likenesses of the marines who were killed. After the war, Congress, prodded by lobbying from military and government officials, passed a joint resolution commissioning de Weldon to create an outdoor memorial to the Marine Corps with his statue based on Rosenthal's photograph as the centerpiece.

It took more than nine years for de Weldon and his team to complete the bronze statue. The casting alone lasted three years. The one-hundred-ton, forty-eight-foot-high statute was finished in 1954 and dedicated as the Marine Corps War Memorial on a hillside near Arlington National Cemetery by President Eisenhower on November 10, the 179th anniversary of the Marine Corps. No public funds were used to cover the $850,000 cost of the statute and memorial site. Individuals, including many marines and former marines, donated the money.

The memorial, which is under the purview of the National Park Service, is dedicated to all marines who have lost their lives in action since 1775. In 1961, Congress passed a joint resolution and President Kennedy signed a proclamation giving official sanction to flying the American flag twenty-four hours a day from the statue's one-hundred-foot-high flagpole. The "raising of the American flag during that battle," Kennedy said, "symbolizes the courage and valor of the American fighting forces in World War II." The flag flown from Mount Suribachi is in the Marine Corps Museum in Washington. Felix de Weldon died on June 3, 2003, at age ninety-six.

When the war ended with Japan's surrender on August 14, 1945, tens of millions of Americans took to the streets and joined in loud, sustained, wild celebrations. In New York City an estimated two million people jammed into Times Square by ten o'clock that night. They shouted, cheered, danced, paraded, sang, and cried. Servicemen kissed civilian women. Cars blew their horns. Office workers showered the streets with paper, confetti, and streamers. Effigies of Japan's emperor Hirohito burned in the streets. And the American flag was very much in evidence.

A young girl dressed in an American flag dress raised the morale of celebrating GI's at Camp Patrick Henry in Virginia on June 22, 1945. *The Library of Virginia*

"Thousands of pedestrians" in New York "carried small American flags" that day, "and there was hardly a vehicle that did not display the Stars and Stripes," the *New York Times* reported.

Also on that day the American flag that had been lowered from the U.S. Embassy in Tokyo on December 7, 1941—the day Japan bombed Pearl Harbor—was raised over the Ontario County Courthouse in Canandaigua, New York. H. Merrill Benninghoff, an embassy employee, had brought the flag home from Japan in 1942, and county officials decided to wait for an auspicious day to display it. They chose August 14, 1945, the day the emperor of Japan announced his nation's surrender and the end of World War II.

CHAPTER SIXTEEN

The Cold War

★ ★ ★

I never set out to design the flag of the nation. I just wanted to keep
from getting a bad grade in history.

— **Bob Heft, the designer of the fifty-star flag**

WHEN WORLD WAR II ENDED, the United States and its
allies entered into the Cold War against the Soviet Union and its allies. The
Cold War heated up with undeclared shooting wars in Korea and in Vietnam before Soviet communism began to collapse in 1989. During the Cold
War the American flag symbolized a nation that had become the acknowledged No. 1 superpower in what was then known as the "free world."

The flag played a symbolic but important role in the post–World War II
decision to station American troops in the U.S.-controlled zone of Berlin,
located deep inside Soviet-occupied communist East Germany. In 1945,
Berlin was divided into four zones, controlled by Britain, France, the
United States, and the Soviet Union. Walter H. Judd, a former congressman from Minnesota and U.S. delegate to the United Nations, for one, believed that the American flag helped dissuade the Soviet Union from a
military takeover there.

"They can take Berlin any weekend," Judd said in 1970 when the city
was still divided. "We haven't got enough troops there to stop them. Why
don't they do it? Because we do have one regiment in Berlin—and the
American flag." The flag, he said, is "a symbol of American power and interest. If we take everything out of Berlin, that gives them the green light to
come in. So we keep American forces in Berlin—and the flag."

The Stars and Stripes was displayed prominently at many civic and cultural events during the Cold War, including the 1951 Shenandoah Apple Blossom Festival in Winchester, Virginia, in 1951. *The Library of Virginia*

On June 24, 1948, the Soviet Union blockaded Berlin's three western-controlled zones by suspending ground travel into and out of the city. Within days the English, French, and Americans inaugurated a massive airlift to circumvent the blockade and keep their sectors supplied with the necessities of life. The Soviet Union did not end the blockade until May 12, 1949; the Berlin airlift ended on September 30. The flag played a role in the American decision to join the airlift, according to Edloe Donnan, an aide to U.S. Army general Lucius D. Clay, the military governor of Germany at the time.

General Clay "made up his mind . . . with [President] Truman that the American flag was going to stay flying in Berlin," Donnan said in 1995. Clay said, "We are going to keep that flag flying in Berlin and we're going to keep the Berlin people in coal, fuel and what have you."

President Truman's speech at Flag Day ceremonies in San Francisco on June 14, 1948, contained veiled references to the American flag's Cold War role. "That flag has significance now, and has had always a significance that no other flag in the world ever had," Truman said in his remarks at Golden Gate Park. The Stars and Stripes, he said, is "the most beautiful flag in the world, and a flag that stands for everything that is sacred on this continent, and stands for everything the world should strive for as a whole." A year later, on August 3, 1949, Truman signed into law legislation that Congress passed designating June 14th of each year as Flag Day.

Students from John Handley High School in Winchester, Virginia, displayed an enormous American flag at that city's 1951 Shenandoah Apple Blossom Festival during the early years of the Cold War. *The Library of Virginia*

In July 1953, with the Cold War in full swing, Truman's successor, Pres. Dwight D. Eisenhower, signed legislation to amend the U.S. Flag Code. The new language prohibited "the display of flags of international organizations or other nations in equal or superior prominence or honor to the flag of the United States except under specified circumstances, and for other purposes." The measure was intended to set out rules for displaying the American flag in this country when flown with the United Nations flag or with any other national or international flag. It became law despite international flag usage regulations that forbid displaying one nation's flag above another nation's during peacetime. The following year, President Eisenhower signed legislation that added the words "under God" to the Pledge of Allegiance—a move that was widely seen as a response to the officially atheist Soviet Union.

The Korean War began when seven communist North Korean infantry divisions crossed the thirty-eighth parallel and invaded South Korea on June 25, 1950. That brutal, bloody, bitter war lasted until a cease-fire went into effect in July 1953. The United States, which came to South Korea's defense along with fifteen other nations under the umbrella of the United Nations, paid a steep price. More than 33,600 Americans were killed in action fighting the North Koreans and their communist Chinese allies. Some 20,600 Americans died in accidents and from other noncombat causes, and more than 103,000 Americans were wounded. Nearly 226,000 South Korean troops died on the battlefield. The war consisted of ground, air, and naval operations that led to what amounted to a stalemate. When the cease-fire took effect in 1953, the Korean peninsula still was divided at the thirty-eighth parallel.

American troops displayed the Stars and Stripes in Korea. Within a half hour after the first U.S. Marine battalion landed on Wolmi-do Island during the Inchon landing on September 15, 1950, for example, the troops raised an American flag on the island's high ground. But the Korean War produced no widespread displays of the Stars and Stripes after the Americans took back the territory that the North Koreans and Chinese captured in South Korea, either among the troops or among the South Korean people, as was the case in World War II in England and France. Nor was there an iconic flag moment such as the flag raising at Iwo Jima. Because the Korean War sputtered to an inconclusive end, no flag-flying victory celebrations took place at home after the fighting ended.

★   ★   ★

The biggest flag developments during the 1950s involved the pending statehood of Hawaii and Alaska. Hawaii had been a United States territory since 1898. Alaska, which the United States purchased from Russia in 1867, became an official territory in 1912. The first Alaska statehood bill came before Congress in 1916; the first bill for Hawaii statehood was introduced in 1919. Statehood legislation for Hawaii and Alaska came up virtually every year after that, but serious consideration did not take place until after the Korean War ended.

Congress voted to make Alaska the forty-ninth state on July 7, 1958. Since the flag resolutions of 1777, 1794, and 1818 provided no guidance, the questions of the exact arrangement of the stars and who would choose the forty-nine-star design had been debated for several years. In 1953, Congress proposed that a joint congressional committee recommend the official forty-nine-star design, but that panel never was set up. During the 1950s, as statehood legislation seemed to be making progress in Congress, American citizens, schoolchildren, flag manufacturers, and patriotic groups sent hundreds of unsolicited proposed designs to Capitol Hill, to various branches of the federal government, and to the White House. All of them wound up at the Research and Engineering Division of the Pentagon's office of the Quartermaster General, Heraldic Branch, which provides heraldic services to federal government agencies.

On September 27, 1958, President Eisenhower named three members of his cabinet—Secretary of State John Foster Dulles, Secretary of the Treasury Robert B. Anderson, and Secretary of Defense Neil H. McElroy—and the chairman of the Commission on Fine Arts David E. Finley to a commission to recommend the official forty-nine-star flag design. The committee asked the Quartermaster Corps' Heraldic Branch to do the staff work for the proposed new design. Corps officers, including Quartermaster General Maj. Gen. Andrew T. McNamara, sifted through some nineteen hundred proposed designs and came up with several prototype forty-nine-star designs and flags.

The suggested flag designs included many with doves, crosses, shields, eagles, and other symbols, and others with words such as "Peace," "In God We Trust," and "Freedom." Suggested star arrangements included circles, five-pointed stars, and an arrangement forming the letters "U.S.A." The commission presented several options to President Eisenhower on November 18, 1958. "From all these suggestions and from a study of the history and traditions of the flag, it finally was decided to recommend [the] arrangement of the forty-nine stars in seven staggered rows," according to an official Pentagon publication.

The proclamation that the president signed on January 3, 1959, admitting Alaska to the Union contained the design Eisenhower chose that day for the new forty-nine-star American flag, which would be effective on July 4. The forty-eight-star flag, which had become official on July 4, 1912, had the distinction of being the longest official American flag in use since the first Flag Resolution of 1777. It was the nation's official flag for forty-seven years.

On August 21, 1959, President Eisenhower signed a proclamation admitting Hawaii to the Union. At the ceremonies he unfurled the new fifty-star flag, which would become official on the Fourth of July, 1960. That flag, the nation's twenty-seventh, has nine rows of stars, alternating between six and five stars per row. If no other states are admitted to the Union, the fifty-star flag will become the nation's longest-serving flag on July 4, 2007.

The name of the designer of the forty-nine-star flag has not surfaced. But the person who designed the fifty-star flag is a matter of public record: Robert G. (Bob) Heft, a retired high school teacher and former seven-term mayor of Napoleon, Ohio, who today is the education manager for the Saganaw County, Michigan, Junior Achievement program. How Bob Heft's design became the official flag is one of the more intriguing stories in the history of the Stars and Stripes. That's because Bob Heft designed the flag when he was a seventeen-year-old junior at Lancaster High School near Columbus, Ohio, in 1958. He came up with the design as part of an American history project — a history project for which he received a B minus.

"I was the only one in the class who decided to pick a flag for that project," Heft said. "I studied flags as a kid. I was always fascinated with the Betsy Ross story. I was also very interested in politics." At the time it appeared as though Alaska, and not Hawaii, would gain statehood. But Heft believed that President Eisenhower, a Republican, would push to have Hawaii admitted soon after Alaska came into the Union because Alaska was heavily dominated by the Democratic Party and Hawaii was predominantly Republican.

"So I played a hunch," Heft said. "While the professional flag makers were working on the forty-nine-star flag, I decided to make a fifty-star flag."

Heft used his mother's old foot-operated sewing machine to make his flag. "I had never sewn before and since sewing the flag together myself, I've never sewn since then," he said. "I took a 48-star flag that we had in the closet and unsewed the area that separated the blue field from the red and white stripes, and then sewed in a blank blue field." He then cut out a hundred white stars, using a cardboard pattern from the stars on the old flag.

"I took a razor blade and cut [the pattern] real accurately," Heft said. "Then I took a real sharp pencil and I sketched out a hundred stars on the fabric. Then I took a pair of scissors and cut them out. I took a piece of chalk and put a dot on the top of each star. I laid it out with a yardstick and proportionately divided it on the blue field. Then I took the stars and touched them with a hot iron so they would be even and symmetrical. Then I took the hot iron and pressed them on."

The work took about twelve hours to complete over three days. Heft's history teacher, Stanley Pratt, was impressed, but not overly so. "The teacher said, 'Where did you get your crystal ball to make a fifty-star flag?' He gave me a B minus and that was the first time I ever challenged a teacher. He said, 'It's got too many stars on it. You get good grades in here, and you don't even know how many states there are. You've got too many.'" Pratt then told Heft that if Congress accepted the design, he would change the grade to an A.

That turned out to be an incentive for Heft. "If he would have given me an A, I probably would have taken that flag home and put it away," Heft said. "I never set out to design the flag of the nation. I just wanted to keep from getting a bad grade in history. I thought I would do something to prove the teacher wrong."

So Heft sent his fifty-star flag to Ohio's governor, Mike DiSalle, the former mayor of Toledo. "I did it just to verify that the flag was in existence long before it became official," Heft said. He was soon notified, though, that DiSalle had put the flag on display in the Ohio State Capitol Building and later at the Governor's Mansion. After retrieving his flag from the governor, Heft took it to his congressman, Walter Henry Moeller, who lived in Lancaster.

"I put the flag in a box and a letter in the box and I got on my bicycle and rode clear across town. He happened to be back in the district," Heft said. "He came to the door and he was chewing on a chicken leg and said, 'What can I do for you, sonny?'" Heft stammered out his homemade fifty-star-flag story and asked Moeller to take it to Washington.

"I said he could put it in a file cabinet or closet or whatever and if there was ever a need for a fifty-star flag, if there was a contest — I didn't know how they went about it then — this was my concept of what it should look like."

President Eisenhower went back to his four-member committee for a recommendation for the design of the fifty-star flag after Alaska entered the Union and Hawaii was on the way in. "They were charged with the responsibility of taking all of the designs and filtering them through and selecting their top five choices," Heft said, "and the President would select from those five."

The president selected Heft's design, which Congressman Moeller had brought to the design committee for consideration. Heft received a call from the White House with the good news in August 1959, then came to Washington to meet the president and receive accolades for his gift to the nation. Heft stood beside President Eisenhower on July 4, 1960, when the first official fifty-star flag was raised in Washington.

The flag that Heft made for his history project has traveled all over the world. It has flown over the White House, at every state capitol building, and at dozens of American embassies. Bob Heft still has that flag, although he no longer displays it.

"It cost me $2.87 to make," Heft said in 2004. "I had decided never to part with it. I just recently turned down an offer for half a million dollars for it from a museum."

On September 20, 2003, the Ohio Historical Society dedicated an Ohio Historical Marker titled "50 Star American Flag" in front of Lancaster High School. The marker reads, in part: "A national symbol for more than 40 years, the design for the 50-star flag was born at Lancaster High School in 1958. Constructed of an old 48-star flag and some blue and white cloth, student Robert Heft designed the flag for a history project. . . . President Eisenhower made the flag official in 1960. It is the only flag in American history to have flown over the White House under five administrations."

CHAPTER SEVENTEEN

The Generation Gap

★   ★   ★

Millions and millions of Americans regard [the flag] with an almost mystical reverence regardless of what sort of social, political, or philosophical beliefs they may have.

—Chief Justice William Rehnquist, June 21, 1989

T HE YEAR THAT the fifty-star flag made its debut, 1960, the United States had fewer than a thousand military advisers in South Vietnam. They were working with that nation, officially known as the Republic of Vietnam, in its fight against indigenous communist guerrillas, the Vietcong, and their communist allies in the Democratic Republic of (North) Vietnam. The direct American military commitment to South Vietnam had begun in 1954, following North Vietnam's victory over France, Indochina's former colonial ruler.

In the next several years Presidents Eisenhower, Kennedy, and Johnson sent increasing numbers of troops to South Vietnam. President Johnson greatly escalated the war in August 1964 following congressional passage of the Tonkin Gulf Resolution, giving the president the authority to take "all necessary measures to repel any armed attacks against the forces of the United States and to prevent further aggression" in Vietnam.

By 1968, at the height of American involvement, more than 536,000 U.S. Army, Navy, Marine, Air Force, and Coast Guard personnel were on the ground in South Vietnam and its territorial waters. More than 58,000 Americans died in the Vietnam War and some 304,000 were wounded in a conflict that became the nation's longest war. The United States withdrew its combat forces in January 1973; the war ended two years later with the communist takeover of South Vietnam.

The Vietnam War was the most controversial overseas war in American history. Beginning with the rapid troop escalation in 1965, the nation became increasingly split over the question of whether the war should have been fought. The Americans who supported the war (hawks) tended to be older and politically conservative. Those who opposed it (the doves) mainly were of the younger Baby Boom generation (born after 1945); they were college aged and politically liberal. A deep cultural divide—sometimes called the Generation Gap—grew between the hawks and doves.

The American flag became an important symbol for both hawks and doves. Unlike all of the other wars fought by the United States, in which flying the American flag symbolized commitment to the war effort, the flag's role during the Vietnam War was vastly different. By the end of the 1960s what the political scientist Robert Justin Goldstein called "a cultural war using the flag as a primary symbol" had broken out in the nation. The flag, Burt Neuborne of the American Civil Liberties Union said in 1970, "has become a partisan symbol. The pro-war people have adopted the flag as the symbol of their side. The antiwar people would like to have the flag symbolizing their activities as well."

Hawks displayed the flag as the primary emblem of their support for the war, as well as their anticommunism and their disdain for those who spoke out against the war, expressed in phrases such as "Love it or leave it" and "My country right or wrong." Barry Goldwater, the conservative Republican senator from Arizona who ran against Pres. Lyndon Johnson in 1964, for example, began his campaign rallies with a recitation of the Pledge of Allegiance. And he received thunderous applause from campaign audiences when he pledged—as he did at a rally in Los Angeles in March— that he would not tolerate the Stars and Stripes being "torn down, spat upon and burned around the world."

Doves flew the flag as well, but the message they conveyed was not support for the war. To the contrary, doves displayed the flag upside down as a sign of distress; they created posters with the stars arrayed in the peace sign and other forms of protest; they wore American flag shirts and bandannas; or they simply displayed the Betsy Ross and fifty-star flags. The most radical elements of the antiwar movement defiantly displayed the Vietcong flag. Some antiwar protesters burned the Stars and Stripes to protest the American war in Vietnam.

★   ★   ★

Many of those who protested against the Vietnam War used the American flag as a symbol of their cause, including these members of Vietnam Veterans Against the War shown in a 1971 antiwar demonstration in Washington. *Bernard Edelman*

In February 1969, *Reader's Digest* magazine distributed eighteen million flag decals nationwide with the advice to "Fly This Flag—Proudly." Gulf Oil Company soon followed suit, distributing twenty million flag decals of its own. Banks, gas stations, and other businesses across the country offered flag decals as a part of sales promotions. Other organizations, including veterans' and patriotic groups and civic groups such as the Benevolent & Protective Order of Elks, distributed them. The Elks flag decal included the phrase "Love it or Leave." The decals were instantly popular among those who supported the war.

William J. Windecker, who in 1969 chaired the Elks's Americanism

Committee, said that his organization's American flag decal originally was intended as a message to Cuban refugees in Miami. "We had a few resenters about the slogan who thought it was too rough, and we had no right to tell people about this, but we figured the opposition would die out," Windecker said. "There is so much confusion in the country today with antagonistic groups trying to overthrow the government. It's time we stand up and be counted."

Flag decals "have become a fixture on fire trucks, police cars, and motorcycles throughout the country," *Life* magazine reported in an article examining what it called "decalcomania." "Cab drivers and truck drivers are particularly addicted to them. . . . Old Glory, it seems, is putting out a signal of its own and to many it reads, 'My Country, Right or Wrong.'"

★　★　★

Towns and cities across the country began requiring police officers to display American flag decals on their patrol cars and to wear flag shoulder patches on their uniforms. After Macon, Georgia, police began wearing flag patches "not a single police officer has been assaulted in the line of duty, and it has also led the officer to do a better job," Mayor Ronnie Thompson said. The reason, he said, had to do with the patriotism "all Americans have and recognition that the policemen and his shield are direct representatives of the flag."

Some Americans were troubled by decalcomania. That included the outspoken Major League baseball player, Jim Bouton, whose iconoclastic book, *Ball Four*, was published in 1970. Bouton, in his journal of the 1969 season, said he and others who were against the war in Vietnam were "troubled by the stiff-minded emphasis on the flag that grips much of the country these days." A flag, he said, "after all, is still only a cloth symbol. You don't show patriotism by showing blank-eyed love for a piece of cloth. And you can be deeply patriotic without covering your car with flag decals."

The folk music singer/songwriter John Prine satirized decalcomania with the antiwar song "Your Flag Decal Won't Get You into Heaven Anymore." The chorus goes:

> *But your flag decal won't get you*
> *Into heaven any more.*
> *They're already overcrowded*
> *From your dirty little war.*

Now Jesus don't like killin'
No matter what the reason's for,
And your flag decal won't get you
Into heaven any more.

TIME magazine, in its January 5, 1970, issue that named "Middle Americans" as its 1969 "Person of the Year," singled out the importance of the flag in that choice. "Everywhere they flew the colors of assertive patriots," the magazine noted. "Their car windows were plastered with American-flag decals, their ideological totems. In the bumper-sticker dialogue of the freeways, they answered Make Love Not War with Honor America. . . ."

President Nixon spoke out during the war in praise of Middle Americans and others who flew the flag, saying they made up the "Great Silent Majority" who patriotically supported the nation and the war effort in Vietnam. "I don't believe that I have ever seen in any American city, either here or anyplace else, more American flags than I saw today," Nixon said on May 25, 1971, as he arrived for a visit to Birmingham, Alabama. "I know what that flag means to you. It means that you love your country, that you want your country to be strong, that you want your country to work for the great cause of peace in the world, as well as peace for America—that cause we are dedicated to and that we are going to bring."

An incident involving the American flag sparked the ensuing bloody riot in the streets of Chicago during the Democratic National Convention in August 1968. On Wednesday, August 28, two days after the convention opened, some ten thousand demonstrators gathered at the band shell in Chicago's Grant Park for an antiwar rally. During the rally a young man wearing an army helmet started to climb a flagpole near the band shell to lower the American flag. When police moved in to arrest him, a group of men surrounded the flagpole, lowered the flag, and replaced it with a red T-shirt. The police then charged the crowd, beating and arresting protesters. That set in motion the events of that night and the next two days during which twelve thousand police officers used clubs, dogs, and tear gas to attack and arrest hundreds of protesters.

Police officials later said that disrespect for the flag was the primary reason that they took physical action against the antiwar demonstrators. The "profanity and spitting" by the demonstrators "did not have the same effect on the police that incidents involving the flag did," a Chicago police official later testified. "Abuse or misuse of the flag deeply affected the police."

Jasper Johns, one of the nation's leading artists, had used the American flag in his work—usually classified as Pop Art—since the mid-1950s. Johns's paintings of white flags, flags on orange backgrounds, flags with sixty-four stars, flags in superimposed triplicate, and other flag images were nonpolitical, the artist and the art establishment agreed.

In 1969, however, the Leo Castelli Gallery in New York, which had represented Johns since 1957, asked him to design a poster for the planned nationwide series of antiwar demonstrations held October 15, 1969, known as Moratorium Day. The colors of the fifty-star flag in Johns's poster, titled "Moratorium," make a subtle antiwar statement. The stars and six stripes are black; seven stripes are done in a green camouflage pattern. The canton's field is painted orange. The word "Moratorium" is stenciled underneath.

"Johns's print successfully became a symbol of protest," the artist Debora Wood wrote, "because he changed his approach. The image is immediately recognizable as a symbol for America, but there is obviously something wrong because the colors are distorted. A single word 'Moratorium' requires no complex analysis."

The popular rock musical *Hair,* which opened on Broadway in April 1968, contained a scene that some Americans—including William F. Buckley Jr., in his review in the *National Review*—believed desecrated the flag. During the musical number "Don't Put It Down" the characters, a group of hippies, hold a satiric flag-folding ceremony during which one of them is wrapped in a flag and then cradled and rocked in it.

When a road version of *Hair* previewed in Boston in February 1970, Suffolk County district attorney Garret Byrne and Boston's Licensing Bureau head Dick Sinnott vehemently objected to the musical's use of obscenities and nudity, as well as its flag scene. "Most sickening was the manner in which the American flag was degraded and used as some sort of symbolic dust rag," Sinnott said. In a speech to a veterans' group in April, Sinnott offered his opinion that anyone "who abuses the American flag should be horsewhipped in public on Boston Common."

The show's producers closed the Boston production on April 10 rather than comply with the district attorney's order to cut out the nude scenes. Legal wrangling over that order wound up in the U.S. Supreme Court where the justices upheld a U.S. District Court ruling that held that the district attorney acted unconstitutionally in ordering the play to cut out the nude scenes and the flag-folding scene.

Two American astronauts, James A. Lovell Jr., and John L. Swigert Jr., walked out on a Broadway performance of *Hair* in June 1970 because the flag scene offended them. "I don't like what you're doing to the flag," Swigert said outside the theater. "I don't like the way they wrapped the flag around that guy."

★   ★   ★

A flag that demonstrators burned at one of the first large antiwar rallies, a gathering of some two hundred thousand people on April 15, 1967, in Central Park in New York City, led to congressional passage in 1968 of the nation's first federal flag desecration law. Several other politically motivated flag burnings and other acts of flag desecration had taken place around the nation since 1965. In Cordele, Georgia, for example, Rufus Hinton was convicted of flag desecration on May 6, 1966, for helping to haul down an American flag and a Georgia state flag at the Crisp County Courthouse during a civil rights demonstration in March of that year. In Seattle, Floyd Turner was convicted in July 1967, for his role in helping burn a flag at a party.

Although flag desecration laws were on the books in every state, the spate of flag burnings and other similar incidents in the mid-sixties led to lobbying by patriotic and veterans' groups, and editorializing by some newspapers, in favor of a federal flag desecration law. "The flag belongs to all the American people and thusly should be protected by national legislation," Veterans of Foreign Wars national Commander in Chief Andy Borg said in 1966. Borg declared that he was "sick and tired of the American flag being burned, stomped upon, torn apart and vilified by communist-inspired peaceniks and others."

Many members of Congress agreed. "Which is the greater contribution to the security of freedom," Republican congressman Dan Kuykendall of Tennessee asked on the House floor. "The inspiring photo of the Marines at Iwo Jima or the shameful pictures of unshaven beatniks burning that same flag in Central Park?" Charles Wiggins, a California Republican, among others, tied flag desecration directly to the war effort. "The public act of desecration of our flag tends to undermine the morale of American troops," he said. "That this finding is true can be attested by many Members who have received correspondence from servicemen expressing their shock and disgust of such conduct."

After a series of hearings in May and June, the House and Senate passed the first federal flag desecration legislation. President Johnson signed the bill into law on July 4, 1968. It provided fines of up to one thousand dollars and one year in jail for anyone who "knowingly" cast "contempt" upon "any flag of the United States by publicly mutilating, defacing, defiling, burning, or trampling upon it."

As was the case during World War I, several states revised their flag desecration laws during the Vietnam War to stiffen penalties. In Alabama, Indiana, Oklahoma, and Illinois the newly revised laws increased the sentences for those convicted of flag desecration from a maximum of thirty days in jail and a hundred-dollar fine to a maximum of between two and five years in jail and fines of three thousand to ten thousand dollars. Virtually all the state flag laws contained language adopted during the first two decades of the century making it illegal to put marks or pictures on the flag, to use the flag commercially, or to burn or otherwise desecrate the flag.

Hundreds of flag desecration prosecutions took place during the Vietnam War. Nearly all of them were "used against 'peace' demonstrations," Robert Justin Goldstein found after studying sixty flag desecration cases adjudicated between 1966 and 1976. Goldstein concluded that officials enforced the state flag protection laws extremely arbitrarily. " 'Establishment' and 'patriotic' elements who wore flag pins in their lapels (including President Nixon and the White House staff and the police departments of Boston and New York City) or flag patches on their shoulders and placed flag decals on their windows and cars by the tens of millions, often in technical violation of the flag desecration statutes, invariably were unhindered," Goldstein said.

On October 3, 1968, three months after Congress passed the first national flag desecration law, Abbie Hoffman, a flamboyant leader of the radical Youth International Party (known as the Yippies), became the first person arrested for violating the new federal statute. That afternoon Hoffman was taking part in a protest demonstration against a House Committee on Un-American Activities hearing outside the Cannon House Office Building on Capitol Hill in Washington. For the occasion he wore a red, white, and blue American flag shirt and buttons that read "Wallace for President: Stand Up for America" and "Vote Pig in Sixty-Eight, Yippie."

As they took Hoffman into custody, District of Columbia police tore off the shirt, which he had purchased in a store. He was held overnight in jail. Hoffman was convicted of flag desecration on November 21 in the Washington, D.C., Court of General Sessions, and sentenced to thirty days in jail.

Hoffman testified that he wore the shirt "to dress symbolically to express the way we felt" in "the tradition of the founding fathers." After his conviction, Hoffman told the court: "I consider this decision ridiculous.

Everyone who wears an Uncle Sam suit is just as guilty." He appealed the verdict. During the appeals process, in the spring of 1969, Hoffman appeared as a guest on Merv Griffin's popular CBS television talk show. Hoffman arrived on the set wearing a jacket, which he took off after the show started to reveal that he was wearing another American flag shirt. When the taped show was broadcast, a blue screen blocked his image.

A federal appeals court in Washington overturned Hoffman's 1968 conviction on March 29, 1971. The three-judge panel ruled that his shirt did not defile or desecrate the flag.

Supreme Court rulings in 1969, 1972, and 1974 found that sections of flag desecration laws in New York, Massachusetts, and Washington violated First Amendment provisions of free speech and were therefore unconstitutional. That led the legislatures in some twenty states to narrow the scope of their flag desecration laws in the next decade. Most of the changes adopted the 1968 federal law's provisions by focusing on flag mutilation and other forms of physical desecration rather than on verbal abuse or commercial or political misuse of the flag.

Fourteen years after the end of the Vietnam War, in a landmark decision, the Supreme Court on June 21, 1989, in *Texas v. Johnson,* ruled 5–4 that burning the flag is a form of symbolic speech protected by the First Amendment. In the case under review, Gregory Lee "Joey" Johnson, a member of the Revolutionary Communist Party, had burned an American flag while participating in a political demonstration during the 1984 Republican National Convention in Dallas. He was convicted of violating Texas's flag desecration law, fined two thousand dollars, and sentenced to a year in jail. The Texas Court of Criminal Appeals overturned the conviction, ruling that Johnson was exercising his First Amendment right of freedom of speech. Prosecutors asked the U.S. Supreme Court to review the decision.

"Johnson burned an American flag as part—indeed, as the culmination—of a political demonstration that coincided with the convening of the Republican Party and its re-nomination of Ronald Reagan for President. The expressive, overtly political nature of this conduct was both intentional and overwhelmingly apparent," Justice William Brennan said in his majority opinion. "Johnson was not, we add, prosecuted for the expression of just any idea; he was prosecuted for his expression of dissatisfaction with the policies of this country, expression situated at the core of our First Amendment values."

Forbidding "criminal punishment for conduct such as Johnson's will not endanger the special role played by our flag or the feelings it inspires,"

Brennan said. "To paraphrase Justice [Oliver Wendell] Holmes, we submit that nobody can suppose that this one gesture of an unknown man will change our Nation's attitude towards its flag." The "flag's deservedly cherished place in our community will be strengthened, not weakened, by our holding today," Brennan said. "Our decision is a reaffirmation of the principles of freedom and inclusiveness that the flag best reflects, and of the conviction that our toleration of criticism such as Johnson's is a sign and source of our strength."

In his dissenting opinion, Chief Justice William Rehnquist offered a brief history of the American flag that included the words to "The Star Spangled Banner" and John Greenleaf Whittier's poem "Barbara Frietschie." For "more than 200 years of our history," Rehnquest said, the American flag "has come to be the visible symbol embodying our Nation." No "other American symbol has been as universally honored as the flag,", he said, pointing out Congress's adoption in 1931 of "The Star-Spangled Banner" as the National Anthem, the 1919 establishment of Flag Day, the 1987 adoption of John Philip Sousa's "The Stars and Stripes Forever" as the national march, the Pledge of Allegiance's inclusion in the U.S. Flag Code, and the fact that the flag "has appeared as the principal symbol on approximately 33 United States postal stamps and in the design of at least 43 more, more times than any other symbol."

The flag, Rehnquist said, "does not represent the views of any particular political party, and it does not represent any particular political philosophy. . . . Millions and millions of Americans regard it with an almost mystical reverence regardless of what sort of social, political, or philosophical beliefs they may have. I cannot agree that the First Amendment invalidates the Act of Congress, and the laws of 48 of the 50 states, which make criminal the public burning of the flag." Since 1777, he said, "the American flag has occupied a unique position as the symbol of our Nation, a uniqueness that justifies a governmental prohibition against flag burning. . . ."

The Supreme Court's decision invalidated the 1968 national flag desecration law, as well as the flag desecration laws on the books in forty-eight states (all except Wyoming and Alaska). In response, Congress passed and Pres. George H. W. Bush signed into law the Flag Protection Act of 1989, which went into effect on October 28, 1989. The next few days saw "perhaps the largest single wave of [flag-burning] incidents in American history," Robert Justin Goldstein noted. Groups of protesters challenging the new law burned American flags in about a dozen cities. Two groups were arrested for doing so in Washington, D.C., and Seattle. Their cases wound up in the Supreme Court, which ruled 5–4 on June 11, 1990, that the 1989 law unconstitutionally violated the protesters' free-speech rights by making it illegal to burn a flag in a public protest.

The 1989 and 1990 Supreme Court decisions overturning the nation's flag desecration laws led to a national movement to bypass the legislative process and amend the U.S. Constitution to make flag desecration illegal. "Congress tried to protect [the flag] by legislation. That legislation did not stand up," Pres. George H. W. Bush said on June 12, 1990, the day after the second Supreme Court ruling. "When it was knocked down by the [Supreme] Court, I feel there's no other way to go but this Constitutional Amendment." In 1989 Bush had termed such an amendment a way "to protect that unique symbol of America's honor." The flag, he said, "is too sacred to be abused."

"I believe," Bush had said at a June 27, 1989, White House news conference, "that the flag of the United States should never be the object of desecration. Flag burning is wrong. Protection of the flag, a unique national symbol, will in no way limit the opportunity nor the breadth of protest available in the exercise of free-speech rights." As president, Bush said, "I will uphold our precious right to dissent, but burning the flag goes too far, and I want to see that matter remedied."

Since 1994, the leading voice in the effort to adopt a flag desecration Constitutional Amendment has been the Citizens Flag Alliance, which was founded in June of that year by the American Legion. The alliance is "engaged in a war to recapture Old Glory," its chairman, retired U.S. Army general Patrick H. Brady, said in 2000. "Our primary task is to capture the constitutional arguments and convince the members of Congress, through common sense and through the people, that the Supreme Court made a mistake and we have an obligation, even a sacred duty, to correct it."

Brady, testifying in favor of a proposed flag protection Constitutional Amendment on Capitol Hill in 2004, said that the 1989 Supreme Court decision "took away a fundamental right of the American people, a right we possessed since our birth as a nation, the right to protect the flag." The decision, Brady said, "was an egregious error and distorted our Constitution. We do not believe the freedom to burn the American flag is a legacy of the freedoms bestowed on us by" the Founding Fathers. "To distort the work of these great men unable to defend themselves, to put flag burning side by side with pornography as protected speech, is outrageous."

The American Legion had begun a lobbying campaign in 1990 to induce the state legislatures to pass memorializing resolutions calling upon Congress to adopt a flag protection constitutional amendment. The Texas Legislature had been the first to do so on July 10, 1989, nineteen days after the *Johnson* decision. By the end of 1993, thirty-five state legislatures had adopted the nonbinding resolutions. In January 2002, Vermont became the fiftieth state to approve a memorializing resolution. The Vermont Legislature ended nearly a decade of often-emotional debate by approving the resolution by a 113–23 vote in the House and a 22–6 vote in the Senate.

Opponents of the resolution in Vermont framed their arguments on First Amendment grounds, as the majority in the Supreme Court had done in 1989 and 1990. "I can't support legislation that would encourage the abridgment of the right of free speech as contained in the First Amendment to the U.S. Constitution," said state representative Betty Nuovo. "Abridging this freedom is desecration of the flag." Supporters of the resolution pointed to the fact that the overwhelming majority of Americans supported flag protection legislation. "Let there be no doubt. The people's House is on record for a Constitutional Amendment to correct the error of the U.S. Supreme Court," said Vermont State representative Duncan Kilmartin.

The first proposed flag desecration Constitutional Amendment — specifying that "the Congress and the States have the power to prohibit the physical desecration of the flag of the United States" — was introduced in the U.S. Congress in the summer of 1990 immediately after the second Supreme Court ruling. It received majority votes in the House and Senate, but not the two-thirds majorities required for constitutional amendments. The amendment has come up in every Congress since, but has failed to gain the needed two-thirds majority votes in both the House and Senate.

★   ★   ★

During the Vietnam War at least one very public display of the American flag was cheered by hawks and doves: the planting of the Stars and Stripes on the Moon on July 20, 1969. At 10:56 p.m. Eastern Daylight Saving Time that day, American astronaut Neil Armstrong became the first human being to set foot on the Moon. Soon thereafter — four days, fourteen hours, and nine minutes into the mission — Armstrong and his fellow Apollo 11 astronaut Buzz Aldrin planted an American flag on the Moon's surface, an event that was broadcast live and beamed back to Earth on television.

The decision to plant the Stars and Stripes on the Moon did not come lightly. The United Nations had adopted a treaty in 1967 denying any nation the right to claim sovereignty over any object in space. Planting an American flag, it was believed, could be construed as an act of taking possession of the Moon.

"There were people at the time, and have been people since then, who thought that planting any flag up there was a bad idea," Chief Historian Roger Launius of the National Aeronautics and Space Administration (NASA) said in 2000. "After the fifteenth century when Europe was pushing outward, the Europeans were planting flags all over the place and claiming the territory for their home countries. They thought that set a bad precedent."

The astronauts themselves had no qualms about planting the flag. "I certainly felt that the American flag is what belonged there," Aldrin said in 1999. "It's a characteristic of previous explorations, to plant a symbol upon arriving at a new shore. And it indeed was a philosophical moment of achievement. It was also a technical challenge."

NASA had set up a Committee on Symbolic Activities for the First Lunar Landing in February 1969 to look into the efficacy of planting a flag on the Moon, given the United Nations' dictum. The committee, after considering options such as leaving miniature flags of all nations or some type of commemorative marker on the Moon, decided that the astronauts would plant only one large American flag. To show that the United States was not trying to take possession of the Moon, the committee also decided that the astronauts would mount an explanatory plaque on the lower half of the lunar module that they left behind on the Moon's surface. The plaque, which contained an image of the American flag, said: "Here men from the planet Earth first set foot upon the Moon July 1969, AD. We came in peace for all mankind."

NASA engineers decided to use a three-by-five-foot nylon flag (purchased commercially for $5.50—accounts differ as to where) and a ten-pound collapsible flagpole with a telescoping horizontal arm designed to keep the flag extended and perpendicular. The folded flag and the pole were placed inside a heat resistant tube attached to the left side of the ladder on the Lunar Landing Module. The flag and its pole survived the Moon landing intact, but the astronauts had trouble planting the flag on the moon's surface.

First, the telescoped rod did not work and was discarded, which is why the flag appears to be rippling in the wind in the photographs beamed back to Earth. Then the astronauts' bulky space suits hindered Armstrong and Aldrin's efforts to plant the flag deeply into the Moon's hard surface. "The flag didn't exactly perform as we put it together," Aldrin remembered thirty years later. "It didn't stick in the ground exactly the way we thought it would." Aldrin and Armstrong persevered though, and left the Stars and Stripes standing on the Moon when they rocketed back to Earth.

"Even though the event took only 10 minutes of the 2½ hour [lunar extravehicular activity], for many people around the world the flag-raising was one of the most memorable parts of the Apollo 11 lunar landing," a NASA report said. "There were no formal protests from other nations that the flag-raising constituted an illegal attempt to claim the moon. Buzz Aldrin, in an article written for *Life* magazine, stated that as he looked at the flag, he sensed an 'almost mystical unification of all people in the world at that moment.'"

American astronauts left five additional Stars and Stripes on the Moon during subsequent lunar missions. Because the first flag was not anchored deeply into the Moon's surface and because of exposure to ultraviolet and solar radiation on the Moon, it is likely that the six Stars and Stripes on the Moon have seriously deteriorated. "My guess is the flags themselves, because they're nylon, the UV rays have probably made them very brittle. Maybe [they] fell off into the dust," Apollo 12 astronaut Alan Bean said in 2001. "I'm sure they've faded to white, but the poles are still there."

★   ★   ★

The most vivid example of the ability of the flag to evoke deep emotions at home during the Vietnam War came on Friday, May 8, 1970, in New York City. Just before noon, some two hundred construction workers—many of whom wore hard hats embossed with American flags—marched through the streets of lower Manhattan carrying large American flags. They converged from four directions on an antiwar rally on Wall Street where they confronted a large group of young demonstrators. Most were college students from New York University and Hunter College. The workers—dubbed "hard hats"—chased and beat dozens of demonstrators with lead pipes and crowbars.

"We came here to express our sympathy for those killed at Kent State and they attacked us with lead pipes wrapped in American flags," Drew Lynch, a nineteen-year-old New York City employee, said.

The workers pushed their way through the demonstrators to Wall Street's Federal Hall National Memorial, the U.S. Subtreasury Building, where George Washington was inaugurated as the nation's first president in 1789. The workers placed American flags on the statue of George Washington that stands on the building's steps. From there, they forced their way into New York's City Hall a few blocks away. A postal worker raised the American flag on the building's roof to full staff. New York City mayor John Lindsay had ordered the flag to be flown at half-staff in mourning for four students who had been shot and killed by National Guard troops during an antiwar demonstration at Kent State University on May 4.

When an aide to Mayor Lindsay lowered the flag to half-staff again, he ignited a small riot outside City Hall. "The mob reacted in fury," the *New York Times* reported. "Workers vaulted the police barricades, surged across the tops of parked cars and past half a dozen mounted policemen. Fists flailing, they stormed through the policemen guarding the barred front doors. Uncertain whether they could contain the mob, the police asked city officials to raise the flag. Deputy Mayor Richard R. Aurelio, in charge during the absence of Mayor Lindsay . . . ordered the flag back to full staff." As the flag went up, "the workers began singing 'The Star-Spangled Banner.'"

Construction workers held other flag-rich rallies in New York's financial district during the next several weeks. At one such event, on May 12, another confrontation took place between construction workers and antiwar demonstrators in the same area of lower Manhattan. With a heavy police presence, this time little violence occurred. That was because, one worker said, "there was no provocation; no one spit on the flag."

The flag and what it stood for was a recurring theme among those who took part in the May 8 and subsequent hard hat rallies. "Outside of God, [the flag] is the most important thing I know," John Nash, a World War II veteran who marched at a May 20 parade in support of the Nixon administration's Vietnam War policies in downtown New York, said. "I know a lot of good friends died under this. It stands for America."

Eighty percent of the American people "are behind America and the flag," said Robert Geary, whose son was killed in Vietnam. The flag, Geary said, "is me. It's part of me. I fought for it myself two or three years in the Second World War." The United States "is the greatest country in the world. All they [antiwar demonstrators] have to do is move out."

Morty Grutman, an electrician who took part in the May 8 hard hat events, said that the antiwar demonstrators' lack of respect for the flag was a prime reason for the construction workers' counterdemonstrations. "A lot of us are World War II vets and fathers and purple hearts," Grutman said. "We're from a generation that believes in the flag over everything."

For a time after the May 8 incident, the hard hat adorned with an American flag decal became a symbol for those who supported the war.

On May 14, at a Conservative Party rally in New York, for example, the event's promoters showed up wearing hard hats decorated with American flags. On May 26 Peter J. Brennan, the president of the Building and Construction Trades Council of Greater New York, and twenty-two other union leaders were guests of President Nixon at the White House. At the end of the meeting Brennan presented the president with a hard hat and placed an American flag pin on his lapel.

Other antiwar demonstrations in the days after the Kent State killings— mainly at more than four hundred colleges and universities across the nation—included emotionally charged, sometimes violent conflicts over the flag. At the University of New Mexico students physically fought over whether the American flag should be lowered to half-staff. Three antiwar students suffered knife wounds.

At Northwestern University—which, like many other colleges, had been shut down due to antiwar unrest—there was a tussle over a flag that protesting students waved upside-down. "A hefty man in work clothes tried to grab the flag, shouting: 'That's my flag! I fought for it! You have no right to it!'" *TIME* magazine reported. "The students began arguing with him. 'To hell with your movement,' the man responded. 'There are millions of people like me. We're fed up with your movement. You're forcing us into it. We'll have to kill you. All I can see is a lot of kids blowing a chance I never had.'"

Philip Caputo, the author and former Vietnam War Marine Corps lieutenant, covered that event as a Chicago journalist. "Flying an upside-down American flag alongside the black flags of the anarchists and the red banners of revolution, the demonstrators mounted makeshift barricades to shout epithets at the police, antiwar chants to whomever would listen," Caputo later recalled. "A stocky, dark-haired man in his early fifties waded into the crowd and seized the U.S. flag, declaring in a voice quavering with rage that he was an electrician and a former marine who had fought for that flag on Iwo Jima, seen it raised on Mount Suribachi, and he was damned if he would allow a mob of long-haired, pot-smoking hippies to desecrate it."

Several demonstrators, Caputo reported, "cried out that the man should be allowed to have his say, but the rest shouted them down, and then the cops waded in with nightsticks."

The Stars and Stripes was a very visible presence at the July 4, 1970, Honor America Day rally held at the Lincoln Memorial and the Washington Monument grounds in the nation's capital. Billed as a nonpartisan celebration, the event was organized by politically conservative supporters of the Nixon administration. The day featured hawkish speeches and ultrap-atriotic comments as well as an antiwar demonstration against the rally that turned violent.

More than 250,000 people attended the rally, which was organized by the head of the Marriott Corporation, J. Willard Marriott, at the behest of President Nixon and by Hobart Lewis, the publisher and editor of *Reader's Digest*. Bob Hope cohosted the day's activities, with the Reverend Billy Graham. The list of performers included politically conservative show business figures Red Skelton, James Stewart, Andy Williams, Kate Smith, Pat Boone, Dinah Shore, and Jack Benny.

In his speech from the steps of the Lincoln Memorial bedecked with American flags, Graham denounced "extremist elements" who had "desecrated our flag, disrupted our educational system, laughed at our religious heritage and threatened to burn down our cities." Newspapers reported that many of those who attended the event displayed the American flag and many others brought along American flag blankets and wore articles of clothing containing images of the flag.

In Vietnam American troops flew the flag as their fathers had done in Korea and in Europe and Japan during World War II and as their grandfathers had done in the trenches in World War I. The flag flew over American bases, remote outposts, and landing zones. Some troops carried small flags into battle, especially during the war's early years before it became controversial at home. During the bloody November 1965 Battle of the Ia Drang Valley, for example, at least one American infantryman displayed a small American flag on his backpack. After the first part of that battle was over, the soldier flew the flag on a tree branch.

"When I saw that [flag] I felt very proud. It's something that always stuck with me," one GI said. It was "just like Iwo Jima, another battle we had won for the United States." That small Stars and Stripes, noted Gen. Hal Moore, who commanded the First Cavalry Division Battalion that fought in that battle, "flew over Landing Zone X-Ray for the rest of the fight, raising all our spirits."

That flag was attached to "a shattered tree . . . about ten feet off the ground," said J. D. Coleman, a former First Cav officer who was on the scene. "True, it was a cliché camera shot from every war movie ever made, but there on LZ X-Ray, in the midst of death, destruction, and unbelievable heroism, its impact transcended the stereotype."

The American flag proved to be an unequivocally positive symbol during the Vietnam War to the men held as prisoners of war in Hanoi. The

U.S. Navy pilot Michael Christian, who was shot down in North Vietnam and taken prisoner on April 24, 1967, was perhaps the most devoted to the flag. When he was held in the infamous Hanoi Hilton prison camp, Christian fashioned an American flag out of a few ragged bits of red and white cloth that he sewed into the inside of his prison-issue blue pajamas with a bamboo needle.

"Every afternoon we would hang Mike's shirt on the wall of our cell and say the Pledge of Allegiance," said U.S. Sen. John McCain, a former navy pilot who was held with Christian. "For those men in that stark prison cell, it was indeed the most important and meaningful event of our day." When prison guards discovered the flag in 1971, they beat Christian mercilessly, battering his face and breaking his ribs. While recovering from his wounds, Christian secretly made a replacement flag.

A few days after the beating, "Mike approached me. He said: 'Major, they got the flag, but they didn't get the needle I made it with. If you agree, I'm making another flag,'" said air force colonel George "Bud" Day, a Medal of Honor recipient held at the Hanoi Hilton from 1967 to 1973. "My answer was, 'Do it.'"

It took Christian "several weeks" to make that second flag, Day said. After he finished it, "there was never a day from that day forward that the Stars and Stripes did not fly in my room, with forty American pilots proudly saluting."

Al Kroboth, a U.S. Marine Corps A-6 navigator, was shot down July 7, 1972, over South Vietnam. Severely wounded, he was forced to march to the Hanoi Hilton where he was held until March 27, 1973, when the North Vietnamese released him and the other American POWs. When he saw the U.S. Air Force transport plane land in Hanoi to pick up the POWs that day, Kroboth said, he did not feel emotional until he noticed the large American flag painted on the airplane's tail.

"That flag," he told the novelist Pat Conroy, a college classmate. "It had the biggest American flag on it I ever saw. To this day, I cry when I think of it. Seeing that flag, I started crying. I couldn't see the plane; I just saw the flag. All the guys started cheering. But that flag . . . that flag."

CHAPTER EIGHTEEN

United We Stand Again

* * *

I always get a chill up and down my spine when I say that Pledge of Allegiance.

— **Pres. Ronald Reagan, June 14, 1985**

O UR LONG NATIONAL NIGHTMARE is over," Gerald Ford said on August 9, 1974, when he was sworn in as president of the United States. Ford was referring to the political and constitutional turmoil that rocked the nation during the Watergate scandal, which had caused Pres. Nixon to resign. But Ford's words easily could have applied to the war in Vietnam, which wound down that summer and would end in April 1975 with the communist takeover of all of South Vietnam.

When the "nightmare" ended for the United States in Vietnam, the antiwar movement, which had been losing strength and adherents since 1971, all but ceased to exist. By the end of the war, too, the American flag all but ceased to be the divisive symbol it was in the late 1960s and early 1970s.

During the late 1970s, things were quiet, too, on the flag desecration front. One notable, widely publicized flag-burning incident did occur though during that period. It took place on April 25, 1976, during a Major League baseball game at Dodger Stadium in Los Angeles. In the bottom of the fourth inning, two men bolted from the stands and ran into the outfield, where they placed an American flag on the ground, doused it with lighter fluid and tried to light it on fire with a match. Before they could do so,

Chicago Cubs center fielder Rick Monday ran over to the men, grabbed the flag, and spirited it to safety.

"To this day, I don't know what I was thinking, except bowl them over," Monday said in 1998. "What they were doing was extremely wrong as far as I was concerned."

Monday received an ovation from the crowd in the stands that day and similar accolades at stadiums around the country during the rest of the 1976 season. Tommy Lasorda, the Los Angeles Dodgers's third-base coach that year who was on the field during the incident, called Monday's actions "One of the most heroic acts ever to take place on the field during a Major League baseball game."

Unlike the Centennial year of 1876, there was no single Bicentennial exhibition celebrating the nation's two-hundredth birthday in 1976. Instead, Americans marked the occasion throughout the year with tens of thousands of flag-rich local special events and celebrations. That included the Bicentennial's first official event, a flag-raising ceremony by National Guard troops at sunrise, 4:31 a.m. on July 4, 1976, at Mars Hill Mountain in Maine. Throughout the year Americans painted the Stars and Stripes on fire hydrants and on locomotives. The American flag appeared on countless T-shirts, ties, jackets, sweaters, and other items of apparel, as well as on dishes, coffee mugs, and countless other consumer products. Network television ran mini–history lessons called *Bicentennial Minutes*, and many schools and colleges offered new or expanded American history courses.

The American Revolution Bicentennial Commission coordinated the state celebrations, as well as the massive event held July 4, 1976, on the Mall in Washington, D.C. Millions attended that and other big Fourth of July 1976 festivities in Philadelphia and in New York City, where thousands of flag-bedecked ships, large and small, converged in New York harbor and the city put on a mammoth fireworks display. The Associated Press called the New York harbor event the "greatest maritime spectacle in American history." The vessels on hand included hundreds of small pleasure craft, a small armada of historic "tall ships," the American aircraft carrier *Forrestall*, and more than fifty warships from twenty-two countries. All of the ships, American and foreign, that day flew the Stars and Stripes. On that day also a record 10,471 American flags flew over the U.S. Capitol, and the Battle of Baltimore—complete with a Star-Spangled Banner withstanding British "bombs" bursting in air—was reenacted at Fort McHenry.

During the eight years that Ronald Reagan was president, from 1981 to 1989, the national mood seemed to reflect the president's conservative, patriotic sensibilities. That included an often-stated reverence for the American flag. The Stars and Stripes, Reagan said on Flag Day, June 14, 1983, for example, stands "for freedom and the forces of good. We apologize to no one for our ideals or our principles, nor the prosperity that we've made for ourselves and shared with the world. Let this grand flag forever be a symbol of the potential before us that free men and women can soar as high as their dreams and energy and ambitions will take them."

The "grand flag" Reagan referred to was a seven-ton Stars and Stripes called the Great American Flag that was displayed on the national Mall in Washington. Billed as the largest American flag ever made, it was more than four-hundred-feet long and 200-feet wide. Each of the fifty stars measured thirteen feet across. The nylon and polyester flag had been manufactured by an Evansville, Indiana, tent manufacturer, Anchor Industries, in 1980, and an organization called the Great American Flag Fund presented it that day to the government.

"I always get a chill up and down my spine when I say that Pledge of Allegiance," Reagan said at the June 14, 1985, Flag Day ceremonies held at Fort McHenry in Baltimore, marking the hundredth anniversary of the first organized Flag Day commemoration in Boston. "From the mountains of Kentucky to the shores of California to the Sea of Tranquillity on the Moon, our pioneers carried our flag before them, a symbol of the indomitable spirit of a free people. And let us never forget that in honoring our flag, we honor the American men and women who have courageously fought and died for it over the last 200 years—patriots who set an ideal above any consideration of self and who suffered for it the greatest hardships. Our flag flies free today because of their sacrifice."

Flag sales rose significantly during the Reagan years. Flag waving reached its zenith during the Reagan administration at the 1984 Summer Olympics in Los Angeles. The United States dominated those games when the Soviet Union and thirteen of its communist allies boycotted the event in retaliation for the American boycott of the 1980 games in protest over the Soviet invasion of Afghanistan.

The Olympic emphasis on the flag began at the White House in Washington on Flag Day, June 14, 1984, when President Reagan presented the Stars and Stripes that would be carried in the opening and closing ceremonies to William Simon, the president of the United States Olympic Committee. "The team, walking behind the banner, our flag, in the opening ceremonies will truly be our team, America's team," the president said. "And I can't help believing that on that day, July 28th, the members of our team will feel all of us there with them—all of us behind them. They'll feel our pride in them, and they'll feel the unity, the patriotism, and the deep love we share for America, for our land of the free."

American athletes took home an unprecedented 174 medals at the Los Angeles Olympics, including 83 first-place gold medals. American fans cheered on those victories with displays of waving American flags that appeared prominently in ABC Television's extensive coverage of the games and in newspaper accounts for sixteen days, beginning with the July 28 opening ceremonies. Winning American athletes waved large and small flags and posed for victory celebrations in front of giant Stars and Stripes. Perhaps the games' most publicized image was track star Carl Lewis, who won four gold medals, taking a large American flag from a spectator in the stands after one of his victories and waving it triumphantly over his head as he took a long, slow victory lap around the Los Angeles Coliseum track.

Since the mid-nineteenth century, virtually every major party presidential candidate had used the Stars and Stripes in advertising and as a prop at campaign stops. Ronald Reagan, though, put the flag to extraordinarily wide use during his successful 1984 reelection campaign against Democratic nominee Walter Mondale. It was not uncommon for the President and Mrs. Reagan to appear at campaign rallies in 1984 holding small American flags with a gigantic Stars and Stripes serving as a backdrop. A widely used campaign ad pictured the president's visage atop the White House with an American flag arrayed behind him and the words "REAGAN FOR PRESIDENT: Let's make America great again."

On May 12, 1986, President Reagan issued a proclamation, following congressional passage of a joint resolution asking him to do so, proclaiming 1986 the Year of the Flag. "There is no greater, more beautiful, and instantly recognizable symbol of our nation and its ideals, traditions and values than the flag of the United States," the president said. "Let [1986] be the year we as a people commemorate our flag as the proud banner that the winds of freedom lovingly caress, for which generations of patriots have fought and died—the sign and symbol of a people ruled by a Constitution that protects all and enshrines our hopes and our history."

★   ★   ★

The flag played a significant role in the 1988 George H. W. Bush–Michael Dukakis presidential election campaign. Vice President Bush and his supporters—including his vice presidential running mate Sen. Dan Quayle of Indiana, Education secretary William Bennett, and Pres. Ronald

Reagan—made former Massachusetts governor Dukakis's 1977 veto of a bill that would have required the Pledge of Allegiance to be recited in Massachusetts's public schools into one of the main issues of his campaign. Congressman Newt Gingrich of Georgia raised the issue for the first time in Washington on May 19, when he circulated a copy of Dukakis's eleven-year-old veto message. "I would just love to see him explain on national television for three or four minutes why a bill requiring the Pledge of Allegiance at the beginning of the school day is unconstitutional," Gingrich, who later became Speaker of the House, said. "When the country realizes that the lawyers who advised him to veto that bill are the people he'd put on the Supreme Court, we've won the South."

Bush kept the issue alive in speeches throughout the summer. In his acceptance speech at the Republican National Convention in New Orleans in August Bush asked rhetorically: "Should public school teachers be required to lead our children in the Pledge of Allegiance? My opponent says no—I say yes." Bush ended that speech by leading delegates in the Pledge. He went on to recite it regularly at campaign rallies, where Bush also continued to condemn the 1977 veto. "What is it about the Pledge of Allegiance that upsets him so much," Bush said at an August 24 rally in Los Angeles with Pres. Ronald Reagan at his side. "It is very hard for me to imagine that the Founding Fathers—Samuel Adams and John Hancock and John Adams—would have objected to teachers leading students in the Pledge of Allegiance to the flag of the United States."

Bush highlighted his attachment to the flag by paying a campaign visit in September to the Annin and Co. flag factory in Bloomfield, New Jersey, and making an appearance at the Flag City Festival in Findlay, Ohio. That northwest Ohio city had been designated "Flag City USA" by a U.S. House of Representatives Joint Resolution in 1974 in honor of the fact that since the mid-1960s city residents displayed some fourteen thousand flags every year on Flag Day.

During the campaign, a Bush ally, Republican senator Steve Symms of Idaho, accused—falsely, as it turned out—Dukakis's wife Kitty of burning an American flag at an antiwar demonstration in the 1960s, a charge that he later withdrew. Speaking at the Veterans of Foreign Wars annual convention on August 22 in Chicago, Bush made a reference to flag burning in his heated response to allegations that Senator Quayle had avoided service in the Vietnam War by joining the National Guard. "He did not go to Canada," Bush said of Quayle. "He did not burn his draft card and he damn sure did not burn the American flag."

Quayle brought the flag into the October 5 nationally broadcast vice presidential debate with Dukakis's running mate, Sen. Lloyd Bentsen of Texas. In his closing statement Quayle contrasted the two presidential nominees. Dukakis, Quayle said, stood for "bigger government, higher taxes" and "cuts in national defense." Bush, he said, stood for "an America second to none, with visions of greatness, economic expansion, tough laws, tough judges, strong values, respect for the flag and our institutions."

George Bush denied that he used the flag for partisan political purposes during the election campaign. "I don't view that as partisanship," he said at a June 27, 1989, White House news conference. "I think respect for the flag transcends political party. It isn't Republican or Democrat; it isn't liberal or conservative. And I just feel very, very strongly about it." During the campaign, he said, "I didn't put it on the basis that Republicans are for the flag and Democrats not."

Bush's patriotic embrace of the flag resonated with many voters. "I like Bush's attitude," a voter in Modesto, California, said during the campaign. "It's the patriotism thing, the flag—you know, the Pledge of Allegiance and all that. I'm not sure he'll be able to do much about the deficit, which worries me a lot, but he's patriotic, so I'm sure that he'll try."

                        ʌ   ʌ   ʌ

In February 1989, a month after George Bush had taken the presidential oath of office—and as the *Johnson* case was pending before the U.S. Supreme Court—an exhibit featuring the American flag at the School of the Art Institute of Chicago stirred up a great deal of outraged protest. The work in question, an installation called "What is the Proper Way to Display a U.S. Flag?" was created by a student at the school, Scott Tyler, who used the name Dread Scott. The three-part installation consisted of a photomontage of South Korean students burning American flags and six American flag-draped coffins in a military transport plane hanging on the wall. Below it was a blank-paged book and pens on a shelf. A three-foot-by-five-foot American flag sat on the floor in front of the book and montage. The artist asked visitors to write their responses to the installation's titular question in the book. While doing so, they could choose to stand on the American flag.

The school began having second thoughts about Scott's artwork before the show opened on February 17. Officials asked Scott to substitute another work, but he declined to do so. Several veterans' groups, including the Veterans of Foreign Wars, the American Legion, and VietNow, filed suit in

Cook County Circuit Court to close the show. A judge dismissed the suit. Newly installed President Bush spoke out on the issue, calling the show "disgraceful." Congress in March added an amendment to the 1968 federal Flag Protection Act making it illegal to place a flag on the floor. Bob Dole, the Senate Minority Leader, said the amendment would apply to "the so-called 'artist' who has invited the trampling on the flag."

The Illinois and Indiana Legislatures and the Chicago City Council passed resolutions condemning the exhibition. The Illinois Legislature also cut the Art Institute School's state funding from seventy thousand to one dollar. Some five thousand people mounted a protest demonstration on March 12, and smaller protests took place every day the exhibit was open to the public.

For its part the Art Institute school maintained that Scott's installation, no matter how provocative, did not desecrate the flag. "We are trying to defend the notion that all art, provocative art, can be displayed," said James McManus, chairman of the school's Liberal Arts Department.

The artist has exhibited the installation thirteen times since 1989. He maintains it is a political work that is designed to prompt debate about the meaning of the Stars and Stripes. "My intent with the work was to open up discussion about America, U.S. patriotism, and the U.S. flag," Scott said in 2003. "My intent was neither to desecrate, nor not to desecrate the flag." Scott, who describes himself as a "revolutionary," said that he "has no love for this flag" because "America has committed towering crimes" under it and the nation "is profoundly unjust." As for the installation, he characterized it as "a participatory work" that "in some respects doesn't reflect—and has little to do with—my personal view of America or its flag."

Scott said he "had no idea, and nobody else did either, that this work by an unknown artist would become the center of a national controversy." When he designed the installation in 1988, Scott said, "the first George Bush was campaigning for president and stopping in all these flag factories." By "placing the flag on the ground and enabling people to walk on it and including pictures of South Korean students burning flags, the work enables those who are oppressed by America to know that their thoughts and ideas are welcome within the context of the work. Normally these voices are silenced in any discussion of the flag. This art brings these voices into the debate within the broad range of people who interact with the work."

Although his intent "was not to desecrate the flag," Scott said, the work "welcomes the sentiments of those who would and encourages many to think about why some may want to do so."

★   ★   ★

The first Persian Gulf War, the fighting portion of which was known as Operation Desert Storm, began in the early morning hours of January 17, 1991. It ended on March 3, after coalition forces, led by the United States, pushed Iraqi president Saddam Hussein's troops out of Kuwait. That conflict, the first large-scale war fought by the United States since the Vietnam War, liberated Kuwait with minimal American casualties. Fewer than three hundred American military personnel died in Desert Storm and fewer than five hundred were wounded.

Americans, partly in reaction to the negative reception given to Vietnam War veterans by many doves and even by some hawks, rallied around the troops who fought in Operation Desert Storm. While there was some criticism of the efficacy of the war, there was near unanimity in the outpouring of support for the American men and women who fought in Kuwait and Iraq in 1991. A good portion of that support was expressed using the American flag.

As was the case with the Civil War in the North and World War I throughout the nation, Americans of all walks of life displayed the Stars and Stripes at the outset of the 1991 Persian Gulf War. "Our pride in the skill and professionalism of our troops has stirred a renewed sense of patriotism throughout our country and is reflected in the tremendous number of American flags that now fly daily over homes and businesses," Congressman C. W. "Bill" Young, a Florida Republican, said on the floor of the House of Representatives on June 19, 1991. "We will forever remember the site of the Kuwaiti people rejoicing as American troops, flying the American flag, triumphantly entered a newly liberated Kuwait City and hoisted the flag over the American Embassy."

At home, sports teams at every level showed their patriotism and their support for the troops during the Persian Gulf War by adding American flags to their uniforms and showcasing the Stars and Stripes at athletic events. "There is hardly a pro or college team in the land that hasn't made some symbolic gesture in support of the U.S. forces," *Sports Illustrated* reported on February 25. "Flag decals and patches are everywhere, from the helmets of NFL players to the backboards of NBA arenas, from the shoe of a high school wrestler to the jersey of Waad Hirmez, the Iraqi-born soccer star of the San Diego Sockers."

Crowds of families and friends, many waving American flags, emotionally and enthusiastically welcomed the 467,000 American troops who served in the Persian Gulf when their units returned home in the spring of 1991. Later the troops took part in flag-rich welcome-home parades across the nation, including the nationally televised "Operation Welcome Home" ticker tape parade in New York City on June 10 and the National Victory Celebration in Washington, D.C., on June 8.

The Wm. Wrigley Jr. Company of Chicago commissioned a massive, eight-story-high, four-story-wide American flag to display at that city's welcome home parade for Operation Desert Storm veterans on May 10. Wrigley, the world's largest chewing gum manufacturer, had the flag made by Flags Unlimited of Saint Charles, Illinois. The enormous flag consisted of seventy different pieces of material sewed together with more than a mile of thread. It was suspended by cables and hung from the Wrigley Building on North Michigan Avenue.

*   *   *

For a decade after the end of Operation Desert Storm, the United States was at peace. The flag did not come up as a political issue in the 1992, 1996, or 2000 presidential elections. There were no flag controversies or changes in the flag during the eight years, 1993–2001, during which Bill Clinton served as president. The most memorable flag-related event of the Clinton presidency came on July 13, 1998, when he gave a speech at the Smithsonian Institution's National Museum of American History at ceremonies marking the start of the restoration of the Star-Spangled Banner.

"You can neither honor the past, nor imagine the future, nor achieve it without the kind of citizenship embodied by all of our memories of the flag," Clinton said that day. "So as you see this flag and leave this place, promise yourself that when your great-grandchildren are here, they'll not only be able to see the Star Spangled Banner, it will mean just as much to them then as it does to you today."

*   *   *

In the wake of the events of September 11, 2001, the American flag became an instant and widely used symbol of a nation united against terrorism. Within days after the attacks in New York, Washington, and Pennsylvania, millions of Americans proudly and defiantly unfurled American flags in every corner of the country. Flags appeared on cars and trucks, on front lawns, and hung from living room windows, office buildings, and in commercial establishments of every stripe. People stuck small flags into their hats and taped them to their computers at work and at home. Police departments, departments of corrections, and other state and local agencies directed employees to wear American flag patches on their uniforms.

Flags flown at the World Trade Center and the Pentagon became instant and widely seen symbols of American patriotism, defiance, and resolve in the face of the attacks. Those attacks took the lives of more than three thousand civilians and rescue workers—more than the number of Americans who died in the War of 1812, the Spanish-American War, or in the first Persian Gulf War.

The day after the attacks, firefighters at the Pentagon unfurled a twenty-by-thirty-eight-foot Stars and Stripes—a garrison flag that had been used by the U.S. Army Band as a concert backdrop—from the roof of the building's western wall. That was where the Al Qaeda terrorists had crashed an American Airlines jet, killing 189 people in the plane and in the building. The flag hung on the Pentagon until October 11. Pentagon officials then turned it over to the U.S. Army Center of Military History and displayed it at the Smithsonian Institution's National Museum of American History in Washington in the same spot where the Star-Spangled Banner had hung from 1964 to 1998.

A tattered flag, the only one flying outside the World Trade Center when the terrorist attacks took place, was rescued from the buildings' rubble three days later. The flag was given to the Port Authority Police and displayed at funerals and memorial services for the thirty-seven Port Authority Police officers who perished September 11 at the World Trade Center. The flag flew over Yankee Stadium during the three games of the 2001 World Series in October. "We wanted a place America could see this flag," said Port Authority sergeant Antonio Scannella, who escorted the flag to Yankee Stadium. "So they could see the rips in it, but it still flies."

The flag was then displayed at the New York City Veterans Day Parade, the Macy's Thanksgiving Day Parade, during the singing of the National Anthem at the Super Bowl in New Orleans on February 2, 2002, and at the NCAA college championship basketball game in Atlanta on April 1. Eight athletes, escorted by a phalanx of New York City firefighters and police officers, carried the flag into Rice-Eccles Stadium on February 8 during the opening ceremonies of the 2002 Winter Olympics in Salt Lake City.

"It was pretty emotional," said army sergeant Kristina Sabasteanski, one of the eight Olympians who carried the flag that day. "This is the World Trade

Center flag and it represents the power of America that we can come back. Then you're thinking this flag was what was left of three thousand lives. One second you'd be inspired, elated, and the next you're choking back tears."

Another flag recovered in the World Trade Center debris—along with a Marine Corps flag from the Pentagon, an American flag donated by the state of Pennsylvania and six thousand small American flags—was taken aboard the shuttle *Endeavour* on its December 5, 2001, mission to the International Space Station. Soon after the Russian and American astronauts returned to Earth on December 17 NASA distributed the small flags to families of the September 11 victims.

On October 2, 2001, the U.S. Postal Service (USPS) unveiled a new thirty-four-cent stamp with an image of a waving red, white, and blue American flag and the words "United We Stand." Hundreds of millions of those stamps were soon in post offices around the nation. "It is fitting that the U.S. Postal Service—which has served the people of this nation since the dawn of our republic—is planning to issue the 'United We Stand' postage stamp," Robert F. Rider, the chairman of the USPS Board of Governors, said October 2. "For our primary job has always been 'to bind the nation together.' Today, more than ever, the people of America are united in their purpose, their pride, and their determination. This postage stamp is graphic representation of that unity."

On October 9, U.S. secretary of education Rod Paige sent a letter to more than hundred thousand public and high school principals across the nation encouraging them to be a part of an event that was similar to the National Columbian Public School Celebration of October 21, 1892. Paige asked the schools to take part in a "Pledge Across America" program by participating in a synchronized Pledge of Allegiance at two o'clock in the afternoon Eastern time on Columbus Day, October 12. The secretary also contacted governors, state legislators, mayors, and state education heads, asking them to join the event, which Celebration USA, a California-based patriotic group, organized.

Teachers nationwide, Paige said in his October 9 letter, "have been working with students to help them understand what happened on September 11, and to overcome their fears and concerns. They have also worked to teach them more about our proud and rich national history and the foundations of our free society. Today, I ask students, teachers, parents, and other proud Americans across the country to join me in showing our patriotism by reciting the Pledge of Allegiance at a single time and with a unified voice. . . . Together, we can send a loud and powerful message that will be heard around the world: America is 'one nation, under God, indivisible, with liberty and justice for all.' "

In the months following September 11, 2001, several states adopted new laws mandating or encouraging the use of the American flag. The Mississippi State Legislature, for example, enacted a law in 2002 requiring that the Stars and Stripes be displayed in all public school classrooms at all times while schools were in session. The same law required Mississippi school districts to provide instruction to students on flag etiquette and to recite the Pledge of Allegiance daily at the beginning of class.

Many Americans followed the lead of Pres. George W. Bush, who— along with the White House staff and many administration leaders and members of Congress—began wearing American-flag-shaped lapel pins on their suit jackets after September 11. Television news reporters and anchors, including the entire staff of *FOX News*, also sported the small but very visible flag lapel pins. When *ABC News* barred its journalists from wearing the flag pins on the air in the name of objectivity, *FOX News* correspondent Brit Hume criticized the network on the air for doing so.

At the same time, the television evangelist Rev. Jerry Falwell offered free Pray for America flag lapel pins to those who pledged to pray for the nation and its leaders. A Gallup survey taken four days after the attacks reported that 82 percent of those polled said they had flown or planned to fly the American flag in response to the attacks.

Not surprisingly, sales of flags soared, and flag manufacturers across the nation were inundated with orders. Many retail outlets sold out of American flags within days after the terrorist attacks. Wal-Mart, the nation's largest retailer, reported that it sold some 450,000 American flags in the three days after September 11. In the next twelve months, Wal-Mart stores sold more than 7.8 million American flags.

In the summer of 2002, the nation's top flag manufacturer, Annin & Co., reported that its factory in Coshocton, Ohio, was turning out more than 250,000 flags a week—flags the company supplied to large retailers such as Wal-Mart. The plant produced flags ranging in size from four-by-six inches to four-by-six feet; the most popular was the three-by-five-foot flag most often displayed from front porches. "We've been running two ten-hour shifts six days a week to keep up with the demand," said plant manager Richard Merrell.

Aside from millions of small, medium, and large-size flags, a spate of gigantic American flags made appearances around the nation in the days, weeks, and months after September 11. In Fayetteville, North Carolina, for example, more than a dozen volunteers helped paint a forty-six-foot-wide, eighty-six-foot-long flag on the roof of a barn on Joe Gillis's farm. "We were just trying to say, 'Hey, we're right here, nobody's going to tread on us,'" Gillis said. "We couldn't pick up a rifle and go yonder, but we wanted everybody to know we were supporting them."

In October 2001, Ricoh Corporation, the office machine company, and Tahari Fashions cosponsored the display of the largest American flag ever flown in New York City, a five-story, one-hundred-fifty-foot-long, fifty-two-foot-high Stars and Stripes that was draped over the office building the two companies shared at Fifth Avenue and Forty-third Street. The flag was made of see-through mesh material. The company's president and CEO said the huge flag was meant to be "another way to show the [human] spirit" that was alive in the city after September 11.

The Adera Corporation of Las Vegas produced dozens of enormous American flags in the weeks after September 11. The largest, commissioned by Siebel Systems of San Mateo, California, measured twenty thousand square feet—one hundred feet high and two hundred feet wide. The flag was produced with a special wide-format ink-jet printer on perforated window vinyl. It was installed at a Siebel office building close to Interstate 80 in Emeryville, near San Francisco, and was visible to some 293,000 freeway drivers every weekday.

On Flag Day, June 14, 2002, Duck Tape brand duct tape showed off the world's largest American flag made of the familiar gray-colored adhesive in New York City's Union Square Park. The fifty-by-ninety-five-foot flag, produced by the duct tape artist Todd Scott, consisted of 1,120 rolls of duct tape—some thirteen miles of it—and weighed more than five hundred pounds. On Friday, May 23, 2003, the start of Memorial Day weekend, Marshall Field's department store flew a fifty-by-one-hundred-foot American flag from the seventh floor of its store on State Street in Chicago. The massive Stars and Stripes, billed as the largest American flag ever displayed in a department store, flowed down to the first floor. It revived a tradition dating to World War I. "Marshall Field's is proud to resurrect a tradition that began at the State Street store in 1916 when the first fifty-by-one-hundred-foot American flag was hoisted in honor of this holiday," said Ralph Hughes, the store's regional director.

A 940-pound, football-field-size flag, measuring 255 by 505 feet, which had been displayed at events such as the Super Bowl and the World Series and at the Washington Monument and Hoover Dam, made an appearance in Ocean City, Maryland, on Sunday, May 25, 2003. Some five hundred volunteers displayed the flag on the beach, a first for that gigantic Stars and Stripes, which cannot be unfurled in winds of over twenty-five miles per hour.

The large flags were not confined to large cities and metropolitan areas. On September 21, 2002, more than thirteen hundred people holding red, white, and blue pieces of paper formed a human American flag at Nara Park in Acton, Massachusetts, west of Boston. The event, part of the annual Acton Day festivities, was recognized as the "largest human national flag" by the Guinness organization until September 10, 2003, when 10,371 spectators at a European Championship soccer match in Dortmond, Germany formed the black, red, and gold German flag.

A thirty-by-sixty-foot American flag was raised on Flag Day 2003 at Wylie Park outside of Aberdeen, South Dakota. Local schoolchildren raised the funds to purchase the flag in conjunction with the National Flag Foundation's Flags Across America program. After September 11, Elizabeth Barnes of Norfolk, Virginia, conceived of a giant cross-stitched American flag, made up of squares containing the names of Americans killed in terrorist incidents since 1971. With the help of many volunteers, Barnes completed the flag, measuring thirty-five by sixty feet, in 2002. Since then, it has been displayed in Jacksonville, North Carolina, and Chambersburg, Pennsylvania, among other places.

"Originally, I was going to make little flags for victims of the Pentagon," Barnes said, "but then I decided to do one flag remembering the victims of September 11. It snowballed into this huge flag."

On June 2, 2003, a thirty-by-sixty-foot American flag, billed as the largest in the state of Wisconsin, was raised near Interstate 43 in Sheboygan on a one-hundred-fifty-foot flagpole, the tallest in the state. ACUITY, a regional insurance company, sponsored the flag and flagpole, which received a twenty-one-gun salute from an Army Reserve Rifle Team and a flyby from four F-16 Wisconsin Air National Guard jets. The company announced it would replace the flag every month and that sixteen one-thousand-watt spotlights would illuminate it at night.

The American Legion's Americanism Division in Indianapolis was inundated with questions about flag usage in the days after the September 11 attacks, according to Michael Buss, the division's assistant director. "I normally answer twenty-five to thirty questions, at most, about the flag by email or telephone each week," Buss said. "After 9/11 for a good month, we were averaging two or three hundred questions a week. I couldn't get off the phone quick enough with reporters wanting to know this and that."

Most of the questions from the media and the public, Buss said, involved displaying the flag. "Right after 9/11, the President issued a proclamation to display the flag at half staff, so people wanted to know how long it was to be and how to do it, especially with the house set, a flag on a pole attached to the porch. The physical make-up of that type of display pretty much prohibits it being placed at half staff." There were also questions about displaying the flag at night, and the propriety of wearing a flag patch.

Soon the Legion was fielding questions about the proper way to dispose of flags that had been torn or tattered. "We point them in the direction of the American Legion headquarters in their state and they can try and get them in contact with a post that does that service," Buss said.

Section 3 of the U.S. Flag Code prohibits the manufacture, sale, or exposure for sale (or to public view) of any article of merchandise "upon which shall have been printed, painted, attached or otherwise placed a representation" of the flag. In the wake of the September 11 events, though, that stricture (which, as is the case with the entire code, is not enforceable) was widely disregarded amid the explosion of American flag images that adorned products of virtually every description. That included countless items of apparel, led by the ubiquitous American flag T-shirt.

The list of post–September 11, 2001, flag-adorned consumer items also included:

- American flag contact lenses from CooperVision, with net proceeds temporarily going to the United Way September 11 fund.

- Tootsie Rolls in Stars and Stripes wrappers sent to American troops in Afghanistan in February 2002.

- Little Patriot disposal diapers in red, white, and blue from Paragon Trade Brands, with 10 percent of the proceeds going to the Red Cross.

- A Luciano Barbera cashmere American flag blanket, retail price: $1,995.

- Hallmark greeting cards adorned with the flag and other patriotic symbols.

- A special edition "American Patriots" Hummel figurine of two boys marching side by side, one playing a drum, the other holding a waving American flag.

Very few Americans objected to the fact that these and other consumer items violated the U.S. Flag Code. Traditionally patriotic segments of society wholeheartedly embraced the American flag. That included country music performers such as Alan Jackson, Toby Keith, Darryl Worley, and the duo of Brooks & Dunn, all of whom featured large American flags, patriotic songs, and flag-waving montages in their music videos and stage acts. Keith's song, "Courtesy of the Red, White, and Blue (The Angry American)," written a week after the September 11 terrorist attacks, became a huge hit the following year and was the centerpiece of Keith's popular concert shows. Keith strummed an American flag–embossed acoustic guitar at his live performances, which also featured a rendition of "The Star-Spangled Banner" by his guitarist and explosions of red, white, and blue confetti.

Politically liberal Americans—many of whom a generation earlier had used the American flag to voice their dissatisfaction with the Vietnam War—also embraced the Stars and Stripes after the terrorist attacks. "September 11 made it safe for liberals to be patriots," the critic George Packer wrote in late September. American academics, many of whom are politically liberal, are "not noted for [their] public display of patriotic sentiments," Walter Berns, a resident scholar at the conservative American Enterprise Institute, said after September 11. "So I was pleasantly surprised by the public response to 9/11, particularly the extent to which the flag was displayed." As Berns indicated, many politically liberal Americans changed their thinking about the meaning of the flag in the wake of the terrorist attacks and flew the Stars and Stripes out of respect to those who lost their lives and in resolve to back the nation's future fight against terrorism.

Not all former flag-flying disdainers felt that way, however. Katha Pollitt, a columnist for the liberal magazine *The Nation,* objected when her high-school-aged daughter suggested flying the flag from their living room window in New York City. "Definitely not, I say: The flag stands for jingoism and vengeance and war," Pollitt wrote. "There are no symbolic representations right now for the things the world really needs—equality and justice and humanity and solidarity and intelligence."

★　　★　　★

When the United States began military operations against Iraq in March 2003, the American people again reacted with a large showing of the American flag in support of the troops. Flag sales increased markedly, flags were displayed nationwide in abundance, and there was another spike in the popularity of flag-embossed clothing and other consumer items. Some Americans, though, in actions similar to what happened during the Vietnam War, used the flag to protest the preemptive military strike into Iraq designed to oust the nation's repressive leader Saddam Hussein and to seize his regime's weapons of mass destruction.

Antiwar activists lowered flags to half-staff or flew them upside down in protest. At a U.S. Army and Marine Corps recruiting station in a Lansing, New York, shopping mall, protesters splattered human blood onto an American flag. Some, including Arizona State University students at a rally in Tempe on March 20, burned the Stars and Stripes in protest. The war also sparked some Americans to speak out about ubiquitous flag waving.

"The flag's been hijacked and turned into a logo, the trademark of a monopoly on patriotism," Bill Moyers, the PBS TV commentator, said several weeks before the war began, on the February 23, 2003, edition of *NOW With Bill Moyers*. "On those Sunday morning talk shows, official chests appear adorned with the flag as if it is the *Good Housekeeping* Seal of Approval. . . . When I see flags sprouting on official lapels, I think of the time in China when I saw Mao's little red book on every official's desk, omnipresent and unread."

Moyers, who wore a flag pin on his lapel on the program, said he did so "as a modest riposte to men with flags in their lapels who shoot missiles from the safety of Washington think tanks, or argue that sacrifice is good as long as they don't have to make it [and] to remind myself that not every patriot thinks we should do to the people of Baghdad what Bin Laden did to us." The flag, Moyers said, "belongs to the country, not to the government. And it reminds me that it is not un-American to think that war—except in self-defense—is a failure of moral imagination, political nerve and diplomacy."

Retired U.S. Army general Wesley K. Clark, a candidate for the 2004 Democratic Party presidential nomination, spoke out strongly in the fall and winter of 2003 against politicians who figuratively wrapped themselves in the American flag for political purposes in the wake of the Iraq war. In late November Clark began integrating what journalists called a "grasp the flag and talk" segment into his campaign speeches.

"That's the flag I served under. That's the flag I fought for," Clark said, for example, at a December 5 campaign stop in McMinnville, Tennessee, as he held an American flag. "It's going to be about the Republicans trying to take away our flag and patriotism and our faith from us. With me as your candidate, I'm not going to let them do that."

The American flag, Clark said later that month in a speech at Phillips Exeter Academy in New Hampshire, "doesn't belong to the Republican

Party." As he had done earlier, Clark had stopped his speech, turned from the lectern, and grabbed a Stars and Stripes displayed at the back of the stage. Clark then asked veterans in the audience to stand. "That's our flag," he said. "We saluted that flag. We served under it. We fought for it. We watched brave men and women buried under it. And no [Republican House Majority Leader] Tom Delay or [U.S. Attorney General] John Ashcroft or George W. Bush is going to take this flag away from us."

The political essayist and social critic Barbara Ehrenreich spoke in February 2003 of a "virus-like proliferation of American flags." The flag, she said, "has, through sheer repetition, been reduced to the equivalent of wallpaper: flag sweaters, flag pins, flag earrings, flag Christmas lights, flag bathing suits, flag sweatshirts, flag underwear. Inevitably, this results in flag burning, since almost any random mound of garbage you ignite is bound to contain some flag or flag-like representation."

A collegiate basketball player, Toni Smith of Manhattanville College in New York, created a mini national stir when she began turning her back to the American flag during the playing of the National Anthem before her team's games in February. "A lot of people blindly stand up and salute the flag, but I feel that blindly facing the flag hurts more people," Smith said. "There are a lot of inequities in this country and these are issues that need to be acknowledged. The rich are getting richer and our priorities are elsewhere." Veterans and others criticized Smith's actions, but she was allowed to continue her silent protests. "It is not about the flag to us," Richard A. Berman, the president of Manhattanville College, said. "We support our troops, but I think it is healthy to have kids on college campuses expressing their views. That's where the energy comes from."

In Iraq itself, American troops, whose uniforms contained an American flag patch on the right sleeve, were—for perhaps the first time since the military began flying the national flag in the War of 1812—under orders not to fly the Stars and Stripes. The reason: not to give the impression that the Americans were leading an invasion of Iraq. "It's imposing enough that we're coming into another society," said U.S. Army captain Frank Stanco, a 101st Airborne Division artillery unit commander. "I tell our soldiers we want to maintain our professionalism. We could be making history. I call it being quiet professionals."

The non–flag-flying directive was not strictly followed. Some American troops defiantly carried the Stars and Stripes with them into Iraq. That included Cpl. Edward Chin of the U.S. Marine Corps's First Tank Battalion. On April 2, Chin and another marine climbed to the top of a large statue of

Saddam Hussein in Firdos Square in Baghdad as a crowd tried to dismantle it. Chin covered the statue's face with an American flag just before the statue came down. The flag was only on the statue for a few minutes before it was replaced by an Iraqi flag, but Abu Dhabi Television broadcast the image live.

"You can understand these Marines who have put their lives on the line, sweated with blood and guts for the past three weeks wanting to show the Stars and Stripes in this moment of glory," *FOX News* television anchor David Asman said of Chin's actions. "It is understandable, but no doubt [the Arab television network] Al-Jazeera and others will make hay with that."

Two weeks later, when a group of marines unfurled an American flag as they took over a regional governor's office in Mosul, Iraqis began a violent street protest over the flying of the Stars and Stripes. In the ensuing firefight at least seven Iraqis were killed. "You must respect the flag," an Iraqi said. "They say to us they want to leave our country soon. How can we believe them if they put up the American flag?"

The Pentagon continued its policy of not showing the flag in Iraq following the June 28, 2004, transfer of sovereignty to an interim Iraqi government. That policy included a special order issued on July 4 at the First Cavalry Division's Forward Operating Base (FOB) Eagle near Sadr City. The words "You cannot display an American flag outside the FOB" were written in red marker on a message board outside one platoon's barracks. Inside the compound the American troops celebrated the Fourth with modest displays of the flag, including a card table–size cake depicting the Stars and Stripes.

On the day that the transfer of sovereignty was official, June 30, U.S. Marines raised an American flag at the new U.S. Embassy in Baghdad — the first time the Stars and Stripes had flown there since the start of the first Persian Gulf War in 1991. The new U.S. Embassy was housed temporarily in a former palace of the ousted Iraqi leader Saddam Hussein in the heavily fortified area known as the Green Zone.

When the war began, the U.S. military brought a supply of American flags to Iraq for the grim purpose of covering the caskets of Americans killed there. The custom of using a flag as a pall to cover the body or the coffin of a fallen soldier dates from the time of the Romans. "We believe that the original form of the pall was a Roman soldier's cloak that was draped over his body as it was carried in procession to the grave," said Jon N. Austin, the director of the Museum of Funeral Customs in Illinois. "The cloak gave way to a rectangular piece of cloth emblazoned with the arms of the deceased or parish guild prior to the general use of a coffin or burial container."

In a sense, Austin said, "the use of the American flag probably has ancient military origins in which the deceased veteran is figuratively wrapped
in his country's colors in recognition of service to his country."

Historians believe that the custom of draping military caskets with national flags began during the Napoleonic Wars in the late-eighteenth and
early-nineteenth century. In this country the tradition likely began during
the Civil War. "It was simply a matter that there was a shortage of caskets,
predominately in the North, and flags were used to cover the bodies," said
Tom Sherlock, the historian at Arlington National Cemetery.

American military funeral flags are provided to family members by the
branch of service of those who are killed on active duty. The U.S. Department of Veterans Affairs provides the flags for other veterans' funerals.
When the flag is draped over a casket in a military funeral, it is placed so
that the canton is at the head and over the left shoulder. The flag, which is
not allowed to touch the ground, is not placed in the grave. It is folded thirteen times into the shape of a triangle and presented to the next of kin at the
end of the funeral.

The origin of the custom of folding the American flag into the shape of
a triangle at the end of military funerals and on other occasions is unknown. Some have postulated that it is a tribute to the tricornered hats
wore by patriots during the American Revolution. "There is no meaning to
the triangle," according to Whitney Smith. "It's simply a matter of conve-
nience that [the] military came up with."

Historians believe the flag-folding ceremony probably originated during World War I, a period of time when the flag was heartily embraced as
the nation's symbol. There is a reference to the custom in James A. Moss's
1930 book, *The Flag of the United States: Its History and Symbolism*. Widely
promulgated flag-folding ceremonies developed by the American Legion
and the National Flag Foundation, which give a meaning for each of the
thirteen folds, are not based on any provisions of the U.S. Flag Code nor on
any official government flag etiquette edict.

The American flag has been used in a much more positive manner during the Iraq war—to greet troops as they return home. Individuals and
"Support Our Troops" groups across the nation organized the flag-waving,
welcome-home celebrations. Members of those groups and others also have
waved flags and displayed patriotic signs near military installations. Scores
of "Support Our Troops" rallies featuring American flags took place nationwide after the fighting began in March 2003. That included a large flag-
waving rally held March 22 at Cathedral Square in Milwaukee. On April 5,

2003, a crowd of some two hundred, many waving American flags, gathered in the parking lot of the La Mesa, California, American Legion post to sing patriotic songs and hear speeches in support of the war effort. Most of the more than two hundred people who marched in a Support Our Troops rally on April 13 in Grand Island, Nebraska, wore red, white, and blue clothing and many carried American flags.

★   ★   ★

It's difficult to believe that the members of the Continental Congress who resolved on June 14, 1777, that "the flag of the United States be thirteen stripes, alternate red and white: that the union be thirteen stars, white in a blue field representing a new constellation" envisioned that the emblem they created would become the most revered symbol of the nation they created and would play a pivotal role in the nation's political and cultural history into the twenty-first century. Old Glory, in its unparalleled position as *the* symbol of the United States, has become one of the lasting legacies created by our Founding Fathers—even though we are not certain exactly which of those fathers (or mothers) conceived of the design.

The flag's design is at once simple and meaningful. The constellation of stars representing the states has more than stood the test of time as it grew from thirteen to fifty. For whatever reason, as the nation has grown from a feisty group of thirteen colonies into the world's most powerful nation during the last 227 years hundreds of millions of American have found special meaning in the red, white, and blue colors and the stars-and-stripes motif. They have risked their lives to defend it and clung to it with emotional white heat in times of national crisis.

Why did this flag—which began almost as an afterthought, and which was used almost exclusively as a military and government banner from 1777 to the start of the Civil War—take on such powerful meaning to millions of Americans beginning in 1861?

There is no definitive answer, probably because the underlying reasons are psychological, social, spiritual, and political. People, whatever nation they live in, have an emotional need to attach themselves to a unifying symbol. But that doesn't explain why Americans have a unique, special feeling for our national flag and why that situation continues as strong as ever in the first decade of the twenty-first century.

One important part of the answer has to do with the fact that the United States is a nation of immigrants. As the nation grew, state by state, and as the stars on the flag grew accordingly, the continuous updating of the nation's banner helped create a lasting, emotional attachment to the flag among those in the new and existing states, and particularly among the new arrivals to these shores, tens of millions of whom ventured here to live under the freedom and democracy that the Stars and Stripes stands for.

"An immigrant comes to the country, moves to a territory that becomes a state, and then becomes part of that flag," said Jeffrey Kohn. "I don't know of any other national flag that's that way."

The children of those immigrants who came to this country beginning in the early 1890s were the first to pledge allegiance to the flag. One of the Pledge of Allegiance's goals, in fact, was to help Americanize the newcomers to these shores. The Pledge itself certainly has been an important factor in promoting devotion to the American flag. The Pledge has evolved from a schoolchildren's ritual to a mantra that is recited by adults today throughout the nation in state and local legislative bodies, the U.S. House and Senate, and at meetings of veterans' and patriotic groups.

The Stars and Stripes has had special meaning for another group of immigrants, slaves. Some slaves fought under the flag for the North in the Civil War; virtually every slave viewed the banner as a symbol of the freedom that would come with the end of slavery. Civil Rights advocates displayed the red, white, and blue at rallies and demonstrations in the mid-twentieth century, again to symbolize the promises of freedom Old Glory stands for.

The simple fact is that—despite its changing meaning over the years—since 1777 the American flag has symbolized the values and ideals upon which this nation was built. Those who display the flag today do so, in nearly every instance, to call attention to those admirable qualities. Others fly the flag to associate themselves or their commercial products with the nation's most important symbol. Others show the flag to demonstrate their belief that the nation is not living up to what the flag symbolizes.

The American flag—whether it is an enormous banner stretched across a football field, a head-to-toe Uncle Sam suit, or a huge Stars and Stripes flying over a used car lot, the U.S. Capitol, or at a demonstration or political rally—represents the American nation's great experiment in democracy.

Appendix:
Stars and Stripes

THE NATION'S THIRD AND FINAL FLAG ACT, which became law on April 4, 1818, mandated that one star be added to the American flag "on the admission of every new state into the Union," and that the addition of the star would take effect "on the fourth of July then next succeeding such admission." What follows is a list of the dates that the stars were added to the flag, as well as the dates that the individual states were admitted to the Union.

13 Stars — June 14, 1777
15 Stars — January 13, 1795
20 Stars — July 4, 1818
21 Stars — July 4, 1819
23 Stars — July 4, 1820
24 Stars — July 4, 1822
25 Stars — July 4, 1836
26 Stars — July 4, 1837
27 Stars — July 4, 1845

28 Stars — July 4, 1846
29 Stars — July 4, 1847

30 Stars — July 4, 1848
31 Stars — July 4, 1851
32 Stars — July 4, 1858
33 Stars — July 4, 1859
34 Stars — July 4, 1861
35 Stars — July 4, 1863
36 Stars — July 4, 1865

37 Stars — July 4, 1867
38 Stars — July 4, 1877
43 Stars — July 4, 1890
44 Stars — July 4, 1891
45 Stars — July 4, 1896
46 Stars — July 4, 1908
48 Stars — July 4, 1912
49 Stars — July 4, 1959
50 Stars — July 4, 1960

1. Delaware — December 7, 1787
2. Pennsylvania — December 12, 1787
3. New Jersey — December 18, 1787
4. Georgia — January 2, 1788
5. Connecticut — January 9, 1788
6. Massachusetts — February 6, 1788
7. Maryland — April 28, 1788
8. South Carolina — May 23, 1788
9. New Hampshire — June 21, 1788
10. Virginia — June 25, 1788

11. New York — July 26, 1788
12. North Carolina — November 21, 1789
13. Rhode Island — May 29, 1790
14. Vermont — March 4, 1791
15. Kentucky — June 1, 1792
16. Tennessee — June 1, 1796
17. Ohio — March 1, 1803
18. Louisiana — April 30, 1812
19. Indiana — December 11, 1816
20. Mississippi — December 10, 1817

21. Illinois—December 3, 1818
22. Alabama—December 14, 1819
23. Maine—March 15, 1820
24. Missouri—August 10, 1821
25. Arkansas—June 15, 1836
26. Michigan—January 26, 1837
27. Florida—March 3, 1845
28. Texas—December 29, 1845
29. Iowa—December 28, 1846
30. Wisconsin—Mary 19, 1948

31. California—September 9, 1850
32. Minnesota—May 11, 1858
33. Oregon—February 14, 1859
34. Kansas—January 29, 1861
35. West Virginia—June 29, 1863
36. Nevada—October 31, 1864
37. Nebraska—March 1, 1867
38. Colorado—August 1, 1876
39. North Dakota—November 2, 1889

40. South Dakota—November 2, 1889
41. Montana—November 8, 1889
42. Washington—November 11, 1889
43. Idaho—July 3, 1890
44. Wyoming—July 10, 1890
45. Utah—January 4, 1896
46. Oklahoma—November 15, 1907
47. New Mexico—January 6, 1912
48. Arizona—February 14, 1912
49. Alaska—January 3, 1959
50. Hawaii—August 21, 1959

Notes

THIS WORK IS INTENDED for a general audience, not a scholarly one. That is why there are no footnotes in the text. However, I have tried to be as thorough as possible in researching the vast amount of primary and secondary material dealing with the history of the American flag. This book, therefore, builds upon the work of historians, vexillologists (flag experts), journalists, and others who have gone before me. It also is based on interviews I conducted in 2003 and 2004 with historians, researchers, and other American flag specialists.

For the first seven chapters, I learned a great deal from the work of the nation's — and perhaps the world's — top vexillologist, Whitney Smith, in his *The Flag Book of the United States* (Morrow, 1975). Smith, a former Boston University political science professor, has run the Flag Research Center in Winchester, Massachusetts, since 1970. He is the author of many other books and pamphlets on the American and other flags and has advised organizations such as the United Nations, the Smithsonian National Museum of American History, national Olympic committees, and the U.S. Department of Defense on matters of "vexillology," a word he invented. Among his other accomplishments, Smith designed the national flag of the nation of Guyana.

For the chapters on the history of the flag through the Civil War, I also made extensive use of the first fully researched history of the American flag, Rear Adm. George Henry Preble's *Origin and History of the American Flag* (Nicholas L. Brown, 1917), Vol. I., first published in 1871. Admiral Preble, the nephew of Commo. Edward Preble, commander of the U.S. naval forces during the 1803-4 Battle of Tripoli, conducted an exhaustive study of the American flag, including its origins, during his retirement.

There is also excellent material on flags flown during the colonial period and in the nation's early years through the Civil War in *Standards and Colors of the American Revolution* (University of Pennsylvania Press, 1982) by Edward W. Richardson, an encyclopedic reference book focusing on the various designs of the early flags, and in *So Proudly We Hail: The History of the United States Flag* (Smithsonian Institution Press, 1981) by Rear Adm. William Rea Furlong, Commo. Byron McCandless, and Harold D. Langley, which also is encyclopedic in its detailed descriptions of eighteenth-century American flags.

Boleslaw and Marie-Louise D'Otrange Mastai's *The Stars and the Stripes: The American Flag as Art and as History from the Birth of the Republic to the Present* (Knopf, 1973), also contains a great deal of information about the origins of the flag and its early history, along with many illustrations from the late authors' extensive collection of historic American flags. Scot Guenter's *The American Flag, 1777–1924: Cultural Shifts from Creation to Codification* (Fairleigh Dickinson University Press, 1990) is a thoroughly researched history of the American flag that stands as the best reference work on the changing uses, customs, and meaning of the flag from the beginnings to 1924.

One: Antecedents

7.   The flag of today represents: Frederic J. Haskin, *Flags of the United States* (National Capital Press, 1941), p. 2.

7.   It is believed that the ancient Chinese: See Ralph D. Sawyer, translator, *Sun-tzu: The Art of War* (MetroBooks, 1994); D. C. Lau and Roger T. Ames, *Sun Pin and the Art of Warfare* (Ballantine, 1996).

10.   It is believed that the *Mayflower* flew: See Hugh F. Rankin, "The Naval Flag of the American Revolution," *The William and Mary Quarterly* (July 1954): pp. 339–53.

12.   Gadsden appointed Esek Hopkins of Rhode Island: For data on Continental navy ships, see the nine-volume *Dictionary of American Naval Fighting Ships*, U.S. Naval Historical Center, 1959–91.

14.   "Certainly Trumbull, like many artists": Smith, p. 47.

17.   An English ship in the harbor reported: A detailed accounting of the Saint Eustatius naval saluting, based on contemporary records, is contained in "Where our Flag Was First Saluted," William Elliot Griffis, *The New England Monthly* (July 1893), pp. 576–85.

17.   "it is expected that you contend warmly": Marine Committee to Nicholas Biddle, February 15, 1777, in Charles Oscar Paullin, ed., *Out-Letters of the Continental Marine Committee and Board of Admiralty* I (1914), p. 76.

18.   In his January 1776 report: "A British Spy in Philadelphia," *Pennsylvania Magazine of History and Biography* (January 1961), p. 22. See also, David McCullough, *John Adams* (Simon & Schuster, 2001), pp. 96–97.

Two: The Birth of a Symbol

22.   Three weeks earlier, on Saturday, June 14, 1777: See Smith, pp. 42–68; Scott M. Guenter, *The American Flag, 1777–1924* (Fairleigh Dickenson University Press, 1992), pp. 15–24; and Preble, pp. 259–89.

23.   "The American flag as a sovereign flag": Henry Moeller, author interview, June 9, 2003. See also Moeller's book, *Shattering an American Myth: Unfurling the History of the Stars and Stripes* (Amereon House, 1995). Moeller, a member of the North American Vexillogical Association, is professor emeritus of marine biology at Dowling College in Oakdale, New York. He has studied the origins of the American flag for more than twenty-five years.

25.   "The most powerful motive . . . I had or have": Library of Congress, *Thomas Jefferson Papers*, Series 1, General Correspondence, 1651–1827, John Trumbull to Thomas Jefferson, June 11, 1789.

27.   Historians believe though that it dates from the War of 1812: See Furlong, et al., p. 113.

28.   However an investigation of the flag: See Furlong, et al., pp. 133–34. "The problem with Maryland's 'Cowpens Flag'": Letter

dated March 23, 1984, from Gregory C. Stiverson to Robert P. Kelm, State of Maryland, Department of General Services, Hall of Records.

28. "As for the Colours": *George Washington Papers at the Library of Congress, 1741–99*, Series 4, General Correspondence. 1697–1799, Continental Congress War Board to George Washington, May 10, 1779.

29. However a significant clue as to who designed: See Richard S. Patterson and Richardson Dougall, *The Eagle and the Shield: A History of the Great Seal of the United States* (U.S. Department of State, 1978).

33. "Accept my thanks": Library of Congress, *Thomas Jefferson Papers*, Series 1, General Correspondence, 1651–1827, Thomas Jefferson to Francis Hopkinson, March 13, 1789.

33. "Francis Hopkinson . . . designed the flag": Whitney Smith quoted in Michael Corcoran, *For Which It Stands: An Anecdotal Biography of the American Flag* (Simon & Schuster, 2002), p. 34. For an in-depth examination of Francis Hopkinson's role in designing the Stars and Stripes, see Earl P. Williams Jr., "The 'Fancy Work' of Francis Hopkinson: Did He Design the Stars and Stripes?" in *Prologue: Quarterly of the National Archives*, Spring 1988, and George E. Hastings, *The Life and Works of Francis Hopkinson* (University of Chicago Press, 1926), pp. 240–54.

Three: Mother of Invention

37. Betsy Ross sewed the first American flag: The Betsy Ross Homepage Web site, www.ushistory.org/betsy/index.html

37. There is no substantiation for the legend: Milo M. Quaife, et. al., *The History of the United States Flag* (Harper & Row, 1961), p. 98. William C. Kashatus's "Seamstress for a Revolution" in the August 2002 issue of *American History*, pp. 20–26, contains excellent biographical information on Betsy Ross.

40. When college students were asked: Michael Frisch, "American History and the Structures of Collective Memory: A Modest Exercise in Empirical Iconography," *The Journal of American History* (March 1939), p. 1,144. Frisch interviewed more than one thousand students at the State University of Buffalo in the study.

41. "The next and last resort then of the historian": The text of William Canby's paper may be found at www.ushistory.org/betsy/more/canby.htm; Canby's argument is spelled out in more detail in *The Evolution of the American Flag* (Ferris and Leach, 1909), written by William Canby's brother George Canby and Lloyd Balderson. Letters Canby wrote to Admiral Preble elaborating on the story on March 29, 1870, and November 9, 1871, may be found in Preble, pp. 266–67.

43. Betsy Ross "became America's founding mother": quoted by Valerie Reitman in "Tale of Betsy Ross It Seems Was Made Out of Whole Cloth," the *Wall Street Journal,* June 12, 1992.

43. "The flaglets were made by": Jeffrey Kohn, author interview, September 4, 2003.

44. The "construction of the first national standard of the United States": H. K. W. Wilcox, "National Standards and Emblems," *Harper's New Monthly Magazine* (July 1873): p. 181.

45. That painting "is the primary reason that the circle of stars": Edward W. Richardson, *Standards and Colors of the American Revolution* (University of Pennsylvania, 1982), p. 269.

45. Weisgerber's inspiration . . . according to family lore: See interview with Charles H. Weisgerber Jr. in the *Philadelphia Inquirer,* September 27, 1997.

46. The *Philadelphia Ledger* reported that the city's two councils: Reprinted in the *New York Times,* December 15, 1895.

46. . . . as his promotional literature put it: Betsy Ross Memorial Association, Library of Congress, Printed Ephemera Collection; Portfolio 160, Folder 45.

46. The *New York Times* in 1908 called six-year-old Vexil Weisgerber: The *New York Times,* July 5, 1908.

47. . . . Kent, who led a fund-raising effort: Atwater Kent, an inventor, industrialist, and philanthropist, in 1938 bought a nearby building on Seventh Street, the original home of the Franklin Institute, and donated it to the city of Philadelphia. Today it is the Atwater Kent Museum, which tells Philadelphia's cultural and industrial history.

47. "When I first learned of the condition of the Betsy Ross House": Quoted in the *New York Times,* February 14, 1937.

48. "Birth of Our Nation's Flag," is "important": Stevens and Weisgerber quoted in Amy Worden, "Betsy Ross Painting Finds New

Home in Pennsylvania's State Museum," Knight Ridder/Tribune News Service, December 27, 2001.

49. ... Canby's Betsy Ross story "a fake of the first water": Quoted in the *New York Times,* June 19, 1908.

49. "So, of course, she's saying, 'I made the flag' ": Lisa Moulder, author interview, January 28, 2004.

49. The brochure notes: "The Betsy Ross House," brochure published by the American Flag House & Betsy Ross Memorial, 2003.

50. "There are elements of the Betsy Ross story": Richardson, pp. 272–73.

50. On the other hand, Smith said: Smith, p. 68.

51. ... an exhaustive study undertaken by Henry Moeller: "A List of Pennsylvania Flag Makers, 1775–1777," paper presented at the Sixth Annual Flag Symposium, March, 28–29, 2003, Harrisburg, Pennsylvania.

51. Margaret Manny, who began making jacks: Ernest C. Rogers, *Connecticut's Naval Office at New London During the American Revolution* (New London Historical Society, 1933), pp. 130–31.

51. "Everyone knows about Betsy Ross": Barbara Tuchman, *The First Salute: A View of the American Revolution* (Knopf, 1988), p. 47.

52. "Would that it were true": A search done by Mark Benbow, the historian at the Woodrow Wilson House in Washington, D.C., of the sixty-volume *Papers of Woodrow Wilson,* Wilson's Flag Day speeches of 1916 and 1917, his books on the Revolutionary War, and other sources came up with no evidence that Wilson made the remark.

Four: First Additions

53. "At this time we had no national colors": Preble, p. 264.

54. A letter dated October 9, 1778, from Benjamin Franklin and John Adams: Library of Congress, U.S. Congressional Documents and Debates, 1774–1875, "The Revolutionary War Diplomatic Correspondence, Vol. II—Franklin and Adams to the Ambassador of Naples."

54. Some flags had emblems sewn into them: Preble, pp. 288–89.

54.   A twenty-four-year-old American, Elkanah Watson: Watson's
        journal and an 1836 magazine article about it are discussed in
        "The First American Flag Hoisted in Old England" by Jane Car-
        son in *The William and Mary Quarterly* (July 1954), pp. 434–40.

55.   It was "the first vessel": Preble, p. 291.

56.   The House of Representatives took up: The debate over the Sec-
        ond Flag Act may be found in the *Annals of Congress*, House of
        Representatives, 3rd Congress, 1st Session, pp. 164–66.

57.   The fight was waged by a heavily outnumbered force: See
        Joseph Wheelan, *Jefferson's War: America's First War on Terror,
        1801–1805* (Carroll & Graf, 2003), pp. 282–85.

57.   . . . supported by three U.S. Navy ships, the *Argus*, the *Hornet*,
        and the *Nautilus:* The *Argus* went on to become one of the most
        successful American ships that confiscated British merchant
        ships in the English Channel during the War of 1812. See Ira
        Dye, *The Fatal Cruise of the* Argus: *Two Captains in the War of 1812*
        (Naval Institute Press, 1994).

Five: Our Flag Was Still There

59.   And it was true with the War of 1812: A comprehensive, well-
        written, well-documented history of the Star-Spangled Banner,
        the flag, is contained in Lonn Taylor's *The Star-Spangled Banner:
        The Flag That Inspired the National Anthem* (National Museum of
        American History/Harry N. Abrams, 2000). Taylor is a histo-
        rian in the Division of Social History at the Smithsonian Insti-
        tution's National Museum of American History where the
        Star-Spangled Banner is preserved. Other good sources
        are Scott S. Sheads, *The Rockets' Red Glare: The Maritime Defense
        of Baltimore, 1814* (Tidewater, 1986) and Walter Lord, *The
        Dawn's Early Light* (Norton, 1992). Sheads is a historian and
        park ranger at the Fort McHenry National Monument and
        Historical Shrine.

62.   " . . . hoisted a splendid and superb ensign": Robert J. Barrett,
        "Naval Recollections of the Late American War," *United Service
        Journal* (April 1841): p. 460. See also Taylor, p. 21.

64.   "The following beautiful and animating effusion": Photostat of
        Baltimore Patriot and Evening Advertiser, September 20, 1814, part

of uncatalogued clippings and photostats relating to the Star Spangled Banner, Music Division, Library of Congress.

64.   The article indicated that the song was meant: For an overview of the history of the song, see Irwin Molotsky, *The Flag, The Poet and the Song* (Dutton, 2001). The National Anthem contains four verses, but the last three are rarely sung in public. The entire song's words are:

Oh, say can you see by the dawn's early light
What so proudly we hailed at the twilight's last gleaming?
Whose broad stripes and bright stars through the perilous fight,
O'er the ramparts we watched were so gallantly streaming?
And the rocket's red glare, the bombs bursting in air,
Gave proof through the night that our flag was still there.
Oh, say does that Star-Spangled Banner yet wave
O'er the land of the free and the home of the brave?

On the shore, dimly seen through the mists of the deep,
Where the foe's haughty host in dread silence reposes,
What is that which the breeze, o'er the towering steep,
As it fitfully blows, half conceals, half discloses?
Now it catches the gleam of the morning's first beam,
In full glory reflected now shines in the stream:
'Tis the Star-Spangled banner! Oh long may it wave
O'er the land of the free and the home of the brave.

And where is that band who so vauntingly swore
That the havoc of war and the battle's confusion,
A home and a country should leave us no more!
Their blood has washed out of of their foul footsteps' pollution.
No refuge could save the hireling and slave
From the terror of flight and the gloom of the grave:
And the Star-Spangled banner in triumph doth wave
O'er the land of the free and the home of the brave.

Oh! thus be it ever, when freemen shall stand
Between their loved home and the war's desolation!
Blest with victory and peace, may the heav'n rescued land

Praise the Power that hath made and preserved us a nation.
Then conquer we must, when our cause it is just,
And this be our motto: "In God is our trust."
And the Star-Spangled banner in triumph shall wave
O'er the land of the free and the home of the brave.

66. In 1917 the army and navy officially named: See George J. Svejda, *History of the Star-Spangled Banner from 1814 to the Present* (U.S. Department of the Interior, 1969), and Taylor, pp. 37–38.

67. Rep. Jefferson Levy, a New York: For a comprehensive post-Jefferson history of Monticello, see Marc Leepson, *Saving Monticello: The Levy Family's Epic Quest to Rescue the House That Jefferson Built* (Free Press, 2001; University of Virginia Press, 2003).

67. " 'The Star-Spangled Banner' suggests that patriotism": Quoted in Molotsky, p. 157.

67. The VWF had been on record as early as 1917: At its 1917 national convention in New York City, the VWF sent a letter of complaint to the Cathedral of Saint John after its bishop had forbidden the playing of "The Star-Spangled Banner" because he believed it "created an enthusiasm for war." See "Say Bishop Barred Anthem: Veterans of Foreign Wars Ask Why Star-Spangled Banner Was Stopped," the *New York Times*, August 29, 1917, p. 8.

67. "There is a powerful and well-financed propaganda emanating from pacifist sources": Quoted in the *New York Times*, December 28, 1926.

68. . . . "to refute," the *New York Times* said: the *New York Times*, February 1, 1930, p. 1.

68. "She sewed the Star Spangled Banner flag": Sally Johnston, author interview, May 27, 2003.

70. Mary Pickersgill was born on February 12, 1776: For a brief biography of Mary Young Pickersgill, see her entry in the Maryland Archives "Maryland Women's Hall of Fame" series, Maryland Commission for Women, 2002.

70. "All kinds of colours, for the Army": A copy of the ad is reproduced in Furlong, p. 136.

72. "Snipping," said Marilyn Zoidis: Marilyn Zoidis, author interview, June 14, 2003.

73. With great pomp and ceremony the Old Defenders . . . paraded the flag through the streets of Baltimore: On the first anniversary of the Battle of Baltimore, September 12, 1815, the city celebrated that day with a parade, called the Defender's Day Cavalcade, which then became an annual event. In the late-nineteenth century tens of thousands took part in that patriotic celebration as municipal employees and schoolchildren were given the day off. But interest waned in the twentieth century and today the celebration is muted, although the 2003 celebration included a reenactment and fireworks display at Fort McHenry.

74. . . . one of the oldest surviving fifteen-star, fifteen-stripe flags: The Fort Niagara Flag, which was made in 1809 and is housed today at the Old Fort Niagara Historic Site in Youngstown, New York, is believed to be the oldest surviving fifteen-star, fifteen-stripe flag. George Armistead, the commanding officer of Fort McHenry, served at Fort Niagara before and during the War of 1812, prior to taking over Fort McHenry in 1813.

75. As Pres. Bill Clinton put it in 1998: Speaking at the National Museum of American History, July 13, 1998.

Six: Additions and a Subtraction

77. . . . Wendover submitted a resolution in the House: *House Journal* (Monday, December 9, 1816).

78. In his motion asking for the committee: *Annals of Congress*, House of Representatives, 14th Congress, 2nd Session, December 12, 1816, p. 268.

82. According to his own account of the matter: Reid offered his version of his role in creating the flag in a letter he wrote on February 17, 1850, to his son Sam. It may be found in the Library of Congress Manuscript Division and on line at www.loc.gov/exhibits/treasures/trmo98.html

83. On May 18 the office issued: Navy Commissioner's Office circular, dated May 18, 1818. See Preble, p. 349.

84. "Before the Civil War especially": Smith, p. 75.

84. Small boats in the U.S. Navy: See Grace Rogers Cooper, *Thirteen-Star Flags: Keys to Identification* (Smithsonian Institution Press, 1973), p. 1.

86.   . . . the "most beautiful of all flags": W. S. Henry, *Campaign Sketches of the War with Mexico* (Harper & Brothers, 1848), p. 215. See also Cecilia Elizabeth O'Leary, *To Die For: The Paradox of American Patriotism* (Princeton University Press, 2000), p. 22.

86.   The flag, while still primarily used: See Guenter, pp. 49–65.

87.   One campaign ribbon contained: See Roger A. Fisher and Edmund B. Sullivan, *American Political Ribbons and Ribbon Badges: 1825–1981* (Quaterman, 1985), pp. 55–56 and O'Leary, p. 21.

88.   "Each new election [after 1844]": Guenter, p. 52.

88.   . . . used the American flag as one of its primary symbols: For a history of the Know-Nothing party, see Ray Allen Billington, *The Protestant Crusade, 1800–1860: A Study in the Origins of American Nativism* (Macmillan, 1938); Carleton Beals, *Brass-Knuckle Crusade: The Great Know-Nothing Conspiracy, 1820–1860* (Hastings House, 1960); Mark Voss-Hubbard, *Beyond Party: Cultures of Antipartisanship in Northern Politics Before the Civil War* (Johns Hopkins University Press, 2002), and David Harry Bennett, *The Party of Fear: From Nativist Movements to the New Right in American History* (University of North Carolina Press, 1988).

88.   Its avowed purpose: Quoted in Nelson Manfred Blake, *A History of American Life and Thought* (McGraw-Hill, 1963), p. 174.

Seven: A House Divided Against Itself

91.   In short order, the Stars and Stripes became: Robert E. Bonner's detailed, inclusive look at the Confederate flag, *Colors and Blood: Flag Passions of the Confederate South* (Princeton University Press, 2002), also has a good deal of information about flag matters in the North during the Civil War. I used this excellent book as a road map for this chapter.

91.   The Civil War, Whitney Smith said: Quoted in Corcoran, p. 77.

92.   In his January 10 speech: The *Congressional Globe*, 36th Congress, 2nd Session, January 10, 1861, pp. 306–12.

92.   As the flag was unfurled, Anderson wrote: Anderson letter of December 30, 1860, quoted in Preble, p. 421.

92.   The last book Davis had checked out: Bonner, p. 8.

95.   If war with a foreign nation came: Quoted in Preble, p. 404.

95.   "I could not help hoping that there was": Preble, p. 411.

95. On that same day in New Orleans: Mastai, p. 124.

95. At Fort Sumter itself: Quoted in Bruce Caton, *The Coming Fury, The Centennial History of the Civil War* (Doubleday, 1961), pp. 174–75.

96. . . . quickly dismissed a resolution: *Journal of the Confederate Congress* (February 13, 1861).

98. Anderson, a Kentucky-born professional soldier: For more details on the fighting at Fort Sumter, see Caton, *The Coming Fury;* Robert Hendrickson, *Fort Sumter: The First Day of the Civil War* (Scarborough House, 1990); and Maury Klein, *Days of Defiance: Sumter, Succession, and Coming of the Civil War* (Knopf, 1997).

99. Watching this unfold from the USS *Pawnee*: U.S Naval War Records Office, *Official Records of the Union and Confederate Navies of the Rebellion,* Series I, *Operations on the Atlantic Coast, January 1, 1861 to June 7, 1861,* p. 255.

100. Jefferson Davis had bitterly derisive . . . words: Jefferson Davis, *The Rise and Fall of the Confederate Government* (Da Capo Press, 1990), p. 252. The book was originally published in 1881.

100. "When the stars and stripes went down at Sumter": Preble, p. 453.

100. "Romantic flag-waving rhetoric": James M. McPherson, *What They Fought For: 1861–1865* (Anchor, 1995), p. 42.

101. He never dreamed his brother would "raise a hand": Quoted in James McPherson: *For Cause and Comrades: Why Men Fought in the Civil War* (Oxford University Press, 1998), p. 15.

101. The "rebels know," the magazine said: *Harper's Weekly* (May 4, 1861).

102. On April 12, the day the attack on Sumter had begun: Quoted in the *New York Times,* April 17, 1861.

102. In Boston flags "blossomed everywhere": Mary A. Livermore, *My Story of the War* (Arno Press, 1972), p. 90. The book was first published in 1889. See also Guenter, p. 69.

102. The flag, one observer said, "flew out to the wind from every housetop": Quoted in Jacob D. Cox, "War Preparation in the North" in Robert Underwood Johnson and Clarence Clough Buel., eds., *Battles and Leaders of the Civil War* (Castle Publishing, 1991), p. 84. See also Harold Holzer, "New Glory for Old Glory: A Lincoln-Era Tradition Reborn," *White House Studies,* Spring 2002.

103.   "The national banners waving from ten thousand windows":
            Quoted in Preble, p. 457. Six months later, on October 21,
            1861, Baker, serving as a major general in the Pennsylvania
            Volunteers, was killed at the Battle of Balls Bluff near Leesburg
            in northern Virginia.

103.   Another speaker urged the crowd to: Quoted in Mark E. Neely
            Jr., and Harold Holzer, *The Union Image: Popular Prints of the
            Civil War North* (University of North Carolina Press, 2000), p. 4.

Eight: Flagmania

105.   . . . what the *New Orleans Picayune*: April 17, 1861. See also,
            Bonner, p. 59.

106.   "I wear one pinned to my bosom": Sarah Morgan Dawson, *A
            Confederate Girl's Diary* (Houghton Mifflin, 1913), p. 24.

106.   Send-offs were similar in the North: Milton S. Lytle, *History of
            Huntingdon County in the State of Pennsylvania From the Earliest
            Times to the Centennial Anniversary of American Independence*
            (W. H. Roy, 1876), pp. 190–91.

106.   The Stars and Stripes began to appear on stationery: See James
            Parton, "Caricature in the United States," *Harper's New Monthly*
            (December 1878), p. 39.

107.   Mark Twain, then a reporter: Writing in the *San Francisco Daily
            Morning Call,* July 6, 1864. See also: Edgar M. Branch, *Clemens
            of the 'Call': Mark Twain in San Francisco* (University of California
            Press, 1969).

108.   Among the other songs published: The Public Domain Music
            Web site, www.pdmusic.org, created by Benjamin Robert
            Tubb, contains a comprehensive list of Civil War songs, based
            on original sheet music sources.

110.   The commander of the New York Fire Zouave's First Regiment:
            "The Murder of Colonel Ellsworth," *Harper's Weekly* (June 15,
            1861). Ellsworth had gained national fame in 1859–60 as the
            founder and leader of United States Zouave Cadets, a group of
            young men recruited from the Illinois State Militia that special-
            ized in close-order drills. They wore flamboyant uniforms that
            Ellsworth designed featuring fezzes, balloon pants, and red vests,
            and performed in front of large, adoring crowds. The name came

from a regiment of the French colonial army made up of fierce warriors from the Kabyli tribe that lived in the hills of Algeria and Morocco. The French Zouaves made their reputation during the Crimean War of 1854–56.

110. One of Ellsworth's men, Private Francis E. Brownell: For his actions that day, Pvt. Brownell was awarded the Medal of Honor, the first given in the Civil War. See the *New York Times*, March 16, 1894.

111. "When the President was reviewing some troops": Julia Taft Bayner and Mary A. Decredico, *Tad Lincoln's Father* (University of Nebraska Press, 2001), pp. 39–40. A fragment of that flag is on exhibit at the Fort Ward Museum in Alexandria, Va.

111. "If anyone attempts to haul down the American flag": Quoted in Robert Underwood Johnson and Clarence Clough Buel, eds., *Battles and Leaders of the Civil War* II (Castle Books, 1985), p. 147.

111. Farragut also ordered, in Monroe's words: New Orleans Public Library, City Archives and Louisiana Division Special Collections, *Correspondence between the Mayor and Federal Authorities relative to the Occupation of New Orleans together with the Proceedings of the Common Council, 1862*, p. 6. For a complete account of New Orleans's fall to Farragut, see Chester G. Hearn, *The Capture of New Orleans, 1862* (Louisiana State University Press, 1995).

113. "His hanging of Mumford for hauling down the flag": "The Redemption of New-Oreans," editorial, the *New York Times*, December 7, 1862, p. 4.

113. "The name of Mumford": Preble, pp. 473–74.

115. They waved the Confederate flag: In a letter to the *Washington Star*, February 9, 1869. See Preble, pp. 489–90.

116. He flew Old Glory on those days: Mary J. Driver Roland, *Old Glory: The True Story* (privately printed), 1918, p. 27. A copy of this book may be found in the Library of Congress in Washington, D.C.

118. Although his grave is not one of the places: There are only eight sites in this country where the flag is flown twenty-four hours a day under specific legal authority; that is, by law or by presidential proclamation. They are: Fort McHenry National Monument in Baltimore: (Presidential Proclamation No. 2795, July 2, 1948); Flag House Square (Mary Pickersgill's "Star Spangled"

House) in Baltimore (Public Law 83-319, March 26, 1954); the U.S. Marine Corps Memorial (Iwo Jima) in Arlington, Virginia (Presidential Proclamation No. 3418, June 12, 1961); on the Green of the town of Lexington, Massachusetts (Public Law 89-335, November 8, 1965); The White House (Presidential Proclamation No. 4000, September 4, 1970); the Washington Monument (Presidential Proclamation No. 4064, July 10, 1971); U.S. Customs Ports of Entry (Presidential Proclamation No. 4131, May 5, 1972); and Valley Forge, Pennsylvania (Public Law 94-53, July 4, 1975). The flag also is flown at many other sites day and night, including the U.S. Capitol and at William Driver's grave, without the benefit of legal sanction. See John R. Luckey, "The United States Flag: Federal Law Relating to Display and Associated Questions," Congressional Research Service, Library of Congress, June 14, 2000, p. 9.

120. That arm, "with which he bore the colors": John Brown Gordon, *Reminiscences of the Civil War* (Scribner's, 1904), p. 114. Electronic Edition, Academic Affairs Library, University of North Carolina at Chapel Hill, http://docsouth.unc.edu/gordon/gordon.html

120. On July 4, 1864, for example: Preble, p. 491.

120. The American flag, historian Scot Guenter observed: Guenter, p. 77.

120. After 1863, when Lincoln allowed blacks to fight: Bonner, pp. 145, 147.

121. During one such occasion: Thomas Wentworth Higginson, *Army Life in a Black Regiment* (Norton, 1984), p. 46. Higginson originally published his Civil War memoir in 1869. See also: Christopher Looby, ed., *The Complete Civil War Journal and Selected Letters of Thomas Wentworth Higginson* (University of Chicago Press, 1999).

122. The "torn and tattered battle-flags": Gordon, p. 444.

122. The Confederate soldiers, Chamberlain said: Joshua Lawrence Chamberlain, *The Passing of the Armies: An Account of the Final Campaign of the Army of the Potomac, Based Upon Personal Reminiscences of the Fifth Army Corps* (Bantam, 1993), p. 196. Chamberlain's memoirs were first published in 1915.

123. Then the old flag, Admiral Preble wrote: Preble, p. 452.

Nine: A Band of Brothers

125.   ... patriotic groups like the Union veterans: Cecilia Elizabeth
            O'Leary, "The Radicalism of Patriotism, 1865–1918," in John
            Bodnar, ed., *Bonds of Affection: Americans Define Their Patriotism*
            (Princeton University Press, 1996), p. 61.

125.   That flag was produced by the newly founded: That flag was
            auctioned on October 11, 2001, for $58,250 by Sotheby's in
            New York. The buyer was Ames Stevens, a great great grand-
            son of General Butler. Stevens donated it to the American Tex-
            tile Museum in Lowell, Massachusetts. General Butler resigned
            from the army in November of 1865 and went into politics. He
            was elected to the U.S. Congress, serving from 1867 to 1875
            and 1877 to 1879. A Radical Republican, he was a leader in the
            impeachment trial of Pres. Andrew Johnson. Butler later be-
            came a Democrat and was elected governor of Massachusetts in
            1882. The business records of the United States Bunting Com-
            pany are in the files of the American Textile Museum in Lowell,
            Massachusetts.

126.   In it the bunting: *Scientific American,* October 2, 1869, p. 218.

126.   "Wherever the flag of the United States": Orra L. Stone, *His-
            tory of Massachusetts Industries: Their Inception, Growth and Success*
            (S. J. Clarke, 1930), p. 748.

127.   "Every person in the column": Preble, p. 591.

127.   One of the clearest examples: See Irwin Ross, "The Most Sen-
            sational Walk in American History," *The Old Farmer's Almanac,*
            1974.

127.   "Bates is to carry the flag unfurled": Quoted in the *New York
            Times,* March 5, 1868.

128.   Mark Twain, the great American humorist and writer: Writing
            in the *Virginia City Territorial Enterprise,* February 27, 1868. The
            article was dated January 30 and was written from Washing-
            ton, D.C.

129.   At the latter event Bates met: the *New York Times,* July 8, 1868.

130.   When Bates arrived in London: Reprinted in the *Washington
            Post,* July 14, 1881.

130.   Bates, who appeared to be drinking heavily: Ibid.

131.   ... the Order of Cincinnati, also known as the Society of the
            Cincinnati: The last full member of the group died in New York

in 1854. The society has been active continuously since then as a hereditary organization based in Washington, D.C. It supports educational, cultural, and literary activities that, in the society's words, "promote the ideals of liberty and constitutional government." See Wallace Evan Davies, *Patriotism on Parade: The Story of Veterans' and Hereditary Organizations in America, 1783–1900* (Harvard University Press, 1955).

132.   That year he also helped found: For a concise history of the Grand Army of the Republic, see: "The Grand Army of the Republic and Kindred Societies," Library of Congress, Bibliographies and Guides, compiled by Albert E. Smith Jr., Humanities and Social Sciences Division, 2001. See also O'Leary, pp. 35–48.

133.   "The most notable act of [Logan's] administration": George S. Merrill, "The Grand Army of the Republic," *The New England Magazine*, August, 1890, p. 614.

134.   "Patriotic color," the historian Robert E. Bonner noted: Robert E. Bonner, "Star-spangled Sentiment," www.common-place.org, January 2003.

Ten: The Hundredth Anniversary

136.   Thirty-seven nations took part: See Robert W. Rydell, *World of Fairs: The Century-of-Progress Expositions* (University of Chicago Press, 1993).

136.   The city of Philadelphia decked itself out in American flags: *Philadelphia Public Ledger,* May 11, 1876.

138.   Another flag falsehood: See Preble, pp. 280–82, Quaife, pp. 100–101, and Guenter, pp. 99–101.

139.   Before the war he had worked: See James F. Ryder, "The Painter of 'Yankee Doodle,'" *The New England Magazine* (December 1895): pp. 483–94.

139.   "The centennial year was approaching": Quoted in the *Washington Post,* July 21, 1912.

140.   The Bowery's "exhibition of patriotism is of the most effusive sort": the *New York Times,* July 3, 1876, p. 8.

140.   In Los Angeles, bunting and flags "were liberally used" throughout the city that day: "Celebrations of Old-Time Days Recited," *Los Angeles Times,* July 3, 1927, p. G1.

142.   In Portland, Oregon: See Joseph P. Gaston, *Portland, Oregon: Its History and Builders* (S. J. Clarke, 1891), p. 369.

142.   The "flag," Admiral Preble wrote: Preble, p. 600.

Eleven: The Golden Age of Fraternity

143.   Sometimes referred to as the "Golden Age of Fraternity": The term was first used by W. S. Harwood in his article, "Secret Societies in America," which appeared in *The North American Review*, April 1897, p. 623.

143.   . . . the rapid growth of the organization in the 1880s and 1890s: Merrill, p. 620. The GAR, which restricted its membership to Civil War veterans, held its final encampment in Indianapolis in 1949. When its last member, Albert Woolson, died in 1956, the GAR dissolved.

144.   During the Twenty-sixth National GAR Encampment: the *Washington, D.C. News*, September 23, 1892.

144.   "American flags fluttered everywhere": "Keep Step to Memories of Days of Sixty-One," *San Francisco Chronicle*, August 20, 1903, p. 1. See also O'Leary, p. 58.

144.   In 1897 one observer estimated: Harwood, p. 617.

145.   The DAR's mission included: O'Leary, p. 79.

146.   "I wish that every citizen of our great republic": Quoted in the *New York Times*, June 15, 1877.

146.   The idea for a national Flag Day was revived in 1885: See Gregory Presto, "The Stars and Stripes Forever," *Northwestern Alumni News*, Summer 2003; Ernest Hooper, "Flag Day Memories," *St. Petersburg Times*, June 18, 2002; and the National Flag Day Foundation Web site, www.flagday.org

146.   . . . at the one-room Stony Hill Schoolhouse: The last class was held at the schoolhouse in 1916. The building stood empty for many years until it was restored in 1952. Today it resembles the structure in which B. J. Cigrand held the first Flag Day observance in 1885. Every year a special commemorative program is held there on the Sunday before June 14.

147.   . . . American Flag Day Association with William T. Kerr of Pittsburgh: Kerr, who worked for the Pennsylvania Railroad, was president of the association from 1898 to 1950. He lobbied during that time for a national Flag Day celebration.

147.   "I would specially recommend that the flag be raised on each school building": Quoted in the *New York Times*, June 14, 1896.

149.   He called on Republican state central committees throughout the nation: Quoted in the *New York Times*, October 27, 1896.

150.   "A whole lot of houses on Connecticut Ave: Letter from Mabel Hubbard Bell to Alexander Graham Bell, November 1, 1896, The Alexander Graham Bell Family Papers, Library of Congress, Mabel Hubbard Bell, Family Correspondence, November 1–17, 1896.

150.   "Although members of both parties": Guenter, p. 135.

151.   "I regard this day as a day of rededication": "A Flag Day Address," June 14, 1916, in Arthur R. Link, ed., *The Papers of Woodrow Wilson, Vol. 37, May 9–August 7, 1916* (Princeton University Press, 1981), pp. 224–25.

155.   As one late-nineteenth-century reference book for advertisers: See Robert Justin Goldstein, *Saving "Old Glory": The History of the American Flag Desecration Controversy* (Westview Press, 1995), p. 9, and Guenter, pp. 138–39.

156.   The first attempt to legislate against: Guenter, p. 140.

156.   Beginning in the mid-1895s: See Davies, p. 221.

156.   In 1895 Reade: Goldstein, p. 31. Goldstein is a professor of political science at Oakland University in Rochester, Michigan, who has specialized in the flag protection movement. In addition to *Saving "Old Glory,"* his books on that subject include *Flag Burning and Free Speech: The Case of* Texas v. Johnson (University Press of Kansas, 2000), *Burning the Flag: The Great 1989–1990 American Flag Desecration Controversy* (Kent State University Press, 1998), and *Desecrating the American Flag: Key Documents of the Controversy from the Civil War to 1995* (Syracuse University Press, 1996).

157.   Prime became the Flag Association's founding president: Goldstein, *Saving "Old Glory":* p. 35.

158.   Henderson, a colleague said: See Guenter, p. 143.

158.   On March 4, 1907, the U.S. Supreme Court: U.S. Supreme Court: *Halter v. Nebraska*, 205 U.S. 34, 1907.

160.   The song was a huge success: See John McCabe, *George M. Cohan: The Man Who Owned Broadway* (Doubleday, 1973), p. 72 and Guenter, pp. 156–57.

160.   . . . which became the nation's official march: U.S. Code, Title 36, Section 10, Paragraph 188.

161.   Former Confederate general John Brown Gordon: Quoted in Bonner, *Colors and Blood*, p. 165.

161.   The "greatest good" the Spanish-American War did: Roosevelt was the guest of honor at a flag-waving National Army Day celebration in Chautauqua, New York. His speech was quoted in the *Chautauqua Assembly Herald*, August 19, 1899.

161.   . . . a spate of extraordinarily large flags: See Mastai, p. 226.

Twelve: One Nation Indivisible

164.   "At that time," said John W. Baer: Author interview, May 12, 2003. Baer, a retired university professor, is the author of the well-researched, detailed account of the history of the Pledge of Allegiance, *The Pledge of Allegiance: A Centennial History, 1892–1992*. Several chapters of the book are available online at: http://history.vineyard.net//pdgecho.htm; another excellent source of information on the pledge is Margarette S. Miller's *Twenty-Three Words* (Printcraft Press, 1976). The book is written in the first person from Francis Bellamy's point of view. It contains many primary source materials, including newspaper articles and many of Bellamy's letters and speeches. Bellamy's family papers are in the Rare Books, Special Collections and Preservation Department at the University of Rochester's Rush Rees Library.

164.   The Grand Army of the Republic . . . joined the movement. See Guenter, p. 105.

164.   Balch, who also was a teacher: Guenter, p. 117.

164.   By 1893 some six thousand students: See O'Leary, p. 154.

164.   It sold six-foot-long flags: Premium offer in *The Youth's Companion*, September 29, 1892.

165.   That campaign was successful: See John Baer, *The Pledge of Allegiance: A Short History* (1992).

166.   October 21 was chosen: Colorado in 1907 was the first state to adopt October 12 as a state holiday. New York followed in 1909. Columbus Day has been a federal holiday since 1971; it is celebrated on the second Monday in October.

166.   "I am very much pleased with the idea": The letter is reproduced in Miller, p. 102.

167.   The GAR commander in chief; Miller, p. 96.

168.   Bellamy looked for inspiration in choosing those words: Quoted by Baer, *The Pledge of Allegiance: A Short History.*

169.   The World's Columbian Exposition: See Donald L. Miller, "The White City," *American Heritage* (July–August 1993) and Stanley Appelbaum, *The Chicago World's Fair of 1893* (Dover Publications), 1980.

170.   The forty-eight-page book contains a section on the American flag: "Citizenship Syllabus Now Being Distributed," the *New York Times,* April 2, 1916.

172.   The historian Arthur M. Schlesinger Jr., for example: Arthur M. Schlesinger Jr., "The Flag: Who Owns Old Glory?" *Rolling Stone,* May 15, 2003.

172.   . . . justice Robert H. Jackson, in fact, prominently cited the First Amendment: *West Virginia State Board of Education v. Barnette,* 319 U.S. 624 (1943).

172.   In the 2002 and 2003 legislative sessions, seven states: Jennifer Piscatelli, "Pledge of Allegiance," *StateNotes,* Education Commission of the States, August. 2003.

173.   "At this moment in our history the principles": U.S. Congress, House of Representatives, *Congressional Record,* 83rd Congress, 2nd Session, June 7, 1954, p. 7,763.

174.   "Since the Soviet Union was avowedly atheistic": In an April 13, 2001, lecture at the 27th National Convention of American Atheists. Reprinted in "One Nation Under God: The Crusade to Capture the American Flag," *American Atheist* (Summer 2001), p. 18.

175.   "The justices ducked this constitutional issue today": Quoted in the *Washington Post,* June 15, 2004.

175.   Dukakis, Bush said, his opponent "isn't willing to let the teachers lead the kids": Quoted in the *Los Angeles Times,* September 3, 1988.

176.   "The U.S. Senate started reciting": Baer, author interview, May 12, 2003.

Thirteen: The Great War

177.   The American flag "had a certain sacred symbolism": Marie Peary Stafford, "The Peary Flag Comes to Rest," *National Geographic,* October 1954, p. 519.

178.   The "Stars and Stripes" that the Peary party planted: Peary
          gave his flag, minus the six pieces he had cut out, to his wife,
          Josephine, after he returned from the North Pole. The family
          permitted the flag to be exhibited at the Smithsonian Institution
          in Washington, and in 1954 turned it over to the National Geo-
          graphic Society in the nation's capital.

178.   That act captured the public imagination: Mastai, p. 226.
          See also Wally Herbert, *The Noose of Laurels: Robert E. Peary and
          the Race to the North Pole* (Atheneum, 1989) and Robert
          M. Bryce, *Cook and Peary: The Polar Controversy Resolved* (Stack-
          pole, 1997).

178.   A government study undertaken: See Quaife, et al., p. 109.

179.   Taft's order cut the number of official government flag sizes to:
          The sizes and proportions were slightly modified in a second
          Taft executive order on October 29, 1912, and a third by Presi-
          dent Wilson on May 29, 1916. See Furlong, et al., p. 212.

179.   He took his flag to President Taft: Quoted in the *Washington
          Post*, May 10, 1914, p. M3.

180.   The parade was led by: See *National Geographic* (October 1917).

180.   The profusion of flags in the city: See Ilene Susan Fort, *The Flag
          Paintings of Childe Hassam* (Los Angeles County Museum of
          Art/Harry N. Abrams, 1988).

181.   "The American flag," the art critic Ilene Susan Fort noted: Fort,
          p. 11. See also Lynn Dumenil, "American Women and the
          Great War," *OAH Magazine of History*, October 2002.

184.   The creed contains words and phrases: The American's Creed,
          in its entirety, reads:

          > I believe in the United States of America as a Govern-
          > ment of the people, by the people, for the people, whose
          > just powers are derived from the consent of the gov-
          > erned; a democracy in a Republic; a sovereign Nation of
          > many sovereign States; a perfect Union, one and insepa-
          > rable; established upon those principles of freedom,
          > equality, justice, and humanity for which American pa-
          > triots sacrificed their lives and fortunes.
          >
          > I therefore believe it is my duty to my Country to love
          > it; to support its Constitution; to obey its laws; to respect
          > its flag, and to defend it against all enemies.

185.   World War I created an "unprecedented demand: See *Prices of American Flags*, a report to the U.S. Senate, 65th Congress, 1st Session, July 26, 1917. See also Guenter, p. 163.

185.   Businesses, including Wanamaker's Department Store: See Guenter, pp. 162–63.

185.   Men went off to war with: Reprinted in the *Congressional Record*, September 6, 1917.

186.   "Material manifestation of the patriotism of the Negroes": "5000 Delaware Colored People Honor 'Flag Day,'" *Cleveland Advocate*, June 22, 1918.

186.   Libby grew up on a ranch: See Frederick Libby's memoir, *Horses Don't Fly: A Memoir of World War I* (Arcade, 2000).

186.   An English RFC major "suggested that I use [the flag] as a streamer": Libby, p. 216.

187.   When Libby took the Carnegie Hall stage at the October 17, 1918, fund-raiser: Libby, pp. 260–61.

187.   As the bidding . . . began, someone in the audience shouted: See the *New York Times*, October 18, 1918.

188.   "The Stars and Stripes almost instantaneously broke out": Burton J. Hendrick, *The Life and Letters of Walter H. Page* (Doubleday, 1923).

189.   In 1918 Congress passed and President Wilson signed: *Statutes at Large*, Washington, D.C., 1918, p. 553.

189.   Three years later Frederick Shumaker Jr.: See Guenter, p. 168 and O'Leary, p. 235.

190.   Texas's Disloyalty Act, which became law on March 11, 1918: See Goldstein, *Saving "Old Glory,"* p. 80 and O'Leary, pp. 234–35.

191.   The day the war ended, November 11, 1918: See "Showdown in Burrton, Kansas" by James C. Juhnke in John E. Sharp, *Gathering at the Hearth: Stories Mennonites Tell* (Herald Press, 2001) and James C. Juhnke, "John Schrag Espionage Case," *Mennonite Life* (July 1967): pp. 121–22.

191.   The most egregious incident involving the flag: "Illinoisan Lynched for Disloyalty," *Chicago Daily Tribune*, April 5, 1918. See also: "German Enemy of U.S. Hanged by Mob," *St. Louis Globe-Democrat*, April 5, 1918, and "German Is Lynched by an Illinois Mob," the *New York Times*, April 5, 1918.

Fourteen: One Hundred Percent Americanism

193. Not long after hostilities ended: Nine years after the end of
World War II, in 1954, President Eisenhower signed a bill that
changed the name of Armistice Day to Veterans Day to honor
all of the nation's veterans. As part of the Uniform Holiday Bill
in 1968, Congress moved the national commemoration of Veterans Day to the fourth Monday in October effective in 1971. But
many states kept the traditional November 11 date. So in 1975
President Ford signed legislation restoring Veterans Day to
November 11 beginning in 1978. The official national Veterans
Day commemoration takes place at the amphitheater of the
Tomb of the Unknowns at Arlington National Cemetery. It features a flag ceremony with a color guard and the laying of a
presidential wreath.

194. . . . a group of army officers and enlisted men: See Anne Cipri-
ano Venzon, ed., *The United States in the First World War: An Encyclopedia* (Garland, 1999), pp. 29–30.

194. . . . the spiritual successor of the Grand Army of the Republic:
The GAR limited its membership to Union veterans of the Civil
War, thus ensuring its own demise as an organization. Its last national encampment took place in 1949. Six of its remaining sixteen members attended. The last GAR member died in 1956.
The American Legion originally was open only to World War I
veterans, but changed its charter to admit veterans of World War
II in 1942, and again during the Korean and Vietnam Wars and
the conflicts in the 1990s, including the Persian Gulf War.

194. Within a year after the Paris caucus met "the Legion established
itself": John Lax and William Pencak, "Creating the American
Legion," *The South Atlantic Quarterly* (Winter, 1982): p. 44.

195. Mayor Ole Hanson, calling the strikers anarchists: See Lynn
Dumenil and Eric Foner, eds., *The Modern Temper: American Culture and Society in the 1920s* (Hill and Wang, 1995), p. 219.

196. . . . was setting up its Americanism Committee: The American
Legion's National Americanism Commission today is made up
of thirty-two volunteer members from around the nation. The
commission provides guidance to the Legion's Americanism,
Children and Youth Division staff at the group's national headquarters in Indianapolis.

197.   Even though President Taft's 1912 executive order: Quoted in Corcoran, p. 139.

197.   American Legion national commander Alvin Owsley: Quoted in the *New York Times*, June 15, 1923.

198.   Harding administration secretary of labor James J. Davis: Quoted in the *New York Times*, June 15, 1923. See also Goldstein, p. 86.

198.   In the weeks after the 1923 conference: See Guenter, pp. 177–78.

198.   Although the Flag Code is a national public law: The American Legion's National Americanism Commission's booklet, *Let's Be Right on Flag Etiquette* (January 2002), provides a clear explanation of the many facets of the U.S. Flag Code.

198.   "It is a set of guidelines": Whitney Smith, *Honor the Flag! The United States Code Annotated and Indexed* (Flag Research Center, 1998), p. 5.

199.   Those words were contained in a letter presented to: The *Nevada News*, November 2, 1922.

200.   . . . according to an account in the *Sidney Daily News*: August 16, 1923. See also David M. Chalmers, *Hooded Americanism: The First Century of the Ku Klux Klan, 1865–1965* (Franklin Watts, 1965).

200.   A report in the May 31, 1924, Klan publication: See Arthur J. Hope, *Notre Dame—One Hundred Years* (University of Notre Dame Press, 1999).

200.   The KKK still exists today: The flag remains an important part of the Ku Klux Klan today, as evidenced by the following statement that appears on the Web site (http://www.unitedknights .org/Our Flag.html) of the United Knights of the Ku Klux Klan:

> One of the very finest things about the Klan is that its every act and throughout its every ritual it inculcates an abiding love for country and flag. No communist can be a true Klansman for from the first time he enters a Klavern till the last time he is around the Klan he is confronted with the flag and required to salute it. It means so much to us—it typifies the finest country in all the world. . . . There's something within that majestic emblem which causes the heart of every Klansman to swell

with conscious pride when the flag of our country is unfurled and takes its rightful place at the head of our
parading legions. My, it's great to be a Klansman! IT's
great to serve our country! IT's great to own such a
flag — our flag — America's flag.

201.   When asked why there was a need for the association: Quoted
        in the *New York Times*, April 20, 1925.

201.   "The Association was mostly a one-man effort": Guenter,
        pp. 179–180.

201.   "Flags made in Japan," the statement said: Quoted in the *New
        York Times*, December 21, 1924.

202.   It focused on "helping to create and galvanize": Reprinted in
        the *Congressional Record*, 74th Congress, 1st Session, July 10,
        1935.

203.   The National Flag Foundation bills itself: National Flag Foun-
        dation brochure, "Pledge Allegiance to the Flag! Join the Na-
        tional Flag Foundation," 2003.

203.   The Veterans of Foreign Wars: The VFW's origins date to 1899
        with the founding of the Veterans of the Spanish-American War
        and the Philippine Insurrection and their affiliated organiz-
        ation, the American Veterans of Foreign Service. That group in
        1913 joined forces with the Colorado Society and the Army of
        the Philippines and adopted the name, the Veterans of Foreign
        Wars of the United States.

204.   "The fact that our population is becoming more varied as immi-
        gration continues": Quoted in the *New York Times*, June 14,
        1926.

Fifteen: United We Stand

206.   "If there was ever a time in the history of the Nation": Quoted
        in the *Christian Science Monitor*, February 24, 1942, p. 4.

207.   Walter B. Kerr, the *New York Tribune* foreign correspondent:
        "War Posters Bring U.S. Flag to Russia Again," *Washington Post*,
        December 8, 1941.

207.   Pres. Franklin D. Roosevelt, on June 22, 1942: Proclamation
        No. 2605, "Flag of the United States," February 18, 1944.

208.   The action was taken after City Councilman: See the *Los Angeles Times*, March 12, 1942, p. 1.

208.   "Everybody flew the flag during the last war": Quoted in the *New York Times*, January 25, 1942.

211.   "People saw in the red, white, and blue": Quoted in Emily Gold Boutilier, "The Symbol: What One Man's Obsession Reveals About the Stars and Stripes," *Brown Alumni Magazine* (May/June 2002). Rev. Kreitler loaned about a hundred magazines from his collection to the Smithsonian Institution's National Museum of American History for its exhibit, "July 1942: United We Stand," which ran from March to October 2002. See also, Fred L. Schultz, "United We Stood," *Naval History* (August 2002).

212.   "They did it in every Broadway theater": Sally Sherman, author interview, November 12, 2003.

212.   "They wore American flags on their right shoulder": Dale Dye, author interview, November 15, 2003. Dye served twenty years in the U.S. Marine Corps, was the editor of *Soldier of Fortune* magazine, and in 1986 reinvented the concept of cinematic military technical advising when he worked with Oliver Stone on his acclaimed Vietnam War film, *Platoon*. Among many other films, Dye was in charge of the military details on Stephen Spielberg's *Saving Private Ryan* (1998). That includes the opening scene, the D day landing, which is widely considered the most realistic depiction of that event on film.

213.   The flag "exemplifies all that they struggled for": Quoted by Stacy Barnwell, "The Admiral Nimitz Museum and Historical Center," *American History*, June 2000, p. 14.

213.   "They gave us small American flags to put in one of the zippered pockets": Quoted in Corcoran, p. 174.

213.   In his World War II memoir: William Manchester, *Goodbye, Darkness: A Memoir of the Pacific War* (Little Brown, 1980), p. 173.

214.   When it was over: Statistics from John Whiteclay Chambers II, ed., *The Oxford Companion to American Military History* (Oxford University Press, 1999), p. 344. See also: Eric Bergerud, *Touched with Fire: The Land War in the South Pacific* (Penguin Books, 1997).

214.   That's when marines Ira Hayes, Franklin Sousley, Harlon
         Block, Michael Strank, Rene Gagnon, and . . . John Bradley:
         The Stars and Stripes the 5 marines and 1 navy corpsman
         raised actually was the second American flag displayed on the
         mountain that day. The first one, which was raised by marines
         who secured the crest of Mount Suribachi under the com-
         mand of First Lt. Harold G. Schrier of Company E., Second
         Battalion, Twenty-eighth Marines, was too small to be recog-
         nized at a distance. The second, larger flag came from the
         navy landing craft, *LST-779*. The craft's communications offi-
         cer, Lt. J. G. Alan Wood, gave the flag to a marine who "was
         dirty and looked tired and had several day's growth of beard
         on his face," Wood later said. When Wood asked the marine
         why he needed the flag, he replied: "Don't worry. You won't
         regret it." See R. C. House, "Iwo Jima: Its Heroes and Flag,"
         World War II magazine (January 2000).

215.   "People ask, 'Was the picture posed?'": Quoted in the *Christian
         Science Monitor,* September 6, 1950, p. 9.

215.   "People would always remember where they were": James
         Bradley with Ron Powers, *Flags of Our Fathers* (Bantam Books,
         2000), p. 220.

215.   "It meant we secured the island": Quoted in the *New Britain Her-
         ald,* February 23, 2004.

216.   "When it was sent to Washington": Speaking at a June 19,
         1998, Marine Corps ceremony honoring him in Arlington, Vir-
         ginia. Quoted in Fred Carr, "Marine Corps War Memorial
         Sculptor Honored at Sunset Parade," *Henderson Hall News,* June
         12, 1998.

Sixteen: The Cold War

219.   "They can take Berlin any weekend": Oral History Interview,
         April 13, 1970, Truman Presidential Museum and Library.

220.   General Clay "made up his mind . . . with [President] Truman":
         Oral History Interview, November 26, 1995, National Security
         Archive.

222.   Within a half hour after the first U.S. Marine battalion landed
         on Wolmi-do Island: See Roy E. Appleman, *United States Army in*

the Korean War: South to the Naktog, North to the Yalu (June–November 1950), U.S. Army Center of Military History, 1961, p. 506.

223. "From all these suggestions and from a study": John D. Martz Jr., "The Story Behind a New Star for the Flag," *Army Information Digest* (July 1959).

224. . . . the new fifty-star flag, which would become official: Section 1 of the U.S. Flag Code still contains the words used when it was codified in 1942: "The flag of the United States shall be thirteen horizontal stripes, alternate red and white; and the union of the flag shall be forty-eight stars, white in a blue field." The president of the United States, however, has the power, under Section 10 to change "any rule or custom" in the code. See Whitney Smith, *Honor the Flag! The United States Flag Code Annotated and Indexed* (Flag Research Center, 1998), p. 7.

224. "I was the only one in the class who decided to pick a flag": Robert Heft, author interview, May 8, 2003.

226. "It cost me $2.87 to make": Quoted in the Newark, Ohio, *Advocate*, June 2, 2004.

Seventeen: The Generation Gap

227. The year that the fifty-star flag made its debut: See the following Vietnam War reference books: Harry G. Summers Jr., *Vietnam War Almanac* (Facts on File, 1985); Marc Leepson, ed., *The Webster's New World Dictionary of the Vietnam War* (Macmillan, 1998); and Spencer C. Tucker, ed., *Encyclopedia of the Vietnam War: A Political, Social, and Military History* (ABC-CLIO, 1998).

228. . . . "a cultural war using the flag as a primary symbol": Goldstein, *Saving "Old Glory,"* p. 148.

228. The flag, Burt Neuborne of the American Civil Liberties Union said in 1970: Quoted in the *Wall Street Journal*, June 12, 1970.

228. . . . he received thunderous applause from campaign audiences: Quoted in the *New York Times*, March 23, 1964.

230. Flag decals "have become a fixture on fire trucks": "Decalcomania over the American Flag," *Life* (July 18, 1969): p. 32.

230. . . . Mayor Ronnie Thompson said: Thompson and Windecker quoted in the *New York Times*, July 4, 1969.

230.   ... "troubled by the stiff-minded emphasis on the flag": Jim
           Bouton, *Ball Four* (Wiley, 1990), p. 59.

230.   ... "Your Flag Decal Won't Get You": copyright John Prine,
           lyrics used by permission of Oh Boy Records, Inc.

231.   President Nixon spoke out during the war: Nixon mentioned
           the "great silent majority" for the first time in a November 3,
           1969, televised address to the nation on his Vietnam War policy
           during a period of intense antiwar activity. "Tonight, to you, the
           great silent majority of Americans, I ask for your support," the
           president said near the end of his speech. "I pledged in my cam-
           paign for the Presidency to end the war in a way that we could
           win the peace. I have initiated a plan of action which will enable
           me to keep that pledge. The more support I can have from the
           American people, the sooner that pledge can be redeemed. For
           the more divided we are at home, the less likely the enemy is to
           negotiate. . . ."

231.   During the rally a young man ... started ... to lower the
           American flag: See Terry H. Anderson, *The Movement and the
           Sixties* (Oxford University Press, 1996), p. 223.

231.   The "profanity and spitting" by the demonstrators: See Charles
           Kaiser, *1968 in America: Music, Politics, Chaos, Counterculture, and the
           Shaping of a Generation* (Weidenfeld & Nicolson, 1988), p. 240.

232.   "Johns's print successfully became a symbol of protest": Deb-
           ora Wood, "Art and Transformation," 1998, online at http://
           users.rcn.com/erebora/debora/transform.html

232.   "Most sickening was the manner in which the American flag
           was degraded": Quoted in *Variety*, February 25, 1970.

233.   "I don't like what you're doing to the flag": Quoted in the *New
           York Times*, June 6, 1970.

233.   "The flag belongs to all the American people": See Goldstein,
           Saving "Old Glory," p. 119.

233.   "Which is the greater contribution to the security of freedom":
           Kuykendall was speaking during a House debate on June 20,
           1967, *Congressional Record*, 113th Congress, p. 16,446; Wiggins
           remarks, p. 16,459.

234.   Nearly all of them were "used against 'peace' demonstrations":
           Goldstein, p. 153.

234.   ... he wore a red, white, and blue American flag shirt: See
           Jonah Raskin, *For the Hell of It: The Life and Times of Abbie Hoff-
           man* (University of California Press, 1996), pp. 178–79.

235.   "Johnson burned an American flag as part": Supreme Court of the United States, *Texas v. Johnson, 38–155,* argued March 21, 1989; decided June 21, 1989.

236.   . . . "perhaps the largest single wave of [flag-burning] incidents": Goldstein, *Saving "Old Glory,"* p. 215.

237.   Their cases wound up in the Supreme Court: Supreme Court of the United States, *United States v. Eichman, 89–1433* and *United States v. Haggerty, 89–1434,* decided June 11, 1990. The votes on the *Johnson* and *Eichman* cases were identical. In both cases Justice William Brennan delivered the majority opinion, joined by Justices Thurgood Marshall, Harry Blackmun, Antonin Scalia, and Anthony Kennedy. Chief Justice William Rehnquist John Paul Stevens, Byron White, and Sandra Day O'Connor dissented.

237.   "Congress tried to protect [the flag] by legislation": In an exchange with reporters in the White House's Rose Garden, following his remarks after receiving a replica of the Marine Corps (Iwo Jima) Memorial.

237.   In 1989 Bush had termed such an amendment: In his remarks to the American Legion Annual Convention in Baltimore, September 7, 1989.

237.   The alliance is "engaged in a war to recapture Old Glory": Citizens Flag Alliance, "Let the People Decide," 2000, pp. 1–2. The Citizens Flag Alliance was chartered in May 1994 by the American Legion to promote a Flag Desecration Constitutional Amendment and to foster flag education.

237.   . . . "took away a fundamental right of the American people": Testifying March 10, 2004, before the Senate Judiciary Committee.

238.   . . . two-thirds majority required for constitutional amendments: Once passed by two-thirds majorities in the House and Senate a proposed amendment to the Constitution does not become effective until it is ratified by the legislatures of three-fourths of the states within seven years after it is submitted for ratification.

239.   "There were people at the time, and have been people since then": Quoted in Steven Siceloff, "Stars and Stripes in Space," *Florida Today,* July 4, 2001, n.p.

239.   "I certainly felt that the American flag is what belonged there":
        Appearing on *NewsHour with Jim Lehrer,* PBS-TV, July 20, 1999.

240.   "Even though the event took only 10 minutes": Anne Platoff,
        "Where No Flag Has Gone Before: Political and Technical As-
        pects of Placing a Flag on the Moon," NASA Contractor Re-
        port 188251, August 1993.

240.   "My guess is the flags themselves, because they're nylon":
        Quoted in *Florida Today,* July 4, 2001.

240.   "We came here to express our sympathy for those killed at Kent
        State": Quoted in the *Wall Street Journal,* May 11, 1970.

241.   That was because, one worker said: Quoted in the *Wall Street
        Journal,* May 13, 1970.

241.   "Outside of God, [the flag] is the most important thing I know":
        Quoted in the *New York Times,* May 21, 1970.

241.   "A lot of us are World War II vets and fathers": Quoted in the
        New York Post, May 9, 1970.

242.   At the end of the meeting Brennan: See Fred J. Cook, "Hard-
        Hats: The Rampaging Patriots," *The Nation* (June 15, 1970).

242.   At the University of New Mexico: See "At War with War,"
        TIME (May 18, 1970): n.p.

242.   Philip Caputo, the author: In a lecture given at the U.S. Air
        Force Academy, April 27, 2000. See U.S. Air Force Academy,
        War, Literature & the Arts (Spring–Summer 2000), p. 25.

243.   It was "just like Iwo Jima": Quoted in Harold G. Moore and
        Joseph L. Galloway, *We Were Soldiers Once and Young* (Random
        House, 1992), p. 169.

243.   That flag was attached to "a shattered tree": J. D. Coleman,
        Pleiku: The Dawn of Helicopter Warfare in Vietnam (St. Martin's,
        1988), p. 226.

244.   "Every afternoon we would hang Mike's shirt": Senator McCain
        first told the story of Mike Christian at the 1988 Republican
        National Convention. A copy of that speech is on his "Straight
        Talk America" Web site: www.straighttalkamerica.com

244.   A few days after the beating: From a letter written by Colonel
        Day, submitted in testimony on the flag protection Constitutional
        Amendment before the U.S. Senate Judiciary Committee. See
        Citizens Flag Alliance undated booklet, *Let the People Decide.*

244.   "That flag," he told the novelist Pat Conroy, a college classmate:
        Quoted in Pat Conroy, *My Losing Season* (Bantam, 2002), p. 371.

Eighteen: United We Stand Again

246.   "To this day, I don't know what I was thinking": Quoted in the
         Everett, Washington, *Herald*, June 14, 1998.

246.   ... "one of the most heroic acts ever to take place": Testifying
         before the U.S. Senate Judiciary Committee, July 8, 1998, in
         favor of a flag desecration Constitutional Amendment.

246.   On that day also a record 10,471 American flags flew over the
         U.S. Capitol: Americans may purchase flags that have been
         flown over the U.S. Capitol through the offices of individual
         members of Congress. Every day, three sizes of cotton and nylon
         flags—three-by-five feet, four-by-six feet, and five-by-eight
         feet—are run up a Capitol Building flagpole on the House side
         for less than a minute by staffers in the office of the Architect of
         the Capitol. The practice began in 1937. Today some 350 flags a
         day are raised over the Capitol and sold for less than twenty dol-
         lars apiece. Each flag comes with a certificate noting that if flew
         over the U.S. Capitol and the date that it was flown. At a "Salute
         to Heroes Night" charity auction in Washington, D.C., on
         March 4, 2004, a flag that flew over the Capitol on September
         11, 2002, in honor of those who perished in the September 11,
         2001, terrorist attacks sold for more than five thousand dollars.

249.   "I would just love to see him explain on national television":
         Quoted in the *New York Times*, May 20, 1988.

249.   In his acceptance speech at the Republican National Conven-
         tion: Quoted in the *Washington Post*, August 24, 1988.

249.   "What is it about the Pledge of Allegiance": Quoted in the *New
         York Times*, August 24, 1988.

249.   During the campaign, a Bush ally, Republican Senator Steve
         Symms: See John L. Sullivan, Amy Fried, and Mary G.
         Dietz, "Patriotism, Politics and the Presidential Election of
         1988," *American Journal of Political Science* (February 1991):
         pp. 200–234.

250.   "I like Bush's attitude.": Quoted in the *New York Times*, October
         30, 1988.

251.   "We are trying to defend the notion that all art": Quoted in
         "Flag-on-the-Floor Furor," *TIME* (March 13, 1989): p. 27.
         Scott's installation also was met by vehement protests from vet-
         erans and others when it was part of eighty-one works of art

that made up a show called "Old Glory: The American Flag in Contemporary Art" at the Phoenix Art Museum in March and April 1996. Veterans' groups led peaceful protests when the installation was included in a show called "Vexillology: The American Symbol in Art" at the Nassau County Community College's Firehouse Art Gallery in Garden City, Long Island, New York, in September and October 2003.

251.   "My intent with the work was to open up discussion about America": Dread Scott, author interview, December 5, 2003.

251.   When he designed the installation in 1988: Quoted in *Newsday,* September 16, 2003.

252.   "There is hardly a pro or college team in the land: Steve Wulf, "Old Glory and New Wounds: The True Meaning of the Flag is Lost in the World of Sports," *Sports Illustrated,* February 25, 1991, p. 7.

254.   "We wanted a place America could see this flag": Quoted in the *Albuquerque Journal,* November 23, 2001.

254.   "It was pretty emotional": Quoted in Brian Lepley, "Soldier Carries WTC Flag at Olympic Opener," Armed Forces Press Service, February 11, 2002.

256.   A Gallup survey taken four days after the attacks: Quoted in Lisa Sanders, et al., "All-American Ads," *Advertising Age,* September 24, 2001.

256.   "We've been running two ten-hour shifts six days a week": Quoted in the *Akron Beacon-Journal,* July 3, 2002.

257.   "We were just trying to say": Quoted in the *Fayetteville Observer,* November 30, 2003.

257.   The company's president and CEO said: Kirk Yoshida, quoted in Business Wire, October 18, 2001, p. 2,352.

257.   "Marshall Field's is proud to resurrect a tradition": Quoted in the *Chicago Sun-Times,* May 24, 2003.

258.   "Originally, I was going to make little flags": Quoted in the Waynesboro and Greencastle (Pennsylvania) *Record Herald,* June 24, 2003.

258.   "I normally answer twenty-five to thirty questions, at most": Michael Buss, author interview, July 12, 2003.

259.   " . . . the President issued a proclamation to display the flag at half staff": According to W. G. Perrin in his book, *British Flags* (Cambridge University Press, 1922), flying a flag at half-staff

(also known as "half-mast") to honor the death of an individual dates from 1612 when a British sailing master was murdered by Eskimos in present-day Canada and the captain of his ship flew his flag halfway down on the mast as a sign of mourning. Many nations honor their dead in this fashion today, including the United States.

The U.S. Flag Code provides specific, detailed instructions on flying the flag at half-staff.

The Code authorizes the president of the United States to order that the flag be flown at half-staff "upon the death of principal figures" of the federal and state governments and for the deaths of notable private citizens. The flag is flown at half-staff for thirty days from the day of death of the president or a former president; for ten days on the death of the vice president, the chief justice, a retired Supreme Court chief justice, or the speaker of the House of Representatives; from the day of death until the burial of an associate justice of the Supreme Court, a member of the cabinet, a former vice president, the president pro tempore of the Senate, the majority and minority leaders of the Senate, or the majority and minority leaders of the House; and on the day of death and the next day for a senator, representative, territorial delegate, or resident commissioner.

The Code does not prohibit private individuals from displaying a flag at half-staff.

As far as flags that are permanently attached on a pole, two black ribbons may be tied on the flagpole—not on the flag—because the flags cannot be physically flown at half-staff, according to the National Flag Foundation.

"The flag, when flown at half-staff, should be hoisted to the peak for an instant, then lowered to the half-staff position," half the distance between the top and bottom of the staff, the Code notes. "The flag should be again raised to the peak before it is lowered for the day."

260.   "September 11 made it safe for liberals to be patriots": George Packer, "Recapturing the Flag," the *New York Times Magazine*, September 30, 2001, p. 15.

260. "So I was pleasantly surprised:" Quoted in "Patriot Practitioner," *American Enterprise,* September 2002.

260. "Definitely not, I say": Katha Pollitt, "Put Out No Flags," *The Nation,* October 8, 2001.

261. "That's the flag I served under": Quoted in The *Tennessean,* December 6, 2003.

262. "That's our flag," he said: Quoted in the *Washington Post,* December 22, 2003.

262. The flag, she said, "has, through sheer repetition, been reduced": Barbara Ehrenreich, "Citizen Curmudgeon," *Progressive,* February 2003.

262. "A lot of people blindly stand up and salute the flag": Quoted in the *New York Times,* February 26, 2003.

262. . . . whose uniforms contained an American flag patch on the right sleeve: Those patches show the flag with the canton on the right, in the "reversed field" position. That is because the flag is on the uniform's right sleeve and is intended to look as though it is blowing in the wind as the person who wears the flag walks forward. Flag patches worn on the left sleeve should have the canton on the left. Reversed field flags also appear on the right side of vehicles and planes, including Air Force One.

262. "It's imposing enough that we're coming into another society": Quoted in the *New York Times,* March 20, 2003.

263. "You can understand these Marines who have put their lives on the line": Quoted in the *New York Times,* April 3, 2003.

263. "You must respect the flag": Quoted by Reuters News, April 23, 2003.

263. . . . "You cannot display an American flag outside the FOB": Quoted in the *Washington Post,* July 5, 2004.

263. "We believe that the original form of the pall": Jon Austin, author interview, May 13, 2003.

264. "It was simply a matter that there was a shortage of caskets": Tom Sherlock, author interview, May 6, 2003.

264. It is folded . . . and presented to the next of kin at the end of the funeral: See "Flag Facts: Folding the United States Flag," National Flag Foundation, 2001.

264.   "There is no meaning to the triangle": Quoted in Corcoran,
         p. 143.
266.   "An immigrant comes to the country, moves to a territory": Jef-
         frey Kohn, author interview, September 4, 2003.

Bibliography

Books

Adams, Gridley, *So Proudly We Hail,* United States Flag Foundation, 1953.

Anderson, Terry H., *The Movement and the Sixties: Protest in America from Greensboro to Wounded Knee,* Oxford University Press, 1995.

Appleton, Nathan, *The Star-Spangled Banner,* Lockwood, Brooks, 1877.

Balch, George T., *Methods of Teaching Patriotism in the Public Schools,* D. Van Nostrand, 1890.

Barry, John W., *Masonry and the Flag,* The Masonic Service Association, 1924.

Beath, Robert Burns, *History of the Grand Army of the Republic,* Bryan, Taylor & Co. 1888.

Bennett, Mabel R., *So Gallantly Streaming,* Drake, 1974.

Berns, Walter, *Making Patriots,* University of Chicago Press, 2001.

Blumenthal, Sidney, *Pledging Allegiance: The Last Campaign of the Cold War,* HarperCollins, 1990.

Bodnar, John, ed., *Bonds of Affection: Americans Define Their Patriotism,* Princeton University Press, 1996.

Boime, Albert, *The Unveiling of National Icons: A Plea for Patriotic Iconoclasm in a Nationalist Era,* Cambridge University Press, 1998.

Bonner, Robert E., *Colors and Blood: Flag Passions of the Confederate South*, Princeton University Press, 2002.

Bradley, James, *Flags of Our Fathers*, Bantam, 2000.

Canby, George and Lloyd Balderston, *The Evolution of the American Flag*, Ferris & Leach, 1909.

Cooper, Grace Rogers, *Thirteen-Star Flags: Keys to Identification*, Smithsonian Institution Press, 1973.

Corcoran, Michael, *For Which It Stands: An Anecdotal Biography of the American Flag*, Simon & Schuster, 2002.

Cortwright, Edgar M., *Apollo Expeditions to the Moon*, U.S. Government Printing Office, 1975.

Crouthers, David D., *Flags of American History*, Hammond & Co. 1962.

Curtis, Michael Kent, ed., *The Constitution and the Flag*, Garland, 1993.

Davies, Wallace Evan, *Patriotism on Parade: The Story of Veterans' and Hereditary Organizations in America, 1783–1900*, Harvard University Press, 1955.

Dearing, Mary R., *Veterans in Politics: The Story of the G.A.R.*, Louisiana State University Press, 1952.

Delaplaine, Edward S., *Francis Scott Key: Life and Times*, Willow Bend Books, 2001.

Detzer, David, *Allegiance: Fort Sumter, Charleston, and the Beginning of the Civil War*, Harcourt, 2001.

Drake, Joseph Rodman, *The American Flag*, James G. Gregory, 1861.

Druckman, Nancy, and Jeffrey Kenneth Kohn, *American Flags: Designs for a Young Nation*, Abrams, 2003.

Eggenberger, David, *Flags of the U.S.A.*, Crowell, 1964.

Elliott, Peter, *Home Front: American Flags from Across the United States*, University of Chicago Press, 2003.

Fischer, David Hackett, *Washington's Crossing*, Oxford University Press, 2004.

Fisher, Leonard Everett, *Stars & Stripes: Our National Flag*, Holiday House, 1993.

Foner, Eric, *The Story of American Freedom*, W. W. Norton, 1998.

Fort, Ilene Susan, *The Flag Paintings of Childe Hassam*, Horizon Books, 1990.

Fow, John H., *The True Story of the American Flag*, William J. Campbell, 1908.

Freeman, Mae Blacker, *Stars and Stripes: The Story of the American Flag*, Random House, 1964.

Furlong, William Rea and Byron McCandless, *So Proudly We Hail: The History of the United States Flag*, Smithsonian Institution Press, 1981.

Goldstein, Robert Justin, *Burning the Flag: The Great 1989–1990 American Flag Desecration Controversy,* Kent State University Press, 1998.

Goldstein, Robert Justin, ed., *Desecrating the American Flag: Key Documents of the Controversy from the Civil War to 1995,* Syracuse University Press, 1996.

Goldstein, Robert Justin, *Flag Burning and Free Speech: The Case of Texas v. Johnson,* University Press of Kansas, 2000.

Goldstein, Robert Justin, *Saving Old Glory: The History of the American Flag Desecration Controversy,* Westview Press, 1995.

Gordon, John B., *Reminiscences of the Civil War,* Charles Scribner's Sons, 1904.

Guenter, Scot M., *The American Flag, 1777–1924: Cultural Shifts from Creation to Codification,* Associated University Press, 1990.

Hannings, Bud, *The Story of the American Flag,* Seniram, 2001.

Hastings, George E., *The Life and Works of Francis Hopkinson,* University of Chicago Press, 1926.

Healy, Nick, *The American Flag,* Lake Street Publishers, 2003.

Hendrickson, Robert, *Fort Sumter: The First Day of the Civil War,* Scarborough House, 1990.

Hickey, Donald R., *War of 1812: A Forgotten Conflict,* University of Illinois Press, 1989.

Higham, John, *Strangers in the Land: Patterns of American Nativism, 1860–1925,* 2nd ed., Rutgers University Press, 1988.

Hinrichs, Kit, and Delphine Hirasuna, *Long May She Wave: A Graphic History of the American Flag,* Ten Speed Press, 2001.

Hobswam, Eric, *Nations and Nationalism Since 1780: Programme, Myth, Reality,* Cambridge University Press, 1990.

Horner, Harlan Hoyt, *The American Flag,* State of New York Education Department, 1910.

Johannsen, Robert W., *To the Halls of Montezuma: The Mexican War in the American Imagination,* Oxford University Press, 1985.

Johnson, Willis Fletcher, *The National Flag: A History,* Houghton Mifflin, 1930.

Jones, Richard Seely, *A History of the American Legion,* Bobbs-Merrill, 1946.

Kazin, Michael, *The Populist Persuasion: An American History,* rev. ed., Cornell University Press, 1998.

Kohn, Hans, *American Nationalism: An Interpretive Essay,* Macmillan, 1957.

Kreitler, Peter Gwillim, *United We Stand: Flying the American Flag,* Chronicle Books, 2002.

Krythe, Maymie R., *What So Proudly We Hail: All About Our American Flag, Monuments, and Symbols*, Harper & Row, 1968.

Lord, Walter, *By the Dawn's Early Light*, W. W. Norton, 1972.

Lorenz, Lincoln, *John Paul Jones: Fighter for Freedom and Glory*, U.S. Naval Institute, 1943.

Manwaring, David Roger, *Render unto Caesar: The Flag Salute Controversy*, University of Chicago Press, 1962.

Marling Karal Ann, *Old Glory: Unfurling History*, Bunker Hill, 2004.

Marvin, Caroline and David W. Ingle, *Blood Sacrifice and the Nation: Totem Rituals and the American Flag*, Cambridge University Press, 1999.

Mayer, Jane, *Betsy Ross and the Flag*, Random House, 1952.

Mastai, Boleslaw and Marie-Louise D. Mastai, *The Stars and Stripes: The American Flag as Art and as History from the Birth of the Republic to the Present*, Alfred A. Knopf, 1973.

McCabe, John, *George M. Cohan: The Man Who Owned Broadway*, Doubleday, 1973.

McPherson, James M., *For Cause and Comrades: Why Men Fought in the Civil War*, Oxford University Press, 1998.

McPherson, James M., *What They Fought For: 1861–1865*, Anchor, 1995.

Miller, Margarette S., *Twenty-Three Words, A Biography of Francis Bellamy: Author of the Pledge of Allegiance*, Printcraft Press, 1976.

Moeller, Henry, *Shattering an American Myth: Unfurling the History of the Stars and Stripes*, Amereon House, 1992.

Molotsky, Irwin, *The Flag, The Poet, and the Song: The Story of the Star-Spangled Banner*, Dutton, 2001.

Morison, Samuel Eliot, *John Paul Jones: A Sailor's Biography*, Little, Brown, 1959.

Morris, Robert, *The Truth About the Betsy Ross Story*, Wynnehaven, 1982.

Moss, James A., *The Flag of Our United States: Its History and Symbolism*, Rand McNally & Co., 1940.

Moss, James A., *Our Country's Flag: The Symbol of All We Are — All We Hope to Be*, United States Flag Association, 1937.

Muller, Charles G., *The Darkest Day: 1814*, Lippincott, 1963.

O'Leary, Cecilia E., *To Die For: The Paradox of American Patriotism*, Princeton University Press, 2000.

Parrish, Thomas, *The American Flag: The Symbol of Our Nation Throughout Its History*, Simon & Schuster, 1973.

Parry, Edwin S., *Betsy Ross: Quaker Rebel*, John C. Winston Company, 1930.

Patterson, Richard S. and Richardson Dougall, *The Eagle and the Shield: A History of the Great Seal of the United States,* United States Department of State, 1976.

Pencak, William, *For God and Country: The American Legion, 1919–1941,* Northeastern University Press, 1989.

Perrin, W. G., *British Flags,* Cambridge University Press, 1922.

Pitch, Anthony, *The Burning of Washington: The British Invasion of 1814,* Naval Institute Press, 2004.

Preble, George Henry, *Origin and History of the American Flag,* 2 vols., Nicholas L. Brown, 1917.

———. *The History of the Flag of the United States,* A. Williams and Co., 1880.

Quaife, Milo M., Melvin J. Weig, and Roy E. Appleman, *The History of the American Flag; From the Revolution to the Present, Including a Guide to Its Use and Display,* Harper and Row, 1961.

Randall, Ruther Painter, *Colonel Elmer Ellsworth: A Biography of Lincoln's Friend and First Hero of the Civil War,* Little, Brown, 1960.

Richardson, Edward W., *Standards and Colors of the American Revolution,* University of Pennsylvania, 1982.

Robinson, Marlyn and Christopher Simoni, eds., *The Flag and the Law: A Documentary History of the Treatment of the American Flag by the Supreme Court and Congress,* vols. 1–4, William Hein & Co, 1992.

Roland, Mary J. Driver, *Old Glory: The True Story,* self-published, 1918.

Rowan, Bob, *Old Glory and Friends,* Unique Printing Services, 2002.

Rubin, David S., ed., *Old Glory: The American Flag in Contemporary Art,* Cleveland Center for Contemporary Art, 1994.

Schneider, Dick, *Stars & Stripes Forever: The History, Stories, and Memories of Our American Flag,* Morrow, 2003.

Sedeen, Margaret, *Star-Spangled Banner: Our Nation and its Flag,* National Geographic Society, 1993.

Skinner, Peter, ed., *God Bless America: The American Flag Book: 120 Stories, Poems and Quotations About the American Flag,* Megapolis, 2002.

Smith, Whitney, *The Flag Book of the United States,* Morrow, 1975.

———. *Flags and Arms Across the World,* McGraw-Hill, 1980.

———. *Flags Through the Ages and Across the World,* McGraw-Hill, 1975.

———. *Honor the Flag: The United States Flag Code Annotated and Indexed,* Flag Research Center, 1998.

Sollod, Celeste, ed., *The American Flag,* Friedman / Fairfax, 2001.

Sonneck, Oscar George Theodore, *Report on "the Star-Spangled Banner" "Hail Columbia" "America" "Yankee Doodle,"* Dover, 1972.

Stewart, Charles W., *Stars and Stripes: A History of the United States Flag*, Boylston Publishing Co., 1915.

Taylor, Lonn, *The Spangled Banner: The Flag That Inspired the National Anthem*, Harry N. Abrams, 2000.

Tuchman, Barbara W., *The First Salute: A View of the American Revolution*, Alfred A. Knopf, 1988.

Virga, Vincent, *Eyes of the Nation: A Visual History of the United States*, Alfred A. Knopf, 1997.

Waldstreicher, David, *In the Midst of Perpetual Fetes: The Making of American Nationalism, 1776–1820*, University of North Carolina Press, 1997.

Whipple, Wayne, *The Story of the American Flag*, Henry Altemus, 1910.

Williams, Earl P. Jr., *What You Should Know About the American Flag*, Maryland Historical Press, 1987.

Zaroulis, Nancy and Gerald Sullivan, *Who Spoke Up? American Protest Against the War in Vietnam, 1963–1975*, Doubleday, 1984.

Articles, Reports, and Studies

American Vexillum magazine, selected issues.

Baer, John, *The Pledge of Allegiance: A Centennial History*, 1992, published online at http://history.vineyard.net/pdgecho.htm

Bonner, Robert E., "Flag Culture and the Consolidation of Confederate Nationalism," *Journal of Southern History*, May 2002.

Boutilier, Emily Gold, "What One Man's Obsession Reveals About the Stars and Stripes," *Brown Alumni Magazine*, May / June 2002.

Brandt, Nat, "To the Flag," *American Heritage*, June 1971.

Carr, Fred, "Marine Corps War Memorial Sculptor Honored at Sunset Parade, *Henderson Hall News*, June 12, 1998.

Carlson, Sarah-Eva H., "Preparing for War: Ellsworth, the Militias, and the Zouaves," *Illinois History*, February 1996.

Carson, Jane, "The First American Flag Hoisted in Old England," *The William and Mary Quarterly*, July 1954.

Clausen, Christopher, "Pledge of Allegiance," *The American Scholar*, Winter 2003.

Conniff, Ruth, "Patriot Games," *The Progressive*, January 2002.

Conover, Kirsten A., "Fluent in the Language of Flags: Every Year Is a Banner Year for Whitney Smith," *Christian Science Monitor*, July 2, 1990.

"Decalomania Over the American Flag," *Life*, July 18, 1969.

Dougherty, Steven, "When the World Runs Something New Up the Flag-pole, Scholar Whitney Smith Is the First to Salute," *People Weekly*, June 17, 1985.

Fawcett, Charles, "The Striped Flag of the East India Company and Its Connection with the American 'Stars and Stripes,'" *The Journal of The Society for Nautical Research*, October 1937.

Fetto, John, "Patriot Games," *American Demographics*, July 2000.

Flag Bulletin, The, selected issues.

"Flag Facts," National Flag Foundation, 2001.

"The Fort Sumter Flags: A Study in Documentation and Authentication," U.S. Department of the Interior, National Park Service, Harpers Ferry Center 1981.

Gelb, Norman, "Reluctant Patriot," *Smithsonian*, September 2004.

Gitlin, Todd, "Patriotism Is Sticky," *The American Scholar*, summer 2003.

Goldstein, Robert Justin, "The Great 1989–90 Flag Flap: An Historical, Political and Legal Analysis, *University of Miami Law Review*, vol. 45, September 1990.

Goldstein, Robert Justin, "The Vietnam War Flag Flap," *The Flag Bulletin*, vol. 153, August 1993.

"The Great Seal of the United States," U.S. Department of State, Bureau of Public Affairs, July 2003.

Griffis, William Elliot, "Where Our Flag Was First Saluted," *The New England Magazine*, July 1893.

Grossman, Lloyd, "Why We Love the Flag and the Frontier," *New States-man*, December 17, 2001.

Haskin, Frederic, J., "Flags of the United States," National Capital Press, 1941.

Hayes, Stephen F., "Fly the Flag — Or Else," *Reason*, April 2001.

Holzer, Harold, "New Glory for Old Glory: A Lincoln-Era Tradition Reborn," *White House Studies*, spring 2002.

House, R. C., "Iwo Jima: Its Heroes and Flag," *World War II*, January 2000.

Jones, Jeffrey Owen, "The Pledge's Creator," *Smithsonian*, November 2003.

Jost, Kenneth, "Patriotism in America," *CQ Researcher*, June 25, 1999.

Kashatus, William C., "Seamstress for a Revolution: An Intriguing Controversy Surrounds Betsy Ross and the Making of the First American Flag," *American History*, August 2002.

Kaufmann, Bill, "The Bellamy Boys Pledge Allegiance," *The American Enterprise*, October–November 2002.

Kazin, Michael, "A Patriotic Left," *Dissent*, fall 2002.

Kernan, Michael, "Saving the Nation's Flag," *Smithsonian*, October 1998.

Kohn, Jeffrey Kenneth, "Stars & Stripes: Star-Spangled Style Has Inspired Artisans and Advertisers Alike," *Country Living*, July 2002.

Lax, John and William Pencak, "Creating the American Legion," *The South Atlantic Quarterly*, winter 1982.

"Let's Be Right on Flag Etiquette," National Americanism Commission, The American Legion, January 2002.

"Let the People Decide," The Citizens Flag Alliance, 2000.

Luckey, John, "Flag Protection: A Brief History and Summary of Recent Supreme Court Decisions and Proposed Constitutional Amendments," Congressional Research Service, Library of Congress, January 27, 2003.

Luckey, John, "The United States Flag: Federal Law Relating to Display and Associated Questions," Congressional Research Service, Library of Congress, June 14, 2000.

Marling, Karal Ann, "The Stars and Stripes, American Chameleon," *The Chronicle of Higher Education*, October 16, 2001.

Martz, John D. Jr., "The Story Behind a New Star for the Flag," *Army Information Digest*, July 1959.

"The Middle Americans: Person of the Year," *TIME*, January 5, 1970.

"Old Glory: A Beloved National Symbol Woven into the Fabric of American Life," U.S. Postal Service, 2003.

Old Glory News, Citizens Flag Alliance, selected issues.

"Old Glory's Strength," *The Economist*, July 3, 1999.

Packer, George, "Recapturing the Flag," *The New York Times Magazine*, September 30, 2001.

Park, Edwards, "Our Flag Was Still There," *Smithsonian*, July 2000.

Paul, Marilyn H., "I Pledge Allegiance . . . ," *Prologue: Quarterly of the National Archives*, winter 1992.

Platoff, Anne, "Where No Flag Has Gone Before: Political and Technical Aspects of Placing a Flag on the Moon," NASA Contractor Report 188251, August 1993.

Presto, Gregory, "The Stars and Stripes Forever," *Northwestern*, summer 2003.

Rankin, H. F., "The Naval Flags of the American Revolution," *William and Mary Quarterly*, vol. XI, July 1954.

Rogers, John, "New Wave," *Landscape Architecture*, July 2003.

Ruffin, Edmund, "The First Shot at Fort Sumter," *William and Mary Quarterly Historical Magazine,* October 1911.

Ryder, James F., "The Painter of 'Yankee Doodle,'" *The New England Magazine,* December 1895.

Sanders, Lisa, *et al.,* "All-American Ads: Marketers Rally Around Flag but Try Not to Push Patriotism, Too," *Advertising Age,* September 24, 2001.

Schlesinger, Arthur M. Jr., "The Flag: Who Owns Old Glory?" *Rolling Stone,* May 15, 2003.

Schultz, Fred L., "United We Stood, 1942," *Naval History Magazine,* August, 2002.

Smith, Whitney, "One Nation Under God: The Crusade to Capture the American Flag," *American Atheist,* summer 2001.

Solis-Cohen, Lisa, "More Flags at Sotheby's," *Maine Antique Digest,* October 2002.

Southgate, M. Therese, "Allies Day, May 1917," *Journal of the American Medical Association,* May 24–31, 2000.

Stafford, Marie Peary, "The Peary Flag Comes to Rest," *National Geographic,* October 1954.

"Stars and Hypes," *Forbes Magazine,* December 24, 2001.

"The Story of the American Flag," *National Geographic,* October 1917.

Sullivan, John L., Amy Fried, Mary G. Dietz, "Patriotism, Politics and the Presidential Election of 1988," *American Journal of Political Science,* February 1992.

Svejda, George J., "History of the Star-Spangled Banner from 1814 to the Present," U.S. Department of the Interior, 1969.

Timmons, Carlin and Sandy Pusey, "Fort Sumter National Monument's New Facility at Liberty Square," *Cultural Resource Management,* National Park Service, vol. 25, No. 4, 2002.

Wellner, Alison Stein, "The Perils of Patriotism," *American Demographics,* September 2002.

Whiteside, Rob, "Through the Perilous Fight: When Americans Suit Up in the Flag, *Harper's Magazine,* July 2002.

Williams, Earl P., Jr. "The 'Fancy Work' of Francis Hopkinson: Did He Design the Stars and Stripes?" *Prologue: Quarterly of the National Archives,* spring 1988.

Wilson, Jim, "Defending the Flag: Conservators Work to Preserve and Restore the Original American Flag," *Popular Mechanics,* July 2000.

Wolkomir, Richard, "Near and Far, We're Waving the Banner for Flags," *Smithsonian,* June 1997.

Wu, Corinna, "Old Glory, New Glory: The Star-Spangled Banner Gets Some Tender Loving Care," *Science News*, June 26, 1999.

Wulf, Steve, "Old Glory and New Wounds: The True Meaning of the Flag Is Lost in the World of Sports," *Sports Illustrated*, February 25, 1991.

Index

ABC News, 256
ACUITY, 258
Adams, Pres. John, 17, 29, 54
Adams, Col. John Quincy, 49
Adera Corporation, 257
Admiral Nimitz Museum, 213
advertising, flag in, 86, 155–56, 189, 210
African Americans, as soldiers, 18, 120–22, 185–86
Air Force, U.S., 213
Alabama, 94, 128, 234, 269
Alaska, 222–25, 236, 269
Aldrin, Buzz, 238–40
Alexandria, Va., 110
Alfred (ship), 16–17, 51
Alley, James P., 195
America Flag Movement, 203
American Civil Liberties Union, 228
American colonies, flags of, 10–12
American Defense Society, 180
American Enterprse Institute, 260

"American Flag, The" (song), 108
American Flag Association, 157–58
American Flag Day Association, 4, 147
American Flag House and Betsy Ross Memorial Association, 44–47
American Indians, 23, 164
Americanism programs, 2, 194–97, 204, 258
American Legion, 2, 4, 67, 118, 171, 191, 194–97, 237, 250, 258, 264, 294
American Party, 88–89
American Protective League, 196
American Revolution, 144, 210, 246
Americans, special feeling of, for flag, 1–2, 5, 265–66
American's Creed, 184, 292
American Standard magazine, 147
"America the Beautiful" (song), 67
Amoskeag Manufacturing Company, 180
Amsterdam Chamber flag, 9
Anacreontic Societies, 64

Anchor Industries, 247
Anderson, Major Robert, 92, 95, 98–99,
    102–3, 122–23
Anderson, Robert B., 223
Andrew Doria (ship), 16, 17
Annin & Co., 86, 249, 256
Antarctica, exploration of, 84
Anthony, Susan B., 43
"Appeal to Heaven" (motto), 14–15
Appleton, Eben, 72–73
Appleton, Georgiana Armistead, 72, 73
Appleton, Nathan, 146
Argus (ship), 57, 277
Arizona, 170, 178, 269
Arkansas, 94, 199, 269
Arlington National Cemetery, 133–34,
    216
Armistead, Maj. George, 60, 71
Armistead, Louisa Hughes, 71–72
Armistice Day (November 11), 193, 294
Armstrong, Neil, 2, 238–40
Army, U.S., 66, 83, 212–13
Arnold, Gen. Benedict, 18
art, flag in, 3, 180–83, 232, 250–51, 303
Art Institute of Chicago, School, 250–51
Art of War, The, 8
Ashburn, Joseph, 38
Ashcroft, John, 175
Atlanta, Ga., 127
Aurelio, Richard R., 241
Aztec Club, 131

Baer, John W., 164, 167, 176
Bahamas, 17, 18
Baker, Sen. Edward Dickinson, 103
Balch, George T., 164
Balderson, Lloyd, 44
Baltimore, Md., 72–73, 180
Baltimore & Ohio Railroad, 135
Barbara Frietsche (play and films), 114,
    236
Barbara Frietsche House and Museum,
    115
Barber, Rep. Hiram, Jr., 156
Barkley, Gilbert, 18
Barnes, Elizabeth, 258
Barrett, William, 51
Barry, Capt. John, 17
Barton, William, 31

Bassett, Rep. Burwell, 78
Batchelor, William, 28
Bates, Gilbert H., 127–30
Bates, Katharine Lee, 67
"Battle Cry of Freedom, The" (song),
    105, 107
"Battle Hymn of the Republic, The"
    (song), 107
Battle of Baltimore, 60–64, 73, 246, 280
Battle of Bennington, 26
Battle of Brandywine, 26–27
Battle of Bull Run, First, 97
Battle of Bunker Hill, 14
Battle of Cowpens, 28
Battle of Fredericksburg, 120
Battle of Gettysburg, 120
Battle of Lexington, 13
Battle of Nashville, 117
Battle of Valcour Island, 18
Beall, C. C., 215
Beanes, Dr. William, 63
Bear Flag Revolt, 85
Beauregard, Gen. P. G. T., 97, 98–99
Bedford (ship), 55
Bedford flag, 11
Beecher, Henry Ward, 123
Belgium, 187
Bell, Alexander Graham, 150
Bell, Mabel Hubbard, 150
Bellamy, Francis, 4, 166–69, 175
Bellamy salute, 168, 171
Bellotti, Francis X., 175
Bennett, William, 248
Benninghoff, H. Merrill, 218
Bennington flag, 26, 35
Benton, Sen. Thomas Hart, 85
Bentsen, Sen. Lloyd, 250
Berlin, 219–20
Berns, Walter, 260
"Betsy Ross" (film), 39
Betsy Ross House and American Flag
    Memorial, 45–49, 47, 147
"Betsy Ross" thirteen-star flag, 2, 39, 139
Bible flag, 92
Bicentennial Year (1976), 246
Birth of Our Nation's Flag (painting), 45, 48
Blaine, James G., 154
Bliss, Gov. Aaron T., 151
Block, Harlon, 214

Boggs, Margaret Donaldson, 42
bonds, wartime, 186, 215–16
Bonhomme Richard (ship), 24
  supposed flag of, 138
Bonner, Robert E., 120, 134
Booth, John Wilkes, 123–24
Borden, Ann, 32
Borg, Andy, 233
Boston, Mass., 14, 18, 102, 142, 146, 148, 232
Boston Gazette, 24
Boudinot, Elias, 31
Boudlin, Grace Evelyn, 68
Bourne, Rep. Benjamin, 57
Bouton, Jim, 230
Bradley, James, 215
Bradley, John, 214–16
Bradley, Sen. Stephen Row, 55–56
Brady, Gen. Patrick H., 237
Brandywine flag, 26–27, 27
Breckinridge, Joseph C., 158
Brennan, Peter J., 242
Brennan, Justice William, 235–36
Bridges, Cornelia, 51
Britain, 54–55, 59, 129–30, 187, 206–7
  colonial rule in America, 12
  flags of, 8–10
British United East India Company, flag of, 11–12, 15–16
Brooke, Lt. Col. Arthur, 61
Brooke, Walter, 96
Brown, Henry K., 103
Brown, O. B., 109
Brownell, Pvt. Francis E., 110
Bryan, William Jennings, 148
Bryant, Mayor A. J., 136
Buckley, William F., Jr., 232
Bucks of America, 18
Bugs Bunny, 40
bunting, 125–26, 161
Bush, Pres. George H. W., 175, 236–37, 248–50
Bush, Pres. George W., 256
Butler, Gen. Benjamin Franklin, 112–13, 125–26, 286
Byrne, Garret, 232

Cabot, John, 9
Cabot (ship), 16

Cahill, George F., 203
Caldwell, Rep. John Alexander, 156
California, 85, 174, 269
Cambridge flag, 15
Campbell, William J., 49
Canada, 187
Canby, George, 44, 48–49
Canby, Jane, 39
Canby, William J., 40–42, 45, 140
canton (union) of flag, 11
Capitol, U.S., 184, 208, 303
Caputo, Philip, 242
Cara, 18
Carney, Sgt. William, 121–22
Cartier, Jacques, 9
cartoons, political, 12, 182, 195
Cashmore, John, 206
Cassel, John H., 195
celebratory flags, 135
Centennial Exhibition (Philadelphia, 1876), 136–37, 139
Centennial flags, 135
Centennial Legion of Historical Military Commands, 141
Centennial Year (1876), 135–42
Chamberlain, Maj. Gen. Joshua Lawrence, 122
Champlain, Samuel de, 9
Chapin, Henry Sterling, 184
Charles Doggett (ship), 116
Charleston, S.C., 22, 127
Chicago, Ill., 168, 209, 250–51
  Democratic Convention (1968), 231
Children's Aid Society, 164
Chin, Cpl. Edward, 262–63
Chinese, ancient, 7–8
Christian, Michael, 244
Cigrand, Bernard John, 146–47, 185
Citizens Flag Alliance, 2, 237
Civil Rights movement, 266
Civil War, 3–4, 43, 91–125
  reconciliation of North and South after, 160–61
  sites, 132
Clark, Gen. Wesley K., 261–62
Clay, Henry, 88
Clay, Gen. Lucius D., 220
Claypoole, John, 38–39, 51
Cleveland, Pres. Grover, 166, 169

Clinton, Pres. Bill, 75, 253
Cochrane, Sir Alexander, 60, 61
Cody, Buffalo Bill, 130
Cohan, George M., 3, 159–60, 212
Cold War, 174, 219–22
Colonial Dames of America, 144
Colorado, 135, 269
color companies, 118–20
colors of flag
   dyeing process, 126
   meaning of, 3, 35–36, 53
Columbia (ship), 55
Columbus, Christopher, 8
Columbus (ship), 16
Columbus Day, 166–68, 290
Communism, 194–95
Confederate Army, 120, 122
Confederate Battle Flag, 97–98, 122, 200
Confederate States of America, 92,
   96–98, 109
   flags of, 96–98, 105–6, 122, 200
Congress, U.S.
   bills about National Anthem, 66–68
   Pledge of Allegiance recited, 175–76
Connecticut, 268
Constitution, U.S., 53
Constitution (ship), 57
Continental Army, 3, 15, 24–29, 140
Continental Colors (American Revolution
   flag), 15–19, 21, 36, 50, 93
   flag makers, 51
   identification problem, 17–18, 22
Continental Congress, 12, 15, 17, 21–23,
   28–29, 50
Continental Navy, 12, 14–15, 32
Coolidge, Pres. Calvin, 201
Copley, John Singleton, 55
country music performers, 260
Cowpen's Flag, 28
Cox, Rep. Samuel Sullivan, 156
Crusades, 8
Culpeper County, Va., 12
Curtis, Mayor Edwin, 148

Dallas, George M., 88
Daughters of the American Revolution
   (DAR), 118, 144, 145, 153, 157, 169,
   171, 184, 197
Davis, James J., 198

Davis, Jefferson, 92–94, 100, 113, 127
Dawson, Sarah Morgan, 106
Day, Col. George "Bud," 244
Death of Warren, The (painting), 14
"decalcomania," 230–31
Declaration of Independence, 21, 27
Decoration Day, 133–34
"Defence of Fort M'Henry" (song), 64
"Defend the Stars and Stripes" (song), 108
Delaware, 268
Delaware River, 23, 25
Democratic Party, 86, 150, 231, 261–62
Denny, Col. Thomas, 201
Devin, 20
de Weldon, Felix, 216
Dewey, Comm. George, 161, 178
Dickinson, John, 210
Dickson, Rev. J. D., 108
DiSalle, Gov. Mike, 225
Dix, John A., 111
Dobbins, Bernard, 215
Docherty, Rev. Dr. George M., 173
Dole, Sen. Bob, 251
Donnan, Edloe, 220
"Don't Tread on Me" (motto), 12, 13
Doubleday, Capt. Abner, 99
Douglas, Sen. Stephen, 103–4
Driver, William, 116–18
Duck Tape company, 257
Dukakis, Kitty, 249
Dukakis, Michael, 175, 248–50
Dulles, John Foster, 223
Dunlap, John, 24
Du Simitière, Pierre Eugène, 30
Du Souchet, Henry A., 39
Dutch United East India Company, 9
Dye, Dale, 212, 297

eagle emblem on flags, 54
Easton flag, 27–28
Eaton, Gen. William, 58
Edes, Benjamin, 63–64
Egyptians, ancient, 7
Ehrenreich, Barbara, 262
Eisenhower, Pres. Dwight D., 173–74,
   216, 221–22, 223–24, 225–26, 227
Eliza (ship), 57
Elizabeth I of England, 11
Elks, Order of, 229–30

Ellsworth, Col. Elmer, 110, 283
emblems on flags, 54, 154
Endicott, John, 10
England
  Great Seal of, 29
  See also Britain
ensign (type of flag), 8–9
Espionage Act, 189, 191
Establishment Clause, 174
"Etiquette of the Stars and Stripes"
  (booklet), 204
Eutaw flag, 141
Evans, Raymond O., 195
Everett, Edward, 105
explorers, flags used by, 9, 239

Falwell, Rev. Jerry, 256
Farragut, Flag Officer David G., 111–12
Farrington, DeWitt C., 126
Faucette, F. W., 120
feminist movement, 43
Ferdinand and Isabella of Spain, 8
Field, James T., 109
Fillmore, Nathaniel, 26
Fillmore flag, 26
Findlay, Ohio ("Flag City USA"), 249
Finley, David E., 223
First Amendment, 172–73, 174, 235, 238
Fisher, Harrison, 183
Fitch, Clyde, 114
Flag, The (film short), 40
flag, U.S., 164
  12–star (spurious), 138
  13–star, 13–stripe, 84, 267
  15–star, 15–stripe, 57, 267
  20–star, 13–stripe, 81, 267
  21–star, 267
  23–star, 267
  24–star, 267
  25–star, 267
  26–star, 84, 267
  27–star, 84, 267
  28–star, 85, 267
  29–star, 267
  30–star, 268
  31–star, 268
  32–star, 268
  33–star, 92, 268
  34–star, 94, 268
  35–star, 94, 268
  36–star, 94, 268
  37–star, 126, 135, 268
  38–star, 135–36, 268
  39–star (unofficial), 135–36
  43–star, 136, 268
  44–star, 268
  45–star, 161, 268
  46–star, 178, 268
  48–star, 178–79, 223–24, 268
  49–star, 223–24, 268
  50–star, 224–26, 268
  adding stars and stripes to, 56–57,
    77–83, 267–69
  in combat, 26–27, 85, 212, 243
  cult of, 3, 4
  death in defense of, 118–20
  early makers of, 18, 21–22, 37–52
  elements and proportions of, 4, 22–23,
    53–54
  flown with other flags, 206–7, 221–22
  hours for flying, 118, 216, 284
  lack of uniformity of, in early Republic,
    53–54, 79, 84, 178–79
  manufacture of, 84, 86, 125–26, 201,
    208
  meaning of elements of, 35–36
  myths and legends about, 3, 34–35,
    37–52, 114, 137–40
  in nation's iconography, 2–3, 5, 86, 107
  Northern defense of, 100–109
  origins of, 3, 16, 29–35, 37–52, 137–38
  public displays of, 2, 183–84, 252–54
  sales of, 185, 208–9, 247, 256, 260
  saluting, 168–69, *170*
  size and dimensions of, 83–84
  slogans and emblems on, 154
  Southerners' feelings about, 109–17,
    127–29
  violence provoked by, 109
  See also flags
Flag Certificates, 165
Flag Code, 2, 4, 171, 198, 207, 221–22,
  236, 259–60, 299, 305
Flag Day (June 14), 4, 44, 52, 153, 175,
  184, 186, 209, 221, 236
  first, and passage of Flag Act, 22–23
  first celebration (1877), 142
  national holiday proposed, 145–53

flag decals, 229–31, 234, 252
flag desecration
  burning of flag, 228, 233, 235, 236–37,
    245–46, 261
  legislation against, 156–59, 189–90,
    196–97, 233–38
  prosecutions for, 234–37
  punishment for, 111–13, 189–91, 208
  and vigilantism, 190–91
Flag Desecration Amendment
  (proposed), 2, 176, 237–38
flag etiquette, 153, 197–98, 258–60
flag firsts
  appearance on consumer items, 58
  fatal incident during Civil War, 110
  flown alongside Union Jack, 187–88
  flown in England, 54–55
  flown in other countries, 54–55, 57
  foreign gun salute to, 17
  largest human, 258
  made with all-American material,
    125–26
  not flown in (Iraq) War, 262–63
  overseas victories, 17
  president born under (Van Buren), 87
  raised on naval vessel, 16–17
  raised over captured fort, 18, 57–58
  Stars and Stripes flown by American
    troops in battle, 85
  Stars and Stripes flown in
    Revolutionary War battle, 26–27
  taken around the world, 55
  taken to Europe, 17
  used for longest period, 223–24
  used under most administrations, 226
Flagg, James Montgomery, 181
flag image
  on clothing, 106, 216, 234–35
  commercialization of, 153–56
  on consumer items, 58, 86, 259–60
  on relief supplies, 207
  on sports clothing, 195, 252
  on stationery, 106–7, 155
  on uniforms, 212, 252, 262
flaglets, 43–44
"flagmania," 103, 105–9
Flag of the United States, The (book), 264
flag patches, 234
flag pins, 234, 256

flag plazas, 203
Flag Protection Act of 1989, 236–37, 251
flag protection movement, 153–59, 201
Flag Resolution (First, of June 14, 1777),
  22–24, 41, 53, 142
Flag Resolution (Second, of 1794), 56–57
Flag Resolution (Third, of 1818), 77, 81,
  267
flags
  disposal of used, 259
  flown by private individuals, 3, 87,
    183–84, 206
  folding of, 264
  at half-staff, 304–5
  history of, up to 1776, 7–15
  other nations' attitudes, 1–2
  parts and designations of, 11
  preservation of, 73, 74
  snipping from, 72
  upside-down, 242
  used by military for communication,
    identification, and burial, 7–8, 23,
    78, 119, 263–64
  very large, 161, 247, 256–58
Flags Across America program, 203
Flags of Our Fathers (book), 215
Flagstaff, Ariz., 141–42
flagstaffs and flagpoles, 165
Flags Unlimited, 253
Flag Week, 153, 202–3
Fleeson, Plunkett, 51
Fletcher, Rachel, 42
fleurs-de-lis, 9
Florida, 84, 92, 269
Flower, Gov. Roswell P., 147
Folger, Rep. Walter, Jr., 80
Ford, Daniel Sharp, 163, 166
Ford, Pres. Gerald, 245
Forster, Maj. Israel, 13
Forster flag, 13
Fort, Ilene Susan, 181
Fort McHenry, 2, 60–64, 69, 71, 247, 280
Fort Niagara Flag, 280
Fort Pickens, 98
Fort Sumter
  fall of, 98–100, 105–7
  flag at, 4, 92–93, 95, 103, 107
  reraising of flag over, 122–23
Fowler, Amelia Bold, 73

FOX News, 256
France, 12, 187, 188–89
    flags of, 9, 181, 188
Franklin, Benjamin, 12, 16, 17, 29, 35, 54, 137
Franklin (ship), 15
fraternal organizations, 143–45
Frederick, Md., 113, 115
freedom of speech, 172–73, 235, 237
Freeman, Bishop James E., 201
Freemasonry, 35
Frelinghuysen, Theodore, 88
Frémont, Jessie Benton, 85
Frémont, John C., 85, 107
French and Indian War, 12
French Revolution, 57
Frietschie, Barbara, 113–16
funeral flags, 263–64

Gadsden, Christopher, 12
Gagnon, Rene, 214–16
Gallway, Pvt. Edward, 99
Garfield, Pres. James, 133, 143
Garner, Patricia, 210
General Armstrong (ship), 82
Generation Gap, 227–28
George III of England, 54–55
George Washington, Jr. (musical), 159–60
George Washington (ship), 57
George Washington Crossing the Delaware (painting), 25
Georgia, 94, 128, 133, 230, 233, 268
German-Americans, in World War I, 189–91
Germany, 193, 213
Gibson, Charles Dana, 181
Gilchrist, Capt. Robert C., 141
Giles, Rep. William Branch, 56
Gillis, Joe, 257
Gingrich, Rep. Newt, 249
Glory (film), 121
Goldstein, Robert Justin, 156, 228, 234, 236
Goldwater, Sen. Barry, 228
Gompers, Samuel, 197, 201
Goodhue, Rep. Benjamin, 56
Gordon, Maj. Gen. John Brown, 122, 161
Graham, Billy, 243
Grand Army of the Republic (GAR),

132–34, 143–45, 148, 153, 157, 164, 167, 194, 288, 294
Grand Review of Union troops, 131
Grand Union flag, 15
Grant, Gen. and Pres. Ulysses S., 122, 133, 136, 143
Gray, Capt. Robert, 55
Great American Flag, 247
Great Depression, 205
Great Seal of the United States, 29–31, 31
Great Silent Majority, 231, 300
Great Union flag, 15
Greeley, Horace, 88
Green, William, 23
Green Mountain Boys, 26
Griffin, Merv, 235
Guenter, Scot, 88, 120, 150, 161, 164, 201
Guillot, Francis, 21
Gulf Oil Company, 229
Gumpert, G., 109
Gustrine, Charles, 185

Hague (ship), 17
Hair (musical), 232–33
Halter v. Nebraska, 158
Hamilton, Schuyler, 92
Hamlin, Hannibal, 154
Hancock, John, 35
Hancock (ship), 15, 17
Hanna, Mark, 148–49
Hanson, Mayor Ole, 195
hard hats, and protestors, 240–42
Harding, Pres. Warren G., 118, 197–98
Harlan, Justice John, 143, 158–59
Harper's Weekly, 101
Harris, William, 166
Harrison, Pres. Benjamin, 143, 166
Harrison, Benjamin (18th c.), 16
Harrison, William Henry, 86–87
Harrison (ship), 15
Hart, Luke E., 173
Hartford, Conn., 145
Haskins, Frederic J., 7
Hassam, Childe, 3, 180–81
Hawaii, 222–25, 269
Hayes, Ira, 214–16
Hayes, Pres. Rutherford B., 143
Heft, Robert G. (Bob), 219, 224–26
Henderson, Rep. David B., 157–58

Henry, Alexander, 109
Henry, Patrick, 13
Henry, Capt. W. S., 86
Hewes, Joseph, 18
Heyman, I. Michael, 59
Higginson, Col. Thomas, 121
Hildebrant, Sophia B., 42
Hinton, Rufus, 233
Historical Society of Pennsylvania, 40
History of the American Flag (book), 92
Hoar, Sen. George F., 157–58
Hobart, Garret A., 149
Hodges, Leigh Mitchell, 178
Hoffman, Abbie, 234–35
Honor America Day (1970), 242–43
Hoover, Pres. Herbert, 68, 201, 205
Hopkins, Esek, 12, 16–17
Hopkinson, Francis, 30–34, *30*
Hopwood, Mary, 115
Hough, Pvt. Daniel, 99
House of Representatives, 56–57, 175–76
Houston, William Churchill, 30
Howe, Julia Ward, 107
Howe, Gen. William, 18
Howells, William Dean, 136
Howes, C. G., Company, 206
Hudson, Henry, 9
Hughes, Justice Charles Evan, 201
Hurley, Patrick J., 202
Hussein, Saddam, 3, 252, 261, 263

Idaho, 269
Illinois, 133, 158, 234, 251, 269
Illinois Flag Day Association, 147
immigrants, 89, 164–65, 204, 265–66
Independence Hall Association, 39
India, ancient, 8
Indiana, 77, 234, 251, 268
"In God We Trust" (motto), 174
Iowa, 269
Iraq War (2003), 3, 260–65
Iwo Jima, 2, 213–15, 216

Jackson, Alan, 260
Jackson, James W., 110
Jackson, Justice Robert H., 172
Jackson, Gen. Thomas J. Stonewall, 114
James I of England, 9–10
Jamestown Island, Virginia, 10

Japan, 11, 201, 213, 216–18
Jasper, John, 147
Jefferson, Thomas, 25, 29, 33
Jehovah's Witnesses, 171–72
Johns, Jasper, 3, 232
Johnson, Pres. Andrew, 129
Johnson, Gregory Lee, 235
Johnson, Pres. Lyndon, 227, 228, 233
Johnston, Gen. Joseph E., 97
Johnston, Sally, 68
Joliet, Louis, 9
Jones, John Paul, 16–17, 24, 35, 51, 138
Jorss-Reilley, Elsie, 68
Joyce, Walter I., 68
Judd, Walter H., 219
July 4 celebrations, 22

Kansas, 94, 170, 189–90, 199, 269
Keith, Toby, 260
Kelly, Judge Robert F., 173
Kendrick, Capt. John, 55
Kennedy, Pres. John F., 216, 227
Kent, A. Atwater, 47–48, 275
Kent State shootings, 240–41
Kentucky, 55, 268
Kerr, William T., 147
Key, Francis Scott, 59, 62–64
Kilmartin, Duncan, 238
King, Anne, 51
Knights of Columbus, 173
Know-Nothings, 88–89, 147
Knoxville, Tenn., 142
Kohn, Jeffrey, 44
Korean War, 222
Kreitler, Paul, 211
Kroboth, Al, 244
Ku Klux Klan, 196, 199–200, 295
Kuykendall, Rep. Dan, 233

Ladies Memorial Association, 132
Lady Washington (ship), 55
Lafayette, Marquis de, 71
Lambkin, Cpl. Price, 121
La Motte Piquet, Admiral, 24
La Salle, Sieur de, 9
La Tourette, Herman R., 68, 204
Launius, Roger, 239
Laws and Customs Regulating the Use of the Flag (pamphlet), 185

League to Enforce Peace, 180
Learned, Col. Ebenezer, 18
Lee, Arthur, 31
Lee, Gen. Robert E., 113, 122, 133
Lee (ship), 15, 17
Lend-Lease Aid, 207
Leo Castelli Gallery, 232
Leutze, Emanuel Gottlieb, 25
Levy, Rep. Jefferson M., 67
Lewis, Carl, 248
Lewis, Hobart, 243
Lexington (ship), 17
Libby, Frederick, 186–87
liberals, 260
Liberia, 97
liberty flags, 12, 13–14
"Liberty or Death" (motto), 13
"Liberty Song, The" (song), 210
liberty trees, 13–14
Lincoln, Pres. Abraham, 92, 95, 96, 98,
    107, 110, 113, 125, 126, 138, 154
    assassination of, 123–24
Lincoln, Mary Todd, 110–11
Lincoln, Tad, 111
Lindsay, Mayor John, 241
Linthicum, Rep. J. Charles, 68
Little Johnny Jones (musical), 159
Livermore, Mary A., 102
Livingston, Robert, 35
Logan, Gen. John A., 131–33, 154
Logan, Mary Simmerson Cunningham,
    133
Lone Star flag, 85
Los Angeles, Calif., 140–41, 208
Louisiana, 77, 94, 268
    flag of, 111–12
Lovell, James, 30
Lovell, James A., Jr., 232–33
Lovell, Gen. Mansfield, 111
Loyal Legion, 157
Lyceum League of America, 165
Lyman, Rep. William, 56
Lynch, Thomas, 16
Lynch (ship), 15
Lytle, Pvt. Milton Scott, 106

MacArthur, Gen. Douglas, 205
MacNamara, Paul, 210
Madison, Pres. James, 56, 59, 60, 63

magazines, flag on covers of, 210–11
Maine, 246, 269
Manchester, William, 213
Mandelberg, W. A., 208
Manly, Capt. John, 17, 53
Manny, Margaret, 18, 51
Marine Band, U.S., 66, 160
Marine Corps War Memorial, 216
Marines, U.S., 57–58, 183, 213–16
Markoe, Capt. Abraham, 14, 35
Marquette, Jacques, 9
Marriott, J. Willard, 243
Marshall, V.P. Thomas R., 201
Marshall Field & Co., 185, 257
Marshall House Incident, 110
Maryland, 170, 172, 268
    military units, 28, 63
Mason, Rep. James Brown, 78, 79
Mason, Gen. John, 63
Massachusetts, 15, 165, 172, 195, 235,
    268
    colonial, 11
    military units, 18, 121
Massachusetts Bay Colony, 10, 14
Massachusetts Red Ensign, 11
Massachusetts Spy, 24
Mayflower (ship), 10
McCain, Sen. John, 244
McCandless, Lt. Cmdr. Byron, 185
McClelland (ship), 111
McDowell, Gen. Irvin, 97
McDowell, William, 169
McElroy, Neil H., 223
McKinley, Pres. William, 138, 143,
    148–50
McLean, Maj. George W., 141
McManus, James, 251
McMillan, Thomas F., 141–42
McNamara, Maj. Gen. Andrew T., 223
McPherson, James M., 100
Memminger, Christopher, 96
Memorial Day, 132–34
Memphis, Tenn., 110
merchant flags, 9
Merrill, Maj. George S., 133, 143–44
Metcalfe, James, 160
Mexican War, 85–86, 131
Mexico City ("Halls of Montezuma"), 86
Meyer, Dietrich, 208

Michael, Barbara Trayer, 146
Michigan, 84, 151, 269
Middleton, Arthur, 31
Middleton, Rep. Henry, 78
Mietike, George A., 109
Miles, William Porcher, 96–97
Military Academy, U.S. (West Point), 66
Miller, Charles Kingsbury, 156
Miller, Clyde R., 67
Miller, Merrill, 212
Minersville School District v. Gobitis, 171–72
Minnesota, 269
Mississippi, 78, 109, 128, 132, 268
Missouri, 269
Moeller, Henry, 23, 50, 273
Moeller, Rep. Walter Henry, 225–26
Mondale, Walter, 248
Monday, Rick, 246
Monroe, Pres. James, 25, 57, 83
Monroe, Mayor John T., 111–12
Montana, 136, 190, 269
Montgomery, Ala., 128
Montgomery, Rep. G. V. Sonny, 175–76
Mooers, Capt. William, 55
Moon, flag on, 2, 238–40
Moore, Gen. Hal, 243
Morgan, Brig. Gen. Daniel, 28
Morgan, Fred, 195
Morgenthau, Henry, Jr., 210
Morris, Robert, 41
Morse, Samuel F. B., 94–95
Moss, Col. James A., 200–203, 264
Mother's Day, 184
Moulder, Lisa, 49
Mountain, Thomas S., 142
Mount Suribachi flag-raising, 2, 213–15, *214*, 298
movies, flag in, 211–12
Moyers, Bill, 261
Mumford, William, 113
Mund, Charles P., 45
musicals, flag in, 159–60
My Maryland (musical), 114

"Name of Old Glory, The" (poem), 117
Napoleonic Wars, 60
NASA, 239–40, 255
Nast, Thomas, 103, 182
National Anthem, 2, 4, 66–68, 236

National Bank of Commerce, 187
National Council of '76, 202
National Education Association, 166
National Flag Conference, 170, 197–98
National Flag Day Foundation, 2
National Flag Foundation, 2, 203, 258, 264
National Geographic magazine, 185
National Liberty Pole and Flag Raising Ceremony, 169
National Museum of American History, 68, 72, 74, 254
National School Celebration, 166–68
National Security League, 151, 180
National Victory Celebration (1991), 253
National Woman Suffrage Association, 43
nativism, 44
Naval Academy, U.S., 66
Navy, U.S., 3, 12, 16–17, 57–58, 66, 83, 216
Nazi flag, 171, 200
Nebraska, 126, 158, 269
Neuborne, Burt, 228
Nevada, 94, 269
Newbury, Mass., flag, 11
Newdow, Michael A., 174
New England flag (1686), 14
Newfoundland, 8, 9
New Hampshire, 268
    military units, 119–20
New Haven, Conn., 54
New Jersey, 32, 208, 268
    military units, 120
New Mexico, 178, 269
New Orleans, La., 95, 111–13, 180
Newton, Rep. Thomas, Jr., 79
New York, N.Y., 102–3, 140, 149, 151, 164, 168, 180–81, 206, 218, 240–42, 246, 257
New York (state), 133, 134, 147, 170, 235, 268
    military units, 110
New York City Teachers' Association, 146
New York Times, 101, 129, 146, 149, 161
Nicholson, Joseph Hopper, 63–64
Nicolay, John G., 123
Niles, Rep. Nathaniel, 56

Nixon, John, 32
Nixon, Pres. Richard, 231, 234, 242–43, 245, 300
North, the
    pre-Civil War, 95
    rallying around the flag, 100–109
North Carolina, 18, 94, 128, 268
    military units, 120
North Dakota, 136, 269
North Pole, flag on, 177–78
Northwestern University, 242
Noyes, Capt. Thomas, 11
Nuovo, Betty, 238

O'Bannon, Lt. Presley N., 58
O'Connell, Card. William Henry, 201
Ohio, 77, 268
Oklahoma, 178, 234, 269
"Old Glory" flag (Driver's), 116–18
Old Guard, The (3rd U.S. Infantry), 134
O'Leary, Cecilia Elizabeth, 125, 145
Olmstead, Frederick Law, 107
Olympia (ship), 161
Olympic Games, 247–48
Operation Desert Storm, 252
Order of Cincinnati, 131, 286–87
Order of the Eastern Star, 35
Order of the Star-Spangled Banner, 88
Oregon, 269
"Our Country's Flag" (song), 109
Owsley, Alvin, 197

pacifism, 67–68
Packer, George, 260
Page, Walter H., 188
Page, William Tyler, 184
Paige, Rod, 255
Paine, Tom, 18
Palmer, John, 167
Pan American Airways, 210
Pascal, Margaret, 164
Patents and Trademarks Commission, 158
patriotic elements of society, 260
Patriotic Heroes' Battalion, 148
Patriotic Order Sons of America, 147
patriotic organizations, 156–58
Peace Flag (Whipple's), 179
Peale, Rembrandt, 45

Pearl Harbor attack, 206, 218
Peary, Josephine, 177–78
Peary, Robert Edwin, 177–78
Pennsylvania, 54, 133, 153, 158, 171, 172–73, 268
    military units, 13, 106
Pentagon, flag display after 9/11, 2, 254
People's Flag (of Samuel Reid), 82
Perry Mason Company, 163
Pershing, Gen. John Joseph, 193
Persian Gulf War (1991), 252–53
Persians, ancient, 7
Peters, Richard, 28–29
Philadelphia, Pa., 21–22, 109, 136–37, 141, 148, 246
Philadelphia Light Horse Troop, 14, 35
Pickersgill, Mary Young, 68–71, *69*
pine tree flags, 12, 14–15
Pittsburgh, Pa., Flag Plaza, 203
Pledge of Allegiance, 4, 44, 168, 228, 236, 249, 255–56, 266
    authorship of, 175
    mandating of, 170–75
    recited in Congress, 175–76
    words of, 168, 171, 173–75, 198, 222
Plymouth Colony, 10
poetry, flag in, 113–16, 117, 178
Poincare, Raymond, 188
Poindexter, Rep. George, 79, 80
political campaigns, flag in, 86–89, 148–50, 154–55, 248–50
Polk, Pres. James K., 88
Pollitt, Katha, 260
Populist Party, 150
Portland, Ore., 142
postage stamps, flag on, 130, 236, 255
postcards, flag on, 155
posters, flag in, 181–83, 185–86, 209–10, 215
Powell, Garland W., 197
Prager, Robert Paul, 191
Pratt, Stanley, 225
Preble, Admiral George Henry, 16, 73, 100, 113, 123, 142
Preparedness Parades, 151, *152*, 179–81
Prescott, Col. William, 14
Preston, Mayor James H., 184
Prince, Mayor Frederick O., 142, 146
Prine, John, 230

prisoners of war, American, 213, 243–44
Pritchard, Sen. J. C., 185
Proctor, Col. John, 13
Prohibition Era, 67
protestors, 228, *229*, 231–35, 240–43, 245, 261
Providence, R.I., 35, 180
Providence (ship), 18
Provincetown, Mass., 13
Purdy, Caroline Pickersgill, 70–71
Puritans, 10

Quaife, Milo M., 37
Quantrill, Mary A., 115
Quartermaster Corps, Heraldic Branch, 223
Quayle, V.P. Dan, 248, 249–50

Rabaut, Rep. Louis C., 173
Ranger (ship), 24
Rasmussen, Carl, 208
Rathbone, Maj. Henry, 123
Rathburne, Capt. John Peck, 18
Raven flag, 8
Reade, Capt. Philip H., 156–57
Reader's Digest, 229, 243
Reagan, Pres. Ronald, 36, 153, 175, 235, 245, 246–49
Reconstruction Period, 126–29
recruiting, military, 209–10, 261
"Red, White & Blue of '61" (song), 108
Red Cross, 183
Red Scare (1920s), 195
Reed, Col. Joseph, 15
regimental colors, 28–29
Rehnquist, Justice William, 227, 236
Reid, Capt. Samuel Chester, 81–83, *81*
Renaissance, 8
Reprisal (ship), 17
Republican Party, 92, 148–50, 235, 261–62
Revere, Paul, 35
Revolutionary War, 3, 54–55, 80, 93, 97, 114, 127, 131, 141
flags of, 12–52, 53–54
Rheimer, Henry, 190–91
Rhode Island, 170, 268
military units, 13, 18
Richards, Capt. William, 22–23

Richardson, Edward W., 45, 50
Richmond, Va., 129
Ricoh Corporation, 257
Riley, James Whitcomb, 117
Roach, John, 24
Robinson, Capt. Isaiah, 17
Roland, Mary Jane Driver, 116–18
Romans, ancient, 8
Roosevelt, Pres. Franklin D., 198, 201, 206, 207, 208, 209, 215–16
Roosevelt, Pres. Theodore, 145, 161, 167, 179
Roosevelt, Col. Theodore, Jr., 194
Root, Elihu, 201
Root, George F., 105, 107
Rosenthal, Joe, 215
Ross, Elizabeth Griscom (Betsy), 22, 37–52
legend of, 39–52, 140, 202
Ross, Col. George, 41–42
Ross, Rep. John, 79
Ross, John (Betsy Ross's husband), 37–38
Ross, Maj. Gen. Robert, 60, 61
Rowan, S. C., 99
Rutledge, John, 31
Ryder, James F., 139–40

Saalburg, Allen, 209, 211
St. Andrew's Cross, 10
Saint Eustatius (island), 17
St. George's Cross, 8–9, 10
St. Mark, flag of, 9
Saltonstall, Capt. Dudley, 16
Sandwich Islands, 97
San Francisco, Calif., 107, 136, 144, 207–8
Sanitary Commission, U.S., 107, 138
Sargent, Gov. Francis W., 172
Satterthwaite, Susanna, 39
Savage, John, 109
Saybrook, Conn., flag, 11
Schlesinger, Arthur M., Jr., 172
schools, flags in, 91, 163–68, 170–75
Schrag, John, 191
Schrier, Lt. Harold, 298
Scotland, 9–10
Scott, Gustave A., 108
Scott, John Morin, 30
Scott, Todd, 257

Scott, Gen. Winfield, 86, 107
seals, official, 29
Seattle, Wash., 195, 237
secession (or peace) flag, 94–95
Sedition Act, 189
Senate, U.S., 176
September 11, 2001, terrorist attack, 2, 134, 172, 253–60
Service for God and Country (book), 197
Seventh Regiment Departing for the War (painting), 103
Shafter, Gen. William, 161
ships, flags of, 14
Shumaker, Frederick, Jr., 189–90
Siebel Systems, 257
Simmons, Col. William Joseph, 199
Simon, Rabbi Abram, 201
Simon, William, 247
Sinnott, Dick, 232
Skinner, Charles R., 147
Skinner, Col. John S., 63
slaves, 89, 91, 266
Smith, Gov. Alfred E., 201
Smith, Sen. Bob, 176
Smith, Rep. Israel, 56
Smith, John Stafford, 64
Smith, Gen. Samuel, 60, 80
Smith, Toni, 262
Smith, Whitney, 14, 33, 50, 84, 91, 174, 197, 198, 264
Smithsonian Institution, 59, 68, 72, 73, 118, 138
snake image (on flags), 12–13
snipping of flags, 72
Societies of the Armies of Ohio, Cumberland, and Tennessee, 131
Society of Colonial Dames, 148
Society of Colonial Wars, 144, 156
Society of Friends (Quakers), 37–39
Somerville flag, 15
songs, the flag in, 3, 107–9
Sons of Liberty, 13–14, 35
Sons of Revolutionary Sires, 141
Sons of the American Revolution (SAR), 141, 144–45, 147, 148, 151, 153, 156, 157, 169
Sons of the Revolution (SR), 144, 148, 157
Sousa, John Philip, 3, 160, 236
Sousley, Franklin, 214

South, the, 95
"flagmania" in, 105–6
Reconstruction Period, 126–29
U.S. flag in, after Civil War, 127–29
See also Confederate States of America
South Carolina, 92, 109, 120, 128, 268
military units, 121
South Dakota, 136, 158, 269
Southern Cross, 97–98, 106
Southworth, Mrs. E.d.e.n., 115
Soviet Union, 174, 207, 219–20
Spain, royal standard of, 8
Spanish-American War, 66, 160–61, 203
Spirit of '76 (painting), 139–40
sporting events, flag at, 1–2, 66
Stafford, James Bayard, 138
Stafford, Marie Peary, 177–78
Stafford, Samuel Bayard, 138
Stafford, Sarah Smith, 138
Stainless Banner, 98
Stamp Act, 13
Stamp Act Congress (1765), 14
Stanton, Edwin M., 123
Stanton, Elizabeth Cady, 43
Stark, Brig. Gen. John, 26
Stark flag, 26
Starr, E. V., 190
"Starry Flag, The" (song), 109
Stars and Bars, 97, 106, 180
Stars and Stripes
erroneously represented in art, 25
foreign flags based on, 97
replacing Continental Colors, 18
"Stars and Stripes, The" (song), 109
"Stars and Stripes Forever, The" (song), 3, 160, 236
stars on flag
arrangement of, 53–54, 83–84, 178, 202, 223
meaning of, 3, 15, 35, 179, 266
number of points, 42, 53
Star-Spangled Banner (Fort McHenry flag), 59, 68–69, 142, 185
making and history of, 68–74
preservation efforts, 74–75, 253
"Star-Spangled Banner" (song), 2, 4, 64–68, 107, 190, 211–12, 236, 262
as National Anthem, 66–68
text of, 278–79

Star-Spangled Banner Flag House (Baltimore), 68, 70, *70*

"star-spangled march" (Bates's), 127–29

state laws
  celebrating Flag Day, 151, 153
  on flag desecration, 158–59, 189–90, 196–97, 233–36, 238
  on the Pledge of Allegiance, 170–75
  on school flags, 165, 256

states
  joining the Union, 55–57, 77, 78, 84–85, 222–25, 266, 268–69
  seceding from the Union, 94

states' rights, 91, 92

Stevens, Ames, 286

Stiles, Ezra, 54

Stiverson, George A, 28

Stokley, Mayor William S., 136

Strank, Michael, 214

streamers (Libby's), 186–87

"Stripes and the Stars, The" (song), 109

stripes on flag
  colors of, 53
  meaning of, 3, 35

Sullivan, Major Gen. John, 13

Sun Pin, 8

Sun Tzu, 8

Support Our Troops groups, 264–65

Supreme Court, U.S., 158, 171–72, 174–75, 235, 237

Surrender of General Burgoyne at Saratoga (painting), 25

Surrender of Lord Cornwallis at Yorktown (painting), 25

Swigert, John L., Jr., 232–33

symbolic speech, 235

Symms, Sen. Steve, 249

Taft, Pres. William Howard, 179, 197

Tahari Fashions, 257

Tansill, George, 138

Taunton, Mass., 14

Taylor, Rep. John W., 78

Taylor, Pres. Zachary, 86

Tennessee, 77, 94, 110, 116–17, 268

terrorism, 253–54

Texas, 85, 94, 190, 238, 269

Texas v. Johnson, 235–36

Thomas, Isaiah, 24

Thompson, Mayor Ronnie, 230

Thomson, Charles, 31, 35, 54

Thurmond, Sen. Strom, 176

TIME magazine, 231

"To Anacreon in Heaven" (song), 64

Tocqueville, Alexis de, 5

Today's Flag Day, June 14th (pamphlet), 201–2

Towne, Benjamin, 23

Tripolitan War (Barbary War), 57–58

Troy, N.Y., 102

Truman, Pres. Harry, 153, 216, 220–21

Trumbull, John, 14, 25

Tuchman, Barbara, 51

Tuffley, Edward W., 137–38

Tupper, Martin Farquhar, 137

Turner, Floyd, 233

Twain, Mark, 107, 128

Tyler, John, 86

Tyler, Scott (Dread Scott), 250–51

Uncle Sam figure, 181–82

"under God," 173–75, 222

uniforms, flag worn on, 212, 252, 262

Union Army, 107, 118–20

Union Flag. *See* Continental Colors (American Revolution flag); Union Jack (British flag)

Union Jack (British flag), 9–10, 12, 21, 36, 181, 187–88, 206

Union Jack (emblem in flags), 15, 22

Union Veteran League, 131

United Nations, 221, 239

United States
  flag as symbol of, 5, 107
  symbols of, other than the flag, 58
  See also flag, U.S.

United States Bunting Company, 125–26

United States Flag Association, 175, 193, 200–203, 206, 208, 211

United States Flag Foundation, 203

United We Stand campaign, 210–11

University of New Mexico, 242

Upham, James B., 163, 165, 166, 169, 175

Utah, 269

Van Buren, Martin, 86–87
Vandegrift, Gen. Alexander, 216
Vermont, 55–56, 238, 268
Verrazzano, Giovanni da, 9
Veteran Brotherhood, 131
Veterans Day, 294
Veterans of Foreign Wars (VFW), 2,
    67–68, 203–4, 233, 250, 296
veterans' organizations, 131–34, 156–58,
    194
Veterans' Rights Union, 131
vexilla, 8
Vietnam War, 227–35, 240–44, 245
VietNow, 250
Vikings, 8
Virginia, 94, 109, 128, 132, 268
    military units, 133
Virginia Company, 10
Vogel, Morris, 43

Walker, Leroy Pope, 98
Wal-Mart, 256
Ward, Rep. Artemas, Jr., 78
Ward, Col. DeWitt C., 164
Ward, Samuel A., 67
War Department, 198
Warner, Charles Dudley, 145
Warner, Seth, 26
Warner, William, 164
War of 1812, 2, 28, 59–64, 82, 131
Warren (ship), 15
Washington, D.C., 144, 168, 184, 237
Washington, Gen. and Pres. George, 14,
    15, 17–18, 28–29, 32, 35, 50, 53, 57
    and Betsy Ross legend, 41, 44, 49
    family coat of arms, 34–35, 137–38
    flags used by troops, 24–25, 28
    as symbol of the nation, 58
Washington, William, 141
Washington (state), 136, 235, 269
Washington: A Drama in Five Acts (play),
    137
Washington on Horseback (sculpture), 103
Watson, Elkanah, 54–55
Watts, Rep. John, 57
WAVEs, 209
Weisgerber, Charles H., 45–48
Weisgerber, Charles II, 48

Weisgerber, Vexil, 46
Welsh, James and John, 100–101
Wendover, Rep. Peter, 77–83
Westmoreland County, Pa., 13
West Virginia, 94, 171–72, 269
*West Virginia State Board of Education v.
    Barnette*, 172
Wharton, John, 32
Whig Party, 86
Whipple, Wayne, 179
Whipple flag, 179
White House, 208
Whitman, Walt, 135
Whittier, John Greenleaf, 113–16, 236
Wickes, Capt. Lambert, 17
Wiggins, Rep. Charles, 233
Wilcox, H. K. W., 44
Wilkes, Lt. Charles, 84
Willard, Archibald M., 139–40
Williams, Roger, 10
Williamsburg, Va., 18
Wilson, Capt. Robert, 27
Wilson, Samuel ("Uncle Sam"), 182
Wilson, Pres. Woodrow, 51–52, 66,
    151–52, 177, 179, 184, 189, 190
Winchell, Walter, 211
Windecker, William J., 229–30
Winder, Gen. William, 60
Wisconsin, 165, 269
Wolverton, Rep. Charles, 173
Woman's Relief Corps, 145, 148, 164
Women's Army Corps (WAC), 209
Wood, Lt. Alan, 298
Wood, Debora, 232
Wood, Gen. Leonard, 179
Woolson, Albert, 288
World's Columbian Exposition (Chicago,
    1893), 45, 166, 168–70
World Series (1918), National Anthem
    at, 66
World Trade Center, flags pulled from, 2,
    254–55
World War I, 66, 151–52, 179–94
World War II, 2, 73, 205–18
Wright, Rep. Jim, 175–76
Wrigley Comany, 253
Wyeth, N. C., 114
Wyoming, 236, 269

"Yankee Doodle" (song), 67
Yankee Doodle Dandy (movie), 212
Year of the Flag (1986), 36
Young, Rep. C. W. "Bill," 252
Young, Eliza, 69, 71
Young, Margaret, 71
Young, Rebecca (flag maker), 51, 70, 71

"You're a Grand Old Flag" (song), 3,
159–60, 212
Youth's Companion (magazine),
163–67

Zoidis, Marilyn, 72, 74
Zouaves, 110, 283–39

CPSIA information can be obtained
at www.ICGtesting.com
Printed in the USA
LVOW07s2341100118
562566LV00003B/322/P